Slavery, Slaveholding, and the Free Black Population of Antebellum Baltimore

Ralph Clayton

HERITAGE BOOKS
2015

HERITAGE BOOKS
AN IMPRINT OF HERITAGE BOOKS, INC.

Books, CDs, and more—Worldwide

For our listing of thousands of titles see our website at
www.HeritageBooks.com

Published 2015 by
HERITAGE BOOKS, INC.
Publishing Division
5810 Ruatan Street
Berwyn Heights, Md. 20740

Copyright © 1993 Ralph Clayton

Heritage Books by the author:

Black Baltimore, 1820–1870
Cash for Blood: The Baltimore to New Orleans Domestic Slave Trade
Free Blacks of Anne Arundel County, Maryland 1850
Slavery, Slaveholding, and the Free Black Population of Antebellum Baltimore
CD: *African-Americans in Anne Arundel County and Baltimore, Maryland*
CD: *Black Baltimore, 1820–1870*
CD: *Free Blacks of Anne Arundel County, Maryland 1850*
CD: *Slavery, Slaveholding and the Free Black Population of Antebellum Baltimore*

All rights reserved. No part of this book may be reproduced or transmitted in any form or by any means, electronic or mechanical, including photocopying, recording or by any information storage and retrieval system without written permission from the author, except for the inclusion of brief quotations in a review.

International Standard Book Numbers
Paperbound: 978-1-55613-868-3
Clothbound: 978-0-7884-6258-0

For my beloved Detria

Table of Contents

Foreword vii

Acknowledgements ix

Part I
The Slaveholders of Antebellum Baltimore

1   The Slaveholders 1
2   The Hiring out of Slaves 13
3   The Sale of Slaves 25
4   The Slave Trade Hierarchy 29
5   The Slave Jails 35
6   Fugitive Slaves - Modes of Escape 37
7   Fugitive Slaves - Frequency 41
8   The Kidnapping of Free Blacks 45
9   The Sale of Free Blacks and Slaves for Crimes Committed 51
10 Research Techniques for Locating Slaveholders 59
11 Slavery in Baltimore's Mount Vernon Area - A Focused Study 63
12 Slaveholders of Baltimore, 1840 & 1850 113

Part II
The Free Black and Slave Population of Antebellum Baltimore

13 Baltimore County Applications for Certificates of Freedom 147
14 Maryland Colonization Society Gleanings from the *Baltimore Sun* 169
15 The Baltimore Census of 1830: The Free Black Population 177
16 The Baltimore City Directory of 1831: The Free Black Population 209
17 Black Property Holders of Baltimore City, 1850 251
18 Black Real Estate and Personal Estate Holders in the Census of 1860 259
19 Mortality in the Free Black and Slave Population of Baltimore, 1850 327

Notes to Chapters 1 - 9 343

Bibliography 349

Index 351

Bibliography 349

Index 351

List of Tables and Indexes

Index of Slave Schedules for the 11th ward, 1860
Individuals listed in 1858 field assessor book but not on slave schedules
Slaveholding Households in Baltimore, 1840
Index to Baltimore County Applications for Certificates of Freedom
Cross-Index to Baltimore County Applications for Certificates of Freedom 1840-1864
Index to the Free Black Population in the 1831 City Directory
Index of Black Property Holders in 1850
Index to Black Real Estate and Personal Estate Holders in the Census of 1860

Legend

Chapter 1
●   Marks the most frequently cited occupations of slave holders.

Chapters 10 and 11
■   Indicates that the head of household is black.

Chapter 12
▲   Indicates a slave holder who is recorded as holding slaves in 1850 as well as in 1860.

Chapter 13
◆   Indicated a manumitted slave who bears the same surname as his or her manumitter.

Foreword

This work represents the culmination of five years of research in documents that reflect the lives of thousands of individuals in antebellum Baltimore. The slave, slaveholder, slave trader, and free Black community are represented. During the compilation of this work numerous records were studied: applications for certificates of freedom, slave schedules, field assesser work books, census schedules, mortality schedules, general property tax records, city directories, newspaper advertisements and articles, the Schomburg collection, original letter manuscripts, and acts of the General Assembly of Maryland.

The following text is not intended to present or prove a particular thesis concerning any period in Baltimore's history. The author's intention is to provide the researcher with a number of files of varying content that hopefully stimulate further research and study in related fields. Therefore this material is presented as a reference work, a series of seperate studies in which facts are collected, collated, and presented in an organized fashion. Although a small number of secondary references are cited in this work, the overwhelming majority of essay and file materials evolved from more than 2,000 hours of research in the aforementioned primary documents.

During the course of this research a number of records reflected words or names which had been clearly misspelled in the originals. There were occassions when quotes may have included errors in spelling. In both instances the author has retained the original spelling in order to transcribe, as accurately as possible, the information as it was initially recorded.

Acknowledgements

I wish to thank the staff of the Enoch Pratt Free Library, Baltimore, one of the finest reference libraries in the United States. More than 95% of the documentation for this book was discovered in the records of that institution. My heartfelt thanks to Pratt's former director, Mrs. Anna Curry, for her continuing support and encouragement.

Other staff members who have lent their support are Mikele Delmore, Eva Slezak, Jeff Korman, Daphne Hurd, Jerome Teagle, Walter K. Wilson, Sharon Mewshaw, Vince Snowden, John Sondheim, David Tirschman, Marc Sober, and Bob Burke. A particular note of thanks to Eleanor Swidan and Vincent Fitzpatrick for their editorial suggestions.

I would also like to thank the staffs of the of the Maryland Historical Society and the Baltimore City Archives for their assistance.

Last but not least thanks to Agnes Callum and James Dilts.

Credits

Portions of the following articles were reprinted here with the kind permission of the *Flower of the Forest - Black Genealogical Journal*:

Mortality Schedules For the Free Black and Slave Population of Baltimore v. 1, no. 6, 1987.

Baltimore County Applications For Certificates of Freedom 1840 - 1864 v. 1, no. 8, 1989.

Maryland Colonization Society Gleanings from the Sun Newspaper v. 1, no. 9, 1990.

The Black Real Estate Holders of Baltimore - 1850 v. 1, no. 9, 1991.

Photo Credits

Photos of the Augustus Kilty slave quarters and the William H. DeCoursy Wright house (the Eubie Blake Museum) by Mr. Tom Lauer.

Photo of William H. DeCoursey Wright courtesy of the Maryland Historical Society.

1
The Slaveholders

A study of the slaveholders of Baltimore reveals that the practice of slaveholding existed at all levels of society; the wealthy and poor of both African-American and European families participated. Although it is safe to say that the upper and upper-middle classes accounted for most of the slaveholding population, carters, sailors, hod carriers, and common laborers with little or no real estate are also documented as slaveholders.

The motivations for holding slaves reflect great diversity as well. Slaves represented not only an important status symbol but also an inexpensive source of help in the workplace or in the home. The latter factor was particularly important when the practice of "hiring out" became widespread (see Chapter 2). For African-American slaveholders, humanitarian concerns often influenced the decision to acquire slaves. The following text sets forth a variety of documents and specific cases that help to characterize the Baltimore slaveholder.

Occupations of Slaveholders, 1850

A study of *Baltimore City slaveholders of 1850* in conjunction with the *Federal Census Population Schedules* of the same year affords the researcher insight into the occupations of the slaveholder. It is important to note that slaveholding schedules are not necessarily slaveowner schedules. Although a large number of those listed are probably the owners of the slaves listed in their household, it is impossible to distinguish between the two categories strictly through the use of slaveholder schedules.

The most frequently cited occupations were:

Merchant	122
Clerk	42
Grocer	39
Physician	32
Carpenter	22
Tavern Keeper	12
Hotel Keeper	9
Lawyer	9
Shoemaker	9
Butcher	9

Chapter 1

These make up 305 of a total of 887 slaveholders, or 34 %.

The whole list, which represents 646 individuals, more than half of the slaveholding population of Baltimore, identifies 190 occupations and reveals the social status of those involved in the practice.

The number following the occupation indicates the number of times that occupation appeared in the records studied. A ● denotes the occupations most frequently cited.

Occupations of Slaveholders, 1850

Agent	2	Chairmaker	1
Auctioneer	2	Chandler	2
Bailiff	1	China Dealer	1
Baker	2	Clergyman	2
Bank Clerk	1	Clerk	42 ●
Bank Officer	1	Clerk - Dist. Court	1
Banker	2	Clothier	5
Baptist Preacher	1	Coachmaker	4
Barber	1	Coachsmith	1
Beef And Pork Packer	1	Collector	5
Blacksmith	4	Colonel U.S. Army	1
Block maker	1	Comb Store	1
Boarding House Keeper	1	Commercial Agent	1
Boat Builder	1	Commission Merchant	8
Bookkeeper	2	Confectioner	4
Bookseller	2	Conveyancer	1
Boot Maker	4	Copper Works Agent	1
Brewer	2	Coppersmith	1
Bricklayer	3	Cotton Broker	1
Brickmaker	6	Crier - Baltimore	
Broker	4	City Court	1
Builder	3	Currier	2
Butcher	9 ●	Dentist	4
Button Dealer	1	Deputy Collector -	
Cabinet Maker	6	Custom's House	1
Car Driver	1	Druggist	6
Carpenter	22 ●	Dry Goods Merchant	8
Carpet Dealer	1	Engine Builder	1
Carter	1	Exchange Broker	1
Cashier	2	Fancy Goods	1
Cashier - Bank	1	Farmer	4
Cattle Dealer	1	Feed Merchant	1

The Slaveholder

Occupations of Slaveholders, 1850

Fish Inspector	1	Mariner	4
Flour Merchant	1	Mate	1
French cuisine	1	Merchant	122 ●
French teacher	1	Merchant Tailor	3
Furniture Dealer	1	Miller	3
Gentleman	1	Millwright	1
Gilder	1	Morocco Dresser	1
Glass Blower	1	Music Dealer	1
Goldsmith	1	Music Publisher	1
Grocer	39 ●	Musical Instrument Maker	1
Gunsmith	1	Negro Buyer	1
Hack Agent	1	Oyster Dealer	2
Hardware	3	Painter	2
Hatter	5	Paperhanger	1
Hod Carrier	2	Paver	1
Horse Dealer	1	Paymaster	1
Hotel Keeper	9 ●	Physician	32 ●
Huckster	3	Pickle And Preserve Manufacturer	1
Importer Of Furs	2	Pile Driver	1
Inn Keeper	2	Pilot	5
Inspector	6	Planter	1
Insurance Co. Agent	1	Plasterer	2
Iron founder	1	Plow Maker	1
Iron Merchant	2	Portrait Painter	1
Jeweller	2	Post Office Clerk	1
Joiner	1	Postmaster	1
Judge - Orphans Court	1	Preacher	1
Laborer	3	Preserver of Provisions	1
Lawyer	9 ●	Printer	4
Leather Dealer	1	Professor Of Language	1
Lime Dealer	2	Property Agent	3
Lime Inspector	1	Proprietor - Hotel	3
Lime Merchant	1	Proprietor - Iron Furnace	1
Livery Stable Keeper	3	Protestant Episcopal Clergyman	2
Locksmith	1	Publican	4
Lumber inspector	1	Publisher Of *Baltimore American*	1
Lumber Merchant	6	Restaurant	2
Machinist	3		
Magistrate	1		
Manufacturer	2		
Marble Cutter	1		

Chapter 1

Occupations of Slaveholders, 1850

Rope Maker	1	Stock Broker	1
Saddler	2	Stone Cutter	2
Sailmaker	1	Stone mason	1
Sailor	6	Store keeper	1
Salesman	1	Stovemaker	3
Salter	1	Superintendent of the	
Sawyer	1	B+O Railroad	
Sea Captain	8	Company	1
Seaman	1	Tailor	8
Sexton	1	Tallow Handler	1
Ship Builder	4	Tanner	4
Ship Carpenter	7	Tavern Keeper	12 ●
Ship Chandler	1	Teacher	4
Ship Joiner	3	Tobacco Merchant	1
Shipping Master	1	Tobacconist	2
Shipping Merchant	1	Trader	4
Shipsmith	1	Turner	1
Shipwright	1	Upholsterer	1
Shoe Factor	1	U. S. Army	1
Shoemaker	9 ●	Waggoner	1
Silversmith	1	Waiter	1
Soap And Candle		Watchmaker	4
Manufacturer	1	Watchman	1
Soldier	1	Waterer	1
Spirit Dealer	1	Wood Dealer	2
Stable Keeper	1	Wood Inspector	1

Although the names of most of the above occupations are self-explanatory, several might be puzzling to readers unfamiliar with nineteenth-century terminology. Below are partial excerpts of definitions located in the *Webster Encyclopedic Dictionary Of The English Language.* [1]

Chandler: makes or sells candles.
Commission Merchant: buys or sells goods for another on commission
Gilder: overlays objects (pages of a book, for instance) with a thin sheet of gold.
Hod Carrier: carries brick or mortar to a mason in a trough fixed to the end of a pole and borne on the shoulder.
Huckster (similar to a hawker or peddler): retailer of small articles. Frequently does not operate from a store.
Joiner: A mechanic who does the woodwork on houses.

The Slaveholder

Morocco Dresser: leather craftsman, using goats leather to bind books, upholster furniture, make ladies shoes, etc.
Publican: tax collector.
Salter: seller of salt
Tallow Handler: separates (renders) the harder and less fusible fat of animals from the fibers or membranes.
Turner: uses a lathe to form wood for table legs, etc.

Of the top thirty-eight slave holders in the city in 1850 (holding 6 or more slaves) three were slave traders. The remaining thirty-five were dispersed throughout the city:

Ward 1	0	Ward 11	8
Ward 2	0	Ward 12	1
Ward 3	1	Ward 13	2
Ward 4	3	Ward 14	0
Ward 5	3	Ward 15	3
Ward 6	0	Ward 16	0
Ward 7	1	Ward 17	0
Ward 8	0	Ward 18	4
Ward 9	5	Ward 19	1
Ward 10	1	Ward 20	2

In some cases it is difficult, through the use of census schedules, to determine which slaveholders held slaves from one decade to another. Through the use of census schedules from 1850 and 1860, however, it is possible to positively identify 140 slaveholders who were repeaters. The numbers of repeaters ward by ward are as follows:

Ward 1	4	Ward 11	17
Ward 2	4	Ward 12	6
Ward 3	14	Ward 13	5
Ward 4	7	Ward 14	9
Ward 5	6	Ward 15	19
Ward 6	8	Ward 16	11
Ward 7	1	Ward 17	0
Ward 8	3	Ward 18	3
Ward 9	6	Ward 19	1
Ward 10	13	Ward 20	3

The list on the next page identifies (through the use of the census slave schedules for Baltimore in 1850 and 1860) those 140 repeaters.

Chapter 1

This particular list was created by using the 1850 schedules in conjunction with census records and city directories for the same year.

Longterm slaveholders (1850-1860)

Name	Ward	Occupation
Adkinson, William	ward 2	
Applegarth, William	ward 2	commission merchant
Arnold, George W.	ward 13	baker and confectioner
Aspril, D. T.	ward 3	clerk
Bankard, Jacob	ward 1	
Berkely, E.	ward 20	merchant
Berry, John H.	ward 15	grocer
Berry, Walter W.	ward 15	commission merchant
Boston, Esau	ward 11	
Boston, John B.	ward 3	hatter
Bouldin, A. J.	ward 6	surveyor
Bruff, John W.	ward 14	merchant
Calloway, William	ward 8	plasterer
Campbell, B. M.	ward 13	slave trader
Carroll, Charles	ward 11	
Carroll, Charles R.	ward 11	
Carroll, Henry D. G.	ward 9	
Carroll, Judith C.	ward 10	
Cator, Elizabeth	ward 15	
Caughey, Michael	ward 6	clothier
Clark, Mathew	ward 18	
Clifford, Sylvester	ward 16	property agent
Cockey, Edward	ward 11	
Cole, William P.	ward 5	hatter
Conway, John R.	ward 15	merchant
Cooper, James	ward 9	
Cottman, James S.	ward 11	
Crichton, William	ward 11	
Cunningham, Martha	ward 4	
Diggs, Richard H.	ward 3	ship carpenter
Doane, Mary	ward 11	
Donovan, Joseph S.	ward 15	slave trader
Dorsey, Comfort W.	ward 10	
Dorsey, Edward H.	ward 15	
Dushane, John	ward 15	carpenter
Duvall, William B.	ward 11	merchant
Ehlen, John H.	ward 12	
Elmore, James	ward 1	butcher

Longterm slaveholders (1850-1860)

Emory, Arthur	ward 16	merchant
Evans, William	ward 15	carpenter
Fairbanks, William	ward 3	
Ferguson, Joshua	ward 4	
Flack, Thomas J.	ward 15	spirit dealer
Forrest, Moreau	ward 14	physician
Frazier, J. B.	ward 2	
Fuller, Richard	ward 14	Baptist clergyman
Gambrill, Charles A.	ward 14	
Gibson, Dr. George	ward 11	physician
Gittings, John S.	ward 11	
Grafton, Samuel H.	ward 15	stove dealer
Griffin, R. B.	ward 12	merchant
Griffith, John	ward 11	
Grindall, John T.	ward 15	clerk
Groverman, Anthony	ward 4	
Hall, Elizabeth A.	ward 9	
Hall, Hester	ward 3	
Hall, Sarah	ward 18	
Hardesty, Richard S.	ward 14	merchant
Harrison, Mary	ward 20	
Henderson, James A.	ward 9	
Holmes, Victor	ward 5	
Hooper, E.	ward 12	
Hooper, Thomas	ward 15	merchant
Howard, Charles	ward 11	orphan's court judge
Ireland, Edward	ward 11	
Isaac, Richard	ward 16	merchant
Jackson, Molly	ward 10	
Jacobs, Samuel	ward 15	merchant
James, Ann M.	ward 6	coachmaker
Jenkins, Austen	ward 11	
Johnson, William H.	ward 5	boatmaker
Johnson, William	ward 5	
Johnson, William	ward 6	
Jones, Sarah A.	ward 15	
Kane, George	ward 4	
Keene, John	ward 16	
Kirby, John	ward 14	tanner
Lambdin, Ann	ward 4	
Lanahan, William	ward 16	confectioner

Chapter 1

Longterm slaveholders (1850-1860)

Leary, William D.	ward 4	
Lee, Thomas	ward 20	Broker
Levering, Thomas W.	ward 16	merchant
Long, H. R.	ward 10	lawyer and magistrate
Maddox, Charles T.	ward 10	Postmaster
Manly, John	ward 16	blacksmith
Martin, William H.	ward 8	post office clerk
McElderry, Henry	ward 6	
McKim, John	ward 11	
McMullen, John	ward 10	cabinet maker
McPherson, Samuel	ward 1	
Merryman, George	ward 10	
Miles, Samuel G.	ward 15	grocer
Miller, Decatur H.	ward 13	tobacco merchant
Mitchell, John	ward 10	confectioner
Monmonier, John	ward 3	
Morris, John B.	ward 11	bank officer
Orndorff, Samuel	ward 14	
Patterson, Edward	ward 9	iron merchant
Patterson, Sarah A.	ward 11	
Pearson, Joseph	ward 13	importer of furs
Pendleton, Robert W.	ward 13	
Perine, Thomas J.	ward 16	trader
Pindle, James	ward 3	
Polk, James	ward 10	lawyer
Porter, Robert	ward 18	commission merchant
Price, A.	ward 1	
Price, William	ward 8	
Raborg, Henrietta	ward 16	
Redgrave, Samuel H.	ward 16	collector
Rose, Peter	ward 5	boatmaker
Rose, William H.	ward 10	publican
Sherwood, Richard P.	ward 10	publican
Skinner, James A.	ward 15	shipbuilder
Slator, James	ward 3	salter
Smith, George M.	ward 15	
Smith, Jacob	ward 12	
Stansbury, J. E.	ward 2	hack agent
Stevenson, Elizabeth	ward 6	
Stewart, Charles	ward 7	upholsterer
Story, Anna	ward 9	

The Slaveholder

Longterm slaveholders (1850-1860)

Street, Thomas	ward 5	hotel keeper
Sturgeon, Edward G.	ward 15	
Suter, Henry	ward 6	turner
Swann, Horace D.	ward 6	merchant
Taylor, William S.	ward 16	
Thomas, John A.	ward 3	ship carpenter
Townsend, Samuel	ward 14	clerk
Trotton, Thomas	ward 3	store keeper
Tucker, Gassaway	ward 3	
Walker, Joshua	ward 4	
Ward, William	ward 10	
Warfield, Daniel	ward 10	miller
Waters, Rebecca	ward 3	
Waters, William C.	ward 15	merchant
Watkins, John W.	ward 12	bricklayer
Waugh, James B.	ward 14	
Welch, J. B.	ward 3	commission merchant
Wright, W. H. D. C.	ward 11	merchant

African-American slaveholding in the city was largely humanitarian in nature. Relatives or friends could be purchased (when economically and politically feasible) in order to keep them out of the hands of a white slaveholder until manumission could be successfully obtained. This phenomenon can be studied in a number of sources in the State: manumission records, applications for certificates of freedom, and laws enacted by the General Assembly of Maryland.

There are a number of examples of acts passed by the State Legislature that allowed for the manumission of slaves by free Blacks, most of whom were family members. The following examples are illustrative of the legislation.

One such act, passed by the State Legislature in February 1842, manumitted a number of slaves that had belonged to Caleb Batson *"A free man of color."* According to the Act, he had purchased the slaves from a man in Charles County in 1821. The Act names the slaves: *"A woman named Letty and her six children, Martha, Adaline, Daniel, Caleb, Duke and William, being his (Batson's) wife and children."* After the purchase in 1821, Batson and his wife, who was then still a slave, had four more children: Brice, Granville, Thomas, and Granville.

Both Caleb Batson and his wife Martha died in 1832. Caleb had never manumitted his wife, children or grandchildren in the eleven

Chapter 1

years between the purchase and his death.

Although the Act does not explain why, one of the major reasons that free Blacks held family members as slaves was that they were concerned about the possibility that the State might force the manumitted slaves to leave Maryland. In fact in 1831 and act was passed that ordered manumitted slaves to leave the State within a certain period of time after their manumission.

When the Administrator of the Will of Caleb Batson determined that his outstanding debts had been paid and the sale of his slaves would not be necessary to balance the account, the state honored a letter left by Batson on his death bed which indicated his desire to see his children and grandchildren freed.

The manumission and proviso in the Batson case reads as follows:

> Be it enacted by the General Assembly of Maryland, That the aforesaid Letty Batson, Adaline Batson, Daniel Batson, Caleb Batson, Duke Batson, William Batson, Brice Batson, Granville Batson, Thomas Batson, Galen Batson, Jim Buckanan, John Henry Buckanan, George Washington Buckanan and Lloyd Buckanan, be and they are hereby declared free; provided, that within twelve months from the passage of this act, they leave the State of Maryland and never return thereto. [2]

Three additional cases in which free black men requested the manumission of slaves can be documented as follows:

> A petition on behalf of a deceased Black man by the name of Isaac Burroughs, alias Isaac Cothell was placed before the General Assembly in February of 1847 requesting that Burroughs' slaves, his wife and children be manumitted. When it was determined that he had died without debt that would require their sale, and the Bill of Sale of the slaves was confirmed, they manumitted the slaves under the proviso that the slaves be subject to provisions of the act relating to people of color, passed at the December session, eighteen hundred and thirty one. [3]

> When Peter White, a free Black man of Somerset County, died he held a bill of sale on his two slaves. The slaves, White's niece and nephew were manumitted subject to all the provisions of the act entitled, and act relating to the people of color of this State, passed at the December session, eighteen hundred and thirty one. [4]

The Slaveholder

In March of 1856 the slaves of Arnold Cottman, a deceased free Black man of Somerset County, were manumitted by an Act of the General Assembly. The slaves, Cottman's wife and children were manumitted under the Proviso that they be subject to an act relating to the people of color of this State, passed at the December session, eighteen hundred and thirty-one. [5]

When the General Assembly determined that the slaves who were to be manumitted were too young to support themselves, other options could be exercised, as the case of Jack Die and his sons illustrates. Jack Die, a free Black man of Queen Anne's County, died intestate, leaving two 16-year-old sons (his slaves for life). In light of the fact that the mother of the two slave boys was also deceased, the General Assembly determined that there were no representatives capable of taking care of John and Joseph Die. As a result the Orphan's Court of Queen Anne's County was ordered to "bind the said Negroes, until they shall attain the age of twenty-one years, as apprentices to one or more white male citizens." [6]

Applications for certificates of freedom as well as manumission records also reflected the ownership of slaves by free blacks. For a more detailed example of such cases see Part II, Chapter 13: *Baltimore County Applications For Certificates of Freedom.*

2
The Hiring out of Slaves

The hiring out of slaves was the practice by which employers purchased, through contract, the services of slaves belonging to someone else. Although the practice of hiring out slaves existed throughout most of the history of slavery, its increase was most assuredly ascribed to the tremendous influx of German and Irish nationals into the United States in the 1840's, forming a seemingly inexhaustible pool of inexpensive labor.

For the slave community of antebellum Maryland, the process of hiring out provided blessings as well as curses. At times the process fragmented families or friends geographically; a proportion of the slave family was in constant danger of separation in spite of the fact that slaveholders would often advertise their desire to keep a family together. In the long run, however, hiring out was certainly preferable to the possibility of being sold out of state or to a local trader. [7]

FOR HIRE,

NEGRO GEORGE, a No. 1 Bricklayer, Brick Burner, Plasterer, &c., &c.

jan. 3—4t   H. A. NEALE.

The hiring out process was also largely responsible for a urban phenomenon known as absentee ownership. In this case slaves were allowed to live in households separate from those of their owners or employers. The census schedule affords the researcher examples that fall into two categories.

The first category is one in which households are occupied by slaves only. In the second category free blacks and slaves live within the same house. There are two possible reasons for the second category. One is absentee ownership, a situation wherein the owner lives in his own household and has allowed his trusted slaves to live separately from him, with their free Black families or friends. The second possible reason is that of free Black ownership of slaves, much of which was (as previously discussed) humanitarian in nature.

The census schedules in conjunction with city directories provide us with excellent examples of this phenomenon in the city of Baltimore. A

13

Chapter 2

sample study of the 1830 census for Baltimore, wards 3 and 5, reveals a number of households where slaves and free Blacks lived together without whites present in the household. [8]

For instance: James Harden is the head of a household where one free female between the ages of 24 and 36 years and 1 free female under 10 reside. The city directory indicates that he is a waiter living on Gay Street. There is one male slave 24 - 36 living in the household. It is easy to ascertain that that slave is Harden when we see that the census reveals a total population in the house of 3 (1 male and 2 females). [9]

Although the census enumerators were not to record slaves by name in the schedules, that rule has clearly been broken in this case. It is wrong to assume that this was an oversight for several reasons. One, it occurred quite regularly as we shall see later. Two, if an enumerator were interviewing a male head of house and was told that the only residents were 2 free females and one male slave, he would surely have to assume that the head of house was a slave. In the city the enumerator made a fee by the head count, not the household. To eliminate households where the head of house was a slave by not naming the slave would mean he would have lost a considerable amount of money by the time he completed his sector.

Other examples include:

Benjamin Cooper, listed as a sawyer living on Aisquith Street in the third ward. The household is listed as having 1 free male under 10, 1 free female 24 - 36, and 1 slave male 36 - 55. [10]

Thomas Fleetwood was a ship carpenter residing in Apple Alley in the third ward. The records indicate that there is 1 free female 10 - 24, 1 free female 36 - 55, and 1 slave male 36 - 55 living in the household. [11]

William Allen was a Tallow Chandler residing on Forest Street in the fifth ward. There is 1 free female under 10, 1 free female 24 - 36, and 1 male slave 24 - 36 in the household. [12]

Carter Woodson explored similar occurrences in the 1830 Census in the *Journal of Negro History* in 1924. [13] What must not be overlooked when one reviews his work is that he considered households where free Blacks and slaves lived together as the households of free Blacks who owned their own slaves. Although that may have been the case in some instances, it is not necessarily the case all of the time.

Although the vast majority of slaves in Baltimore lived in small alley houses attached to the rear of their owners' / employers' houses, there were dozens of cases of absentee ownership in the city. Woodson's work will afford the researcher a overview of these incidents throughout the country in 1830. [14]

The influx of inexpensive immigrant labor (mostly Germans and Irish) into Baltimore starting in the 1840's decreased the need for male slave labor and contributed to the variety of "relatively inexpensive" hiring out contracts being offered.

Greater numbers of "hiring out" advertisements began to appear in the local papers in the late eighteen forties and early eighteen fifties. A study of the variety of these advertisements clearly indicates the flexibility of the hiring out contract.

The following advertisement stipulates hiring out by the month or the year.

> *To Hire ... By the month or year, a Colored boy, about 16 years old - has been brought up to wait in the house; and, if necessary, can attend to and drive a Horse and Carriage. A home in the country would be preferred. Apply at 124 Light Street Wharf, near Lee.* [15]

The second type of advertisement offered a choice of hiring or buying a slave.

> *Negro. For Sale Or Hire ... Advertiser has a strong and able bodied young Negro Man, which he would sell or hire for a term of years to a kind master and a good home. He would make an excellent farm hand, having until within the last year been employed in that capacity. Apply at the office of the Patriot.* [16]

Also

> *A Slave For Sale Or Hire ... A young healthy woman with her infant two months old; the woman is a good cook. She will be sold for a term of nine years or hired yearly at moderate rates. A home in the country preferred but the owner would not object to a good home in the city. Apply at the Sun office.* [17]

Infrequently the advertisements would announce the terms of the cash requirements for the hiring to be accomplished. This was usually discussed after the contact had been made as a result of the advertisement. Here is an exception:

Chapter 2

> For Hire ... A likely Negro Girl, about 16 years of age, of good character, (from the country), a slave for life, Terms $5 per month. Apply at #78 Light Street Wharf ... upstairs. [18]

Advertisements in the *Baltimore Sun* appeared with addresses on the light Street wharf where a number of business offices were located. Businesses often offered their slaves for hire during slack economic periods.

> For Hire ... Two young Negro Men, slaves - one is a good house servant, the other a laborer, and would make an excellent porter. Apply to R. T. Ross, at Duvall, Rogers and Co., # 321 Baltimore Street. [19]

Some, on the other hand, sought to hire.

> Wanted To Hire ... A colored young Man, to take charge of a Horse and Dray. None need apply but such as can give the very best in recommendations. Apply at #232 Baltimore Street. Watkins, Dungan and Wafsche. [20]

Slaves were often used as waiters, professionally as well as in the private home. If someone were in the market for waiters, he had options short of buying the slave.

> For Hire ... A likely young mulatto Man, to serve as WAITER. Apply at #7 Counsellor's Hall, Lexington Street. [21]

Also

> For Hire ... Two servant men to act in the capacity of waiters. Apply at 7 South Broadway. [22]

And

> A Coachman To Hire ... He is careful and honest, and understands the treatment of horses, and is handy at any service. Can wait and market. [23]

Some owners were able to offer a great deal of versatility in the jobs that their slaves were able to perform.

The Hiring out of Slaves

Several Servants To Hire. Good cooks, washers, ironers and house servants; Also, a good Servant Man, who can do any kind of work, from driving a carriage to waiting in the house; Also, Boys, one of whom speaks French and German. The best of references required. Apply at the offices of the Sun. [24]

Advertisements offering slaves for sale or hire as well as rewards for runaways offer insight into the kind of occupations that slaves held. The following is a sampling of such advertisements from the Baltimore Sun between 1850 and 1854. The advertisements show the ratio of female slaves being hired out during the ante bellum decade was 3 to 1 over male slaves.

body servant	for sale	6 / 21 / 50 - 3
carriage driver	for sale	6 / 19 / 50 - 2
carriage driver	for hire	5 / 27 / 52 - 4
chambermaids	for sale	6 / 2 / 52 - 2
chambermaid	reward	4 / 24 / 52 - 3
chambermaid	reward	4 / 24 / 52 - 3
chambermaid	for sale	12 / 23 / 54 - 3
coachman	for sale	1 / 3 / 51 - 4
cooks	for sale	6 / 25 / 50 - 2
cooks	for hire	5 / 27 / 52 - 4
cooks	for sale	6 / 2 / 52 - 2
cooks	for hire	4 / 11 / 52 - 2
cook	for sale	10 / 19 / 52 - 2
cook	for sale	12 / 18 / 52 - 3
driver	for sale	2 / 6 / 50 - 4
driver	for sale	6 / 2 / 52 - 2
driver	for hire	5 / 19 / 23 - 3
drives carriage	for sale	6 / 21 / 50 - 3
farm boys	for hire	4 / 11 / 52 - 2
field hand	for sale	1 / 7 / 50 - 3
fisher		6 / 2 / 52 - 4
horse attendant	for hire	1 / 1 / 50 - 2
horse attendant	for hire	5 / 19 / 52 - 3
house girls	for hire	4 / 11 / 52 - 2
house keeper	for sale	12 / 18 / 52 - 3
house servants	for hire	5 / 27 / 52 - 4
housework	for sale	2 / 6 / 50 - 4
housework	reward	12 / 23 / 54 - 3
Ironers	for sale	6 / 25 / 50 - 2
Ironers	for sale	6 / 2 / 52 - 2

Chapter 2

Ironers	for hire	5 / 27 / 52 - 4
Ironers	for hire	4 / 11 / 52 - 2
Ironer	for sale	10 / 19 / 54 - 2
laundress	for sale	12 / 18 / 52 - 3
milkers	for sale	6 / 2 / 52 - 2
nurse	for sale	6 / 25 / 50 - 2
nurse	for sale	6 / 2 / 52 - 2
nurse	reward	4 / 24 / 52 - 3
nurse		5 / 15 / 52 - 3
waiter	for sale	3 / 21 / 50 - 3
waiter	for sale	6 / 21 / 50 - 3
waiter	for sale	6 / 2 / 52 - 2
waiter	reward	5 / 13 / 52 - 4
waiter	for hire	5 / 27 / 52 - 4
washer	for sale	6 / 25 / 50 - 2
washer	for sale	6 / 2 / 52 - 2
washer	for hire	4 / 11 / 52 - 2
washer	for hire	5 / 27 / 52 - 4
washer	for sale	10 / 19 / 54 - 2

Some owners placed seemingly impossible restrictions on the hiring of their slaves. One wonders if the next advertisement doesn't reflect an owner who is overly cautious:

> For Hire ... Two very sprightly, neat and good looking colored girl slaves, to light house work. Apply at No. 823 West Fayette Street, for particulars and where they can be seen. None need apply except persons living north of Pratt Street, west of Green Street, and south of Franklin. Good references required. [25]

Slaves were sometimes hired to perform unusual duties, such as the following story of a slave hired to fish for another man.

> Notice. Was committed to jail of Prince George's County, as a runaway, a negro man, about 5 feet 5 inches in height, 24 or 25 years of age, of a copper color. Says he belongs to Mr. McPherson, Canton Avenue, Baltimore City, and that he was hired to a Mr. Cooley to fish for him. The owner of the above described negro is requested to come forward, prove property, pay charges and take him away, otherwise he will be discharged according to law. Charles S. Middleton - Sheriff. [26]

The Hiring out of Slaves

Hiring out was not limited to the slaveholder. It was a practice also entered into by the trader. Hope H. Slatter, the premier trader in Baltimore from 1835 - 1848, moved his business to Mobile Alabama in 1849. This advertisement, reprinted in the Liberator (from a Mobile paper in December of 1849), notes his willingness to hire large numbers of slaves.

To Hire - By month - 70 Negro Men from Virginia Hope Slatter.[27]

John N. Denning, a Baltimore trader whose business was on 18 South Frederick Street, modified his terms from time to time to accommodate those wishing to hire rather than buy.

Negro Woman From The Eastern Shore To Hire By the year only, To a small family, the terms will be made agreeable. John N. Denning [28]

There were several ways in which the "hiring out" process was accomplished. One, the owner signed a binding contract between himself and the employer. This contract allowed for a specified time period for hiring as well as pre-arranged payments to the owner. In this case liability for the slaves' welfare was in the hands of the employer. Two, owners would allow trusted slaves to hire themselves out to employers provided the slave paid, out of his or her earnings, a pre - arranged amount to the owner on a regular basis. Anything left over was his or hers for the taking.

The hiring out process can be viewed through the use of several primary source documents available to the researcher in the city of Baltimore. One of course is the slaveholding schedules. Enumerators in several of the city's wards recorded information on slaves being hired out in the document we know as slave schedules.

Field assessor tax books for the city of Baltimore also reflect the hiring out process. These books were the preliminary field research tools by which the general property tax records for the city were devised. Assessors would go from door to door and ask householders for their real and personal estate holdings. Slaves were considered a form of property and therefore are listed in such records. Although the field assessor's books are preliminary workups for the General Property Tax Records, they offer more complete information on the slave community.

Anderson Ellicott, of Hamilton Street, is listed as holding one 15-year-old male slave named Berry who, as the record continues, "Belongs to Mr. James Johnston of Lexington Street, above Schroeder."[29]

Chapter 2

Solomon Hillen Jr. of ward 11 is listed with one 16-year-old female slave named Lizzy and one 16-year-old male slave named Henson who is "hired." [30]

Dr. Alexander Tyson is listed with one 19-year-old male slave named George "Belonging to Miss McCloskey ... Fremont St. near Franklin." [31]

E. Samuel Rogers is listed as holding one 45-year-old female slave named Jane who is the "Property of M. Palter of Talbot County." [32]

Charles Morton Stewart is listed as holding one 40-year-old female slave named Minty and one 8-year-old male slave named Sam "both belonging to Carrol Spencer." [33]

The Federal Population Census Slave Schedules were not required to record the practice of hiring out. The 1850 schedules completely eliminate any reference to the hiring out process. Although the same requirements existed for the 1860 schedules a number of enumerators chose to record the transaction of employing slaves in Baltimore City. Enumerators in the fifth, sixth, eighth, ninth, tenth, fourteenth, fifteenth, eighteenth, and twentieth wards recorded the names of employers as well as the slaveholders employing their slaves.

It is not safe to say that hiring out did not exist in the other wards as evidenced by the preceding study of tax records for ward eleven in 1858. Ward eleven's hiring out statistics were completely overlooked by the enumerator assigned to cover that geographical area. It is obvious, therefore, that it was the choice of the enumerators in those wards not to record the information.

The following list represents an index to those names that were recorded in nine of Baltimore's twenty wards in 1860. If the ninety-three names recorded are a low estimate of the slaves hired out in those nine wards, it is fairly safe to assume that, city wide, there were well over two hundred slaves being hired at any given time. That number represents approximately 9% of the total slave population in the city.

The index is organized as follows:

Surname and first name of slaveholder, ward of slaveholders residence, employer's name, sex (1f - female slave,

1m - male slave) and age (in parentheses) of slave being hired out.

Slaveholder	Ward	Employer	Slave
Bearn, Mrs.	14	E. Sutton	1f (22)
Belt, T. H.	9	Miss Hall	1f (20)
Brent, George	5+6	N. I.	1f (5)
Brown, Garret	20	Albert Brown	1f (30)
Brown, Lewis	5+6	Franklin Metzger	1m (35)

The Hiring out of Slaves

Slaveholder	Ward	Employer	Slave
Calleday, C.	18	G. Talbot	1f (22)
Cator, M.	15	John Travis	1f (6)
Cecil, W.	15	John Sauner	1f (15)
Cockey, Peter	5+6	Charles Green	1f (18)
Cole, Nancy	5+6	William Winderly	1f (16)
Cole, William	5+6	N. I.	1f (60)
Conley, Emma	8	G. W. Pryor	1f (7)
Crawford, Annabelle	18	D. E. Breck	1f (60)
Cumberland, Mrs. Pigman	14	J. Hoblitzell	1f (57)
Cunningham, James W.	5+6	N. I.	1f (40)
Day, John	5+6	N. I.	1f (8)
Diffendaffer, Mrs.	9	John T. Stewart	1f (20)
Doane, Mrs.	14	Charles Goodwin	1f (42)
Don, Julia	9	Miss Wagerman	1f (66)
Dorsey, Mary A.	20	Levin Gall	1f (28)
Emory, Arthur	5+6	N. I.	1f (14)
Fendall, Philip	20	J. Minnicks	1m (30)
Gault, Dickson	5+6	Sarah Ross	1f (20)
Gault, Dickson	5+6	N. I.	1f (20)
Goodwin, Achsha	8	Mary A. Ault	1f (30)
Goodwin, Achsha	8	Mary A. Ault	1m (5)
Griffiths, Maria	20	C. Coleman	1f (8)
Guadrich, Henry	5+6	N. I.	1f (46)
Hamilton, Mr.	10	Richard P. Sherwood	1m (15)
Hooper, Rachael	20	C. Towson	1f (40)
Hopkins, Dr.	10	Richard P. Sherwood	1m (25)
Hutchins, John	15	William Fosbenner	1f (20)
Johnson, W. L.	14	Mr. Gray	1f (6)
Johnson, William	5+6	William Carter	1f (21)
Jones, Charles	5+6	Rachel Benson	1f (8)
Jones, Dr.	20	Bishop Whittingham	1m (12)
Jones, Mrs.	14	Mr. Gray	1f (40)
Joyce, Henry	5+6	N. I.	1f (14)
Juett, Eliza	14	John K. White	1f (36)
Kane, Mary	5+6	N. I.	1f (13)
Keene, Benjamin	20	B. Tubman	1f (30)
Kimberly, Henry	8	W. H. Kimberly	1f (20)
Kirt, Amelia	20	Philip Coakby	1f (40)
Leach, Matilda	5+6	N. I.	1f (21)
Leary, W.	15	Moses Greist	1f (20)
Lilbrian, John	8	Thomas McCubbin	1f (9)

Chapter 2

Slaveholder	Ward	Employer	Slave
Lilgham, Capt.	14	M. Mildekauff	1f (13)
Mace, Virginia	8	Frances Mace	1f (7)
Maddox, Miss	20	S. Philips	1m (14)
Magruder, Sarah	20	A. Thompson	1f (40)
Malsby, Hannah	10	Richard P. Sherwood	1m (15)
McCormick, Dr.	14	Miss Yerby	1f (40)
McCormick, William	5+6	N. I.	1f (25)
McKay, Miss	9	C. Turnbull	1m (35)
Mills, Ann	5+6	N. I.	1f (14)
Monkeiser, Mrs.	14	Mr. Gray	1m (10)
Moreland, O.	15	John Sauner	1f (19)
Neatell, George W.	5+6	N. I.	1f (10)
Owens, James	18	E. Sekwertz	1f (20)
Patten, Adelaid	5+6	Joseph C. Dugan	1f (25)
Pentz, Samuel	5+6	N. I.	1f (30)
Powell, Mary	5+6	Sarah Ross	1m (21)
Preston, James	5+6	L. P. Keach	1m (28)
Price, William	8	William E. Price	1f (32)
Purnell, Maria	20	J. Minnicks	1f (20)
Rasin, Mary R.	8	Perigine Gorsuch	1f (14)
Redgrave, S.	15	Henry Nolan	1m (8)
Reed, Dr. James A.	8	Ortbridge Gorsuch	1f (11)
Riggins, Ann	20	C. Coleman	1f (13)
Shields, Mrs.	14	A. Barritz	1f (40)
Shipley, Enoch (C0.)	14	J. Kefauver	1f (24)
Shram, Matthew	5+6	N. I.	1m (11)
Spencer, Mrs.	14	A. L. Webb	1m (25)
Stansberg, Nathaniel	10	Richard P. Sherwood	1m (48)
Stenson, Mrs. Dr.	14	H. Heald	1m (19)
Stewart, Mrs.	14	H. A. Stump	1f (24)
Summerville, Mrs.	14	Mr. Shear	1f (25)
Sutton, Andrew	14	G. R. Arsguith	1f (8)
Thomas, Mrs.	16	William Doebaker	1f (50)
Tibbons, Mr.	14	J. Hylett	1f (45)
Traverse, Mason	8	Courtland, James	1m (20)
Turner, Charlotte	14	C. H. Raborg	1f (50)
Turner, Joseph	5+6	N. I.	1f (50)
Wall, Mr.	14	Mr. Angleheart	1f (24)
Watts, Henry	8	Thomas B. Gaither	1f (40)
Waugh, James F.	14	W. Dalrymple	1f (10)
Weeks, Mrs.	14	B. S. Guyton	1f (14)

Slaveholder	Ward	Employer	Slave
West, John	5+6	N. I.	1f (10)
Wilcox, Thomas J.	5+6	N. I.	1f (28)
Wilcox, Thomas S.	5+6	L. P. Keach	1f (28)
Williams, John (Estate)	14	K. Adams	1f (16)
Woolford, William	14	S. Bird	1f (20)
Worrell, Ann	5+6	N. I.	1f (13)

3
The Sale Of Slaves

Slaveholders had several alternatives to consider if they chose not to hire out their slaves. They could sell their slaves to other households, commission merchants, and on occasion, to slave traders with businesses near the Camden - Pratt Street corridor. Personal sales were often initiated through advertisements in the local newspapers. A close scrutiny of these ads reveals a great deal of information on the methods and stipulations of the sale. Individuals would come to Baltimore from outside the city or state, sign in to a hotel, and advertise in the papers their wish to buy or sell slaves. The transactions would often take place within the hotel.

> *Negroes - Negroes ... I wish to buy twenty or twenty five likely young Negroes, from ten to twenty years of age, of both sexes, and would prefer them in families, as they are for my own use. I also wish to buy a good Country Blacksmith. - Those having such property for sale will find me at Miller's Hotel, either by letter or in person, if within ten days time. William Varnee.* [34]

> *Negroes! Negroes! Negroes! ... I am at all times purchasing slaves, paying the highest cash prices. I am also prepared to receive Negroes for safe keeping, having erected a comfortable and secure place for that purpose, on Green Street, near Baltimore, immediately opposite the Western Police Station. Henry Fairbanks, General Wayne Hotel, Baltimore.* [35]

Also

> *Slaves Wanted ... I wish to purchase, for my own domestic use, a lot of Slaves. Persons wishing to sell will do well to call on me at the Eastern And Western Hotel, J. T. Harmon, proprietor, Camden Street, Balto., immediately in rear of the Pratt Street Depot. Liberal Commission will be paid. E. C. Bishop* [36]

And

> *For Sale - A Servant Man ... a slave for life, He is an excellent house servant, and also a good field hand. He is a man of good character, which can be vouched for by his owner and others. Apply to Thomas loyd, Union Hotel, corner of Charles and Pratt Streets.* [37]

Chapter 3

On occasion transactions of slaves for sale at the local hotels were considered newsworthy events. One example of such a sale involved the fugitive slave Arthur Burns who had been returned from Massachusetts. The particulars were as follows:

> *Fugitive Slave Case ... Arthur Burns, the fugitive slave whose trial excited so much attention in Massachusetts about six months ago, was yesterday in this city, and took the cars last evening for Philadelphia, with the intention of proceeding North as far as Massachusetts. It appears that his master did not wish to part with him, but finally agreed to do so, whereupon he was purchased by Mr. McDaniel for $900. The gentleman yesterday reached here, and effected a sale of Burns to Rev. Lloyd A. Grimes, of Massachusetts, for the sum of $1,325. The transaction took place at Barnum's Hotel, and was evidenced by Colonel Houston, one of the clerks. Burns excited considerable attention during the few hours he was here. Upon his arrival North a grand demonstration will be made.* [38]

Persons not wishing to deal directly with traders or commission merchants found it preferable to place their advertisements in the local papers. Slaves were sold for life or for a term of years. Those who wished to retain their anonymity would publish the advertisement with the instructions for persons interested to apply to the office of the newspaper for their address.

> *For sale, a negro woman ... a slave for life. She is a first rate washer and a good general house servant. She will not be sold to go out of the state. For address apply at the Sun office* [39]

Also

> *For sale - A colored boy ... 16 years of age, having eight years to serve. He is one of the best of drivers of a physician's carriage, has acted as nurse and body servant for six months back, and has some pretentions to the business of waiting. Sold now in consequence of the owner being about to travel for health. Inquire at the Sun Office.* [40]

Others did not hesitate to sign their names to their advertisement.

The Sale of Slaves

For sale - A colored girl ... Twenty years of age, tall, stout and very healthy; a slave for 20 years, and without any incumbrance; to be sold for no fault whatever. For a more minute description of the girl and terms of the sale apply to William Burgess, no. 131 Baltimore Street, between Calvert and South Street [41]

Administrators of deceased slave owners' wills seemed inclined to give more particulars in their advertisements such as the following insertion that indicates the names and ages of the slaves involved:

For sale - Three young negroes ... belonging to the estate of the late Robert Alder, deceased. I will sell said negroes at private sale if immediate application be made to me at my residence, 5 miles from Baltimore, between the Falls and York Turnpike roads. The above negroes, respectively named James, aged 20, Aquilla, aged 14, and Eliza, aged 14, will be sold for life to any person or persons requiring their services within the state of Maryland.
Michael Alder
Administrator [42]

Also

The negroes belonging to the estate of William Cecil - slaves for life. Immediately after the sale of the household furniture, as above, the undersigned, administrator of the estate of William Cecil, deceased, will sell by order of the Orphan's Court of Baltimore City the negroes belonging to the estate of William Cecil, most of whom are slaves for life .. as follows:
Negro man, David .. 18 years of age - slave for life
Negro man named William, about 48 years of age - slave for life
Negro woman named Sarah - slave for life
Negro girl named Jane, 23 years of age - slave for eight years
Negro named Andrew - slave for life

We call the attention of those wanting negroes to the above sale. Terms as prescribed by the court - - one third cash, and the balance in two equal payments, on credits of four and eight months, with interest from the day of the sale, and that where credit is given, bond with good security shall be taken.
Owen Cecil, Administrator of William Cecil, deceased.
Adreon and Co. , Aucts. [43]

Chapter 3

The price that a slave would bring was determined by numerous factors: demand, age, sex, health, work experience, size, and the economic conditions of the times. Ads for runaways are not good indicators of true value because the owner was not always eager to pay the full value. Typically, young healthy males between the ages of 18 and thirty would cost more than their female counterparts of the same age. The same male slave who sold for $800 in a period of economic depression would probably sell for hundreds of dollars more in prosperous times. A slave with several years to serve might not bring the price that a slave for life, with comparable experience and qualities, might bring. The pricing of a slave was, therefore, often a result of a number of complex factors. As a consequence it was not often the practice of someone advertising to sell a slave to quote the price beforehand. There were, however, some exceptions.

One slaveholder, offering three slaves for sale through the offices of the Baltimore Clipper, advertised *"a woman to serve about seven years, an excellent cook and washer, price $140. She has lived with a highly respectable minister, who gives her a letter of character."* [44]

In the spring of 1850 a young male slave was advertised to serve four years: *"A good waiter, sober and honest; price $150."* [45]

In the spring of 1858 an anonymous advertiser wishes to sell *"a smart, active Negro boy, aged 16 years. He has been used to attending horses. he has five years to serve."* Price $150. [46]

During the winter of 1850 two females, to serve a term of years, are sold: *"Two women, excellent cooks, washers and ironers - price $125 and $250."* [47] The address clearly indicates that the seller is the slave trader John N. Denning of 18 South Frederick Street.

Several weeks later Denning advertised a number of slaves of all ages and both sexes. It is curious to note that the slave he chose to highlight was an elderly woman: *"An elderly woman, a slave for life, one of the most superior women in the state in all respects, price $250."* [48]

In the fall of 1852 John Denning advertised the particulars of a number of slaves he had for sale. Although Denning did not sign the advertisement, he placed the address of his slave jail, 18 South Frederick Street, as the establishment where the transactions were to take place. Among the many slaves offered he highlights a male slave by saying, *"An excellent cook, a slave for life. He has been accustomed to cook, drive carriage, wait, and is a healthy, hearty man. I will sell for $450."* [49]

Once again, in the late fall of 1854, Denning offers a woman for sale: *"A Negro woman, about 25 years old, a good plain cook, washer, ironer and milker raised in Talbot County: price $250."* [50]

4
The Slave Trade Hierarchy

There was a hierarchy of men who sold slaves throughout the South: Auctioneers; who occasionally received slaves as part of an estate to be sold to the highest bidder, commission merchants; who dealt in almost any product on behalf of a third party for a commission of the profit, general agents; who sold estate and property (including slaves) for a commission, and the major slave traders; whose primary business was the buying and selling of slaves. [51]

Slave trading in Baltimore and the District of Columbia was a big business in which large profits were possible. In the summer of 1850 a major trader in Washington D.C. boasted that he had cleared thirty thousand dollars "In the last few months." [52] For those who had no qualms about selling their slaves to Baltimore's major slave traders, the opportunities were always present. It was unlikely that the terms of such a sale would include the trader's promise not to sell the slave out of state. In personal sales such a stipulation could be, and often was, made. The slave traders of Baltimore advertised daily in the local papers. Although it is obvious from a close study of the advertisements that they often offered similar "bargains" in an effort to compete, several made promises that stretched the imagination.

John Denning kept his slave jail at 18 South Frederick Street through much of the 1840s until his retirement in late 1854 Denning attempted to seize part of the trade by playing on the emotions of slave-owners with promises that would have obviously been impossible to keep. [53] On numerous occasions he advertised "families never separated" [54] and "200 or 300 Negroes wanted for Maryland (not for the Southern trade)." [55] What Denning failed to explain to his potential customers is how he could possibly sell single slaves, both children and adults, without having, at some point, separated them from their families. In one ad he states that he is "buying large or small families or single negroes." [56] In yet another he states "10 boys wanted, 10 - 18 years of age." [57] It would have been impossible for Denning to buy 300 slaves at any one time and insure the seller that not one of them would "go south." Furthermore, it was unlikely that a trader could hold 300 slaves at a time in his jail.

The figures that traders placed in their advertisements for the purchase of slaves were certainly inflated in an attempt to impress the possible seller or buyer into thinking that "his" was the largest trade in the city. Consequently, a number of traders advertised inflated figures throughout the two decades prior to the Civil War.

Chapter 4

Joseph S. Donovan, a trader whose business was located on 13 Camden Street, often advertised the purchase of 500 slaves. [58] Donovan, a leading slave trader in the city throughout the antebellum decade, noted the importance of the proximity of his business to the railroad and harbor.

> Persons bringing Negroes by railroad or steamboat find it very convenient to secure their Negroes, as my jail is adjoining the railroad depot, and near the steamboat landings. [59]

By May of 1854 Donovan had sold his business to two partners who carried on the trade from his jail. Jonathan Wilson and G. M. Duke continued the sell slaves from 13 Camden Street for several years. They, along with all the major traders of the city, maintained a strong business relationship with buyers and sellers in the New Orleans slave market. The Baltimore market was responsible for supplying a large number of slaves to many areas of the Deep South. Commissions were paid to individuals supplying information that resulted in a sale for the traders.

> Cash For Negroes - We want to purchase immediately a large number of likely Young Negroes for the New Orleans market, for which we will pay the highest cash prices. All persons having Slaves for sale will find it to their interest by calling on us at our office, no. 13 Camden Street, (formerly occupied by Joseph S. Donovan) Liberal commission paid for information. All communications promptly attended to. J. M. Wilson G. M. Duke s [60]

By 1857 Wilson had found a new business partner named Hindes. Although the business had moved several doors to 1 Camden Street, the method of advertising did not change considerably.

> Cash For Negroes ... We are at all times purchasing Slaves, paying the highest cash prices. Persons wishing to sell will call at no. 1 Camden Street, Baltimore. Negroes received on board. Communications addressed to Wilson and Hindes. [61]

If politics make "strange bedfellows," so did the slave trade. In June of 1844 Wilson had retired as a working agent for Hope H. Slatter, one of Baltimore's most powerful slave traders. [62] Slatter, a Georgia native, began his trade in Baltimore in the mid eighteen thirties. [63] Slatter was the most widely known trader in the city of Baltimore from 1835 through most of 1848. It was then that he sold his business to Bernard Campbell and opened a new one in Mobile, Alabama. [64] Because of his power and

The Slave Trade Hierarchy

fame (or infamy) Slatter is the trader about whom we have the most information, first - hand information that will help us understand the way in which the system of slave trading worked in Baltimore.

In 1837 Slatter applied to municipal authorities for permission to build his slave jail near the corner of Howard and Pratt Streets. [65] A sign, posted on the outside of the jail, read "Hope H. Slatter, from Clinton, Georgia." [66] The structure was a common one for the period in Baltimore. The front house which contained his offices was a three - story brick structure with a building in the rear of the property that was two stories in height. [67] The back building, which was the actual slave jail, had barred windows and, as one his assistants commented to a visitor in 1846, *"was hot as hell."* [68]

The visitor described a *"paved yard of perhaps 75 feet by 40 where his stock was allowed the range of the courtyard by day."* He continued, *"They beguiled their time with cards, and dance, and fiddle and banjo, and every device that he could suggest or they could devise to while away the time and banish memory and anticipation."* [69] He gathered the slaves until a quota had been reached and delivery was prepared to sail to the Southern market.

In the decades before the Civil War, all of the major traders in Baltimore had strong business ties with New Orleans, where a large number of manifests were shipped. Consequently, large shipments of slaves went South from the port. In order to avoid problems in the inner harbor, where a number of free blacks worked, many of the larger shipments of living cargo sailed from Fell's Point. Each trader had his own method of delivering his slaves to the ships that were anchored off the Fell's Point. Some would march the slaves, chained together, down Pratt Street on foot. [70] Hope Slatter delivered his slaves down Pratt Street to Fell's Point in a unique manner. He used rented omnibuses, privately owned horse drawn vehicles that carried a considerable number of people in Baltimore's first experience with "mass transit." An eyewitness account describes Slatter's method of delivering his slaves to the Point on January 19, 1847:

> *The vessel General Pinkney lay anchored off the point awaiting her cargo ... A train of omnibuses crowded with human beings was seen travelling toward the point. Following the train was a tall, gray headed old man (Slatter) on horseback. The trader's heart was callous to the wailings of the angujished mother for her child. He heeded not the sobs of the young wife for her husband. I saw a mother whose very frame was convulsed with anguish for her first born, a girl of 18, who had been sold to this dealer and was among the number then shipped. I saw a young man who kept pace with*

Chapter 4

the carriages, that he might catch one more glimpse of a dear friend, before she was torn forever from his sight. As she saw him, she burst into a flood of tears, sorrowing most of all that they should see each other's faces no more. [71]

In his fascinating study entitled Manifests of Slave Shipments Along the Waterways 1808 - 1864, Charles H. Wesley states:

> The coastwise trade on its largest scale set out from the ports of Baltimore, Alexandria, Richmond and Charleston. The extant manuscript manifests are largely those which name New Orleans as the main port of destination for ships from the upper South and the main port of embarkation to ports of the lower South. [72]

Manifests in the Manuscript Division of the Library of Congress reflect the numerous shipments that left the port of Baltimore, often on ships owned or rented by the major traders such as Slatter. A portion of one such manifest is shown below. There are several interesting things to notice about the manifest. The manifest in this case specifically notes the slaves by their full names and ages, together with a brief description. Hope H. Slatter is noted as the owner and shipper of the slaves. [73]

No. of Entry	Names	Sex Male	Sex Female	Age	Height Feet	Height Inches	Whether Negro Mulatto or Person of color	Owner or shipper Name Residence
27.	Mary Dorsey		"	18	5	1	Black	Hope
28.	Charlotte Morgan		"	26	5	5	"	H.
29.	Edward Nelson	"		Infant			"	Slatter
30.	Adaline Francis		"	6	3	7	"	(shipper)
31.	Catherine Hogan		"	4	3	1	"	
32.	Elisha Shorter		"	30	5	4	"	
33.	Asbury Shorter	"		11	4	6	"	

Examined and found correct
S. W. Pops April 9, 1845
G. M. Browsrich
Brig. Off.

As mentioned previously, most traders denied their willingness to break up families and to sell single young "negroes." Of course this type of advertisement was a ruse as one can see by taking a close look at this manifest. Adaline Francis (aged 6) and Catherine Hogan (aged 4) are both offered up for shipment. This is particularly interesting in light of the fact that Slatter was on record as saying that he was "utterly opposed to the sale of children." [74]

In his book *Slave-Trading In The Old South* Frederic Bancroft relates two more stories about Slatter. The poet Whittier and a Quaker named Joseph Sturge visited Slatter at his jail on Pratt Street. He told them that he was in favor of compensated emancipation and that he never divided families. Bancroft relates that Sturge wrote that after leaving Slatter's impressed they were reliably informed that he had *"purchased a free negro's slave wife and child and had sent them off to New Orleans."* [75]

Another story that Bancroft relates refers to an account of an antislavery observer recalled by a man named Daniel Drayton. He states that Slatter was in the Washington D. C. station of the Baltimore and Ohio R. R. with about 50 slaves he was about to take to Georgia to sell:

About half of them were females, a few of whom had but a slight tinge of African blood in their veins, and were finely formed and beautiful. The men were ironed together, and the whole group looked sad and dejected. At each end of the car stood two ruffianly - looking personages, with large canes in their hands ... While observing this old, gray headed villain (Slatter, who was styanding in the middle of the car) ... the chaplain of the Senate entered the car - a Methodist brother, - and took his brother Slatter by the hand, chatted with him for some time, and seemd to view the heart rending scene before him with little or no concern as we should look upon cattle ... Some of the colored people outside, as well as in the car, were weeping most bitterly. I learned that many families were seperated ... A husband, in the meridian of life, begged to see the partner of his bosom. He protested that she was free - That she had free papers, and was torn from him, and shut up in the jail. He clambered up to one of the windows of the car to see his wife, and, as she was reaching her hand forward to him, the black hearted villian, Slatter, ordered him down. He did not obey. The husband and wife, with tears streaming down their cheeks, besought him to let them converse for a moment. But No! a monster more hideous, hardened and savage, than the blackest spirit of the pit, knocked him down from the car and ordered him away. [76]

By July of 1848 Slatter had sold his "stand" to Bernard and Walter L. Campbell. [77] So great had been the influence of Slatter on the slave trade in the South that Campbell continued to use Slatter's name in his adver-

Chapter 4

tising for the next four years. [78] The slave schedules of 1860 list Campbell with twenty-four female and twenty-six male slaves. [79] A close scrutiny of news accounts as well as advertisements in the local newspapers indicates that Bernard Campbell became one of the leading slave traders in the city. The Campbells had a business in New Orleans where most of their sales were made. The slaves were in Campbell's jail on Pratt Street, where they were visited, on occasion, by Dr. Willis, of New Market, Frederick County. Willis took care of the health problems of Campbell's slaves while they were in Baltimore. In return, Willis would take some of the slaves out to his farm when their was need for extra labor. [80]

In 1862 Congress adopted compensation for emancipation in the District of Columbia. Bernard Campbell was so influential in the slave trade that he was invited to Washington to help decide the prices of slaves formulated by a special commission. [81] In the summer of 1863, after the Battle of Gettysburg, Union soldiers marched into Baltimore and freed the slaves in Campbell's jail and enlisted the male slaves into the Union Army. So ended the career of one of the leading traders of the South, a career that spanned two decades. [82]

5
The Slave Jails

Slave jails in the city of Baltimore housed slaves for a variety of reasons. One function provided by all major traders was to supply a reasonably secure place to house or board slaves while an owner was out of town on business or for pleasure. The accepted rate that the traders were charging throughout the mid nineteenth century was $.25 a day. [83] Joseph Donovan, previously mentioned, advertised, *"I will receive and keep Negroes comfortable, at the usual rates."* [84] Many traders also offered their jails for the temporary incarceration of suspected runaways or abducted slaves. Slaves who were convicted of crimes were sent to the Penitentiary and often "sold South" on the Penitentiary steps after serving their term for a second felony. [85] (See Chapter 9 *The Sale of Free Blacks and Slaves For Crimes Committed*.)

Examples of slaves being placed in private slave jails can be examined throughout the antebellum decades. The following cases illustrate the practice. During the summer of 1849 Thomas Mitcell, a former fugitive slave residing in Pennsylvania for a number of years, was arrested and brought to Baltimore where he was *"handed over to Mr. Donovan's (Joseph Donovan) prison keeper, as a fugitive slave."* [86]

In August of 1850 five slaves were captured between New Market and Shrewsbury, Pennsylvania. They were returned to Baltimore in a locked freight car attached to the back of a passenger train. The slaves, from Calvert, Prince George's, Montgomery, and Baltimore Counties, were manacled upon arrival in Baltimore and *"immediately taken to one of the private prisons to await the orders of their masters."* [87]

In the late summer of the same year James Hamlett, a fugitive slave whose owner, Mrs. Mary Brown, lived in Baltimore, was apprehended in New York and returned to the city. Mrs. Brown, who had knowledge of his location some time before the arrest, was advised by the private police firm she had employed to wait for the passage of the Fugitive Slave Act before attempting Hamlett's capture. When the bill passed, a representative of the police firm secured certification from the State Department and proceeded to New York where the arrest was made. Upon his return to Baltimore James Hamlett was deposited in Joseph Donovan's jail. [88]

In the late fall of 1852 a watchman was informed that a slave was going to attempt to escape by rail. Officer William Snyder succeeded in arresting the suspected slave near the railroad depot after which *"he was*

Chapter 5

safely lodged in the establishment of Messrs. Campbell (Bernard and Walter Campbell), Pratt Street." [89]

In early 1856 two families were arrested at the depot of the Baltimore and Ohio, and Philadelphia railroads. They were from Staunton, Virginia and Charleston, South Carolina. Apparently they were trying to make their escape north through the rail system in Baltimore. Some of them had already obtained through tickets to New York when they were apprehended. The article ends by stating: *"They are at present confined in this city in a private jail."* [90]

Later that same year an interesting case appeared on the front page of the Baltimore Sun. It involved the abduction of five slaves from the Charles Street residence of their owner, Joseph C. Wilson. Ironically, Wilson had been one of the city's leading slave traders in the previous decade. It seems that the five slaves were taken to a frame building on South Eutaw Street opposite the rail depot (Camden Station). They were held there for a week and then removed to a place in Baltimore County. A man named Redgraves approached Mr. Wilson with information that led him to believe that Redgraves knew of their whereabouts. Redgraves forced Joseph Wilson to sign an agreement promising he would increase the reward from $500 to $800. Wilson agreed and the slaves were returned to Baltimore where they were *"safely confined in Mr. Campbell's jail."* [91]

Wilson then refused to pay the reward and alleged that Redgraves was in collusion with other parties to abduct the slaves and then return them for the reward money.

Ironically it was a brother of one of the slaves who had talked them into running away so that he could obtain part of the reward money on their return. Several arrests were made, and the slaves returned to Mr. Wilson.

Articles such as these abound in the period after the passage of the Fugitive Slave Act. One of the leading candidates for incarceration in the private jails of traders was the fugitive slave. These suspected runaways were often placed in the jails until their owner came forth or they were sold at public auction. Although the problem of fugitive slaves was always apparent in a border state such as Maryland, the situation deteriorated by the early 1850's.

6
Fugitive Slaves - Modes of Escape

One of the most fascinating escapes in the infamous history of slavery in America was provided by Henry (Box) Brown. Born a slave in Virginia in 1816, Henry purchased the freedom of his wife and three children from their owner. Upon returning from work one day he was alarmed to find that his family had been sold on the auction block to "Go South"(a term which meant to sell a slave to someone residing in one of the slave states other than the state of the slave's residency).

Heartbroken, he sought any way possible to escape his ruthless owner. Henry paid a friend, James A. (Boxer) Smith, $80 to assist him in his escape. [92] On March 29, 1849 James A. Smith placed Henry Brown in a large box and forwarded the box to Philadelphia. [93] After a thirty - seven hour journey from Richmond that took Brown by rail, steamboat, and overland in a nailed crate, the package arrived in Philadelphia. Antislavery agents received the box and freed the much shaken Brown.

After the passage of the Fugitive Slave Act several unsuccessful attempts to capture Brown were made! One final attempt was made on August 30, 1850. [94] In the fall of 1850, Henry (Box) Brown and James A. (Boxer) Smith travelled to England with a show entitled the *Panorama Of Slavery* in an attempt to raise money for the abolitionist cause. [95] Brown's penchant for notoriety made him a hero overnight. The story of his daring escape was the subject of numerous narratives and articles in 1849 and 1850. Although other slaves attempted to escape in the same manner, few succeeded. What makes the Brown escape of particular interest to our study of fugitives in the city of Baltimore is that he was not the first to have succeeded in such an escape.

In the spring of 1845, four years prior to Brown, a young female slave escaped from Baltimore by placing herself in a large box that was invoiced to be delivered to York, Pennsylvania.

The female was a slave belonging to Benjamin Ross, a wealthy merchant living in the city at the time. Following are the exact transcripts of the articles that appeared in the Baltimore Sun newspaper.

New Mode Of Transportation
Information was yesterday received in town of a negro servant girl, belonging to Mr. Benjamin Ross, who has been missing for some time. It appears from the facts which have transpired that she had been safely delivered in York Pennsylvania, as per invoice, snugly packed away in a good sized box adapted to her dimensions.

Chapter 6

> *This is an entirely novel style of abducting slaves we apprehend, and may serve as a caution to common carriers, as the same system might possibly be practiced with some success upon a larger scale, unless the living mummy should be too roughly handled, in transit, and be induced to squeal from very necessity, in the present case, the mode of conveyance was private it is believed, and it seems quite successful.* [96]

The Novel Transportation
The York Pennsylvania Republican, noticing an article which appeared in this paper some days ago, relative to the transportation of a negro woman in a box to that borough says:

> *A vehicle bearing very much the appearance of a furniture wagon, and marked 15, came to town, from the direction of Baltimore, in the afternoon of that day, and the man driving it having fallen down in a fit on the borders of the borough, somebody was curious enough to raise the lid of a box which it contained, and was not a little surprised to find a colored woman all alive and snugly packed in it. She of course went her way; the wagon and horse were, we believe, deserted afterwards by the driver, and have been sold by an auctioneer.* [97]

A study of the Baltimore Sun for the period from 1845 - 1860 reveals dozens of arrests of fugitive or suspected fugitive slaves. Not only was Baltimore a city in which escaped slaves attempted to blend in with the free community, it was also a city which provided numerous vehicles for escape to the north. Slaves escaping to, from, or through Baltimore used a number of modes of escape. One mode was, of course, the railroad. So great had the problem become that in 1839 an Act *"to prevent the transportation of People of Color, Upon Railroads or steamboats"* was passed by the General Assembly of Maryland. [98]

By this act a penalty of $500 was to be levied against the directors of the railroad or the captain of the steamboat caught allowing slaves to be transported without the slaveowner's written permission. The act also permitted the slaveowner, who lost a slave by such means, to sue the railroad or the steamboat company for the value of the slave.

A variety of records reveal that this law was instrumental in a number of runaway cases. In 1840 the minute books of the B&O Railroad record the claim of a slaveowner whose slave had apparently escaped on the B&O. *"A report was received from J. H. B. Latrobe, counsel, on the claim of Richard G. Brashear for the value of a slave, which was referred to the President for examination and report to the Board."* [99] It didn't take long before the law created hardships for the rail lines as evidenced by this entry in the B&O minute books in the summer of 1841:

> *The President submitted the report of J. H. B. Latrobe, counsel, on the subject of the claim made by W. Maddox for a runaway slave and explained the difficulties & hardships to which the company was subjected under the Act of Assembly relating to the transportation of slaves ... The President was authorized to contest the claim in order that ... The Company's liability in carrying of negroes in the cars may be judicially decided.* [100]

In the following two decades similar judicial decisions were handed down. One decision, indicating that the problem was still troubling the State on the eve of the abolition of slavery was reported in the Baltimore Sun. A slaveowner named Ford had instituted an action to recover for the loss of his slave, transported by the Western Maryland Railroad Company. The slave escaped by rail, without a permit, on Easter Sunday, 1863. The jury returned a verdict of $100 in favor of the plaintiff, Ford. Ironically, a Constitutional provision was cited which stated that, when damages recovered were less than $300, the plaintiff was to pay the court costs. The court costs in this case were $49.27, to be paid by Ford. Therefore, Ford recovered only $51.73 on his loss. [101]

Employees of the rail line were instructed to ask all Black travellers to produce permits or passes before they were allowed to board the train. Slaves were often captured when they could not produce a certificate of freedom or a pass enabling them to travel. The Baltimore Sun relates the case of two families of suspected runaways arrested after buying tickets to New York. The families, one from Charleston, South Carolina, and the other from Stanton, Virginia, were arrested at the depots of the Baltimore and Ohio and Philadelphia railroads. [102]

In February of 1858 two slaves were captured while trying to escape on a train at the President Street Station (initially reported as the Calvert Street Station). In order to obtain their tickets that had to produce a freedom pass (certificate of freedom). They submitted copies that, it was later learned, had been forged by a Mr. Campbell. After submitting the papers they were able to purchase their tickets. The two men were detained when someone in the station noticed that they were acting suspiciously. It was then discovered that they were attempting to escape from their owners, S. Owings Hoffman and Charles Gilmore. Mr. Campbell, who had forged the papers, was arrested and charged with aiding and abetting in the escape of a slave. [103]

Later the same year the Sun published a story of a report of the discovery of a young boy on the "out train" on the Philadelphia road. The

Chapter 6

boy could not prove his identity and was returned to jail in Baltimore for further investigation. [104]

Another mode of escape to, through, or from Baltimore was by steamboat or schooner. In January 1854, the steamer Baltimore entered the port for repairs. During the trip the captain had discovered three slaves hiding in the forecastle. With the help of his men, the captain tied the slaves up and delivered them to the authorities upon the ship's arrival in the port. All three slaves; Richard Bell, Thomas Brooks, and Williard Winfrie, were the property of Newman Newby of Chesterfield County, Virginia. They were later returned to Virginia. [105]

Isaac Queen, a slave from the Eastern Shore of Maryland, was captured and arrested as suspected runaway in March 1856. He asserted that he was free, and coming here upon an Eastern Shore vessel, had been "Frozen In." Nevertheless, Mr. Queen was committed to jail until his freedom could be established or his master found. [106]

In the fall of 1860 the Sun reported the attempted escape of Alexander, a slave to Mrs. Walker of Norfolk. The slave had hidden on the steamer *Adelaide* for the purpose of making his way to Baltimore, and then to Pennsylvania: "This is the second time he has attempted the same thing; having taken passage on the Great Eastern on her trip up the Bay last summer." [107]

In the following article the Sun reported the great lengths to which some slaves would go in order to avoid recapture:

A Disguised Runaway ... Upon the arrival of the steamer Wilson Small at her wharf, foot of Camden Street, on Friday night, the first mate gave into the custody of officer Austin a colored personage attired in full female apparel, but whom he suspected of being a man, which subsequently proved to be the fact. The fellow was full six feet in height, and it was giant like proportions that first excited suspicions as to his sex. He carried in one hand a handbox with two bonnets in it, and in the other a parasol.

To complete the womanly appearance he had stuffed his bosom with old rags for a delicate purpose. He was examined before Justice Showacre, when he gave the name of Irvin, and said he belonged to Dr. Chase Purnell, of Snow Hill Maryland. Irvin was sent to jail in the unbecoming apparel he had assumed to await the requisition of his master. [108]

7
Fugitive Slaves - Frequency of Escape

Although Maryland, as a border state, continually suffered from a high incidence of runaway slaves the problem clearly worsened in the latter eighteen forties. The weekly estimated loss of fugitive slaves from the border counties in Maryland was set at $10,000 by the spring of 1850. [109] As a matter of fact 30 to 40 slaves were reported to have absconded from Prince George's County on August 18 of that same year. [110] Incidences of large number of escaped slaves in a single group can be found throughout the ante-bellum decade. William Lloyd Garrison's *Liberator* copied the following article from the *Charlestown Maryland News* of September 20, 1855:

> *Stampede ... a regular stampede of Negroes was made from this neighborhood on Saturday night last. They were ten in number. They took with them three horses and a double carriage belonging to Ed Ringgold's estate, and a carriage belonging to John Greenwood. They were all valuable Negroes, and it is to be hoped will be recovered; Up to the present time, however, nothing has been heard of them.* [111]

Other large escapes are noted in the runaway advertisements of major newspapers in Baltimore. On occassion the Baltimore Sun ran advertisements that reflected the escapes of large number of slaves. In the spring of 1846 four brothers, ranging in age from eighteen to thirty years, ran away in a group from a plantation in Harford County. A total of four hundred dollars reward was offered for their return. [112]

In the late summer of 1858 Allen Davidson, his wife and four brothers escaped in a group from the estate of M. Tilghman Goldsborough. A total reward of $1,200 (or $200 if captured singly) was offered for their return. [113]

In the late summer of 1848 twelve slaves escaped from two slaveholders in Baltimore County:

> *A Slave Stampede - On tuesday night a stampede took place among the slaves in Baltimore county, twelve having gone without leave from two gentlemen of the county.* [114]

Chapter 7

Although escapes of large groups occurred on occasion, the overwhelming number of escapes involved one to three slaves. A study of runaway advertisements of full - named slaves in the *Baltimore Sun* from 1837 - 1864 provides interesting insight into this phenomonon. [115] A number of Blacks were apprehended if they were not recognized by the neighborhood watch, if they were acting suspiciously, or if they could not provide freedom papers. Many of those apprehended were jailed merely on the suspicion of being a runaway. In the summer of 1848 a small 10-year-old boy was arrested by officer Stocket as a suspected runaway because *"he would give no satisfactory account of himself."* [116]

Harriet Hawkins, a 22-year-old woman, was committed to jail as a runaway when she could not *"establish her freedom by evidence."* [117] William K. Watson was arrested after being involved in disorderly conduct. His arrest was not maintained for the conduct within itself but because he was "under suspicion of being a runaway." [118]

During the summer of the following year Charles Adams was arrested by watchman Schley for disorderly conduct and "with being a runaway." [119] That same summer Joseph Branson was arrested by officer Stapleford on the charge of being a runaway and *"committed to jail in default of security to answer."* [120] George Grings was arrested by two watchmen in December 1856 on the charge of being a runaway. He was committed to jail *"For a further hearing."* [121] In the spring of the following year Margaret Williams was arrested on the charge of being a runaway: *"Justice Mearis committed her to jail subject to a further examination."* [122]

Many blacks who could not prove their identity to the watchman who arrested them were incarcerated in this manner. It was only at a later date that their freedom may or may not have been established. It is impossible to determine how many free blacks were incarcerated in this manner and later sold at auction. The following is a most typical case of a person suffering arrest under these conditions:

> *Alleged Fugitive ... Officer Favier, of the Southern District, yesterday captured a colored man on Light Street Wharf on suspicion of being a runaway slave. He was brought before Justice Boyd where he gave his name as Abraham Prigg, and said he was from New Market, Frederick County, in this state. He was locked up until his right to freedom or slavery can be established.* [123]

There are numerous cases revealed in the Baltimore Sun where very specific information relating a slave to a particular owner is known early in the arrest. It is not clear, in all cases, whether the slave has offered the information or whether an informant has turned the slave in for a possible reward.

Following are excerpts from news items that show a clear identification of the slave with a particular slaveholder early in the arrest. In late December of 1848 Officer McKewan arrested Patsy Ann Reed and charged her with having run away from G. C. Frazier. *"Justice Robbins committed her to jail".* [124]

The following March, Officer Gould arrested William Dison and and charged him with being a runaway from Dr. Robinson. Dison, intent upon not being held, *"attempted to escape by jumping through the window, which he did, carrying with him the whole sash, lights, and fixtures. Officer Gould grabbed him and held on like a stoic until he could draw him back."* [125]

In January of 1857 Moses Cole was arrested by a watchman upon the charge of absconding from Joshua Bosley: *"Justice Mearis committed him to jail for safe keeping."* [126]

In the early spring of the same year George Johnson was arrested by Officer Taylor upon the charge of escaping from John Hart, of Annapolis. *"Justice McAllister committed him to jail subject to the proper orders."* [127]

Several months later Edward Douns was taken into custody at the Lexington Market upon suspicion of being a fugitive from his owner. In this case, when Douns was taken before Justice Root, he quickly declared that he belonged to Joseph Cook, of Queene Anne's County. According to the *Sun*, *"he was committed to await the action of his owner."* [128]

On August 11, 1857 Joseph Lee was arrested for being a runaway. Several days later a Mr. Gardiner *"from the county appeared and claimed him as his property."* [129]

In early September two slaves were arrested within a day of one another in Baltimore and returned to their owners. Eliza Ross was arrested in the western district and charged with being a fugitive from labor and the property of her owner, Dr. W. Griselin of Baltimore County. Nathaniel Bias was also arrested in the western district and charged with being a runaway slave. He was the slave of Reuben Dorsey of Howard County. *"He was committed to jail to await his owner."* [130]

Two officers of the middle district arrested John W. Bordley, a 13-year-old slave. He claimed to *"belong to a captain Gibson, on a line of one of the railroads."* [131]

In August 1860 Dennis Wood was arrested in the western part of the city and charged with *"running away from William Steele, of Carrol County. He confessed the charge and was committed to jail to await the requisition of his owner."* [132]

Ten days later Charles Susker was charged with being a runaway slave, the property of Eli Gaither of Patuxent Forge, Maryland. *"Justice*

Chapter 7

Ensor committed him to jail to await the requisition of his owner." [133]

The cases presented here are just a sampling of the fugitive and alleged fugitive cases covered locally from 1848-1860. There are several important observations. If the number of captured runaways is as high as it appears, then the number of fugitives who escaped detection must also be very high.

Although a number of historians have given in to the temptation to blame the large number of arrests on turncoats in the Black community operating for potential profit, there is minimal hard evidence in the local papers for such a determination. On the contrary, there is only one article in the twelve year period studied which presents such a scenario. It is reprinted here in its entirety.

> *Alleged Absconding Slave ... Policeman Harks, of the Southern District, on Tuesday night apprehended a colored man named Henry Stanley, upon the Oath of Charles Cornish, colored, who charged him with being a fugitive slave from Dorchester County, Maryland. He was taken to the Marshall's office yesterday morning, and from thence committed to jail.* [134]

Not all slaves headed for escape beyond the border with Pennsylvania. Fugitives also fled to the cities in an attempt to blend in with the rest of the free Black community. Baltimore was no exception. Baltimore contained the largest free Black community of any city in the slave states by 1810. *"The Urban Environment permitted many runaways to find a sanctuary within municipal boundaries, either by hiding out in some obscure place or with conivance of other Blacks."* [135]

8
The Kidnapping of Free Blacks

Although integration of the free Black population with slaves was not encouraged it was only rarely resisted. The following chart, gleaned from the Federal Population Census figures, reflects the large population of free Blacks in the city:

Population Statistics for Baltimore 1820-1860 [136]

Year	Total	White	Free Black	Slave
1820	62,738	48,055	10,326	4,357
1830	80,620	61,710	14,790	4,120
1840	102,313	81,147	17,967	3,199
1850	169,054	140,666	25,442	2,946
1860	212,418	184,520	25,680	2,218

The fact that slaves and free blacks lived together was not unusual in Baltimore. This free mixture of the slave and free community evolved with a complex system of labor management. That system intertwined the hiring out of slaves with the binding out or indenturing of free blacks which in itself was a form a quasi-slavery. This informal mixture of the slave and free community of Baltimore created an atmosphere where the illegal kidnapping of free blacks was a constant problem. Kidnappers were not a new phenomenon to Baltimore in the decades before the Civil War. According to Leroy Graham in his book *Baltimore - The Nineteenth Century Black Capital*, kidnapping was reported throughout the early part of the nineteenth century in Baltimore. [137]

In March 1840 the *Colored American* newspaper published an interesting report on the laws that affected Black people, slave and free, in various states. Among the practices addressed in the report was the practice of kidnapping. In the words of the *Colored American*:

> *An able bodied colored man sells in the southern market fro from eight hundred to a thousand dollars; of course he is worth stealing. Kidnapping being a lucrative business it is not strange that it should be extensively practiced.* [138]

The article continued:

45

Chapter 8

> *It is difficult to estimate the extent to which illegal kidnapping is carried, since a large number of cases must escape detection.* [139]

A careful search of the *Baltimore Sun* between 1848 and 1860 indicates that the practice was reaching alarming proportions in Baltimore. We shall see that there were two major ways in which the kidnappings were accomplished. With one, free blacks were literally taken from the streets of Baltimore, forcibly removed to another area and sold. The other was more complex and ingenious. Free blacks who had indentured themselves to whites for a "term of years" were taken outside of Baltimore to another market where the attempt was made to sell them as slaves for life.

The market most often used to dispose of free blacks from Baltimore was the auction blocks in Richmond, a city where transactions on slaves took place daily. It was the closest major slave selling center where kidnappers could take their victims and hope that their ruse was not recognized. The *Liberator*, reprinting a report from the *Richmond Southerner* in February 1849, reveals several cases of kidnapping. The report verifies two cases in which free blacks from Baltimore were taken by separate kidnappers who then made the attempt to sell them in Richmond. In the first case two kidnappers brought a man they claimed to be their slave to Richmond and were in the process of selling him when *"The Negro protested against the act, declaring himself to be free."* The report continues that at that point the kidnappers fled and had not yet been captured. [140]

The article also relates that in a separate incident a *"small Black girl, taken from the same city* (Baltimore)*, now in Richmond, was waiting to be taken back."* [141]

With the potential of considerable profit to consider, even appointed officials became involved in scams or plots to sell free Blacks. In 1857 a free Black man by the name of Talbot was incarcerated in the Cecil County jail for disturbing a religious meeting. Sheriff John Poole, of Cecil County, requested the help of Talbot in an attempt to capture a Black prisoner who had escaped from the jail. Talbot, believing that accepting the Sheriff's invitation would draw him a lenient sentence, consented. When Talbot and Poole left the county, Poole headed for Richmond where they met a man named Beatty. Beatty and Poole immediately attempted to sell Talbot as a slave. The *Baltimore Sun* reported, *"The boy protested that he was free, and told his story so straight as to beget a doubt in the minds of those to whom he was offered."* [142]

After a great deal of investigation on behalf of Talbot, he was returned to Cecil County to await trial on the charges pending against him, a fate far preferable to "going South" as a slave for life. As for Sheriff Poole and Beatty, both were incarcerated, Poole in Baltimore and Beatty in Towsontowne. [143]

A number of free Blacks were being indentured to serve a term of years. One mother, Elizabeth Brown, a free servant of Mr. Williams of French and Center Streets, indentured her son William through the orphan's court, to a man named Ridley. Ridley transferred him to a man named Owings who, in turn, sold his indenture to Lewis F. Bowen of Baltimore County. Bowen transported William Brown to Richmond where he sold him as a slave for life. *"The last named (Bowen) took him to Richmond, where he was sold under the hammer, but some conversation of the boy excited suspicion that he was not a slave."* [144] Bowen and William Brown were returned by the authorities to Baltimore where Bowen was jailed to await trial and the young boy was returned to his joyous mother. [145]

During the summer of 1860 several cases of kidnapping of indentured servants were reported in the local newspapers. The first case involved a young boy apprenticed to S. S. Sanders, of Baltimore. The young apprentice ran away from Sanders and, upon his capture, was sentenced by the Orphan's Court to an extension of his apprenticeship.

However, information was received by the authorities that led them to believe that Sanders was about to take the boy to Virginia and sell him as a slave. A warrant was issued by Justice Boyd in Baltimore and none too soon! Sanders was arrested on the steamer *George Peabody* where he had booked passage to Virginia for himself and the apprentice. Justice Boyd ordered Sanders held on $1,000 bond and the boy was committed to jail for safekeeping. [146]

The second incident, which occurred about a week later, involved a female apprentice indentured to a Baltimore city resident. In the spring of the year Mary E. Johnson applied to George Marshall of 179 Lexington Street in hopes of binding herself out to him for employment. The indentures were drawn up by the court and signed by both Marshall and Johnson.

For some reason, which the reports do not make clear, Mary Johnson soon felt compelled to escape from the employ of Marshall. So great was her desire to leave his employ that she escaped two separate times during the summer. After the second escape, which took place during the first week in August, Marshall placed ads offering a reward for her return. [147]

Upon her recapture the second time Marshall took Mary Johnson to Richmond for the purpose of selling her as a slave for life. While on the auction block Mary's protestations of freedom convinced her potential buyers of the wisdom of checking into the matter. Marshall was arrest-

Chapter 8

ed. It is unclear how the situation that Mary Johnson faced was resolved. [148]

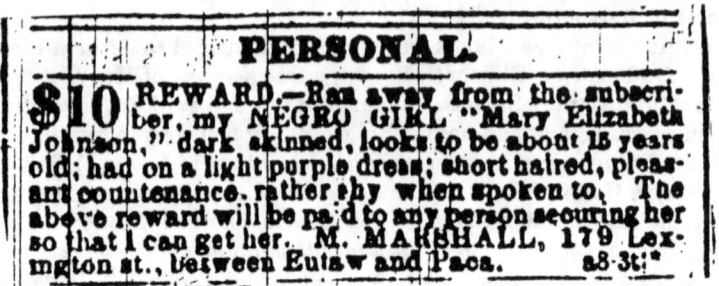

Throughout the antebellum decade there are numerous incidences in which the slave kidnapper attempted to use the auction block in Richmond to sell free Blacks South. The fact that potential slave buyers often chose to check rather than ignore the protests of the free Blacks was not an entirely humanitarian decision. They were well aware of the legal implications of buying someone who was not a slave. Without the appropriate papers, heavy legal fines and the possibility of incarceration awaited those found guilty of buying a free person.

Even in cases where a sale was made and it was determined that the buyer was an innocent (albeit gullible) victim, he ran the possibility of losing his money or facing liability for the costs of the return of the free Black to Baltimore. [149]

A number of kidnappings created great excitement in the state. There was evidence that, in some cases, the same individuals may have been involved in the illegal sale of free Blacks on a number of occasions. An excellent example of this is the kidnapping of Jim Brown, a 7-year-old boy taken from the residence of William Cahill of Centerville, Queen Anne's County. The boy's mother had put him to bed and left the house to visit a neighbor. When she returned, her son was missing. Authorities uncovered an elaborate plot involving the Cahills and several men of Queen Anne's County. The plan was to deliver the boy to Baltimore and sell him South as a slave. By the end of the first day the boy was still missing and the *Baltimore Sun* commented *"while we have no sympathy with abolitionist, who seek to disturb our domestic economy, we have just as little for the kidnapper, who would sell a freeman into slavery."* [150]

The following day the boy was located at the home of one of the alleged conspirators, Thomas Moffit of Spring Street. Moffit turned "state's evidence" and testified against the rest of the conspirators. In an amazing twist to the case, it was learned that the previous summer two free Blacks apprentices, a boy and a girl, had also been "carried off" while working for Cahill. [151]

One of the most unusual kidnapping cases occurred in the early spring of 1852. Joseph Bosley, a white man in the employ of Joshua Marsh of Baltimore County, disappeared from Marsh's house along with a 17-year-old female slave belonging to Marsh.

The pair were discovered about twenty-two miles outside Baltimore at a place called Slade's by James Bennet, a neighbor of Marsh who had been following leads in an attempt to locate them. Bosley threatened Bennet with a sword and eluded capture. A search of buildings in the area was commenced whereupon the two were discovered in a shed *"laying quite cosily together on the top of the hay."* [152]

Both were arrested and taken to Baltimore where the female slave expressed her desire to return to work for the Marsh's in whose family she had been raised. She claimed that Bosley told her he loved her and that he would marry her as soon as they reached Pennsylvania. Bosley's real intentions, however, were to *"take her from Philadelphia to some southern port, and sell her as a slave."* [153]

Individuals involved themselves in elaborate scams in an attempt to make money by selling free Blacks and splitting the proceeds with them after they were released. Sometimes, however, the ruse backfired resulting in the arrest of the parties concerned. Such a case occurred in March of 1859. David Dysert, a white man from Waynesburg, Pennsylvania, took a black man named James Lockwood to the General Wayne Hotel. His object was to sell Lockwood as a slave to Henry Fairbanks, the proprietor of the hotel and much advertised "slave buyer." After the purchase of Lockwood for $1,300 Fairbanks became suspicious and ordered the arrest of Dysert who was located several miles from the city.

Dysert confessed to fraud and implicated Lockwood as an accessory to the sale. It was determined that the ruse was pre-arranged with the understanding that Lockwood, an employee of Dysert, would receive a share of the $1,300 when his freedom had been ascertained and his release accomplished. Both were arrested and the case sent before the Grand Jury. [154]

In a case with some similarities, another slave trader, Bernard Campbell, was the victim of an attempted ruse reported by the *Baltimore Sun* on June 29, 1858. The motives in this case, however, were much more complex than the case previously discussed. Two white men, William Collins and Thomas Hobbs, conspired with a free Black man named Sewell to sell Sewell to Campbell. After the attempted sale and subsequent arrests, the court determined sentencing based upon a complex series of motives which included greed, sorrow, and humanitarianism.

Collins, it was agreed, had acted purely out of sympathy for Sewell

Chapter 8

who was trying to be sold into slavery in order to be reunited to his slave wife. It seems that she had sometime before been sold to a planter on the South. Sewell's motive was, therefore, clearly one of sorrow of a husband for his wife. Hobbs, it was determined, was actually attempting to make a profit from the sale, and was thereby completing a ruse against Campbell as well as his companion, Collins. Hobbs was the only conspirator arrested and bonded for $500 in order to answer the charge.

Some of the saddest cases of kidnapping in the city of Baltimore involved mothers who attempted to kidnap their own children. In the fall of 1853, Catherine Brown (alias Green) kidnapped her three children, was captured, and incarcerated in jail to await trial. Sadly, the three children were jailed "For Identification." [155]

Maria Taylor, in December 1860, was arrested by policeman Barranger on the charge of abducting two young slaves from Zadoc T. Wilburn of Snow Hill, Maryland. Maria alleged that the two boys, her sons, were free. Justice Hiss ordered that Maria be placed in custody until a hearing could be set. [156]

These as well as many other cases reflect one of many threats to the Black family, both slave and free, in the decades prior to the Civil War. It is alarming to consider the number of reported kidnappings that occurred in this period. There are no figures on how many free Blacks were successfully "Sold South" in this manner. It is safe to assume, however, that when the numbers of discovered cases are considered there must have been large numbers of disappearances that were never resolved. For additional stories on kidnappings, refer to the *Baltimore Sun*. [157]

9
The Sale Of Free Blacks and Slaves For Crimes Committed

Prior to 1845 the punishment of slaves for felonies committed was either hanging or being sold outside the state of Maryland. Slaves were not incarcerated in the penitentiary. [158] In his book *The Negro In Maryland* Jeffrey Brackett chronicles Governor Pratt's attempts to have a law instituted that would make the committing of a felony by a slave punishable by imprisonment and sale outside of the state. [159] In March 1845 such a law was passed entitled *An act respecting the punishment of slaves.* [160]

In this legislation the General Assembly agreed with the Governor that banishment from the state was insufficient punishment for slaves guilty of committing serious offenses. Some of the crimes covered by the act were murder, manslaughter, rape, assault with the intent to rob, insurrection, burglary, and arson. The punishment for these crimes was to serve a term in the penitentiary, after which the slave was to be sold "To Go South" (Out Of State). The value of the slave was determined by the courts and payment made to the owner. At the completion of the slave's sentence in the penitentiary he or she was sold at auction. [161]

A 5% fee to the warden was issued from the profits of the sale. After the warden paid the price of advertising the auction the remaining money was reimbursed to the court for having originally paid the slave-owner. [162] This practice can be observed by looking at advertisements in the local newspapers. There are several examples of this practice that can be seen in the files of the *Baltimore Sun*.

In May of 1850 the *Baltimore Sun* advertised the following:

> *Negro Man At Public Sale ... Whereas a negro man, (John Simms) slave of Mrs. Joseph Reynolds, of Calvert County, was, at the October term of the Calvert County Court, for the year 1847, convicted of "assault with intent to kill," and sentenced to two years and seven months imprisonment in the Maryland Penitentiary; and whereas an act of the General Assembly of This State, (ch 340) passed at the December session, 1845, requires that all slaves so offending shall, at the expiration of their terms in the Penitentiary, "be sold to the highest bidder, for cash, for transportation beyond the limits of the State of Maryland," I hereby give notice to all concerned, that I will, in accordance with the requirements of the above recited act, offer at public sale, at the Maryland Penitentiary*

Chapter 9

on Tuesday, the 15th instant, at 10 o'clock, A. M., to the highest bidder, for cash, the said negro man, John Simms, as above described.

Isaac M. Denson, Warden [163]

In May 1854 Robert Diggs, a slave of Charles Bell of Prince George's County, was advertised for sale in a similar manner. The warden, G. P. Merryman indicated that the slave, having served his term for manslaughter, would be sold *"To the highest bidder, for cash."* [164]

In January of 1853 Henry Reynolds was sold by Sheriff Hays for a period of seven years for $302.50, while "Negro Bowen" (also sold by the Sheriff) brought $507.50 for a seven-year term. [165]

The Baltimore Sun of December 1855 indicated that during 1855, seven Negroes were sold out of State, having been twice convicted of larceny." [166]

By the latter part of the antebellum decade legislation ordering the sale of free Blacks into slavery for minor offenses was initiated. Tremendous increases in immigration from Ireland and the German States directly affected the economy of Baltimore and threatened the slaveholders' ability to employ their slaves. [167] A number of free blacks and slaves were forced from the labor market in the city. Incidences of pauperism and crime rose as would be expected when the market in a small geographical area such as Baltimore was glutted with so much inexpensive labor. A depression in 1857 served only to make matters worse. Ironically the slaveholding elite viewed the problem as one initiated by the labor force in the free black community. [168]

Unsuccessful attempts were made to rid the state of the free black population. As crime continued to rise in the city, the Penitentiary quickly became overcrowded with inmates. In *The Negro In Maryland*, Brackett reveals that the executive message of 1858 revealed *"nearly half of the convicts in the penitentiary were negroes, suggesting the courts should again be given the power of selling out of the State slaves convicted of certain felonies."* [169] Now, however, legislation was to be introduced that would also include the sale of free blacks for crimes committed.

A look at the total penitentiary population of 1850 and 1860 reveals some interesting figures. [170]

Year	Total Population	Blacks	Whites
1850	236	123	113
1860	428	109	319

The Sale of Free Blacks and Slaves for Crimes Committed

The drop in the ratio of blacks incarcerated in the prison reflects the willingness of the state to sell free blacks into terms of slavery as an alternative to imprisonment. This came about as a result of an act of the General Assembly passed in March 1858 entitled "An act to modify the punishment of free negroes, convicted of Larceny and other crimes in this State." [171]

The penalties, which provided the alternative to selling a free Black person over incarceration if so desired, were much more severe than those incurred by whites. Simple larceny of $5 value could bring slavery for 2 to 5 years; robbery - ten years in slavery; stealing a mule or horse - 2 to 14 years in slavery; killing or wounding a horse - 2 to 4 years in slavery.

A look at the census of 1860 for the penitentiary in Baltimore's eighth ward reflects the greater average period of incarceration of Blacks over whites.

Race Sex	Number of Inmates	Years (Total)	Average Sentence
wf	9	15.5	1 year, 8 months
wm	308	847.5	2 years, 9 months
bf	13	53	4 years, 1 month
bm	96	424	4 years, 5 months

The following is a list of the 109 Black prisoners incarcerated in the Maryland Penitentiary. [172] The list appeared in the census of ward 8 of Baltimore City in 1860. The index is organized as follows: Surname and first name of inmate, age, occupation at time of arrest, and crime committed.

Inmate	Age	Occupation	Crime
Allen, Margaret	16	Servant	Arson
Armwood, Wellington	31	Farm Hand	Felony
Atkinson, Benjamin	29	Laborer	Stealing
Ballard, Lewis	25	Laborer	Larceny
Banks, George	24	Laborer	Setting Fire
Barton, William	42	Laborer	Attempt To Kill
Benson, Henry	30	Farm Hand	Burglary
Boston, James	29	Laborer	Larceny
Bowen, John	26	Laborer	Setting Fire
Bratton, Stephen	26	Laborer	Stealing

Chapter 9

Inmate	Age	Occupation	Crime
Bright, Dennis	28	Mariner	Attempt To Murder
Bright, Moses	37	Carpenter	Attempt To Murder
Briscoe, Josiah	38	Waterman	Attempted To Kill
Brooks, Charles	21	Cook	Larceny
Brown, John	39	Farm Hand	Entice Slaves To Run
Brown, Mary E.	37	Servant	Murder
Brown, Robert	28	Laborer	Attempt To Kill
Brummell, Charles	25	Sailor	Burglary
Butler, Madeline	25	Farm Hand	Manslaughter
Caldwell, Zacariah	31	Waiter	Larceny
Camphor, William	21	Farm Hand	Stealing
Clarke, Washington	49	Farm Hand	Rape
Cole, Henson	34	Farm Hand	Stealing
Collins, Sarah	18	Servant	Arson
Cooper, James	37	Farm Hand	Robbery
Curtis, John	21	Farm Hand	Stealing
Dorsey, Lorenzo	21	Laborer	Attempt To Rape
Dunbar, George	45	Grain Measurer	Larceny
Foreman, John	35	Butcher	Murder
Frances, Lewis	24	Laborer	Larceny
Frances, Samuel	21	Blacksmith	Murder - 2nd Degree
Frie, Nathan	62	Farm Hand	Murder
Gaddess, Pearce	44	Farm Hand	Murder
Gibbs, Ann E.	18	Cook	Arson
Gibson, Gabriel	22	Laborer	Larceny
Goff, Frank	18	Hay Dealer	False Pretenses
Golder, Samuel	23	Caulker	Larceny
Green, John	31	Farm Hand	Stealing
Green, Samuel	24	Farm Hand	Burglary
Green, Samuel	58	Farmer	Abolition Book
Hanson, Elijah	38	Brickmaker	Stealing
Harris, Ephraim	25	Sailor	Violent Assault
Hawkins, Josiah	21	Ostler	Attempt To Kill
Henney, Henrietta	26	Washerwoman	Murder
Henry, Negro	36	Farm Hand	Arson
Herbert, David	28	Waiter	Attempt To Kill
Hill, William	32	Farm Hand	Rape
Hinney, Esma	30	Waterman	Stealing
Holliday, Joshua	55	Laborer	Stealing
Houston, John	28	Farm Hand	Murder - 2nd Degree
Jackson, Arthur	40	Farm Hand	Larceny

The Sale of Free Blacks and Slaves for Crimes Committed

Inmate	Age	Occupation	Crime
Jackson, Daniel	34	Farm Hand	Intent - Burglarize
Jenifer, Gilbert	32	Farm Hand	Manslaughter
Johns, Othello	37	Carter	Arson
Johnston, William	32	Farm Hand	Larceny
Knocks, Margeret	24	Servant	Murder
Laurance, Joseph	34	Laborer	Murder - 2nd Degree
Lee, George	33	Laborer	Stealing
Lightner, Robert	39	Farmer	Entice Slave To Run
Ligmore, William	41	Farm Hand	Larceny
Long, George H.	31	Ostler	Murder
Lucas, Vincent	44	Farm Hand	Intent to Kill
Mack, Charles	18	Farm Hand	Attempt To Kill
Martin, Andrew	62	Laborer	Attempt To Kill
Miller, Washington	37	Farm Hand	Murder - 2nd Degree
Morgan, James	21	Brickmaker	Larceny
Negro, Clarence	24	Farm hand	Arson
Negro, Dick	26	Farm Hand	Arson
Ockemey, David	31	Farm Hand	Intent To Kill
Palmer, Edward	32	Laborer	Manslaughter
Parker, Charles	21	Farm Hand	Larceny
Parker, Hooper	50	Laborer	Attempt To Kill
Peacock, Jacob	26	Waiter	Burglary
Peck, Theodore	59	Farm Hand	Stealing
Perry, Edward	26	Laborer	Attempted Rape
Queen, George	48	Farm Hand	Murder
Quinn, Robert	18	Brickmaker	Arson
Richardson, Joseph	49	Laborer	Rape
Rumsey, Josiah	30	Waterman	Burning Children
Shark, John	30	Caulker	Attempt To Rape
Skinner, Thomas	36	Wagoner	Entice Slave To Run
Slavey, Cato	27	Laborer	Burglary
Smith, Ann	38	Washerwoman	Larceny
Smith, Charles	16	Loafer	Stealing
Sprouts, Nat	29	Farm Hand	Attempt To Kill
Stewart, Charles	36	Cook	Assist Slave Esc.
Stiles, Joseph	26	Boatman	Burglary
Taylor, Wiliam	58	Waiter	Entice Slave To Run
Thomas, Charles	27	Farm Hand	Murder
Thomas, Henry	27	Laborer	Rob+Intent To Kill
Thomas, Mary C.	23	Servant	Murder
Thompson, Ellen	20	Servant	Attempt To Kill

Chapter 9

Inmate	Age	Occupation	Crime
Tillman, Joseph	24	Drayman	Obtain Goods Falsely
Travers, Henry	40	Laborer	Intent To Kill
Tyler, Stephen	31	Steamboat Hand	Obtain Money Falsely
Walker, John	31	Laborer	Arson
Watkins, Dennis	42	Carpenter	Attempt To Kill
Watts, Peter	19	Farm Hand	Intent To Kill
Webb, Josephine	24	Servant	Murder - 2nd Degree
Wedge, John	27	Farm Hand	Stealing
West, Charles	30	Laborer	Larceny
Wheately, Joseph	28	Farm Hand	Stealing
Wiliams, Amos	27	Laborer	Stealing
Williams, Henry	33	Laborer	Rape
Wilmot, Tilly	47	Servant	Stealing
Wilson, James	22	Laborer	Larceny
Wilson, Sarah	29	Farm hand	Murder
Wyatt, William	30	Plasterer	Murder
Young, Isaac	68	Farmer	Rape

Sales of free blacks for felony convictions were sometimes covered as a newsworthy event by the local newspapers. The Baltimore Sun published a several such sales after the passage of the 1858 act of the General Assembly previously noted. One such article is here reprinted in its entirety:

> *Sale Of Convicts ... The free colored persons convicted at the present term of the Circuit Court of Baltimore County have been sold at the door of the jail in pursuance of the sentence of the court, under the act of the last General Assembly of Maryland.*
>
> *Sarah, alias Emily Taylor, convicted of the larceny of a pocket book, and sentenced to be sold for five years, was purchased by E. C. Wade, for $26.*
>
> *Richard Forti, convicted of stealing a check, and sentenced to be sold for two years, was purchased for $150.*
>
> *Henry Jenkins, convicted of the larceny of a saddle, and sentenced to be sold for five years, was purchased by Mortimer Watkins for $60.* [173]

In another article in the spring of 1860 the Baltimore Sun reported the sale at public auction of three free blacks convicted of petty larcenies.

They were sold into slavery to John Hinesly for 2 years and two months each for a total price of $1,000. [174]

Conclusion

Historians generally agree that the free Black community reached a peak of positive growth by 1830. Two subsequent events, however, had a profoundly negative impact on the free Black population: the Nat Turner insurrection in Southampton, Virginia in 1831; and the introduction of hundreds of thousands of German and Irish nationals into the labor market between 1835 and 1865. For the Black community, which had already endured uncommon adversity, these events brought additional burdens.

The Nat Turner insurrection caused panic, particularly in the slaveholding communities of the South. As a result, tough legislation was introduced throughout the Southern states that further restricted the rights of the free Black person. This legislation, as well as additional acts of the General Assembly of Maryland, reflected the slaveholders' perception that a free Black labor force was a threat to the survival of slavery. A portion of this legislation gave impetus to the newly formed Maryland Colonization Society. Attempts by slaveholders to rid the State of the free Black community also fueled the fire of the colonization cause. The Colonization Society's impact on the removal of manumitted slaves to Liberia was a dismal failure.

By the latter portion of the antebellum decade slaveholders, particularly those with influence in the General Assembly, successfully pressed for the enforcement of vagrancy laws and the creation of new laws that allowed for the enslavement of free Blacks under certain circumstances. In spite of this activity the slaveholders generally agreed that the removal of the free Black population of Maryland would have serious consequences on the economy of the State. However, slaveholders failed to realize that a greater threat was being imposed upon the institution of slavery by immigrants flooding the South with an inexpensive labor force.

Census figures indicate that between 1849 and 1860 almost 3,000,000 immigrants entered into the United States, most of them from Germany and Ireland. Baltimore ship lists indicate that in 1852 alone, more than 13,500 German and Irish citizens entered the port of Baltimore. The population of the resident German and Irish citizens in the city rose from 21,000 in 1850 to 48,000 in 1860. Inexpensive immigrant labor severely impacted the free Black and slave male work force, particularly in the wards encircling Baltimore's harbor.

Occupations of Blacks living in these wards changed dramatically

Chapter 9

during the period between 1850 and 1860. Black laborers, who had formerly worked in shipbuilding and other occupations directly related to the shipping trade, were forced, in increasing numbers, into the role of house servants. By the latter antebellum decade labor riots were common in Baltimore as White males forced Black Males out of a number of occupations that they had held for years.

Although free Blacks in the city were able to secure real estate, buy their own businesses, and operate fraternal orders, the period was filled with potential problems for the Black family. Public education for free Blacks was non existent, with much of the training that was available being offered through the Black Church. This, in light of the fact that the Black populace paid city taxes that supported public education, frustrated many in the community. The children of poor families could be indentured out to a white family, further separating the family unit. A number of mothers chose, voluntarily, to indenture their children, knowing that in such cases there was greater opportunity to make the decision for which white families children would work.

Nevertheless, as we have seen, a number of free Black children were illegally sold South into slavery. Although the numbers of such sales would be impossible to ascertain, the knowledge that such incidences were rising in the antebellum decade placed an additional burden on the family. As the need for slave labor declined in the city, sales of slaves, manumissions, and hirings increased. The slave family, as well as the slave who was married to a free spouse, constantly lived under the fear of forced separation. Slave traders would not hesitate to sell "families or single Negroes" to the highest bidder.

By 1860, the living quarters of a number of slave and free Black families shifted geographically as servants attempted to live close to their employment. Black families in the poorer wards encircling Baltimore's harbor moved to wealthy sections of the city such as the Mt. Vernon area as a greater number of free Black males were forced to seek employment in the households of wealthy white families. Consequently, the slave and free Black population of such areas grew dramatically between 1850 and 1860.

Repressive legislation as well as the entry in Baltimore of a large immigrant labor force, served to fragment the Black family. Although hundreds of Black families managed to remain together in spite of these obstacles, the knowledge of their potential separation was ever present. In a city where slave trading, kidnappings, forced indentures, the legal sale of free Blacks into slavery, and other oppressive measures occurred on a regular basis, the Black families' survival stands, in itself, as their greatest testimonial.

10
Research Techniques For Locating Slaveholders

Numerous documents preserved in a number of locations throughout the state of Maryland afford the researcher vital information on the slaveholder and slaveowner. The researcher must take great care not to assume that an individual owned a slave simply because he or she was enumerated in a household with slaves in the census records and slave schedules. Although the majority of such individual householders were probably slaveowners the possibility exists that they were employers (hiring the slave for a period of time) or free blacks allowed to live with slaves in their own abodes. It was possible for an individual to hold or employ the services of a slave without the burden of ownership. This was accomplished when a prospective employer entered into an agreement with a slaveowner to hire out the slave for a pre-arranged period of time (see the chapter in this book on the hiring of slaves).

There are several examples of records that clearly reflect the ownership of slaves. The deed or will of manumission indicates the owner's name, the slaves name, and the date or temporal conditions of the manumission. It may also reflect other conditions of the transaction. This is an excellent example for which there are numerous surviving records in various archives throughout the state of Maryland. Bill of sales and hiring out contracts generally named the true owner but are not as valuable a source in light of the fact that few such records have survived for study. The same holds true for plantation account ledgers. Among the numerous documents stored at the Maryland Hall Of Records are the Slave Lists compiled in 1864. Anticipating imminent emancipation of their slaves, numerous slaveowners in a number of Maryland counties provided lists of their slaves by name. The lists were intended to provide vital information to the government should they consider partial reimbursement for property lost as a result of the act of emancipation.

The Federal Population Census Schedules are an excellent source by which we can study the slaveholder in the city. Prior to 1850 seperate slave schedules were not collected by the census enumerator. Information indicating the prescence of slaves in the household was collected on the second of a two sheet record available for all households. The first sheet listed white males and females while the second sheet listed male and female slaves followed by free black males and females. All listings, with the exception of the names of the head of house, were by hash

Chapter 10

marks which indicated general age groupings within the aforementioned categories.

A two step proceedure is necessary to retrieve information on householders who had slaves living on the premises. When studying the records from 1790-1840 one must take care to name such individuals as heads of households with slaves. It is impossible to determine the relationship of the head of house to the slaves. Closer scrutiny of these records indicate that the enumerators would, on occassion mistakenly name the slaves themselves as heads of house - a distinction supposedly reserved for free citizens.

The first step of the proceedure is to turn to the second page of the document, the page that indicates the prescence of any slaves that may be in residence. When hash marks are entered indicating the prescence of slaves count the number of columns from the top of the sheet to the column indicating said slaves. list the number of columns from the top (or the bottom) of the page along with the number of slaves found in the appropriate column. For example if 1 male and 1 female slave is found in the third column from the top indicate the listing in your records as

3t - 1f, 1m

During the second step of the proceedure turn back to the first page of the document, the page which indicates the names of heads of house as well as numbers of white male and female inhabitants. Count three columns down from the top of the page and list the name of the head of house indicated in that column. If the name of the head of house was John Doe your first completed entry under the heading heads of households with slaves should read:

Doe, John 1f, 1m

Although the type of entry just indicated would be helpful in the study of these households a list which includes the ward and page number of the findings would open the possibility of sociological studies of extreme importance. Such an entry would read:

Doe, John (10) 1f, 1m (263)

The translation of this information would be John Doe, of ward 10 on page 263, is the head of of a household in which 1 female and 1 male slave reside.

In most cases it is possible to indicate whether John Doe is of European or African Descent (White or black). When the researcher surveys the appropriate column of the first page of the document for the name of the head of house (in this case column three from the top) he or she can tell whether the head of house is of African descent by looking for an abscence of hash marks on that page. If, for example, the first hash mark indicated on either page is of a free black male then we know that the head of house is not of European descent (white). Such a record can be seperated from the rest of the alphabetized list you are compiling by placing an asterisk before or after the name (provided you indicate the reason in the key to your index). Such an entry would read:

■ *Doe, John (10) 1f, 1m (263)*

The translation of this information would be John Doe of ward 10, page 263, is the free black head of house in which 1 female and 1 male slave reside.

Now we can conduct sociological as well as genealogical studies from the information we have obtained. We can compare the prescence of slavery ward by ward in the city, ascertain the total male and female slave population, and highlight the phenomonon (largely urban) in which slaves and free blacks were allowed to live together seperate from a householder of European descent.

Slaveholder schedules for the years 1850 and 1860 were collected as seperate documents from population schedules by the census enumerator. They are known quite simply as slave schedules. Their purported purpose was to name those individuals who were slaveholders in the community. Although the majority of those listed in these schedules are probably owners there is no way to seperate owners from employers with the exception of a few records in the 1860 listings.

Generally speaking these records are easier to index than the records of 1790-1840. Because they are seperate from the main body of population schedules, there are fewer pages to scan for the necessary information. Secondly, the space allocated for information in the records is much greater in 1850 than in previous census years. The larger samples of handwriting make the task of attempting to interpret information easier in most cases.

Slave schedules of 1850 and 1860 do not indicate the race of the slaveholder (whether white or black). It is more difficult, therefore, to determine the households in which potential free black slaveholders or the phenomonon of absentee ownership exists.

Indexing the schedules of 1850 and 1860 is accomplished in similar fashion to previous records. The names, which are grouped by wards, are indexed in the following manner:

Chapter 10

Surname, First name (Ward) and number of slaves.

A typical entry would thus read:

Doe, John (4) 1f, 2m

Translated that would indicate John Doe, residing in the 12th ward, holds 1 female and 2 male slaves in his household.

A number of possibilities now exist for us to use a variety of records (in conjunction with slave schedules);records that focus on the occupations and geographical locations of slaveholders.

Let us use the index to the 1860 slave schedules as a sample study of the technique. The documents that we will be searching are:

1.) Federal Population Census Schedules of 1860
2.) Baltimore City Directory of 1860
3.) General Property Tax Records
4.) Field Assesser Work Book

11
Slavery in Baltimore's Mount Vernon Area - A Focused Study

Our sample study will focus on the slaveholder in the 11th ward of the city of Baltimore. First we will create an alphabetized list of only those slaveholders who reside in the 11th ward. Baltimore's 11th ward was bounded by Howard Street on the west, Franklin Street on the south, Jones Falls on the east, and Biddle Street on the north. It was one of Baltimore's wealthiest neighborhoods with the Mount Vernon area as its centerpiece. Of more than 1,300 slaveholders in Baltimore in 1860 almost 200 resided in the 11th ward. Its dubious record as the largest slaveholding ward in the city was due in part to the overall wealth of many of the residents of the Mount Vernon area.

We will begin the process of focusing on the 11th ward with our alphabetized list of 11th ward slaveholders. Our first step will be to use the alphabetized list to check the index to the 1860 Federal Population Census Schedules. One thing becomes quickly apparent. It is impossible to identify every single slaveholder in our study as we survey the population census. One of the reasons for this is the prevalence of certain names in the records. Names like John W. Brown, and Henry Jones are excellent examples of this. There may be numerous citations of these "common names" in the records of a particular sector of the city. To be as thorough as possible in our process we eliminate the names for which we do not hold a high degree of certainty.

By matching those individuals whose name is unique or whose name is only matched once in the ward in question we are able to locate 73 of the slaveholders in the census records. In many of those cases we are now able to determine the occupation of the slaveholder as well as the real or personal estate holdings.

The Baltimore city directory affords us with an alphabetical listing of individuals followed by their occupation and place of residence. By following our alphabetized list of names we are now able to determine the addresses of a considerable number of our slaveholders within the 11th ward. All such addresses in the city of Baltimore were changed in the year 1886. By scanning a copy of the city directory for 1887 (which published all of the address changes) we are easily able to determine the post 1886 address of the individuals in a large number of cases.

The General property tax records of 1858 for the city of Baltimore allow us some insight into cases where slaveholders claimed their slaves as taxable property. These particular records are alphabetized, creating

Chapter 11

a valuable source for our study. When we use these records it is evident that a large number of slaveholders in the city did not name and claim their slaves as property for tax purposes. When they do claim them the record affords us with some interesting additional information on the practice of slaveholding.

Also available for the year 1858 is the field assessor work book, the preliminary study from which the general property tax records are gleaned. What makes the assessor's books more valuable is that they are more complete, giving us the names and ages of the slaves residing in the household.

The following is an index of the slave schedules for Baltimore's eleventh ward in 1860. The index compiles all available data on the individuals in the census schedules from the four records previously mentioned.

Frances J. Albert ... holds one 45-year-old male slave which the field assessor work book indicates is named Henry.

Thomas S. Alexander ... holds 1 female slave .. He is an attorney living on Charles Street, two doors south of Eager street. The census lists him with real estate valued at $20,000 and personal estate valued at $10,000.

Caroline E. Andrews ... holds 1 female slave.

Hughes C. Armstead ... holds one 20-year-old female slave named Lucy. The field assessor work book indicates that she has 6 1/2 years to serve.

William W. Aubrey ... holds 1 female slave

William D. Barret ... holds 1 female slave .. His dwelling is the northwest corner of Monument and Park. The census indicates that he has a personal estate of $1,000.

Llewellen F. Barry ... holds 1 male slave .. his dwelling is 79 W. Monument (post 1886 address is 103 W. Monument). The census lists him as an attorney with real estate valued at $30,000 and personal estate valued at $10,000.

Joseph Baugher ... holds 2 female slaves .. The field assessor work book indicates that one woman is named Priscilla (40 years of age) and the second woman is named Charlotte (45 years of age). His dwelling is 149 Park. general property tax records note his slaves valued at $400.

James H. Bayfield ... holds 2 female slaves .. his dwelling is 148 N. Howard (post 1886 address is 511 N. Howard). The census lists him as a merchant with real estate valued at $20,000 and personal estate valued at $50,000.

S. Lewis Beatty ... holds 1 female slave .. his dwelling is 139 Washington Place (post 1886 address is 603 N. Charles Street).

The general property tax records indicate he has plates, a watch, and a slave worth a total of $2,000.

Frances W. Bell ... holds 1 female slave.

Catherine Belmore ... holds 3 female slaves .. the census lists her with real estate valued at $12,000 and personal estate valued at $5,000.

Susan G. Boggs ... holds 2 female slaves .. field assessor work books indicate that she has 1 female slave named Dido. The census indicates that she has real estate valued at $6,000 and personal estate valued at $3,000.

Esau Boston ... holds 1 female slave.

Margaret Bradford ... Holds 1 male slave.

William S. Brian ... holds 1 female slave.

William Briscoe ... holds 1 female slave.

John W. Brown ... holds 1 female slave. The field assessor work book indicates that his slave's name is Charlotte.

Steven L. Bird ... holds 1 female slave.

Samuel Burns ... holds 1 female slave .. general property tax records indicate that he has furniture, plates, and slaves valued at $1,800.

Daniel M. Cann ... holds 4 female slaves.

Robert H. Carr ... holds 3 female and 1 male slave .. his dwelling is listed as 118 Cathederal (post 1886 address is 1000 Cathederal). The census lists him as a merchant with real estatevalued at $10,000 and personal estate valued at $11,000. General property tax records indicate that he has slaves valued at $900. The field assessor work book list him with one 10-year-old female slave named Lucy.

Charles R. Carroll ... holds 3 male slaves .. The census indicates that he has real estate valued at $250,000 and a personal estate of $15,000. The field assessor work book indicates that he has three male slaves; Thomas, 50 years of age, Tom, 45 years of age, and John, 30 years of age.

Harry D. G. Carroll ... holds 1 female slave .. his dwelling is on the north side of Monument Street, between Howard and Park. The field assessor work book indicates that he has one 17-year-old male slave (unnamed) and one 16-year-old female slave named Mary Elizabeth.

Judith C. Carroll ... holds 2 female slaves .. Her dwelling is 60 Franklin (post 1886 address is 21 Franklin). The census indicates that he has real estate valued at $30,000.

Thomas J. Carson ... holds 3 female and 1 male slave .. His dwelling is listed as 172 Preston (post 1886 address is 528 Preston). He

Chapter 11

is a banker.

Thomas Carver ... holds 1 female slave.

Benjamin F. Cator ... holds 4 female slaves .. The census lists him as a merchant with $8,000 real estate and $33,000 personal estate. General property tax records indicate that he has slaves and furniture valued at $1,1000.

Francis Churchman ... holds 1 female slave.

Elizabeth Clark ... holds 1 female slave.

Maria Clark ... holds 1 male slave. She is indicated as living in Mt. Vernon Place.

Martha M. Clark ... holds 1 female slave.

Elizabeth Cockey ... holds 1 female slave.

James C. Conn ... holds 1 female slave .. He is a grocer with a dwelling at 287 N. Howard (post 1886 address is 866 N. Howard).

Solomon Corner ... holds 1 female slave .. His dwelling is listed as 122 St. Paul (post 1886 address is 810 St. Paul). The census lists him as a merchant with real estate holdings of $30,000 and personal estate holdings of 10,000.

James S. Cottman ... holds 3 female slaves .. His dwelling is 73 St. Paul (post 1886 address is 333 St. Paul). The census lists him as a merchant with personal estate valued at $5,000. The general property tax records list him as having slaves valued at $250.

Benjamin F. Coy ... holds 1 female slave.

William Crichton ... holds 1 female slave ... his dwelling is listed as Monument street near St. Paul. The census lists him as a merchant with real estate valued at $30,000 and personal estate valued at $20,000.

Edward B. Dallam ... holds 1 female slave ... his dwelling is 89 St. Paul (post 1886 address is 405 St. Paul street. The census lists him as a merchant with $800 real estate and $1,500 personal estate.

John D. Daniels ... holds 2 female slaves ... The census lists him as a brewer with $17,000 real estate and $17,000 personal estate.

Miss Darkins ... holds 1 female slave.

John G. Day ... holds 1 male slave.

Benjamin Deford ... holds 1 male slave ... His dwelling is 105 N. Charles street (post 1886 address is 405 N. Charles street). The census lists him as a merchant with $100,000 in real estate and $200,000 personal estate.

Maria Denham ... holds 1 female slave.

Ann Denmead ... holds 1 male slave.

Ann Denny ... holds 1 female slave ... Her dwelling is 70 St. Paul (post 1886 address is 402 St. Paul). The census lists her with

$20,000 in real estate and $4,000 in personal estate. The field assessor work book indicates that she has one 62-year-old female slave named Charlotte.

Mary Doane ... holds 1 female slave.

Horace Edmondson ... holds 1 female slave.

John B. Egerton ... holds 1 female slave ... The census lists him as a retired broker with $50,000 in real estate and $50,000 in personal estate. The general property tax records list him as having horses and slaves valued at $300. The field assessor work book lists him as having one 45-year-old female slave named Lilly (with 3 years to serve).

Catherine Emory ... holds 1 male slave

Henry M. Emory ... holds 1 male slave.

Walter Fernandis ... holds 1 female slave.

Josiah Ford ... holds 1 female slave.

Moreau Forrest ... holds 1 male slave

Richard France ... holds 3 female and 2 male slaves .. His dwelling is Mt. Vernon Place. The census list him with real estate valued at $400,000 and personal estate valued at $100,000.

Reverend Richard Fuller ... holds 4 female and two male slaves ... His dwelling is 97 Park (post 1886 address is 709 Park). The census lists him as a Baptist clergyman with $20,000 in real estate and $5,000 in personal estate.

Philip T. George ... holds 1 female and 1 male slave .. The census lists him as a merchant with $7,500 in real estate and $12,000 in personal estate.

George S. Gibson ... holds 1 male and 1 female slave .. His dwelling is 116 Park (post 1886 address is 578 Park). The census lists him as a physician with real estate valued at $81,000 and personal estate valued at $4,250. General property tax records list him with slaves valued at $400. The field assessor work book indicates that he has one 26-year-old male slave named Sims and one 13-year-old female slave named Mary.

John S. Gittings ... holds 1 female and 1 male slave ... His dwelling is 149 St. Paul (post 1886 address is 701 St. Paul).

William S. Gittings ... holds 1 male slave ... His dwelling is 338 W. Madison (post 1886 address is 496 W. Madison). The census lists him as a clerk with no real or personal estate.

Henrietta Glenn ... holds 1 female slave.

Mrs. Goldsborough ... holds 2 female and 2 male slaves.

William Gordon ... holds 1 female slave.

Ann Gough ... holds 1 female slave.

Mary Gough ... holds 1 female slave.

Chapter 11

Sarah Green ... holds 1 male slave.

James Gregg ... holds 2 female slaves ... His dwelling is 58 Franklin (post 1886 address is 19 Franklin). The field assesser work book indicates that he has 2 female slaves; Caroline, 16 years of age and Delia, 18 years of age.

John Griffith ... holds 4 female and 1 male slave. The general property tax records lists slaves valued at $2,050.

Michael Griffith ... holds 2 female and 1 male slave.

Henry Grogan ... holds 1 male slave.

Anthony Groverman ... holds 3 female and 1 male slave ... His dwelling is on the Northeast corner of Charles and Eager streets.

Samuel Groverman ... holds 1 female slave.

Mrs. James Hackett ... holds 1 male slave ... The field assesser work book indicates that she has one 21-year-old female slave.

Eliza Hall ... holds 1 male slave.

Robert B. Hallady ... holds 1 male slave.

Mary C. Hamilton ... holds 1 female slave.

Thomas E. Hamilton ... holds 1 female slave.

Thomas Handy ... holds 1 female slave.

Richard S. Hardesty ... holds 1 female slave ... Census list him as a retired merchant with real estate valued at $50,000 and personal estate valued at $50,000.

J. Morrison Harris ... holds 1 male slave ... He is listed as an attorney at law.

Samuel A Harrison ... holds 1 female and 1 male slave ... His dwelling is Charles Street, two doors North of Eager street. The census lists him as a physician with real estate valued at $25,000 and personal estate valued at $5,000. The field assesser work book indicates that he has one 17-year-old male slave named Murray and one 14-year-old female slave named Leona.

Eliza Hayne ... holds 1 female slave ... Her dwelling is 33 Hamilton (post 1886 address is 18 Hamilton).

John H. Heald ... holds 1 female slave ... The census lists him as tanner holding real estate valued at $20,000 and personal estate valued at $3,000. The field asseser work book indicates that he has one 18-year-old male slave named Harrison.

Benjamin Heigh ... holds 2 female and 1 male slave ... His dwelling is 44 Mulberry (post 1886 address is 117 Mulberry). The census lists him as a lawyer with real estate valued at $40,000 and personal estate valued at $15,000.

J. Frisby Henderson ... holds 1 male slave ... The census lists him as a lawyer with real estate valued at $15,000 and personal estate valued at $15,000.

Peter Hernan ... holds 1 female slave.
Charles H. Hey ... holds 3 female slaves.
Dr. James Higgans ... holds 1 male slave ... His dwelling is on the S. E. Corner of Mulberry and St. Paul.
Rebecca A. Hillen ... holds 1 female slave ... The census lists her personal estate valued at $10,000.
Joshua F. Hitchcock ... holds 1 female slave ... His dwelling is 287 Cathederal (post 1886 address is 1409 Cathderal). The census lists him as a lime inspector with personal estate valued at $150.
Elizabeth Hooper ... holds 1 female slave.
Lavina Hopkins ... holds 1 male slave.
Robert Hough ... holds 1 male slave ... His dwelling is 228 N. Charles Street (post 1886 address is 926 N. Charles Street). The census lists him as a merchant with personal estate valued at $60,000.
Benjamin C. Howard ... holds 5 female and 4 male slaves ... His dwelling is 39 Mulberry (post 1886 address is 108 Mulberry). The census lists him as a reporter for the Superior Court with real estate valued at $50,000 and personal estate valued at $25,000.
Charles Howard ... holds 1 female and 1 male slave ... His dwelling is 33 Cathedral (post 1886 address is 809 Cathederal).
Henrietta Howard ... holds 1 female slave.
Mary Howard ... holds 1 female slave.
Ellen M. Hunter ... holds 2 female slave ... Her dwelling is 141 Park (post 1886 address is 835 Park). The census lists her personal estate valued at $5,000. The field assessor work book indicates that she has two female slaves; Rebecca, 50 years of age and Harriet, 12 years of age.
Thomas T. Hutchins ... holds 3 female slaves ... His dwelling is 132 Park (post 1886 address is 708 Park). The census lists him as a lawyer with personal estate valued at $10,000. The field assessor work book indicates that he has one 25-year-old female slave named Sally, one 13-year-old female slave named Laura, and one 9-year-old male slave named John.
Jane Hutton ... holds 1 female slave ... Her dwelling is 123 Park (post 1886 address is 817 Park). The census lists her with real estate vakued at $6,000 and personal estate valued at $2,000.
George Hyland ... holds 1 female slave.
Mary Hyland ... holds 1 female slave ... The census lists her as operator of a boarding house with personal estate valued at $3,000. The field assessor work book indicates that she has one 11-year-old female slave named Ellen and one 14-year-old male slave named Sam.

Chapter 11

Edward Ireland ... holds 2 female slaves ... His dwelling is 232 N. Howard (post 1886 address is 813 N. Howard). The census lists him as a retired merchant with real estate valued at $16,000 and personal estate valued at $4,000. The field assesser work book indicates that he has one 14-year-old female slave named Rachel, one 60-year-old female slave named Phoebe, and one 45-year-old male slave named Aaron.

Mollie E. Jackson ... holds 1 male slave ... The census lists her with real estate valued at $30,000 and personal estate valued at $10,000.

Charles C. Jameson ... holds 3 female and 2 male slaves ... His dwelling is 129 Mulberry (post 1886 address is 514 Mulberry). The census lists him as a bank president with real estate valued at $7,500 and personal estate valued at $30,000. The field assesser work book indicates that he has 3 female slaves (not named in the record) ages 35, 50, and 67 years old.

John Jameson ... holds 1 male slave.

Ann M. Jenkins ... holds 2 female slaves.

Austin Jenkins ... holds 1 female slave ... His dwelling is 128 Park (post 1886 address is 702 Park). The census lists him as a merchant with real estate valued at $40,000 and personal estate valued at $40,000. The Field Assesser Work Book indicates that he has one 20-year-old female slave named Sarah and one 21-year-old female slave named Rose.

Mary A. Jenkins ... holds 1 male slave.

Robert T. Jenkins ... holds 1 female slave ... The census lists him as a merchant with real estate valued at $17,000 and personal estate valued at $70,000. The field assesser work book indicates that he has one 25-year-old female slave named Susan.

The Order Of Jesuits ... holds 1 female slave.

Elizabeth Johnston ... holds 1 female slave.

Henry Jones ... holds 1 female slave.

George P. Kane ... holds 2 male slaves ... The census lists him as Marshall Of Police with real estate valued at $15,000 and personal estate valued at $15,000.

Richard Keene ... holds 1 female slave.

John N. Kemp ... holds 1 female slave ... The census lists him as a waiter with personal estate valued at $40.

Augustus Kilty ... holds 1 female slave ... His dwelling is 41 Mulberry (post 1886 address is 110 Mulberry).

Langford, Henry ... holds 2 female slaves ... The census lists him as a merchant with real estate valued at $8,000 and personal estate valued at $5,000.

William Leach ... holds 1 female slave.
Samuel S. Levering ... holds 1 male slave ... His dwelling is Monument near Calvert. The census lists him as a merchant with personal estate valued at $10,000. The general property tax records note the value of his female slave and a horse at $1,500. The field assessor work book indicates that he has one 13-year-old male slave named David.
Thomas W. Levering ... holds 1 female and two male slaves.
William Loney ... holds 1 female slave ... His dwelling is 237 Madison Ave. (post 1886 address is 1425 Madison Ave.). The census lists him as a Gentleman with real estate valued at $50,000 and personal estate valued at $3,000.
Josiah Lord ... holds 2 female slaves.
Robert H. Love ... holds 4 female slaves ... His dwelling is 138 Park (post 1886 address is 714 Park). The general property tax records note that he has furniture, plates, a watch and slaves valued at $2,100. The field assessor work book indicates that he has one 50-year-old female slave named Charlotte, one 16-year-old female slave named Keziah, one 14-year-old female slave named Rachel, one 60-year-old female slave named Josephine and one 14-year-old male slave named Sidney.
Colin Mackenzie ... holds 2 female slaves ... The census lists him with personal estate valued at $3,000.
Charles T. Maddox ... holds 1 male slave ... He is a judge on the Appeals Tax Court.
Mary Maddox ... holds 1 female slave.
Susan Makepeice ... holds 1 male slave.
J. McKIm Marriott ... holds 1 female and 1 male slave ... His dwelling is on the N. E. corner of Park and Madison. The general property tax records note him with furniture, plates and slaves valued at $2,250. The Field Assessor Work Book indicate that he has one 12-year-old female slave named Hanna.
William Martin ... holds 1 female slave.
Augustas Matthiot ... holds 1 male slave.
Edward Mc Adams ... holds 1 female slave ... He is a soap and candle manufacturer.
John C. Mc Abe ... holds 1 female slave ... He is a Protestant Episcopal clergyman. The general oroperty tax records note him with furniture, library and slaves(no value was indicated).
William W. McClellan ... holds 1 female slave ... His dwelling is 67 Cathederal (post 1886 address is 1007 Cathederal).
John McDevitt ... holds 1 female slave ... His dwelling is 367 E. Eager Street (post 1886 address is 1635 E. Eager street).

Chapter 11

Margaret McElderry ... holds 2 female and 2 male slaves.

John S. McKin ... holds 1 female slave ... His dwelling is Belvedere near North.

Emily McTavish ... holds 1 female and 1 male slave ... Her dwelling is 84 Cathderal Street (post 1886 address is 816 Cathederal street). The census lists her with persoanl estate valued at $10,000. The general property tax records note her with furniture, plates, and slaves valued at $4,650.

Henrietta Medcalfe ... holds 1 male slave.

Decatur Miller ... holds 2 female slaves ... The census lists him as a gentleman with real estate valued at $25,000 and personal estate valued at $10,000. The general property tax records note him with furniture, plates, and slaves valued at $5,720.

Sallie H. Montague ... holds 1 male slave.

John B. Morris ... holds 3 female and 1 male slave ... His dwelling is 22 Mulberry (post 1886 address is 9 Mulberry). The census lists him as a gentleman with real estate valued at $193,796 and personal estate valued at $6, 500. The field assesser work book indicates that he has one 70-year-old female slave named Nelly, one 30-year-old female slave named Betty, and 1 male slave named Edwin (no age indicated).

Richard Munroe ... holds 1 male slave.

Thomas Z. Neale ... holds 3 female slaves.

James N. Nicholson ... holds 4 female and three male slaves ... The census lists him as a lawyer with real estate valued at $36,000 and personal estate valued at $30,000. General property tax records notes him with furniture, plates, and slaves valued at $3,700. The field assesser work book indicates that he has one 70-year-old female slave named Amy, one 58-year-old female slave named Sally, one 33-year-old female slave named Mary, one 31-year-old female slave named Ellen, and one 43-year-old male slave named Henry.

Margaret Nicholson ... holds 1 female slave.

Kennedy O. Norris ... holds 1 female slave.

William H. Norris ... holds 2 female and 1 male slave ... The census lists him as a lawyer with real estate holdings valued at $10,000 and personal estate holdings valued at $9,000. The field assesser work book indicates that he has one 22-year-old female slave named Marsha, one 22-year-old female slave named Molly, and one 19-year-old female slave named Anna.

Robert Pendleton ... holds 2 female amd 1 male slave ... His dwelling is 70 Cathederal Street (post 1886 address is 802 Cathederal Street). The census lists him as a gentleman with real estate valued at $40,000 and personal estate valued at $10,000.

Jane Perkins ... holds 2 female slaves.

William Perkins ... holds 1 male slave.

John B. Piet ... holds 1 female slave ... His dwelling is 49 Mulberry (post 1886 address is 118 Mulberry). The census lists him with real estate valued at $10,000 and personal estate valued at $4,500. The general property tax records note him with a slave valued at $200. The field assessor work book indicates that he has one 14-year-old female slave named Susan and one 14-year-old female slave named Lucy.

Charles M. Plator ... holds 2 female slaves.

Henry Poindexter ... holds 2 females slaves ... The census lists him a s a merchant with real estate valued at $13,000 and personal estate valued at $25,000. The field assessor work book indicates that he has one 22-year-old female slave (unnamed) and one 9-year-old female slave (unnamed).

Maria Porter ... holds 1 male slave.

Marion Price ... holds 1 female slave.

Henry Y. Purviance ... holds 1 male slave ... The census lists hum as a Captain in the U. S. Navy with real estate valued at $45,000 and personal estate valued at $50,000.

William G. Read ... holds 2 female and 1 male slave ... The census lists him as a lawyer with personal estate valued at $15,000.

Andrew S. Ridgely ... holds 1 female slave ... His dwelling is 67 Franklin (post 1886 address is 204 Franklin). The census lisis him as a lawyer with personal estate valued at $2,000.

Mary L. Ridgely ... holds 1 male slave ... Census lists her with real estate valued at $150,000 and personal estate valued at $5,000.

Jesse S. Schofield ... holds 2 females slaves ... The census lists him as a property agent with real estate valued at $5,000 and personal estate valued at $7,000.

Augustas F. Seavers ... holds 1 female slave ... The census lists him as a broker with real estate valued at $10,000 and personal estate valued at $5,000. The general property tax records notes his furniture and slaves valued at $650. The field assessor work book indicates that he has one 10-year-old female slave named Ellen.

Mary Seldon ... holds 1 female slave.

Henry W. Sheffy ... holds 1 female slave.

John Shields ... holds 1 female slave.

Samuel M. Shoemaker ... holds 2 female slaves ... His dwelling is the northeast corner of St. Paul and Read Street. The census lists him as an express agent with real estate valued at $75,000 and personal estate valued at $2,600.

Chapter 11

Dr. Shorb ... holds 1 female slave.
Andrew Shriver ... holds 1 male slave.
Hugh Sisson ... holds 1 female and 1 male slave ... The census lists him as a master stone cutter with real estate valued at $35,000 and personal estate valued at $30,000.
John E. Slade ... holds 1 female slave.
Stephen Sorrell ... holds 1 female slave.
R. Spraights(the estate of) ... holds 1 female and 1 male slave.
Edward Tagart ... holds 2 female and 1 male slave.
Catherine Taskins ... holds 1 female slave.
Ann Taylor ... holds 1 female slave.
Hanson J. Thomas ... holds 2 female slaves.
Susan Thompson ... holds 1 female slave.
William Thompson ... holds 1 female slave.
Charles Tiernan ... holds 1 female and 2 male slaves ... His dwelling is 123 N. Charles (post 1886 address is 517 North Charles). The census lists him as a gentleman with real estate valued at $50,000 and personal estate valued at $55,000.
Charles Tilghman ... holds 1 female slave.
Henry Tilghman ... holds 1 female slave.
Benjaimin Tubman ... holds 1 female slave.
Eliza Veazy ... holds 1 female slave.
Elizabeth Waguarman ... holds 1 female slave.
Josiah Walker ... holds 1 male slave.
George W. Ward ... holds 1 male slave ... His dwelling is 74 Centre Street (post 1886 address is 9 Centre street). The census lists him as a merchant with real estate valued at $500 and personal estate valued at $30,000. The field assessor work book indicates that he has one 35-year-old male slave named Aleck.
Rebecca Waters ... holds 2 male slaves ... The census lists her with personal estate valued at $40,000.
Robert Waters ... holds 5 female and 1 male slave ... The census lists him as a retired farmer with real estate valued at $8,000 and personal estate valued at $11,000.
Dr. William Waters ... holds 1 female slave.
Michael Welling ... holds 1 male slave.
George H. Williams ... holds 1 female and 1 male slave.
John Williams (estate of) ... holds 1 female slave. The field assessor work book indicates that he had one 62-year-old female slave named Sally and one 20-year-old female slave naemd Susan.
Lewis Williams ... holds 2 female and 1 male slave.
Thomas Williams ... holds 2 male slaves.
Thomas Williams ... holds 3 female slaves ... The field assessor work

book indicates that he has one 22-year-old female slave (unnamed) and one 3-year-old and one 6-month-old child (unnamed).
Virginia Williams ... holds 1 female slave.
Robert G. Wilson ... holds 2 female slaves.
Samuel Worthington ... holds 1 female slave.
W. H. D. C. Wright ... holds 5 male slaves ... His dwelling is 109 N. Charles Street (post 1886 address is 409 N. Charles). The census lists him as a merchant with real estate holdings valued at $75,000 and personal estate holdings valued at $52,000. The field assesser work book indicates that he has one 20-year-old female slave named Lizzy and one 20-year-old male slave named Jake.

A close study of the slave schedules in conjunction with the tax assesser's field books lead to several very interesting conclusions. A thorough study of the 11th ward (the area bounded by Saratoga, Howard, Biddle and the Jones Falls) indicate numerous changes in slaveholding in a two year period 1858-1860. The ward was known as one of the wealthiest areas of the city during the period between 1850-1860. Part of that wealth was due to the large slave population; a population that served many of the notable doctors, lawyers, and merchants in that sector.

In 1852 a city ordinance was passed, regulating the values of slaves for the purposes of municipal taxation. Slaves who were unable to serve due to ill health or age were exempt from the tax. Following is a list of the price ranges of slaves (as taxable property) created under this ordinance.

Males
0 - 12 years $75
12 - 21 years $250
21 - 45 years $400
45 - 60 years $160

Females
0 - 12 years $50
12 - 21 years $200
23 - 40 years $300
45 - 60 years $100

By 1853 the personal and real estate value held by the ward eleven's inhabitants exceeded $6,600,000. A portion of a table of statistics from the *Baltimore Sun* of May 7, 1853 reveals the value of slaves and real

Chapter 11

estate througout the city in that same year. The statistics were collected by field assesers using the guidelines of the 1852 Ordinance previously listed.

Wards	Real Estate (Value in Dollars)	Slaves (Value in Dollars)
1st Ward	2,370,829	5,850
2nd Ward	1,969,685	5,950
3rd Ward	2,566,563	12,780
4th Ward	2,181,363	20,160
5th Ward	1,364,148	7,325
6th Ward	1,755,946	13,510
7th Ward	1,653,951	3,975
8th Ward	2,187,497	6,800
9th Ward	7,740,871	8,335
10th Ward	4,309,711	20,735
11th Ward	6,638,512	40,985
12th Ward	3,002,756	23,195
13th Ward	5,321,968	27,970
14th Ward	3,665,877	28,140
15th Ward	3,776,662	31,855
16th Ward	1,821,818	5,950
17th Ward	3,313,685	2,525
18th Ward	4,906,670	34,330
19th Ward	2,416,283	6,445
20th Ward	3,307,064	20,000
Totals	$66,271,259	$326,815

There are a number of individuals claiming to hold or own slaves in the 1858 field assseser's tax book who do not appear in the slave schedules of ward 11 in 1860. Their entries are listed as:

Timothy P. Andrews	West side of Mt. Vernon between St. Paul and Washington Place
	1 male slave, Nathan, 32
	1 female slave, Emily, 18
	1 female slave Cherry, 10
W. H. Beatty	1 female slave, Phoebe
Dr. James Bordley	1 male slave, Tom, 16

Slavery in Baltimore's Mount Vernon Area

Richard P. Bowie	1 female slave, Sophie, 35
	1 female slave, Maria (baby)
	1 male slave, John, 15
	1 male slave, William, 12
A. W. Bradford	*West side of Park*
	1 female slave, Fillis, 50
	1 female slave, Charity, 30
	1 male slave, Billy, 20
Anna M. Brice	1 female slave, Mabel, 50
	1 female slave, Wilona, 18
	1 female slave, Kitty, 17
Dr. John Buckler	1 male slave, Glover, 28
	1 female slave, Priscilla, 27
	1 female slave, Mary, 35
Robert Buckmiller	*East side of North*
	1 female slave, Ann Webster, 45
Charles Carroll	*North Side Mount Vernon Place*
	1 male slave, James, 40
	1 female slave, Harriet, 30
	1 male slave, Austin, 18
	1 male slave, William, 15
	1 female slave, Margaret, 25
	1 female slave, Fisby, 35
	1 female slave, Matilda, 25
	1 female slave, Ann, 14
James Carroll	*S. E. Corner of Monument and Howard*
	1 male slave, James, 58
	1 female slave, 16
	1 female slave, Eliza, 45
Wilson M. Cary	1 female slave, Ann, 30
J. Lyle Clark	1 female slave, Emma, 14
Sophia Clark	*North side of Mount Vernon Place*
	1 female slave, Susan, 17
	1 male slave, Cato, 30
	1 female slave, Chloe, 14
	1 female slave, Emily, 35
	1 female slave, Priscilla, 9
	1 female slave, Matilda, 7
	1 female slave, Anna, 3
Adam Denmead	1 female slave, Susanna, 65
	1 female slave, Deborah, 30
	1 male slave, Jim 5

Chapter 11

Anderson Ellicott	1 male slave, Berry, 15
	1 male slave, Hamilton, 15
	(belongs to James Johnston, Lexington above Schroeder)
William H. Emory	1 female slave, Susan, 28
William Fisher	1 male slave, Daniel, 18
Campbell Graham	1 male slave, John, 25
Henry Hardesty	1 female slave, Esther, 46
Emily Harper	1 female slave, Ellen, 20
H. H. Haydens	1 female slave, Mary, 45
Susan Henderson	1 male slave, (unnamed), 12
Solomon Hillen Jr.	1 female slave, Lizzy, 13
	1 male slave, Henson (hired)
Henry F. Jackson	*North side of Monument Street*
	1 female slave, Dotty
Courtney Jenkins	*S. W. corner of Courtland and Mulberry*
	1 female slave, Eliza, 32
	1 male slave, Henry, 26
E. F. Jenkins	*South side of Monument Street, between Howard and Park*
	1 male slave, John, 6
John Johnston	*N. E. corner of Mount Vernon and Cathederal Street*
	1 female slave, Jane, 50
Joshua Jones	1 female slave, Anna, 26
Catherine Kelly	1 female slave, Madonna, 20
	1 female slave, Mary, 18
Michael J. Kelly	1 female slave, Louisa, 16
Peter Kernan	1 female slave (no name or age indicated)
Charles H. Key	1 female slave, Mabel, 50
	1 female slave, Fanny, 28 (Belongs to Colonel Lloyd, Talbot Co.)
Mrs Frank Key	1 female slave, Annabelle, 22
	1 male slave, Henry, 17
G. W. Levering	1 female slave, Eliza, 35
	1 male slave, Sims, 2
	1 male slave, Dan, 33
Daniel McCann	1 female slave, Elizabeth, 40
	1 female slave, Sophy, 21
	1 female slave, Emily, 21
Hugh McElderry	*St. Paul St.*
	1 female slave, Charlotte, 60
John S. McKim	1 male slave, Joshua, 35

	1 female slave, Josephine, 30
John McTavish	1 female slave, Kate, 70
	1 female slave, Ann, 40
	1 female slave, Polly, 18
	1 female slave, Ann, 15
	1 female slave, Lizzie, 20
	1 female slave, Columbia, 10
Henry S. Mitchell	1 female slave, Sally, 55
	1 female slave, Caroline, 21
	1 male slave, Daniel, 21
	1 female slave, Nelly, 15
Thomas Morris	1 male slave, William, 10
John Murphy	1 female slave, Ellen, 45
Francis Neale	1 female slave, Lucinda, 30
	1 female slave, Rosetta, over 60
Albert A. Nernes	1 female slave, Julia, 50
	1 female slave, Annabelle, 30
	1 male slave, John, 15
	1 female slave, May, 15
Sarah E. Patterson	1 female slave, Dinah, 48
Dr. James Perkins	1 female slave, Ann, 25
William Price	1 female slave, Eliza, 14
	1 female slave, Priscilla, 40
E. Samuel Rogers	1 female slave, Adeline, 19
	1 female slave, Jane, 45 (property of C. M. Plater, Talbot Co.)
Joshua Royston	1 female slave, (unnamed), 35
P. B. Sadtler	1 male slave, Levi, 30
	1 male slave, Jacob, 22
Richard Simmons	1 female slave, Selby, 35
Mr. Sofanchirco	1 male slave, John, 15
	1 female slave, Caroline, 22
B. R. Spalding	1 female slave, Clara, 35
Charles Morton Stewart	1 female slave .. Minty, 40
	1 male slave, Sam, 8 (both slaves belong to Carrol Spencer)
Thomas Swann	*South side of Franklin between Park and Cathederal*
	1 female slave, Lavinia (no age indicated)
William F. Taylor	*East side of Park*
	1 male slave, Isaac, 28
	1 male slave, Dick, 8
	1 female slave, Leah, 26

Chapter 11

Dr. Alexander Tyson	1 female slave, Flora, 4 1 female slave, Liddy, 11 1 male slave, George, 19 (Belongs to Miss McCloskey of Fremont St. near Franklin)
Mrs Jane Von Sprecklesen	1 male slave, Bob, 50
Henry Walton	1 male slave, John, 17
C. A. Williamson	1 female slave, Sidney, 14 (Owned by .. name not discernable)
William H. D. C. Wright	1 female slave, Lizzy, 20 and 1 male slave, Jake, 22

More than 160 (76%) of the slaveholders of the 11th ward listed in the 1860 slave schedules do not appear in the field assesser's work books for 1858. There are several possible reasons for this. By the late 1850's slavery was on the decline in Baltimore. There were sales and hirings of the slaves in the city on a continual basis. The system of slavery in the city was therefore in a constant state of change. As the need for slave labor decreased slaves were hired out to individuals in other areas of the city or surrounding counties. The change can be viewed by looking at the tax records in conjunction with slave schedules for Baltimore.

Another possibility exists that must be explored. Census slave schedules were records that would not affect the individual in any direct or immediate way. The records were collected on the Federal level of government and would not be open for the scrutiny of local individuals. The tax records, on the other hand, would affect the city tax that an individual would have to pay in a more immediate and intrusive manner. It is possible that some of the holders failed to claim their slaves on the one record to avoid paying their city tax and agreed to claim them on the Federal record that would affect them in a less dramatic and immediate way.

With information available from these documents it is easy to see how we can begin to tell a great deal about the nature of slaveholding in an area of particular geographical focus. With post 1886 addresses in hand it is also possible for us to determine, through the use of other records available in the city of Baltimore, which ante bellum structures may still be in existence. Many of the fine old ante bellum houses of Baltimore's wealthy Mount Vernon area stand intact today, along with their slave quarters, so often attached to the rear of the main house.

Many of the more affluent slaveholders of the city took an active participation in affairs of business or petitioning for beneficial changes in Baltimore. They became involved in the drive for the widening of streets as well as improvements and construction of municipal projects.

William H. DeCoury Wright, Baltimore slaveholder, circa 1860. Photo courtesy of the Maryland Historical Society.

Slave quarters attached to the rear of 110 W. Mulberry St. (formerly the Augustus Kilty residence). Photo by Tom Lauer.

409 N. Charles St.; formerly the home of slaveholder William H. DeCoury Wright, now the site of the Euble Blake Cultural Center. Photo by Tom Lauer.

Because of this it is possible to track a number of the more affluent slaveholders through documents filed at the Baltimore City Archives. In light of the fact that a number of the very same slaveholders were professionals (i. e. doctors, lawyers, shipping merchants) correspondence, deeds, and other documentation may have survived in the files of the Maryland Historical Society.

One example of such an affluent slaveholder is William H. DeCoursey Wright. Mr. Wright owned the plantation known as Blakesford, in Queen Anne's County. He also owned a house located in the one hundred block of North Charles Street(Currently 409 N. Charles Street). He was the son of a former governor of Maryland (Robert Wright).

In 1825, William Wright became the consul for the United States to Rio De Janeiro. While in Brazil he formed close business ties with coffee exporters and managed to bring substantial trade between the ports of Baltimore and Rio De Janeiro. As a result, he became a coffee shipping merchant and helped to organize the Maxwell-Wright (coffee importing) company in Baltimore. Upon his death in March of 1864 the Sun reported that he had been a model citizen, always interested in helping the poor in the community.

Records of Mr. Wright's transactions can be found in various documents throughout the city of Baltimore: field assessor work books, population census, slave schedules, city directories, manuscripts including manumission records and letters, newspaper articles, and general property tax records to name a few.

By using records such as city directories, slave schedules, business directories, newspaper accounts, obituaries, tax records and local histories it is possible to focus on information concerning the slaveholder. The key to finding the slaves, therefore, is to work through the records of the slaveholder.

By using the techniques indicated in the chapter on Research Techniques For Locating The Slaveholder we are now able to locate and index the slaveholders of Baltimore in 1840. The index is organized as follows: Surname, then first name of slaveholder, ward number, number of slaves by sex, page number where located in the census schedules of aforementioned ward.

Therefore a sample entry such as

Abercrombie, Mary - w 9, s 1f, p 123

would translate as: Mary Abercrombie, head of house in which 1 female slave resides in the census records of ward 9 of Baltimore city on page 123.

A name with ■ indicates that the head of house is a Black person.

Chapter 11

Slaveholding Households in Baltimore, 1840

Abercrombie, Mary - w 9, s 1f, p 123
Abrahams, Samuel C. - w 3, s 1f, p 121
Adams, David - w 5, s 1f, p 232
Adams, James - w 11, s 4f, p 228
Adams, Philip - w 7, s 1m, p 24
Adams, Stephen ■ - w 8, s 1f, p 62
Adams, William - w 6, s 1f, p 262
Adams, William ■ - w 12, s 1m, p 312
Adams, William F. - w 1, s 1f, p 5
Aisguith, Charlotte - w 9, s 2f, p 108
Albert, Eliza - w 6, s 1m, p 266
Alexander, Ashton - w 7, s 1m, p 5
Allen, Robert W. - w 5, s 1f, p 233
Allender, Mary - w 5, s 2f, p 230
Allison, Mrs. - w 10, s 2f, p 140
Alricks, Hennarus - w 3, s 1m, p 125
Ames, George C. - w 5, s 1f, 1m, p 223
Anderson, James - w 6, s 2m, p 271
Anderson, James M. - w 3, s 1f, p 100
Applegarth, Alexander - w 5, s 1f, p 241
Archer, R. H. - w 7, s 1m, p 17
Arden, David - w 6, s 1f, p 276
Armstrong, James - w 5, s 1f, p 208
Ashton, John - w 6, s 1m, p 261
Ashton, Margaret C. - w 11, s 2f, p 228
Askew, Mrs. - w 10, s 1f, p 156
Atkinson, John H. - w 5, s 1f, p 240
Atkinson, William - w 5, s 2f, p 234
Augustus, Charles ■ - w 8, s 1m, p 40
Ault, Samuel - w 3, s 1m, p 125
Ayers, Charles - w 12, s 1f, p 264
Ayres, L. - w 9, s 1m, p 123
Bachem, Alex - w 9, s 1f, p 129
Bad, R. S. A. - w 9, s 1f, p 102
Badger, Jarret ■ - w 11, s 1m, p 199
Badger, Richard R. - w 11, s 1m, p 198
Baer, Dr. M. S. - w 9, s 2f, p 121
Bailey, George - w 9, s 1f, p 131
Bailey, William - w 5, s 1f, p 251
Baker, David - w 5, s 3m, p 228
Baker, Francis - w 7, s 2f, p 26
Baker, J. S. - w 9, s 1m, p 123
Baker, Maria - w 7, s 1m, p 4
Baker, Peter - w 8, s 4f, 2m, p 60
Baker, Samuel George - w 9, s 1m, p 131
Baldwin, Pierson - w 1, s 1f, p 12
Ball, Walter - w 12, s 3f, p 282
Ball, William Jr. - w 11, s 1m, p 222
Baltzell, Jacob - w 10, s 1f, p 146
Bandel, William S. - w 6, s 1f, p 271
Bandle, William - w 6, s 1f, p 271
Bangs, John - w 11, s 1f, 1m, p 221
Barber, John T. - w 2, s 1m, p 93
Barclay, Mary - w 8, s 1m, p 49
Bardie, Mrs. Jane - w 10, s 1f, p 176
Barker, Elizabeth - w 12, s 1f, p 274
Barnedo, J. W. - w 12, s 1f, p 278
Barnes, Mary - w 1, s 2f, p 4

Slavery in Baltimore's Mount Vernon Area

Slaveholding Households in Baltimore, 1840

Barnett, William - w 10, s 1m, p 168
Barney, John - w 7, s 3f, 1m, p 21
Barney, Lewis - w 10, s 1f, 1m, p 146
Barns, Joseph ■ - w 1, s 3f, p 9
Barrett, Henry - w 11, s 1m, p 227
Barrow, John - w 11, s 1m, p 211
Barry, John - w 12, s 1f, p 303
Barry, Robert - w 8, s 1f, p 43
Bartlett, George - w 9, s 1m, p 130
Barton, Cordelia - w 1, s 1m, p 122
Barton, William - w 3, s 1m, p 142
Bashell, Charles - w 9, s 1m, p 122
Battee, R. H. - w 8, s 1f, 1m, p 41
Bauffre, Mrs. J. D. - w 6, s 2m, p 274
Baughman, Frederick - w 10, s 1f, p 152
Baxter, J. N. - w 7, s 1f, p 17
Bealman, Catherine - w 10, s 1f, 1m, p 168
Beam, Joseph - w 9, s 1m, p 127
Beam, Rick - w 11, s 2f, 3m, p 235
Bean, George - w 1, s 1f, p 33
Bean, Richard - w 1, s 1f, p 11
Beeman, Joseph J. - w 1, s 1f, p 12
Belt, J. H. - w 7, s 2f, 1m, p 28
Bennet, J. - w 11, s 2f, 1m, p 210
Bennett, Prudence - w 8, s 1f, p 71
Bennett, William - w 2, s 1f, s 92
Benson, Joseph - w 9, s 1f, p 122
Benson, Paul - w 1, s 1f, p 25

Benson, Samuel - w 6, s 2f, p 280
Benzinger, M. - w 11, s 1f, p 227
Berger, John - w 4, s 3m, p 193
Bescler, Daniel - w 11, s 1f, p 241
Bevan, Thomas - w 12, s 1f, p 320
Bine, Robert - w 11, s 1m, p 202
Birch, William S. - w 7, s 1m, p 24
Birckhead, Hugh - w 9, s 1f, 2m, p 129
Bizouard, Mrs. - w 10, s 1f, p 158
Black, John - w 1, s 1f, p 12
Black, William B. - w 3, s 1f, p 146
Blacke, John W. - w 4, s 1f, p 191
Blair, James - w 12, s 1m, p 309
Blakely, J. H. - w 7, s 1f, p 10
Blakney, Able R. - w 4, s 1f, 1m, p 190
Blanchard, Elizabeth - w 7, s 2f, p 27
Boardley, D. C. H. - w 10, s 5f, p 168
Boardley, J. B. - w 6, s 1f, p 288
Boarman, G. S. - w 12, s 2m, p 296
Bochmas, Charles L. - w 9, s 3f, p 129
Boggs, Marmomas - w 9, s 1f, 2m, p 114
Boggs, William - w 5, s 1m, p 223
Bolden, Alexander - w 4, s 1f, p 193
Bolling, Larence - w 5, s 1f, p 216
Bolster, Thomas - w 8, s 1f, p 46
Bolton, Hugh - w 5, s 1f, s 250
Bond, Barnet - w 2, s 1m, p 86
Bond, Ellen - w 11, s 1f, p 226
Bond, Thomas W. - w 5, s 2f, 1m, p 210

Chapter 11

Slaveholding Households in Baltimore, 1840

Bond, Z. O. - w 3, s 1f, 1m, p 132
Bool, Henry W. - w 6, s 1f, p 280
Boon, Joshua ■ - w 8, s 1m, p 70
Boone, Nicholas - w 3, s 1f, p 131
Borsch, Henry - w 5, s 1f, p 241
Bosard, Joseph - w 7, s 1m, p 18
Bose, William - w 7, s 1f, p 17
Boses, Louis - w 11, s 1f, p 197
Boslry, James - w 7, s 2f, 1m, p 5
Boston, John - w 5, s 1f, 1m, p 252
Boston, John B. - w 5, s 1f, p 252
Boswell, James - w 3, s 1f, p 145
Boulden, Owen - w 1, s 1f, p 48
Bowen, Richard - w 3, s 1f, p 137
Bowman, Ignatius - w 12, s 1m, p 310
Boyd, Elizabeth - w 7, s 1f, p 4
Boyle, Hugh - w 7, s 1m, p 19
Bradford, A. W. - w 3, s 1f, 1m, p 134
Bradshaw, Catherine - w 7, s 6f, 2m, p 18
Bradshaw, Richard - w 6, s 2m, p 260
Brannan, Alexander - w 6, s 1f, 1m, p 291
Brant, Jacob - w 11, s 2f, 1m, p 202
Brashears, Francis - w 2, s 1f, 1m, p 87
Brawner, Andrew - w 3, s 1m, p 109
Brevitt, Cassander - w 5, s 2f, p 244
Brewer, Edward W. - w 3, s 1m, p 138
Brewer, Elias - w 6, s 1m, p 261
Brewer, Nicholas - w 5, s 1f, 1m, p 250
Briant, John E. - w 6, s 1f, p 273

Brice, Honorable J. - w 7, s 2f, 2m, p 8
Bridges, William - w 91f, p 108
Briggs, Ann - w 8, s 1f, p 54
Bright, Thomas - w 5, s 1m, p 214
Briser, Lewis ■ - w 11, s 3m, p 232
Bromwell, Joseph R. - w 5, s 1f, 1m, p 216
Broom, John - w 1, s 1f, p 4
Broom, Thomas - w 1, s 1m, p 45
Broughton, James - w 5, s 1m, p 249
Brown, Alexander - w 6, s 1f, p 289
Brown, Benjamin - w 9, s 1f, 2m, p 117
Brown, Fisher ■ - w 11, s 2f, p 235
Brown, Garet - w 6, s 1f, p 278
Brown, John - w 5, s 1f, p 227
Brown, John N. - w 11, s 1f, p 224
Brown, John R. - w 1, s 1f, p 224
Brown, John T. - w 9, s 1m, p 101
Brown, Joseph ■ - w 1, s 1m, p 46
Brown, Joshua - w 12, s 1f, p 302
Brown, Mrs. G. J. - w 6, s 1m, p 282
Brown, Richard ■ - w 12, s 1m, p 272
Brown, Robert - w 7, s 2m, p 13
Brown, Sarah - w 11, s 2f, p 229
Brown, William - w 1, s 2m, p 36
Brown, William - w 9, s 1f, p 131
Browne, E. N. - w 9, s 1f, p 131
Browning, Edward - w 8, s 5f, 8m, p 84
Brune, J. C. - w 7, s 1m, p 16

84

Slavery in Baltimore's Mount Vernon Area

Slaveholding Households in Baltimore, 1840

Bruner, Daniel - w 11, s 1f, p 214
Bryden, James W. - w 1, s 1f, 1m, p 47
Buchanan, Elizabeth - w 7, s 1f, 1m, p 4
Buchanan, J. M. - w 7, s 2f, p 28
Buchanan, Miss Sidney - w 6, s 1f, p 282
Buck, Benjamin - w 5, s 2f, 1m, p 220
Buck, Jacob J. - w 7, s 1m, p 10
Buckey, Daniel - w 12, s 3f, p 280
Buckey, Mrs. - w 10, s 1f, p 161
Buckler, John - w 7, s 1f, 1m, p 16
Buckmiller, Robert - w 6, s 1f, p 292
Bujac, Edele - w 3, s 5f, p 132
Bull, G. M. - w 7, s 2f, 1m, p 13
Bull, Harriet - w 3, s 1f, p 108
Bull, Jarrett - w 10, s 1f, p 155
Burk, Margarett - w 10, s 1f, p 146
Burk, Nicholas - w 4, s 1f, p 195
Burk, Washington - w 12, s 1f, p 274
Burk, William - w 3, s 1f, p 143
Burke, John - w 9, s 1f, p 131
Burnes, Francis - w 11, s 1m, p 220
Burneston, Ann - w 12, s 1m, p 262
Burnet, Samuel - w 9, s 1f, p 117
Burns, R. D. - w 9, s 2f, p 132
Burris, John - w 6, s 1f, 1m, p 260
Busk, George W. - w 1, s 2f, 1m, p 9
Butcher, Alsi - w 9, s 1m, p 130
Butler, James ■ - w 8, s 2f, 2m, p 40
Butler, Moses ■ - w 11, s 2f, 2m, p 215
Butler, Thomas - w 9, s 1m, p 120
Clifford, John - w 11, s 1f, p 229
Caduc, John - w 5, s 1m, p 214
Caldwell, Rachel - w 5, s 2f, 3m, p 239
Calhoun, Benjamin C. S. - w 11, s 1m, p 230
Clark, Levin P. - w 5, s 1f, p 245
Cameron, Samuel - w 1f, s 1f, p 124
Campbell, Edward ■ - w 12, s 1m, p 298
Campbell, J. M. - w 7, s 1m, p 16
Campbell, Robert - w 9, s 1f, p 132
Cantwell, Sarah - w 11, s 1f, p 235
Care, Ann - w 7, s 1f, p 13
Carman, Jacob - w 5, s 1f, p 219
Carpenter, Uriah - w 8, s 1f, p 45
Carroll, Cesar ■ - w 12, s 1f, p 298
Carroll, Charles - w 10, s 4f, 3m, p 146
Carroll, H. D. G. - w 6, s 4f, 2m, p 273
Carroll, Mrs. R. - w 7, s 4f, p 14
Carson, George - w 9, s 2f, p 109
Cary, William - w 5, s 1f, p 238
Cassell, Edward ■ - w 12, s 3f, 2m, p 256
Caton, Richard - w 5, s 4f, 6m, p 230
Cator, Joseph - w 11, s 3f, 1m, p 211
Caughey, B. H. P. - w 10, s 3f, p 162
Caughey, Michael - w 6, s 1f, 3m,

85

Chapter 11

Slaveholding Households in Baltimore, 1840

p 268
Chaisty, Edmond - w 10, s 1m, p 185
Chalmers, William - w 4, s 1f, p 202
Chapmon, H. D. - w 11, s 1m, p 206
Chappell, Philip - w 10, s 1m, p 154
Chase, A. H. - w 9, s 1f, p 125
Chase, Britian - w 8, s 2f, 1m, p 36
Chase, Daniel - w 10, s 3f, 2m, p 142
Chase, Thorndick - w 2, s 1f, p 55
Chase, Will - w 11, s 1m, p 225
Chassaing, Edward - w 10, s 1f, p 160
Chew, Samuel - w 10, s 2f, p 141
Childs, James S. - w 8, s 1f, p 66
Christie, Cordelia - w 6, s 2f, 3m, p 288
Clagett, Thomas - w 5, s 2f, p 251
Claggett, Eli - w 5, s 2f, 3m, p 227
Claggett, Sarah - w 7, s 1f, 2m, p 28
Clare, Thomas J. - w 8, s 1f, 1m, p 42
Clark, Alex - w 1, s 1f, p 27
Clark, Charles - w 1, s 2f, p 24
Clark, J. - w 9, s 1f, p 132
Clark, J. F. - w 12, s 1f, p 322
Clark, John - w 5, s 1m, p 243
Clark, Kane M. - w 8, s 1f, p 49
Clark, Maria - w 9, s 1f, p 30
Clark, Mathew - w 12, s 1f, p 251
Clark, Sarah - w 11, s 1f, p 224
Clark, William - w 11, s 1f, p 200
Clarke, Robert - w 3, s 1f, 1m, p 102

Cleary, Jonathan - w 2, s 2f, p 87
Clendenin, David - w 8, s 2m, p 39
Clifford, Sylvester - w 11, s 1m, p 217
Cline, Jacob - w 8, s 1f, p 79
Clopper, Ann - w 7, s 2f, p 15
Cobb, Josiah - w 9, s 1m, p 125
Cobb, Ruth A. - w 7, s 2f, p 26
Cockrill, Rebecca - w 2, s 1f, 1m, p 51
Cocky, Charles E. - w 5, s 1f, p 208
Cocky, John P. - w 5, s 3f, p 232
Coe, A. B. - w 12, s 1f, 1m, p 268
Cohen, Benjamin J. - w 9, s 1m, p 131
Cohen, David J. - w 10, s 2f, p 166
Cohen, E. P. - w 7, s 1f, 1m, p 26
Cohen, Jacob J. - w 7, s 1f, p 19
Cole, Elisa - w 7, s 3f, 2m, p 19
Cole, Isabella - w 11, s 2f, 1m, p 230
Cole, Joshua - w 6, s 1f, p 272
Coles, John - w 9, s 1f, 1m, p 109
Collins, George C. - w 5, s 1m, p 216
Collins, J. W. - w 9, s 5f, p 129
Collins, William H. - w 6, s 3f, 2m, p 290
Conine, William C. - w 6, s 1m, p 278
Conklin, William H. - w 2, s 2f, p 72
Conn, Elizabeth - w 3, s 1f, p 116
Conn, William - w 9, s 1m, p 127
Constable, Benjamin ■ - w 11, s 1m, p 225
Contee, Philip ■ - w 8, s 1m, p 67
Conway, Robert - w 2, s 1f, p 73

Slaveholding Households in Baltimore, 1840

Conway, Thomas - w 12, s 1f, 2m, p 322
Cook, Columbus E. - w 3, s 1f, 1m, p 122
Cook, Mary - w 5, s 1f, 1m, p 217
Cook, W. - w 10, s 1f, p 153
Cooney, Patrick - w 1, s 1f, p 23
Cooper, John - w 3, s 1f, p 119
Cooper, James - w 8, s 1m, p 49
Cooper, John - w 6, s 2m, p 274
Corner, James C. - w 1, s 2f, 1m, p 24
Cosking, F. S. - w 12, s 2f, p 283
Costello, James J. - w 3, s 2f, p 102
Cottrell, Clark - w 8, s 2f, p 57
Coulson, Thomas H. - w 5, s 1f, p 214
Cowpland, William S. - w 1, s 1m, p 10
Cox, C. - w 8, s 3f, 2m, p 92
Cragen, William - w 11, s 2m, p 199
Craig, James L. - w 7, s 2f, 1m, p 24
Cramer, Dora - w 4, s 1f, p 176
Cramer, Edward - w 4, s 1f, p 180
Crandell, John - w 8, s 7m, p 33
Crawford, Alexander - w 7, s 1f, p 27
Crawford, William Jr. - w 7, s 1m, p 5
Crochett, Thomas J. - w 9, s 1f, p 114
Cromwell, Debrow - w 5, s 1m, p 244
Cromwell, Joshua - w 1, s ?, p 35
Cromwell, Mercy - w 3, s 1f, 1m, p 122
Crook, Joseph - w 6, s 2f, p 289
Crook, William - w 5, s 1m, p 218
Crookshanks, John - w 8, s 1f, 1m, p 41
Cross, John - w 5, s 2f, p 244
Croxall, Richard - w 10, s 2f, p 153
Cugle, John - w 9, s 1f, p 119
Cummings, Samuel - w 2, s 1f, p 91
Cummins, Ann - w 6, s 2f, 1m, p 290
Cunningham, John - w 2, s 1f, p 58
Cunningham, John - w 3, s 1f, p 123
Cunningham, Mortimer - w 6, s 3m, p 266
Cunnungham, James - w 3, s 1f, p 123
Cupbord, Ellen - w 6, s 2f, 1m, p 285
Curtain, Lucreta - w 5, s 1m, p 238
Curtain, Thomas - w 3, s 4f, 2m, p 148
Curtis, Levi - w 5, s 2f, 1m, p 241
Cushing, Joseph Jr. - w 8, s 1f, p 45
David, John - w 7, s 1m, p 18
Duhamel, J. - w 10, s 1f, p 158
Dail, Daniel - w 5, s 1f, 1m, p 216
Dailey, John - w 11, s 1f, p 238
Daily, Elijah - w 12, s 1m, p 273
Dallam, F. J. - w 7, s 3m, p 17
Dashields, Mary - w 2, s 2f, 1m, p 63
Davey, Hugh - w 2, s 1m, p 62
Davin, William - w 5, s 1f, p 218
Davis, Catherine - w 12, s 1m, p 264
Davis, Charles S. - w 5, s 3f, p

Chapter 11

Slaveholding Households in Baltimore, 1840

239
Davis, David - w 3, s 1f, p 140
Davis, Fanny ■ - w 5, s 1m, p 249
Davis, Hanna - w 7, s 2f, 3m, p 7
Davis, Jacob G. - w 7, s 1f, 2m, p 14
Davoul, Rubin - w 11, s 4f, p 225
Davy, Hugh - w 2, s 1f, p 57
Dawson, John - w 2, s 1f, p 11
Dawson, William H. - w 8, s 4f, p 46
Dawson, Thomas R. - w 1, s 1m, p 9
DeLaRoche, George - w 5, s 2f, p 223
Deaver, E. K. - w 12, s 1f, p 287
Dekins, Julia - w 8, s 2m, p 72
Delerue, Mrs. - w 10, s 1f, p 148

Deluol, Dr. - w 10, s 2m, p 162
Dempster, John - w 8, s 2m, p 90
Denison, Edward - w 12, s 1f, 1m, p 258
Denison, Marcus - w 6, s 2f, p 273
Denmaker, J. J. - w 8, s 1f, p 77
Denny, Elizabeth - w 2, s 1f, p 87
Denny, Thomas - w 5, s 1f, p 217
Denny, William - w 2, s 1f, 1m, p 95
Deronceray, Charles - w 5, s 1f, p 215
Devries, William - w 12, s 1f, p 251
Dickey, James ■ - w 11, s 1m, p 198
Diffendeffer, Catherine R. - w 5, s 2f, p 242
Diffendeffer, Charles - w 5, s 2f, p 242
Dincan, George - w 12, s 1f, p 322

Dine, Mary H. - w 7, s 3m, p 3
Dobbin, G. M. - w 7, s 2f, 2m, p 16
Donald, Mrs. Ann - w 6, s 1f, p 292
Donaldson, Catherine - w 9, s 3f, p 130
Donaldson, J. J. - w 7, s 3f, 1m, p 23
Donaldson, Samuel J. - w 7, s 1f, p 17
Donnelly, Rean - w 11, s 3f, 1m, p 239
Donnold, Ann - w 12, s 2f, p 322
Donovan, Dr. O. - w 10, s 1f, p 152
Donovan, J. S. - w 8, s 1f, p 76
Dorman, William - w 2, s 1m, p 59
Dorsey, Augusta - w 7, s 1f, p 7
Dorsey, Bartholomew ■ - w 10, s 1f, p 147
Dorsey, Bateman ■ - w 8, s 1m, p 81
Dorsey, Elizabeth - w 1, s 1m, p 32
Dorsey, Jacob - w 8, s 1f, p 76
Dorsey, Joseph - w 7, s 1f, p 13
Dorsey, Loyd - w 5, s 2f, 2m, p 238
Dorsey, Michael - w 8, s 2m, p 54
Dorsey, Mrs. E. - w 7, s 2f, 2m, p 29
Dorsey, Richard - w 10, s 1f, 2m, p 146
Doubledee, Samuel - w 12, s 1f, p 274
Dougherty, Hanna - w 7, s 1m, p 5
Dowell, John - w 4, s 1f, p 172

Slavery in Baltimore's Mount Vernon Area

Slaveholding Households in Baltimore, 1840

Downing, N. - w 10, s 1m, p 141
Doxey, Josiah - w 12, s 1f, p 33
Doyle, William - w 4, s 1f, p 172
Dryden, E. S. - w 9, s 1f, p 123
Dryden, J. - w 9, s 2f, p 130
Dudley, J. L. - w 8, s 1m, p 41
Dugan, F. J. - w 7, s 1f, 1m, p 4
Dugan, Mrs. Cumberland - w 6, s 2f, 1m, p 290
Duhurst, Mrs. Mary - w 6, s 1m, p 281
Dull, James - w 8, s 1f, p 40
Dunan, Emily - w 5, s 1f, p 240
Dunan, Gustavus - w 12, s 1f, p 282
Duncan, Joseph - w 6, s 1m, p 283
Dunham, Thorton C. - w 11, s 2f, p 227
Dunhel, Catherine - w 5, s 2f, 1m, p 239
Dunn, James - w 9, s 1f, 1m, p 114
Dunn, Michael - w 11, s 1f, p 206
Dusenburg, S. B. - w 9, s 3f, 1m, p 125
Dusheve, John - w 9, s 1m, p 112
Dutton, John - w 2, s 1f, p 70
Dutton, Robert - w 2, s 2f, 1m, p 67
Duvall, Richard - w 11, s 1f, p 224
Easter, John - w 10, s 1f, p 140
Eccleston, Samuel - w 10, s 1m, p 153
Eden, William - w 12, s 2f, 2m, p 256
Edes, M. A. - w 6, s 1f, 1m, p 272
Edmondson, John - w 8, s 1f, 2m, p 81
Edwards, Ann - w 12, s 1m, p 316
Egerton, John B. - w 3, s 2f, p 106
Egleston, Rebecca - w 1, s 1f, p 10
Eichelberger, Charles - w 2, s 1f, p 91
Eichelberger, James - w 2, s 1f, p 87
Eichelberger, Martin - w 7, s 1m, p 3
Eichelbuger, John M. - w 12, s 1m, p 304
Elder, Hillary - w 12, s 1f, p 291
Elder, Hussey P. - w 11, s 5f, 9m, p 242
Elderman, Frederick W. - w 6, s 1f, p 289
Ellicott, Samuel J. - w 9, s 1f, p 109
Elmore, James - w 1, s 2m, p 45
Elnese, Basil S. - w 11, s 1f, p 235
Elsworth, Thomas J. - w 6, s 1f, 1m, p 278
Emmers, J. - w 4, s 1f, p 163
Emory, Anna L. - w 9, s 4f, 3m, p 124
Emory, William H. - w 12, s 3f, 1m, p 282
Emrys, Daniel C. - w 11, s 2f, p 224
Ennalls, Margaret - w 6, s 1f, p 282
Estes, E. B. - w 9, s 1f, 1m, p 114
Euhler, Christian - w 11, s 2f, p 230
Evans, David - w 1, s 1f, p 11
Evans, Mary - w 5, s 1m, p 235
Evans, Miss M. - w 7, s 2f, p 3
Evans, Miss M. - w 10, s 1f, p

Chapter 11

Slaveholding Households in Baltimore, 1840

176
Evans, Thomas - w 11, s 1f, p 233
Evatt, Columbus - w 9, s 1f, p 111
Fales, James - w 1, s 2f, p 36
Falls, M. - w 10, s 2f, 1m, p 139
Family, Worden - w 4, s 1f, p 162
Farnandis, Walker - w 9, s 3f, 2m, p 122
Farndon, D. J. - w 9, s 1f, p 104
Farrall, Sarah - w 8, s 1f, p 43
Farrell, Joshua - w 1, s 1f, p 15
Farrow, Joseph - w 6, s 1f, p 283
Faulkner, Thomas - w 5, s 1f, 3m, p 218
Fenby, Peter - w 1, s 1f, 1m, p 19
Fenby, Rebecca - w 6, s 1f, p 284
Fenwick, George - w 11, s 1f, p 241
Ferguson, George - w 8, s 1m, p 46
Ferguson, Thomas - w 7, s 4f, p 21
Fichey, Frederick - w 9, s 1f, 1m, p 131
Fisher, Charles - w 11, s 1f, p 235
Fisher, Henry - w 7, s 1f, p 4
Fisher, James J. - w 7, s 1m, p 16
Fisher, Thomas - w 7, s 1f, p 7
Fites, Mary - w 9, s 2f, p 105
Fitzgerald, Capt. Richard - w 11, s 1f, p 232
Fitzgerald, Henry - w 8, s 1f, p 41
Fitzgerald, John - w 8, s 1f, p 81
Fitzhugh, H. W. - w 9, s 1f, 1m, p 132
Fitzpatrick, John - w 8, s 1f, 1m, p 49

Flanagan, Andrew - w 5, s 1m, p 224
Fleck, James - w 11, s 1f, p 234
Flemming, James - w 5, s 1f, p 253
Floyd, D. J. - w 12, s 1f, p 315
Foley, S. J. - w 8, s 2f, p 43
Ford, George W. - w 8, s 1f, p 44
Ford, Lewis - w 2, s 1f, 1m, p 87
Foreman, Lenard - w 5, s 4f, 1m, p 208
Foreman, Valentine - w 10, s 1m, p 150
Forsyth, Alexander - w 10, s 3f, 3m, p 189
Fowler, Richard J. - w 5, s 1f, p 222
Fowlers, Sarah - w 9, s 2f, 1m, p 114
Franciscus, John - w 6, s 2f, 1m, p 279
Frazier, James - w 1, s 1f, p 14
Frazier, Jeremiah - w 1, s 1m, p 13
Freeland, Egbert - w 9, s 1f, p 132
Frisby, Catherine - w 1, s 1f, p 15
Frisby, L. - w 11, s 3f, p 234
Fry, John - w 1, s 1m, p 14

Fulford, Mary F. - w 7, s 3f, 2m, p 23
Fuller, Horace - w 1, s 1f, p 30
Funk, Frederick - w 4, s 1m, p 192
Gambel, Charles - w 11, s 1f, p 224
Gamble, David - w 12, s 1f, p 274
Gant, Christopher - w 5, s 1f, p 227

Slaveholding Households in Baltimore, 1840

Gardner, John - w 2, s 1m, p 63
Garland, N. - w 7, s 1m, p 16
Garrettson, Bennett - w 11, s 1f, p 223
Gatchell, M. H. - w 7, s 1m, p 23
Geban, Joseph - w 3, s 1f, p 110
Gelson, Hugh - w 10, s 1m, p 150
Gelston, Hugh - w 12, s 2m, p 320
Geoghegan, James - w 8, s 2f, p 42
George, Archabald - w 10, s 2m, p 149
Gepson, Jacob ■ - w 11, s 2f, 2m, p 202
Germaine, Jonathan - w 6, s 1f, p 262
German, Benjamin - w 3, s 1f, p 148
Gibbs, A. C. - w 9, s 1f, p 132
Gibson, Doctor - w 10, s 1f, 1m, p 146
Gibson, Elizabeth - w 1, s 2f, 1m, p 24
Gilbey, Rebecca - w 11, s 1f, p 209
Gildea, John - w 5, s 1f, p 213
Gill, Berson - w 9, s 1f, 1m, p 123
Gillson, Elizabeth - w 11, s 1f, 1m, p 235
Gilmore, Roberet - w 12, s 5f, 3m, p 322
Ginnamon, Patrick - w 11, s 1f, p 201
Gist, Samuel - w 8, s 1f, p 44
Gist, William - w 9, s 2f, p 121
Gittings, John S. - w 6, s 2f, 1m, p 289
Glanville, Mary - w 8, s 1f, p 40
Glenn, Elias - w 12, s 1f, p 322
Glenn, John - w 9, s 2f, 1m, p 132

Goddard, Charles - w 11, s 3m, p 232
Goldsborough, Nicholas - w 10, s 2f, p 154
Goldsmith, Elizabeth W. - w 1, s 3f, 3m, p 47
Gooden, John - w 5, s 2f, p 221
Goodwin, Caleb - w 5, s 1f, 1m, p 217
Goodwin, Eliza - w 4, s 1f, 1m, p 192
Goodwin, Lyde - w 7, s 2f, p 17
Gordon, John M. - w 7, s 1f, 1m, s 16
Gorrell, George - w 2, s 1m, p 91
Gorsuch, Agnes - w 3, s 1f, p 102
Gorsuch, John - w 5, s 1f, p 248
Gorsuch, Peregrine - w 3, s 1f, p 129
Gorsuch, William G. - w 10, s 2m, p 140
Gott, Thomas J. - w 5, s 1f, p 223
Gould, Alexander Sr. - w 8, s 1f, p 82
Gould, Peter - w 7, s 1f, p 8
Gould, Richard ■ - w 12, s 1m, p 289
Goulder, Archibald - w 7, s 1m, p 3
Gover, George P. - w 3, s 2f, 1m, p 134
Grace, Adam ■ - w 1, s 1m, p 16
Grace, Henry - w 3, s 1f, p 126
Grace, John - w 5, s 1m, p 210
Graflin, Jacob W. - w 5, s 2f, 1m, p 244
Grafton, Martha - w 5, s 1f, 1m, p 240
Graham, Elizabeth - w 11, s 1f, p 201
Graham, William - w 2, s 1f, 1m,

Chapter 11

Slaveholding Households in Baltimore, 1840

p 57
Gratts, Sarah - w 10, s 1m, p 147
Gravinstein, James H. - w 5, s 1m, p 247
Gray, Adam - w 5, s 3f, p 223
Gray, Esther - w 9, s 2f, 2m, p 119
Gray, William - w 1, s 1m, p 12
Green, Abraham - w 4, s 1f, p 177
Green, Charles - w 4, s 1m, p 166
Green, Duff - w 5, s 1m, p 233
Green, G. M. - w 12, s 2m, p 305
Gregg, Alexander - w 6, s 1m, p 281
Gregg, T. - w 10, s 3f, p 153
Griffin, E. T. - w 12, s 1f, p 308
Griffith, Allen - w 8, s 2f, p 41
Griffith, Isreal - w 9, s 6f, 3m, p 122
Griffith, R. B. - w 12, s 1f, p 309
Griffith, Susan - w 8, s 1f, p 42
Gross, John T. - w 4, s 1f, p 167
Gross, Lenard ■ - w 11, s 1m, p 211
Grove, Sarah - w 12, s 1f, p 269
Grovermans, A. - w 9, s 2f, 1m, p 120
Gudgeon, Jesse - w 3, s 1f, p 152
Guest, Richard W. - w 9, s 1f, p 121
Gunby, James - w 1, s 1f, p 17
Gunn, AnnMaria - w 9, s 3f, 1m, p 106
Gunther, H. H. - w 8, s 1m, p 35
Gwinn, William - w 12, s 1f, 1m, p 255
Habun, Charles - w 12, s 1f, p 279
Hace, William H. - w 11, s 1f, 1m, p 201
Hack, Ann M. - w 7, s 6f, 1m, p 7
Hack, John - w 12, s 1m, p 280
Haired, John J. - w 9, s 1m, p 127
Hale, Philip M. - w 3, s 1f, p 132
Hall, A. C. - w 10, s 1f, p 166
Hall, Charlotte - w 3, s 1f, p 126
Hall, Chris - w 6, s 1f, p 273
Hall, D. W. - w 12, s 1f, p 260
Hall, Daniel - w 1, s 1f, 1m, p 8
Hall, Elisa - w 9, s 3f, 2m, p 104
Hall, John - w 1, s 1f, p 4
Hall, John - w 4, s 1f, p 178
Hall, Leonard - w 9, s 1f, p 117
Hall, MaryAnn - w 3, s 2f, 1m, p 106
Hall, R. H. - w 12, s 4f, 4m, p 318
Hall, R. W. - w 7, s 1f, 2m, p 14
Hall, Richard M. - w 6, s 2f, p 260
Hall, Robert - w 3, s 1f, p 219
Hamill, James - w 5, s 1f, p 240
Hamilton, Even - w 11, s 1f, p 226
Hamilton, James - w 6, s 1f, p 283
Hamilton, James - w 12, s 1f, 1m, p 315
Hamilton, William - w 7, s 2f, 1m, p 16
Hammond, John - w 5, s 1f, p 214
Hancock, Absalom - w 3, s 1f, 1m, p 138
Hancock, Robert B. - w 5, s 1f, p 220
Handy, S. J. K. - w 10, s 1f, 1m, p 148
Hanimon, Charles - w 12, s 4f, 1m, p 258
Hanville, James - w 6, s 1m, p 271

Slaveholding Households in Baltimore, 1840

Harching, Walter E. - w 5, s 2f, 1m, p 217
Harden, William - w 11, s 1f, p 242
Hardester, Henry - w 5, s 1f, p 251
Hardesty, Henry - w 9, s 2f, p 119
Hardesty, John - w 3, s 1f, p 144
Hardy, John - w 12, s 1f, p 256
Hardy, Priscilla - w 12, s 3f, 2m, p 283
Hardy, Robert - w 7, s 1f, p 12
Hardy, Samuel ■ - w 12, s 1f, p 257
Harison, Thomas - w 12, s 2f, p 299
Harman, John M. - w 7, s 1f, p 27
Harney, E. R. - w 12, s 1f, p 259
Harp, David - w 10, s 2f, p 150
Harper, Mrs. C. C. - w 10, s 4f, p 153
Harris, Eliza ■ - w 8, s 1m, p 46
Harris, James - w 8, s 1f, p 61
Harrison, A. C. - w 7, s 1f, p 16
Harrison, Ann - w 9, s 1f, p 122
Harrison, Benjamin B. - w 2, s 1f, p 60
Harrison, Charles - w 9, s 1f, p 117
Harrison, Nathan - w 3, s 1f, 4m, p 154
Harrison, Thomas - w 1, s 1f, p 13
Hart, Ann - w 3, s 1m, p 120
Hart, Archabald - w 11, s 5f, 2m, p 233
Harvey, Joshua - w 9, s 1f, p 120
Harwood, J. - w 7, s 1m, p 16
Harwood, James - w 10, s 1f, p 149
Haslup, Henrietta - w 3, s 1f, p 131
Haslup, John - w 5, s 1f, p 250
Haslup, Margaret - w 5, s 1f, p 244
Hassleford, Winlo - w 3, s 1f, p 150
Haubert, Elizabeth C. - w 11, s 1f, 4m, p 226
Hawkins, James L. - w 6, s 2f, 1m, p 290
Hawkins, John J. - w 8, s 2f, 3m, p 66
Haynes, C. Y. - w 3, s 1f, p 101
Hays, William - w 4, s 1f, p 181
Heald, William - w 5, s 1f, 1m, p 243
Healy, John - w 9, s 1f, p 108
Heath, Richard - w 11, s 1f, 2m, p 220
Hebb, Hopewell - w 1, s 1f, p 33
Heckrotte, William - w 8, s 3f, p 35
Hederiger, Catherine - w 3, s 1f, p 150
Heigh, Jane - w 8, s 3f, 4m, p 36
Heighe, B. M. - w 10, s 1f, p 145
Helpin, Patrick - w 3, s 1f, p 100
Henderson, James - w 6, s 1f, p 273
Henderson, John - w 5, s 1f, 1m, p 217
Henisler, G. A. - w 10, s 1f, p 169
Henrix, Thomas - w 5, s 1f, p 226
Henry, William - w 9, s 2f, p 128
Herrington, James - w 8, s 1f, 2m, p 79
Herrington, Samuel - w 8, s 1f, p 54
Hess, Joseph Jr. - w 11, s 1f, p 224

Chapter 11

Slaveholding Households in Baltimore, 1840

Hess, S. - w 11, s 1f, p 243
Hickey, Morton - w 11, s 1m, p 199
Hickley, Robert - w 10, s 1m, p 139
Hickman, Nathaniel - w 6, s 1f, p 289
Hicks, Robert ■ - w 2, s 1m, p 81
Hide, Rachael - w 7, s 1f, 1m, p 29
Higens, Richard W. - w 11, s 1f, 2m, p 216
Higgins, Edwin - w 8, s 2f, p 33
Hildebrand, N. W. P. - w 6, s 2f, 1m, p 259
Hill, Pipin - w 6, s 1m, p 281
Hill, Robert M. - w 8, s 1f, p 37
Hillen, John - w 3, s 1f, p 106
Hilliard, B. F. - w 7, s 2f, 1m, p 14
Hindes, Rebecca - w 9, s 1f, p 114
Hinds, James B. - w 11, s 2f, p 226
Hines, Isaac - w 5, s 3f, 1m, p 232
Hinkley, Edward - w 10, s 1m, p 146
Hintze, F. C. B. - w 6, s 1m, p 274
Hiser, H. W. - w 12, s 1f, p 304
Hiss, Elizabeth S. - w 5, s 1f, p 217
Hitch, Charles ■ - w 8, s 1m, p 39
Hitch, William - w 12, s 2f, 1m, p 320
Hobbs, Samuel - w 12, s 1f, p 314
Hodges, B. H. - w 7, s 2f, 2m, p 14
Hodges, B. O. - w 7, s 1m, p 18
Hodges, John - w 11, s 1f, p 218
Hodges, Mary H. - w 12, s 2f, 1m, p 278
Hodges, Samuel ■ - w 12, s 1f, p 257
Hoffman, Charles - w 12, s 2f, p 268
Hoffman, David - w 5, s 2f, 1m, p 239
Hoffman, George - w 10, s 2f, p 153
Hoffman, George L. - w 9, s 1f, p 107
Hoffman, S. O. - w 7, s 1f, p 14
Hogg, John - w 9, s 1f, p 98
Holbrook, Joseph - w 5, s 1f, 1m, p 238
Holdon, Ebenezer - w 9, s 1f, p 106
Holliday, Jesse - w 4, s 1f, p 191
Holliday, Jesse L. - w 4, s 1fm, 1m, p 170
Hollin, Henry ■ - w 11, s 2f, 3m, p 203
Hollingshead, Francis - w 8, s 1m, p 44
Hollingshead, John - w 8, s 1f, p 66
Hollingsworth, May - w 9, s 1f, p 132
Hollins, John S. - w 6, s 1f, 1m, p 290
Hollins, Lieutenant G. - w 7, s 1m, p 29
Hollins, William - w 7, s 1f, p 4
Holmead, J. B. - w 12, s 1f, p 280
Holtzman, J. F. - w 7, s 1m, p 4
Homes, James - w 11, s 2f, p 218
Hoofnagle, Lydia - w 8, s 1f, p 56
Hook, Joseph Jr. - w 12, s 2f, 3m, p 306
Hooker, James - w 4, s 1f, p 201
Hooper, Amasa - w 3, s 1f, p 152

94

Slavery in Baltimore's Mount Vernon Area

Slaveholding Households in Baltimore, 1840

Hooper, Capt. Thomas - w 8, s 2f, p 72
Hooper, James - w 8, s 5f, 1m, p 40
Hooper, James J. - w 12, s 1f, 1m, p 252
Hooper, James Jr. - w 9, s 3f, p 116
Hooper, John P. - w 8, s 1f, p 40
Hooper, Sarah - w 2, s 3f, 3m, p 320
Hooper, William - w 5, s 2f, p 224
Hooper, William E. - w 5, s 1f, p 215
Hopkins, John - w 11, s 2f, 1m, p 222
Hopkins, Johns - w 9, s 1m, p 132
Horn, Benjamin - w 10, s 1m, p 190
Horsey, W. H. - w 9, s 2f, 4m, p 114
Hostman, Charles - w 1, s 1f, p 11
Hough, Robert - w 9, s 1f, p 114
House, Jesse - w 4, s 2m, p 192
House, Samuel - w 8, s 6f, 2m, p 37
House, William A. - w 8, s 1f, p 35
Howard, B. C. - w 7, s 3f, 4m, p 18
Howard, James - w 6, s 2f, 2m, p 273
Howard, Robert - w 4, s 1f, p 162
Howitt, Elmer - w 6, s 1m, p 263
Huges, James - w 1, s 1f, 2m, p 48
Huges, Lydia - w 1, s 1f, p 33
Hughes, Agerellas - w 11, s 1f, p 245

Hugo, Samuel B. - w 6, s 2f, 2m, p 281
Huks, John - w 11, s 1f, p 244
Hulett, J. D. - w 11, s 1f, p 227
Hunt, Sheridan - w 9, s 1f, p 116
Hunter, John - w 5, s 1f, 1m, p 250
Hunter, William - w 5, s 1f, 4m, p 248
Huppman, George - w 9, s 1m, p 123
Hynson, Nathaniel K. - w 6, s 3f, p 278
Idlett, Peter - w 8, s 1f, p 64
Inloes, Henry A. - w 2, s 1f, p 69
Inloes, J. S. - w 8, s 1f, p 39
Inloes, William - w 1, s 1f, p 26
Ironmonger, E. L. - w 9, s 1f, p 128
Jackson, Christopher ■ - w 8, s 1m, p 67
Jackson, William - w 2, s 2f, 2m, p 55
Jacobs, Robert T. - w 9, s 1m, p 99
Jamart, Michael - w 6, s 5f, 5m, p 290
James, Acach - w 9, s 1f, p 98
Jamison, C. C. - w 7, s 1f, p 26
Janney, Sarah ■ - w 11, s 1m, p 198
Jenkins, Alfred - w 9, s 1f, p 105
Jenkins, Courtney - w 10, s 4f, p 152
Jenkins, Edward F. - w 7, s 2f, p 26
Jenkins, James - w 7, s 1, p 6
Jenkins, Joseph - w 3, s 1f, p 150
Jenkins, Joseph - w 7, s 1f, p 26w
Jenkins, Mrs. F. - w 7, s 2f, p 7
Jenkins, Sarah - w 12, s 1f, 1m, p

Chapter 11

Slaveholding Households in Baltimore, 1840

Jenkins, Thomas C. - w 7, s 2f, p 309, 27
Jewitt, Joseph - w 6, s 2f, 10m, p 291
Johns, John - w 3, s 2f, 2m, p 106
Johns, Kensey - w 3, s 1f, 3m, p 151
Johns, Richard H. - w 1, s 1f, 1m, p 17
Johnson, Cassey ■ - w 8, s 2f, p 46
Johnson, David ■ - w 8, s 1m, p 69
Johnson, Gerard - w 3, s 1f, p 119
Johnson, Isaac - w 2, s 2f, p 86
Johnson, James - w 3, s 2f, 2m, p 100
Johnson, James - w 8, s 4f, 4m, p 42
Johnson, Jesse ■ - w 12, s 2f, p 272
Johnson, Julia Ann ■ - w 8, s 1m, p 90
Johnson, M. J. - w 11, s 1f, p 234
Johnson, Reverdy - w 7, s 1f, 1m, p 29
Johnson, William - w 9, s 1f, p 122
Johnston, John - w 6, s 1m, p 261
Johnston, T. D. - w 11, s 1f, p 239
Jones, Elijah - w 8, s 1f, p 90
Jones, Elisa - w 9, s 4f, 2m, p 130
JOnes, Euria - w 11, s 1f, p 246
Jones, George - w 12, s 1f, p 259
Jones, James - w 7, s 2f, p 7
Jones, James - w 8, s 1f, p 40
Jones, James - w 9, s 1m, p 118
Jones, Joshua - w 7, s 1f, p 5
Jones, Samuel - w 11, s 1f, 1m, p 233
Jones, Thomas ■ - w 11, s 1f, p 197
Jones, William - w 7, s 1f, p 29
Jones, Zachariah - w 8, s 3f, 2m, p 41
Jordan, Henry - w 11, s 1f, 1m, p 239
Judlin, Andrew J. - w 3, s 1f, p 125
Kalfus, Daniel - w 12, s 2f, 1m, p 319
Kall, P. T. - w 11, s 1f, p 202
Kane, John K. - w 9, s 1f, p 113
Keenan, Anthony - w 6, s 1m, p 290
Keene, Samuel - w 5, s 3f, 1m, p 223
Keiler, George - w 8, s 2m, p 82
Keilholty, William - w 12, s 2f, p 282
Keisle, Mathew - w 11, s 1f, p 238
Kelley, Mathew - w 2, s 1f, p 67
Kelly, Sarah A. - w 1, s 1f, p 18
Kelly, Timothy - w 9, s 1f, p 129
Kelso, Thomas - w 3, s 1f, 1m, p 124
Kemp, Edward D. - w 7, s 1m, p 17
Kemp, Henry - w 11, s 6f, 1m, p 224
Kemp, Lewis - w 12, s 4f, 3m, p 314
Kemp, Matilda - w 12, s 1f, p 307
Kemp, Thomas - w 11, s 1f, p 210
Kennard, G. J. - w 7, s 1f, p 12
Kennard, Isaac - w 6, s 2m, p 273
Kenny, Thomas - w 2, s 1f, p 87
Kesmon, William - w 11, s 1m, p

Slaveholding Households in Baltimore, 1840

Kessel, Margaret - w 11, s 1f, p 228
Key, Abner - w 12, s 2f, p 261
King, John - w 1, s 3m, p 45
Kiork, Ann - w 9, s 1f, p 122
Kirby, James - w 8, s 1f, p 92
Kirby, John - w 3, s 2f, p 106
Kirk, Samuel - w 7, s 1m, p 13
Kirkland, Alexander - w 5, s 1m, p 216
Kirks, William G. - w 11, s 1f, p 218
Kirkz, Daniel - w 6, s 1f, p 281
Knehson, Smithern - w 11, s 1m, p 199
Knight, Elizabeth - w 1, s 1m, p 44
Knighting, Thomas - w 2, s 2f, 1m, p 94
Krebs, George W. - w 9, s 1f, p 119
Krems, Mrs. C. - w 10, s 1f, p 161
Kune, Marcellus - w 5, s 1f, p 223
Kurk, Benjamin - w 9, s 1f, p 130
La Font, Peter - w 5, s 1f, p 230
Lakeman, John - w 3, s 1f, p 118
Lamb, Daniel - w 11, s 1f, p 210
Lamb, George - w 11, s 1m, p 211
Lamden, Ed S. - w 1, s 1f, p 3
Lamott, M. A. - w 7, s 3f, p 19
Landstreet, John - w 12, s 2f, p 282
Lane, Thomas A. - w 3, s 2f, p 124
Lankford, David - w 6, s 1f, p 283
Laroque, E. R. - w 9, s 1f, p 259
Lathers, Ruth - w 12, s 1f, p 260
Latimer, J. B. - w 7, s 2f, p 26
Latimor, R. W. - w 9, s 1f, p 112
Lauderman, Edwrad - w 2, s 1f, p 245
Laurason, Elizabeth - w 8, s 1m, p 39
Laurenson, Philip - w 11, s 1f, p 245
Law, George - w 12, s 1m, p 266
Law, John K. - w 7, s 1f, p 27
Lawrence, Richard - w 1, s 2f, 2m, p 38
Lea, Pricilla - w 11, s 1m, p 200
Leach, C. L. - w 12, s 2f, 2m, p 258
Leakin, Sheppard C. - w 5, s 1m, p 232
Leaking, Hannah - w 5, s 1f, p 233
Leas, Maria H. - w 9, s 3f, 1m, p 111
Leatherbury, Levin - w 5, s 1f, p 235
LeCount, Ann - w 5, s 1f, p 215
LeCount, Mary - w 5, s 2f, p 235
Lecour, Ellen - w 6, s 1m, p 285
Lee, Beal - w 11, s 1m, p 231
Lee, Hugh ■ - w 9, s 1m, p 116
Lee, Josiah - w 10, s 4f, 1m, p 146
Lee, Z. C. - w 9, s 1f, 1m, p 132
Leloup, Sophia - w 8, s 1f, p 88
Lemmon, Andrew H. - w 3, s 1f, p 126
Lemmon, Richard - w 10, s 1f, p 153
Lemmon, Robert - w 1, s 1f, p 31
Lemmon, William P. - w 10, s 1f, p 144
Lendrune, T. W. - w 12, s 1f, 1m, p 298
Leonard, A. - w 9, s 1f, 1m, p 125
Levering, George A. - w 3, s 1m, p 150

97

Chapter 11

Slaveholding Households in Baltimore, 1840

Levering, T. W. - w 8, s 2f, p 40
Levy, Thomas - w 5, s 1f, 1m, p 234
Lewis, E. W. - w 12, s 1m, p 252
Lewis, James - w 5, s 1m, p 210
Lewis, Joseph W. - w 8, s 1f, p 36
Lewis, Martin - w 9, s 1f, p 120
Leypold, Elizabeth - w 6, s 2f, p 284
Liche, David - w 6, s 1f, p 283
Lindsey, John - w 9, s 1f, p 117
Linthicum, R. - w 9, s 1m, p 110
Lipyer, Onsell - w 8, s 1f, p 57
Livingston, James - w 8, s 1f, p 40
Logue, James - w 6, s 1f, p 272
Loney, John - w 7, s 1m, p 22
Loney, William - w 5, s 1m, p 252
Long, Mary - w 3, s 1f, p 108
Long, Samuel - w 1, s 1f, p 15
Ludlow, A. C. - w 10, s 1f, p 153
Ludlow, Robert - w 9, s 1f, p 122
Lurman, J. W. - w 12, s 1m, p 322
Lusby, William - w 1, s 1m, p 46
Lutand, Angusta - w 11, s 1f, p 231
Lyon, Robert - w 12, s 1f, 3m, p 323
Lytle, Robert A. - w 6, s 1f, p 273
Mablock, R. C. - w 9, s 4f, p 132
Mackall, Benjamin - w 8, s 2f, p 64
Mackall, L. - w 7, s 1f, p 4
Macubbin, Nicholas - w 3, s 1f, p 141
Macubbin, Richard - w 2, s 1f, p 91
Maddox, Charles T. - w 7, s 2f, 2m, p 19
Maddox, Daniel - w 1, s 1f, p 4

Magnas, Fainah - w 11, s 4f, p 205
Magrath, John - w 8, s 1f, p 51
Magruder, John R. - w 8, s 2f, p 37
Magruder, R. B. - w 7, s 1m, p 16
Malcolm, Peter - w 7, s 2f, p 5
Manly, John - w 8, s 4f, 2m, p 87
Mann, George - w 5, s 1f, p 232
Mannor, James B. - w 5, s 2f, p 207
Maran, Robert - w 11, s 1m, p 201
Marbin, Dixon - w 4, s 1f, p 190
Marcilly, Emma - w 7, s 2f, p 8
Maris, George - w 7, s 2f, p 1m
Marriot, Caleb - w 8, s 1m, p 49
Marriott, William H. - w 9, s 1f, 1m, p 129
Marshal, Elizabeth - w 1, s 1m, p 35
Marshal, Henry - w 12, s 1f, p 264
Marshal, Wesley ■ - w 12, s 1m, p 252
Marshall, Tracy - w 3, s 1f, p 119
Marshall, William - w 10, s 1f, p 155
Marshall, William L. - w 10, s 1m, p 154
Martiag, A. - w 7, s 1f, p 22
Martin, Jane - w 5, s 1f, 1m, p 247
Martin, Sally Maria - w 9, s 2f, 3m, p 119
Martin, Susana - w 7, s 1f, p 6
Martin, William - w 7, s 2f, p 6
Mask, William M. - w 8, s 1f, 1m, p 35
Mason, Edward - w 12, s 1f, 1m, p 317

Slavery in Baltimore's Mount Vernon Area

Slaveholding Households in Baltimore, 1840

Mason, William - w 5, s 1f, p 224
Mass, Samuel - w 10, s 1f, p 148
Mathrot, Augustus - w 5, s 1f, p 228
Matthews, J. Jr. - w 8, s 2f, p 40
Matthews, samuel - w 5, s 1f, p 250
Mauro, John - w 9, s 1f, p 132
Mayhew, William E. - w 7, s 1f, p 17
McCauley, Patrick - w 9, s 1f, 1m, p 131
McClellan, Samuel - w 12, s 1f, 1m, p 252
McComas, Ellen - w 12, s 1f, p 278
McComas, James H. - w 5, s 1f, 1m, p 216
McConey, Caroline - w 6, s 2f, p 283
McConn, Charles - w 10, s 1f, p 148
McCormack, Henry - w 10, s 1m, p 148
McCubbin, Aron - w 4, s 1f, p 192
McCulla, Duncan - w 2, s 1f, p 86
McDay, Henry - w 12, s 1m, p 274
McDonald, John - w 12, s 1f, p 258
McDowell, George W. - w 6, s 1f, p 281
McDowell, R. - w 7, s 1m, p 14
McElderry, Henry - w 3, s 2f, 1m, p 131
McElderry, Hugh - w 7, s 2f, 1m, p 26
McFaul, Eneas - w 10, s 2f, 1m, p 148
McGowan, Andrew - w 3, s 1f, p 122
McKanna, William - w 8, s 1f, p 53
McKeen, Ann - w 9, s 1f, 1m, p 124
McKenzie, James - w 3, s 1f, p 100
McKim, John Jr. - w 6, s 2f, 1m, p 289
McKim, John S. - w 10, s 2f, 1m, p 187
McKim, Patrick - w 5, s 1f, p 252
McKinne, David T. - w 6, s 2f, p 281
McKinson, Henry B. - w 11, s 1m, p 225
McLean, William M. - w 9, s 1f, p 113
McLeane, John - w 5, s 1m, p 216
McLoughan, Charles - w 11, s 1m, p 225
McMechen, Mrs. J. - w 7, s 1f, 1m, p 29
McMurray, Samuel - w 10, s 1f, p 177
McNeal, Andrew - w 4, s 1f, p 192
McNeal, James - w 5, s 1f, p 208
McPhail, May - w 9, s 1m, p 127
McPhail, William - w 7, s 1f, p 23
McPherson, John - w 10, s 1f, p 180
McPherson, William - w 12, s 2f, p 322
McTruney, John A. - w 11, s 1f, p 244
McWilliams, Robert - w 8, s 1m, p 56
Meads, William - w 1, s 1f, p 47
Mears, John B. - w 5, s 1f, p 218
Medairy, John - w 9, s 1f, p 117
Medtart, Joshua - w 12, s 1m, p

Chapter 11

Slaveholding Households in Baltimore, 1840

280
Meekins, George - w 8, s 1f, p 61
Meredisk, Joseph P. - w 11, s 1f, p 238
Merrell, Jarmiah - w 11, s 1f, 2m, p 216
Merritt, W. K. - w 11, s 2f, 1m, p 224
Merroken, Joseph T. - w 5, s 2f, 2m, p 226
Mescanden, Alexander - w 11, s 3f, 2m, p 224
Meusham, Rachael - w 9, s 1m, p 110
Michael, Harry - w 9, s 1f, p 108
Middleton, R. - w 7, s 1m, p 26
Milburn, James A. - w 1, s 1m, p 37
Miller, Alfred J. - w 5, s 1f, 1m, p 223
Miller, Catherine - w 3, s 2m, p 105
Miller, J. R. - w 12, s 1f, p 259
Miller, Jacob - w 8, s 1f, p 33
Miller, James - w 11, s 1f, 1m, p 241
Miller, William F. - w 12, s 1f, 1m, p 313
Millholland, Robert D. - w 1, s 1f, p 26
Mills, William P. - w 6, s 2f, 2m, p 282
Mina, Elizabeth - w 5, s 2f, p 217
Mingo, James ■ - w 1, s 1f, p 34
Mister, Abraham - w 8, s 1f, p 41
Mitchell, John - w 7, s 1m, p 13
Mitchell, John - w 9, s 2f, 1m, p 124
Mitchell, Joseph - w 10, s 3f, 2m, p 141
Mitchell, Robert - w 6, s 1f, 1m, p 266
Mitchell, William ■ - w 8, s 1m, p 69
Moal, Samuel - w 10, s 2f, 1m, p 145
Monkur, Dr. J. C. S. - w 1, s 3f, p 18
Moor, William - w 12, s 2f, 1m, p 280
Moore, Ann ■ - w 11, s 2f, p 198
Moore, Delia - w 3, s 1f, p 126
Moore, E. S. - w 9, s 2f, p 130
Moore, Samuel - w 7, s 1f, p 16
Moore, Steven - w 5, s 1f, p 232
Moreland, Joseph S. - w 5, s 1f, p 247
Morgan, Edward - w 3, s 3f, p 134
Morling, G. W. - w 12, s 1f, p 299
Morris, Gary - w 5, s 3f, p 227
Morris, John B. - w 10, s 3f, 1m, p 145
Morris, John G. - w 9, s 1m, p 99
Morrison, Hugh J. - w 5, s 1f, p 243
Mortimore, John - w 1, s 2f, p 152
Morton, James F. - w 11, s 1f, p 218
Morton, John C. - w 10, s 2m, p 165
Mosher, James - w 7, s 1f, p 4
Mott, Rachel J. - w 3, s 1f, p 100
Moxley, Walter - w 2, s 2m, p 62
Muckelroy, John - w 1, s 1f, p 45
Mudd, Mary Ann - w 3, s 2m, p 121
Muller, Lewis C. - w 2, s 1f, p 93
Mullikin, O. M. - w 7, s 1f, p 5
Muncaster, Edward - w 7, s 1f, p 28

Slaveholding Households in Baltimore, 1840

Munday, Sarah - w 11, s 1m, p 243
Munroe, John H. - w 8, s 2f, p 41
Murdock, William - w 12, s 1f, p 320
Murdock, William F. - w 9, s 2f, p 109
Murphy, Jesse - w 4, s 2m, p 198
Murphy, Thomas S. - w 1, s 1f, p 3
Murray, Matthew - w 3, s 1m, p 150
Murray, Patrick - w 9, s 1f, p 127
Murrow, John - w 8, s 1f, 1m, p 41
Murry, A. B. - w 12, s 1m, p 260
Murry, Francis - w 4, s 1f, 3m, p 180
Mushell, Walters - w 7, s 1f, 1m, p 26
Myer, George - w 4, s 1f, p 169
Myer, Godfrey - w 6, s 1f, p 265
Myer, John J. - w 8, s 1f, p 39
Myer, Thomas - w 8, s 1f, p 41
Myers, Charles - w 12, s 1f, 1m, p 317
Myers, Magdalen - 12, s - 2f, p 27
Myers, Maria - w 5, s 2f, 1m, p 227
Myers, Samuel ■ - w 12, s 1m, p 267
Nants, John - w 5, s 2f, p 214
Neal, Francis - w 9, s 1f, p 106
Neal, Richard - w 5, s 1f, p 217
Neale, Mary - w 8, s 3m, p 83
Needham, Asa - w 8, s 1f, p 41
Nesbit, Alexander - w 6, s 3f, 1m, p 273
Newman, Joseph - w 3, s 1f, p 141
Newman, William H. ■ - w 10, s 1m, p 159
Nicholas, J. S. - w 7, s 1f, p 14
Nicholas, John S. - w 7, s 1m, p 16
Nicholson, Elizabeth - w 2, s 1m, p 56
Nicholson, J. J. - w 11, s 1f, p 237
Nickerson, Charles F. - w 9, s 1m, p 99
Ninde, James - w 6, s 1f, p 273
Nixdorff, Tobias - w 12, s 1f, p 259
Nixon, John - w 3, s 1f, p 152
Norris, B. B. - w 11, s 1f, 1m, p 232
Norris, Jamis - w 5, s 1f, p 229
Norris, Richard - w 7, s 1f, 1m, p 8
Norvell, Lorenzo - w 12, s 4f, 3m, p 320
Nulter, Ellen ■ - w 9, s 1f, p 117
Nyser, Thomas - w 3, s 1f, p 153
O'Brien, Isabella - w 3, s 1f, p 124
O'Brien, Josbella - w 3, s 1f, p 115
O'Neal, William - w 11, s 1f, p 246
Occumbaugh, Juliet - w 12, s 1f, p 313
Odonald, Sarah C. - w 12, s 1m, p 260
ODonnell, Columbus - w 7, s 2f, 1m, p 19
Olmere, Femile - w 5, s 1m, p 214
Olney, Peter ■ - w 9, s 1m, p 114
Orndorff, William - w 11, s 1f, p 247
Osborne, Elizabeth - w 7, s 1f, 1m, p 15

Chapter 11

Slaveholding Households in Baltimore, 1840

Owen, William - w 10, s 2f, p 146
Owens, Isaac - w 5, s 2f, 1m, p 215
Owens, Joseph - w 3, s 1f, 1m, p 122
Owens, Sarah - w 1, s 1f, p 25
Owens, William - w 6, s 3f, p 268
Owings, J. W. - w 10, s 2f, 1m, p 139
Owings, S. C. - w 7, s 1f, p 5
Owings, Thomas - w 9, s 2f, 2m, p 126
Paca, Mrs. P. J. - w 10, s 4f, 1m, p 146
Page, Ann - w 7, s 1f, 1m, p 26
Page, Washington A. - w 5, s 1f, p 215
Pairo, C. W. - w 12, s 1f, 1m, p 321
Palmer, E. - w 9, s 1f, p 114
Palmer, William - w 8, s 1f, p 37
Paran, James - w 11, s 1m, p 197
Parks, Abram - w 2, s 1f, p 91
Parnell, John - w 1, s 1f, 1m, p 47
Partridge, Daubner B. - w 1, s 1f, p 34
Pascall, Francis - w 1, s 1f, p 47
Patterson, Ann - w 7, s 2f, p 4
Patterson, Edward - w 6, s 5m, p 292
Patterson, Eleanor - w 8, s 2f, p 41
Patterson, J. M. - w 7, s 3f, 2m, p 7
Patterson, James J. - w 1, s 1f, p 5
Patterson, John - w 7, s 1f, p 7
Patterson, Sarah - w 7, s 2f, p 26
Patterson, William - w 8, s 1f, p 47
Patterson, William - w 11, s 1f, 1m, p 230
Patterson, William P. - w 5, s 1f, 3m, p 250
Patton, James M. - w 9, s 1f, 1m, p 116
Pearson, Andrew - w 9, s 1f, p 111
Peck, John - w 3, s 1f, p 149
Peer, Lydia - w 6, s 1m, p 262
Pendleton, Elizabeth - w 11, s 5f, 2m, p 233
Pendleton, Robert W. - w 10, s 2f, 1m, p 138
Penniman, Thomas - w 9, s 2f, p 131
Penty, John J. - w 3, s 2f, 1m, p 143
Penty, P. Henry - w 3, s 2m, p 143
Peregay, James Sr. - w 12, s 1f, p 257
Perine, D. M. - w 7, s 1m, p 14
Perkins, Ellen - w 12, s 1f, 1m, p 282
Perrine, Thomas J. - w 6, s 1m, p 260
Peters, Ann - w 5, s 2f, p 226
Peters, J. T. - w 12, s 1f, p 308
Philips, Ann B. - w 9, s 1f, 1m, p 129
Phillips, Greenbury - w 6, s 1m, p 266
Phillips, Thomas - w 3, s 1m, p 102
Phillips, William - w 5, s 1f, p 224
Pickering, Samuel - w 5, s 1f, p 223
Picket, John - w 12, s 1f, p 267
Pierce, Stephen A. - w 6, s 1f, p

Slavery in Baltimore's Mount Vernon Area

Slaveholding Households in Baltimore, 1840

Pinckney, Ann - w 7, s 2f, p 272
Pindell, Thomas - w 3, s 1f, p 125
Piper, James - w 12, s 2f, p 279
Pitt, William - w 5, s 2f, p 241
Placide, Henry - w 5, s 2f, 2m, p 220
Plummington, W. - w 11, s 1f, p 22
Pontier, Lewis B. - w 6, s 1f, p 277
Poor, Dudley - w 10, s 2f, p 158
Poor, John H. - w 7, s 1f, p 5
Pope, Folger - w 7, s 1f, p 6
Porter, James - w 1, s 1f, p 32
Porter, Jane - w 6, s 1m, p 273
Potter, John Jr. - w 7, s 1f, 1m, p 7
Potter, Martin - w 1, s 1f, 1m, p 45
Potter, Nathaniel - w 7, s 4f, p 17
Pouder, Mrs. - w 11, s 1f, p 241
Poultney, Samuel - w 10, s 2m, p 145
Powell, John ■ - w 12, s 1m, p 306
Power, Michael - w 7, s 2f, 1m, p 23
Pratt, Henry - w 9, s 1f, p 108
Prentiss, John - w 4, s 5f, 1m, p 198
Preston, Orney ■ - w 1, s 1m, p 5
Price, Augustus M. - w 9, s 1f, p 102
Price, Susan - w 1, s 1m, p 36
Price, William - w 4, s 1f, p 187
Proud, John G. - w 10, s 2f, 1m, p 148
Pryor, George W. - w 7, s 2f, 1m, p 19
Pue, Peggy - w 7, s 2f, 1m, p 19

Pugh, Arthur - w 9, s 2f, 1m, p 123
Purdy, Caroline - w 5, s 3m, p 225
Pursen, William - w 3, s 1f, p 119
Purviance, Robert - w 7, s 3f, p 26
Purvis, James - w 4, s 14f, 7m, p 198
Putman, William - w 6, s 1f, p 272
Quay, John M. - w 2, s 1f, p 55
Qumlix, Leonard G. - w 11, s 3f, 4m, p 244
Raborg, Henrietta - w 9, s 2f, 3m, p 128
Rains, Lewis - w 1, s 1f, p 2
Ramsay, Ann - w 2, s 1f, 1m, p 55
Ramsay, Elizabeth - w 6, s 1f, p 282
Ramsay, Joseph - w 2, s 2f, p 61
Randolph, John W. - w 2, s 1f, p 78
Rayman, Henry - w 12, s 1f, p 271
Raymo, Modest - w 6, s 1m, p 278
Rea, G. - w 11, s 1f, p 210
Readman, Elizabeth - w 5, s 1, p 208
Reaside, Mary - w 5, s 1f, 2m, p 217
Redgraves, Samuel H. - w 9, s 1f, 1m, p 116
Reed, William G. - w 10, s 1m, p 153
Reeder, Amos - w 8, s 1f, p 76
Reese, D. E. - w 9, s 1f, p 107
Reese, Daniel M. - w 11, s 1f, p 210
Reese, John E. - w 8, s 2f, p 48
Reese, John L. - w 9, s 1f, 1m, p

103

Chapter 11

Slaveholding Households in Baltimore, 1840

Reese, John N. - w 11, s 1f, p 228
Reese, William - w 9, s 4f, 2m, p 116
Rehine, Z. - w 8, s 2f, 1m, p 35
Reynolds, J. W. - w 9, s 3f, p 112
Reynolds, James - w 12, s 1m, p 298
Reynolds, William - w 9, s 1f, p 130
Rhobock, Henry - w 10, s 1m, p 167
Rhodes, J. W. - w 8, s 1f, 1m, p 41
Richardson, Beal H. - w 10, s 1m, p 147
Richardson, Eliza - w 12, s 4f, 2m, p 259
Richardson, John W. - w 2, s 1m, p 55
Richardson, William - w 6, s 2f, p 278
Richardson, William R. - w 5, s 1f, p 218
Rick, Arthur W. - w 8, s 2f, 1m, p 36
Ridgaway, Henry - w 2, s 1f, p 55
Ridgely, James L. - w 6, s 1f, 1m, p 278
Ridgely, Noah - w 7, s 1f, p 14
Riggins, Ed - w 9, s 4f, p 101
Riggs, G. W. - w 12, s 2f, p 323
Rigllen, John E. - w 9, s 1f, p 123
Riley, Miss - w 11, s 1f, p 244
Ringgold, Peragrine - w 7, s 1f, p 9
Ringrose, John W. - w 11, s 4f, p 234
Rivers, Robert H. - w 3, s 1f, p 123
Robert, J. G. - w 12, s 1m, p 270
Roberts, Nicholas - w 10, s 1f, p 148
Robins, Stephen ■ - w 8, s 1m, p 91
Robinson, Benjamin - w 8, s 2f, 2m, p 39
Robinson, Dr. A. C. - w 11, s 3f, 1m, p 230
Robinson, Joseph - w 2, s 2f, 1m, p 80
Robinson, Lucy A. - w 8, s 1f, p 46
Robinson, Steven ■ - w 11, s 1m, p 244
Robinson, Thomas - w 2, s 1m, p 93
Roche, John H. - w 9, s 1f, p 122
Rock, James - w 6, s 1m, p 290
Rogers, Ann - w 5, s 1f, p 227
Rogers, Jacob - w 6, s 2f, 3m, p 292
Rogers, Samuel - w 7, s 3f, 1m, p 12
Rogers, Thomas - w 11, s 1m, p 197
Rogers, William S. - w 8, s 1f, p 61
Rollins, James - w 3, s 1m, p 138
Rollins, William - w 2, s 1f, p 86
Roney, William - w 6, s 1m, p 275
Rose, George - w 8, s 1f, 1m, p 85
Rose, P. R. - w 12, s 3f, p 267
Roshen, Bernard J. - w 3, s 1f, p 136
Ross, Benjamin C. - w 6, s 5f, 3m, p 260
Ross, William - w 2, s 1f, 1m, p
Rothock, John - w 11, s 1m, p 232
Rouse, John - w 10, s 1f, p 142
Royston, Joshua - w 6, s 2f, 1m, p

Slaveholding Households in Baltimore, 1840

Rozell, Steven M. - w 5, s 1f, p 283
Ruckle, Paul - w 9, s 1f, p 224
Ruddack, Rebecca - w 9, s 1f, p 113
Ruff, Andrew - w 7, s 3f, p 112
Rugart, Henry P. - w 3, s 1f, p 13
Rutherford, John - w 7, s 1f, p 133
Rutt, Margret - w 12, s 1f, 1m, p 26
Rutter, Thomas B. - w 6, s 1m, p 268
Ryan, William - w 11, s 1f, p 283
Salisbury, Edward - w 5, s 1m, p 245
Salisbury, James - w 4, s 3f, 1m, p 243
Sanders, Charles ■ - w 5, s 1m, p 192
Sanders, Edward - w 5, s 1f, p 207
Sanderson, Henry S. - w 5, s 1f, p 235
Sands, S. - w 3, s 1f, p 244
Sandshale, Marond - w 11, s 5f, 1m, p 106
Sanks, Nicholas - w 11, s 1f, p 233
Sauerhoff, John F. - w 8, s 1f, p 240
Saunders, B. J. - w 3, s 1f, 1m, p 60
Saunders, J. M. - w 7, s 1f, p 123
Saurwine, E. - w 10, s 1f, p 4
Sayers, James - w 11, s 2f, 1m, p 143
Scarf, George - w 10, s 1m, p 220
Schley, Mrs. Jacobs - w 10, s 2f, p 56
Schley, William - w 7, s 2m, p 153
Schoolfield, Luther - w 5, s 2f, 2m, p 14
Schrick, George W. - w 3, s 3f, 2m, p 250
Schrick, Jacob - w 3, s 1f, p 121
Schuarhouse, Edward - w 9, s 1m, p 121
Schulty, J. - w 8, s 1m, p 119
Schwarzauer, Daniel - w 8, s 1m, p 42
Scott, John - w 7, s 1f, p 77
Seamon, William - w 11, s 1f, p 17
Seblar, M. - w 9, s 1f, p 218
Seche, Joseph - w 9, s 1f, p 121
Segler, Frederick - w 9, s 1f, p 101
Seif, Henry - w 9, s 1f, p 101
Seiger, Jacob - w 9, s 1f, p 132
Sellman, James C. - w 7, s 1f, p 127
Selvage, W. - w 11, s 1f, p 16
Semmes, R. - w 7, s 2f, 1m, pg 234
Senall, Pete - w 11, s 1m, p 5
Seward, Hannah G. - w 6, s 1f, p 231
Sewell, Perry ■ - w 8, s 1f, 1m, p 279
Sewell, Pollydore - w 8, s 1f, p 50
Sewell, Thomas - w 10, s 3f, 3m, p 44
Shaneybrook, F. - w 8, s 1m, p 189
Shangurg, William - w 9, s 1f, p 46
Shaw, William - w 1, s 3f, 1m, p 108
Sheppard, Colonel Thomas - w 8, s 1f, 1m, p 48
Sheppard, Thomas S. - w 9, s 2f, p 40
 p 109

Chapter 11

Slaveholding Households in Baltimore, 1840

Shipley, Washington - w 12, s 2f, 1m, p 251
Shipley, William - w 12, s 1f, p 274
Shnehahn, George - w 9, s 3f, 2m, p 131
Shockney, Samuel - w 5, s 1f, p 215
Shoemaker, William S. - w 2, s 1f, 1m, p 61
Shorte, John - w 11, s 1f, p 201
Shriver, J. S. - w 12, s 3f, 2m, p 311
Shroder, William - w 12, s 1f, p 309
Shutt, Augustus - w 6, s 1m, p 271
Simmon, A. - w 11, s 1f, p 206
Simmonds, J. A. - w 9, s 1f, p 131
Simmons, Elijah R. - w 6, s 1f, p 274
Simms, George - w 8, s 1f, p 44
Simpson, John K. - w 7, s 1m, p 7
Sinclair, Edward - w 8, s 1f, p 55
Skinner, Zacariah - w 8, s 1f, p 46
Slater, James - w 2, s 1m, p 83
Slater, John - w 1, s 1m, p 47
Slatter, Hope H. - w 9, s 12f, 10m, p 109
Slingluff, C. D. - w 11, s 1f, p 227
Slingluff, Eporn - w 11, s 1f, 1m, p 238
Slittig, Frederick - w 2, s 2f, p 85
Slothower, George - w 10, s 2f, p 148
Slow, Thomas - w 7, s 1f, p 8
Smith, Alex - w 10, s 1f, 1m, p 147
Smith, Charles - w 1, s 1f, p 2
Smith, Dennis H. - w 9, s 2f, 1m, p 120
Smith, George - w 1, s 1f, p 26
Smith, Henry - w 12, s 1f, p 295
Smith, J. S. M. - w 7, s 3f, p 28
Smith, J. W. - w 11, s 1f, p 229
Smith, J. W. - w 12, s 2f, p 296
Smith, Jacob - w 10, s 1f, 1m, p 158
Smith, Jog - w 5, s 1f, 2m, p 250
Smith, John - w 2, s 2f, p 72
Smith, John - w 3, s 3f, p 106
Smith, John - w 5, s 2f, 1m, p 224
Smith, John A. - w 1, s 2f, 1m, p 25
Smith, John J. - w 7, s 1f, p 6
Smith, Kitty - w 3, s 1f, p 115
Smith, Mrs. E. G. - w 7, s 1f, p 19
Smith, Mrs. Samuel - w 6, s 2f, 3m, p 290
Smith, N. R. - w 9, s 2f, 1m, p 109
Smith, Patrick - w 11, s 1m, p 219
Smith, Robert - w 7, s 2f, 1m, p 5
Smith, Robert M. - w 3, s 1m, p 106
Smith, Samuel - w 7, s 1f, 1m, p 20
Smith, Sarah - w 5, s 1f, p 241
Smith, William - w 11, s 1f, 2m, p 238
Snipp, Dedrick - w 11, s 1m, p 198
Snow, Freeman - w 5, s 1f, p 213
Sollers, Susan - w 4, s 1f, 1m, p 192
Solomon, Benjamin - w 7, s 2f, p 29
Somer, Samuel - w 9, s 1f, p 115
Soran, Charles - w 11, s 1f, p 234
Soulsby, Robert - w 8, s 3f, 1m, p

Slaveholding Households in Baltimore, 1840

Spalding, B. R. - w 7, s 3f, p 28 58
Sparks, Dorcas - w 10, s 1f, 3m, p 139
Spedden, Robert - w 2, s 1f, p 79
Spence, Mary C. - w 7, s 4f, 3m, p 8
Spencer, Catherine - w 1, s 2m, p 22
Spencer, Susan - w 12, s 1f, p 257
Spicer, Thomas - w 10, s 1f, p 191
Spicknell, Richard - w 6, s 1f, p 261
Spiers, Ann - w 1, s 1m, p 47
Sprague, George - w 3, s 1f, p 149
Spreckelsen, George A. - w 2, s 2f, 2m, p 55
Sprigg, Daniel - w 9, s 1f, p 104
Sprigg, Margaret - w 7, s 1m, p 8
Springer, David C. - w 5, s 1m, p 218
Spuner, Enoch L. - w 11, s 1f, p 246
Spurrier, Nelson - w 12, s 1m, p 258
Stalling, Peter - w 11, s 1f, p 218
Stamp, Thomas - w 11, s 1f, p 219
Stannard, McLaughlin - w 7, s 2f, 7m, p 12
Stansbury, Daniel - w 3, s 1f, p 117
Stansbury, Elijah - w 5, s 1m, p 213
Stansbury, John C. - w 2, s 1f, 3m, p 60
Stansbury, Nicholas - w 5, s 1f, 2m, p 250
Stansbury, William - w 1, s 1f, p 35
Starr, Rebecca - w 3, s 1f, 1m, p 106
Strindall, John B. - w 5, s 1f, p 245
Stuart, John A. - w 11, s 2f, p 227
Stuart, Richard - w 7, s 2f, 2m, p 16
Stump, Samuel Sr. - w 8, s 1f, 1m, p 39
Sumerill, John T. - w 9, s 1f, p 116
Summer, Francis A. - w 8, s 1f, p 39
Sumnon, Jacob - w 11, s 1f, p 227
Susby, William - w 7, s 2f, 2m, p 7
Sutliff, Thomas - w 9, s 3f, p 99
Sutton, James L. - w 6, s 1f, p 273
Sutton, Thomas - w 2, s 1f, p 54
Sutton, Vincent - w 9, s 1f, p 123
Swan, James - w 7, s 3f, 2m, p 14
Swann, Thomas - w 10, s 1f, 1m, p 153
Sweeney, Dennis - w 4, s 1f, p 177
Sword, Alex - w 1, s 1f, p 15
Sword, John W. - w 1, s 2f, p 33
Sword, William - w 1, s 1f, p 37
Syeth, John - w 11, s 1f, p 234
Talbot, Joseph - w 9, s 1f, 4m, p 106
Tarence, Ellen - w 9, s 1f, p 131
Tarlton, Elizabeth - w 9, s 1f, p 114
Taylor, George - w 5, s 1f, p 233
Taylor, Henry ■ - w 5, s 1m, p 247
Taylor, J. - w 11, s 2f, p 226

Chapter 11

Slaveholding Households in Baltimore, 1840

Taylor, Jenifer S. - w 8, s 1f, p 48
Taylor, Lemeul G. - w 5, s 2f, p 224
Taylor, Margaret - w 3, s 1f, p 109
Taylor, Robert H. - w 7, s 1m, p 23
Taylor, Thomas - w 7, s 1f, p 18
Taylor, William S. - w 1, s 1m, p 18
Taylor, Levi - w 8, s 1f, p 34
Teackle, St. George - w 10, s 1m, p 168
Teal, Elizabeth - w 8, s 1f, p 46
Tennant, Mrs. THomas - w 6, s 2f, p 282
Thomas, James - w 2, s 2f, 3m, p 74
Thomas, John H. - w 7, s 3f, p 23
Thomas, Lambert S. - w 4, s 1f, p 188
Thomas, Lloyd ■ - w 2, s 1m, p 78
Thomas, Mary J. - w 7, s 1m, p 28
Thomas, Richard ■ - w 12, s 2m, p 319
Thomas, Sterling - w 3, s 1f, p 131
Thomas, William B. - w 1, s 1f, 1m, p 22
Thomas, Elanor - w 7, s 2f, 1m, p 4
Thompson, A. W. - w 12, s 1f, p 303
Thompson, Charles - w 9, s 1m, p 130
Thompson, D. H. - w 9, s 1f, 1m, p 105
Thompson, John - w 5, s 1f, p 216
Thompson, Joseph B. - w 5, s 2f, 1m, p 220
Thompson, Joseph L. - w 3, s 1f, p 104
Thompson, Samuel T. - w 3, s 3f, p 134
Thompson, Thomas F. - w 10, s 1f, p 156
Thrush, Nicholas - w 11, s 1m, p 200
Tier, Washington - w 1, s 1f, p 48
Tiffany, C. L. - w 10, s 1m, p 154
Tilghman, James - w 7, s 1f, p 18
Timmons, John - w 11, s 1f, p 227
Tittle, Jeremiah - w 6, s 3f, p 283
Tolly, Thomas N. D. - w 1, s 2f, p 8
Tomblinson, William - w 8, s 1f, p 41
Torrence, Charles - w 6, s 1f, p 278
Towel, Amelia - w 5, s 1m, p 218
Towson, C. - w 11, s 2f, p 242
Towson, Joshua - w 12, s 1f, 1m, p 268
Travers, Susanna - w 5, s 1m, p 218
Travers, Thomas - w 8, s 2f, p 42
Trigo, Albert - w 11, s 1f, p 218
Tripp, Joseph E. - w 3, s 2f, p 106
Trotten, Thomas - w 1, s 2f, 1m, p 9
Trylon, Phene - w 11, s 1m, p 222
Tucker, Thomas - w 2, s 1f, p 93
Turner, Harry F. - w 3, s 1m, p 150
Turner, John - w 5, s 1f, p 227
Turner, John C. - w 11, s 3f, 1m, p 205
Turner, Joshua - w 3, s 2f, 4m, p 102

Slaveholding Households in Baltimore, 1840

Turner, Joshua M. - w 1, s 5f, 1m, p 45
Turner, Samuel - w 8, s 3f, p 42
Turner, Thomas W. - w 9, s 3f, p 120
Tyler, Isaac ■ - w 12, s 1m, p 276
Tyson, Charles - w 12, s 1f, p 308
Valiant, James H. - w 5, s 1m, p 216
Vallenilla, A. J. - w 10, s 1m, p 153
Vass, James C. - w 12, s 1f, p 308
Vaughn, Susan - w 1, s 1m, p 17
Veasey, George C. - w 8, s 1f, p 38
Vernetson, William - w 6, s 1f, 1m, p 271
Vickers, George R. - w 9, s 1f, p 112
Vickers, Joel - w 9, s 2f, 1m, p 120
Vinton, Perry - w 8, s 2m, p 64
Wade, Mrs. John - w 6, s 1f, p 279
Waggner, George - w 1, s 1f, 1m, p 39
Walker, Abram - w 6, s 1f, p 261
Walker, John W. - w 10, s 1f, p 165
Walker, Joshua - w 9, s 1f, 1m, p 108
Walker, Noah - w 3, s 1f, p 151
Walker, Robert - w 2, s 2f, p 92
Wallace, Ruth - w 5, s 1f, 1m, p 252
Wallace, Samuel - w 8, s 1m, p 74
Wallace, William - w 5, s 1f, p 221
Wallace, William - w 11, s 1f, p 238
Wallis, Phillip - w 7, s 1f, 2m, p 19
Walter, Basil - w 6, s 1m, p 260
Walter, John - w 3, s 1f, p 100
Walton, Charles ■ - w 10, s 1f, p 159
Wanlear, Ann E. - w 7, s 3f, 3m, p 17
Ward, Catherine - w 12, s 1m, p 265
Ward, Elizabeth - w 11, s 1f, p 226
Ward, William - w 5, s 2f, p 217
Warfield, Charles - w 8, s 3f, p 36
Warfield, David - w 7, s 1m, p 17
Warfield, Sarah - w 9, s 2f, 2m, p 131
Warner, Mary Ann - w 6, s 1f, p 280
Warner, Michael - w 11, s 2f, 1m, p 218
Warner, Susan - w 6, s 2f, p 279
Warren, George Jr. - w 11, s 1f, p 217
Washington, James H. - w 5, s 1f, p 222
Watchman, John - w 8, s 1f, 1m, p 57
Waters, Elenor - w 9, s 2f, 1m, p 113
Waters, F. G. - w 10, s 1f, 1m, p 138
Waters, George - w 3, s 1f, p 124
Waters, Joseph G. - w 9, s 1f, p 112
Waters, Tabita - w 3, s 1f, p 150
Waterton, George - w 8, s 1f, p 86
Watkins, George W. - w 10, s 1f, p 156
Watkins, J. W. - w 12, s 1m, p 280

Chapter 11

Slaveholding Households in Baltimore, 1840

Watkins, Thomas - w 7, s 3m, p 3
Watson, William H. - w 2, s 2f, p 86
Watts, Elmer D. - w 5, s 1f, p 227
Watts, William - w 11, s 1f, p 199
Watts, William J. - w 2, s 1f, p 94
Weaver, Mary - w 2, s 1f, p 62
Webb, Charles - w 4, s 1f, p 194
Webb, Jane - w 7, s 1f, p 18
Welch, John - w 1, s 1f, p 31
Welch, Lydia - w 6, s 1f, p 278
Welch, Mrs. M. - w 10, s 1f, p 140
Welles, Andrew - w 12, s 3f, 1m, p 308
Welling, J. W. - w 12, s 1f, 1m, p 260
Wells, Edward A. - w 10, s 1f, p 144
Welsh, John - w 2, s 1f, 2m, p 91
Wernwag, John - w 5, s 1m, p 208
Wetherly, Sarah - w 5, s 1f, p 223
Wheaton, James C. - w 2, s 1f, p 68
Wheeden, Mary Ann - w 1, s 1f, 1m, p 11
Wheeler, Barry - w 3, s 2f, p 133
Wheeler, M. - w 9, s 1f, p 120
Wheelwright, J. W. - w 10, s 1f, p 153
Whelan, Thomas - w 9, s 2f, 1m, p 129
White, James - w 11, s 1f, p 234
White, Mrs. S. - w 7, s 1f, 1m, p 5
White, Thomas ■ - w 1, s 1m, p 27
White, William H. - w 5, s 1m, p 233
Whiteford, D. - w 11, s 2f, p 227
Whiteford, William - w 4, s 1f, 1m, p 198
Whitelock, John - w 5, s 1m, p 253
Whitely, A. - w 11, s 2f, p 226
Whitman, M. - w 7, s 1f, 1m, p 18
Whitney, D. - w 11, s 1f, p 205
Whitney, Daniel - w 11, s 1f, p 218
Whitrodge, Dr. Thomas - w 6, s 1m, p 281
Wickersham, William - w 2, s 1f, 1m, pg 82
Wight, Resin - w 12, s 1mn, p 257
Wight, William J. - w 8, s 1f, p 37
Wilcox, Peter - w 4, s 1m, p 201
Wiley, A. B. - w 10, s 2f, p 138
Wilhelm, Wallace - w 6, s 3f, 2m, p 260
Wilkins, A. - w 10, s 1f, p 146
Wilkinson, James - w 5, s 1f, p 247
Wilks, James - w 11, s 1f, p 233
Willard, Simon - w 5, s 1f, p 211
Williams, C. D. - w 7, s 1f, p 15
Williams, James - w 8, s 1f, 1m, p 39
Williams, Nathaniel - w 7, s 1f, p 14
Williams, Rachael - w 11, s 1m, p 197
Williams, Susan F. - w 7, s 1f, p 28
Williams, Thomas P. - w 9, s 2f, p 131
Williams, William ■ - w 8, s 2f, 1m, p 69
Williamson, Charles A. - w 7, s 2f, p 8
Willmore, E. - w 9, s 1m, p 120
Wilmer, John W. - w 9, s 1m, p 114

Slavery in Baltimore's Mount Vernon Area

Slaveholding Households in Baltimore, 1840

Wilson, G. B. - w 7, s 1m, p 16
Wilson, Henry - w 4, s 1f, 1m, p 193
Wilson, Isaac - w 5, s 1m, p 221
Wilson, J. M. - w 7, s 1f, p 6
Wilson, James - w 6, s 1m, p 291
Wilson, Joseph C. - w 3, s 3f, p 124
Wilson, Joseph S. - w 5, s 2f, p 4m
Wilson, Luther - - w 12, s 1f, p 299
Wilson, P. T. - w 6, s 1f, p 273
Wilson, Peter - w 8, s 4f, 1m, p 35
Wilson, Robert - w 11, s 2m, p 235
Wilson, Robert - w 12, s 1m, p 320
Wilson, Thomas - w 7, s 2f, p 8
Wilson, William - w 1, s 3f, 6m, p 46
Wimmel, George S. - w 2, s 1f, p 93
Winchester, Samuel - w 7, s 1f, 1m, p 19
Wingate, Temperance - w 6, s 1f, p 278
Winingder, Lewis - w 1, s 1f, 1m, p 47
Winn, Susan - w 12, s 1f, p 309
Winter, Gabriel - w 9, s 1f, p 120
Witener, John - w 11, s 2f, p 233
Wollen, Robinson - w 5, s 1f, p 246
Wood, J. - w 11, s 1f, p 229
Wood, Nicholas - w 11, s 1f, p 225
Wood, William - w 11, s 1f, p 221
Wooden, David Manning - w 4, s 2f, 1m, p 162
Woodsell, William - w 9, s 1f, 2m, p 114
Woodward, W. - w 9, s 1f, p 123
Woodworth, Frederick - w 10, s 1f, p 148
Worley, Jacob - w 4, s 1f, p 162
Worthington, Abraham - w 1, s 2f, 6m, p 47
Worthington, Charles - w 9, s 1f, p 11
Wright, Edward - w 7, s 2f, 1m, p 8
Wright, John - w 12, s 1f, p 309
Wright, Mary ■ - w 10, s 1m, p 183
Wright, Thomas H. - w 9, s 1f, 1m, p 105
Wurty, Ann - w 6, s 1f, p 289
Wynn, Christain - w 7, s 1f, p 3
Wysham, E. C. - w 11, s 1f, p 233
Yeats, John L. - w 6, s 1m, p 277
Young, John - w 12, s 1f, p 315
Young, Richard - w 12, s 2f, 2m, p 280

12
Slaveholders Of Baltimore 1840 & 1850

The following is an index of the slave schedules for Baltimore in the 1850 census. This list was compiled by using the slave schedules in conjunction with the population census schedules (when feasible) to compile data on the occupations and estate holdings of the slaveholder. An ▲ denotes that the slaveholder is a repeater (one who also held slaves in 1840). A sample entry reads as follows:

Applegarth, William ▲ *- commission merchant, es $10,000, s 2f, w 2, p 183*

The record translates as follows: William Applegarth, who was also a slaveholder in 1840, is a commission merchant with real estate holdings worth es $10,000. He resides in Ward 2 of Baltimore City. The information recording his household is on page 183 of that ward. He holds 2 female slaves.

Abell, H. - s 1f, w 18
Adams, Bridget - s 1f, w 3
Adams, Jane - es $2,000, s 1f, w 9, p 6
Adams, John T. - Hotel, s 1f, 1m, p 152
Addison, George C. - es $47,000, s 1f, w 15, p 110
Addison, J. A. - 1f, w 11
Adkinson, William ▲ - s 1, w 2
Aiken, R. E. - 1f, 2m, w 19
Aires, Mary - s 1f, w 14
Airy, George - Physician, s 2f, w 14, p 415
Albers, Henry - Physician, s 2f, w 15, p 114
Albertson, J. - s 1m, w 10
Alexander, Thomas - Lawyer, es $2,000, s 3f, 1m, w 10, p 107
Allen, J. - s 1m, w 6

Allen, R. W. - Merchant, s 1f, w 4, p 39
Allen, Solomon - Carpenter, es $2,600, s 1f, w 15, p 99
Allison, James L. - Carpenter, s 1f, w 8, p 406
Allridge, Andrew - s 2f, 1m, w 11
Allyn, Mary - s 1f, w 3, 341
Alnutt, Sarah - s 3f, 2m, w 15, p 104
Amos, Aquila - Grocer, s 1f, w 18, p 72
Amos, Corbin - s 2f, 2, w 12
Amos, James - s 1, w 3, s 312
Anderson, T. P. - U. S. Paymaster, s 2f, 1, w 13, p 348
Applegaith, George - s 1, w 3
Applegarth, William ▲ - Commission Merchant, es $10,000, s 2f, w 2, p 183

113

Chapter 12

Slaveholders of Baltimore, 1840 & 1850

Archer, Robert H. - Teacher, es $600, s 2f, w 10, p 97

Armiger, Joseph - Grocer, s 1f, 1m, w 7, p 325

Armor, George F. - Merchan, s 1f, w 16, p 174

Armour, Mrs. - s 1f, 1m, w 18

Armstrong, Andrew - Merchant, s 2f, 1m, w 15, p 83

Armstrong, Benjamin - s 1f, w 4

Armstrong, J. L. - es $4,000 s 1f, w 12, p 275

Armstrong, William - s 1m, w 17

Arnold, George W. ▲ - Baker, es $2,000, s 2f, 2m, w 13, p 337

Arthur, Anne - s 1f, w 15, p 57

Aspril, D. T. ▲ - s 2f, 1m, w 3

Asquith, Charlotte - s 2f, w 13

Atkinson, Joshua - Property Agent, es $1,500, ?, p 1

Atkinson, Mary - s 1f, w 6

Atkinson, Rev. Thomas - Clergyman, es $300, s 3f, 1m, w 13, p 389

Ault, ▲amuel - Feed Merchant, s 1f, w 8, p 436

Ault, Samuel Jr. - s 1f, w 8

Auodoun, Oliver - Carpenter, es $1,000, s 1m, w 3, p 309

Ayers, Charles C. - Grocer, s 1f, w 16, p 170

Ayers, Jacob - s 2f, 1m, w 13

Ayres, Littleton - s 1f, w 15, p 70

Ayres, Mary - 3f, 3m, w 15, p 109

Baer, Dr. M. S. - 2m, w 13

Bailey, Elijah - Inn Keeper, s 1m, w 17, p 197

Bailey, Margaret - s 1m, w 14

Bain, William - s 1m, w 18

Bake, William - s 1f, 1m, w 19

Baker, David - es $6,000, 2m, w 4, p 22

Baker, Francis H. - Clergyman, es $5,000, s 1f, w 13, p 338

Baker, James - s 1f, w 3

Baker, Maria - s 1f, w 10, p 59

Ball, Walter - s 2f, 1m, w 12

Ballard, Edward J. - Sailmaker, s 2f, w 15, p 97

Bamberger, James - Blacksmith, es $3,500, s 1f, 1m, w 1, p 54

Bandle, R. - s 1f, 1m, w 5

Bankard, Jacob J. - Butcher, s 1f, w 1, p 102

Bankard, Jacob ▲ - s 1f, w 1, p 108

Bankard, William - Butcher, s 1f, w 1, p 107

Barber, Jane - s 1f, w 4

Barber, John T. - es $2,200, s 1m, w 15, p 3

Barker, Rebecca - s 1f, w 3, p 413

Barney, Ann L. - es $20,000, s 1f, 1m, w 11, p 140

Barney, John - s 2f, 1m, w 10

Barrow, Sally - s 1m, w 4

Bastable, Gilbert - Dealer In Cattle, s 5f, 2m, w 18, p 74

Bates, Eliza - s 1f, w 6

Bates, Lawrence W. - Preacher, s 2f, 1m, w 14, p 425

Baughman, H. F. - Stone Cutter, es $4,000, s 1f, w 20, p 284

Baumer, William - s 1m, w 18

Bayne, L. F. - Dry Goods, s 3f, w 18, p 46

Beadel, Dr. John D. - Physician, s 2f, w 13, p 369

Beal, Alexander - Clerk, s 2f, w 4, p 72

Slaveholders of Baltimore, 1840 & 1850

Beam, C. - s 1m, w 1, p 3
Beam, Mary - s 1f, w 14
Beams, J. - s 1f, w 11
Bean, Louisa - s 1f, w 4
Bean, Mrs. - s 1f, w 6
Beard, John - s 1f, w 1f
Beard, Lewis - Sailor, s 1f, w 16, p 182
Beard, Mary A. - es $1,800, s 1f, w 6, p 222
Beasten, George J. - Commission Merchant, s 1m, w 16, p 175
Beckett, William - Merchant, s 3f, w 15, p 113
Behrens, Jacob - Watchman, s 1f, w 5, p 107
Bell, Henry - Boot + Shoemaker, s 1f, w 15, p 7
Bellmear, Catherine - s 2f, w 11, p 115
Bellmear, Mrs. - s 1f, w 11, p 115
Belt, Mrs. T. - s 1f, w 11
Belt, Thomas H. - s 1m, w 11
Bennet, Thomas - s 1f, 1m, w 8
Bennett, Sam - s 1f, w 18
Benning, S. C. - 3f, 3m, w 12
Benteen, F. D. - Music Publisher, s 1f, w 17, p 225
Berkely, E. ▲ - Merchant, s 1f, w 20, p 300
Bernard, Henrietta - s 1m, w 3
Berry, Benajmin - s 1m, w 1
Berry, George R. - Brickmaker, s 1m, w 15, p 79
Berry, James W. - Grocer, s 1m, w 15, p 46
Berry, John H. ▲ - Grocer, s 1f, 1m, w 15, p 98
Berry, Sarah J. - s 2f, w 4
Berry, Walter W. ▲ - Merchant, s 2f, w 15, p 75
Berry, William H. - Merchant, s 1m, w 15, p 64
Berryman, Mrs. - 1f, 1m, w 12
Bery, George W. - 2f, w 6
Bevan, James - Lawyer, s 3f, 1m, w 11, p 197
Bevan, Samuel - Merchant, es $50,000, s 2f, w 11, p 142
Bevan, Thomas - Sea Captain, es $10,000, s 1f, w 3, p 313
Billinglea, Eliza - s 1m, w 3
Birce, N. C. - 1f, w 13
Birckhead, Hugh - s 1m, w 13
Bird, Edward T. - Dry Goods, es $5,000, s 1m, w 13, p 342
Birkhead, William J. - Merchant, s 3f, 1m, w 11, p 150
Biscoe, James - Merchant, s 2f, w 16, p 163
Blackstone, John - Carpenter, s 1f, w 18, p 61
Blair, Henry - s 1f, 1m, w 5
Blake, John S. - Hod Carrier, s 1m, w 12, p 280
Blakely, Samuel H. - 2f, 2m, w 4
Blanch, Jeremiah - s 1m, w 7
Bland, Sarah - s 1?, w 13, p 347
Blunt, Charles - s 1f, w 18
Blunt, Martha - s 1f, w 12
Boardley, Samuel C. - 1f, w 16
Boarman, James - s 1f, w 18
Boggs, A. L. - s 1m, w 6
Boggs, Alexander - s 1f, w 4
Boggs, John - Merchant, s 1f, 1m, w 4, p 40
Bolton, William - Saddler, s 1f, w 3, p 347
Bond, William - Tavern Keeper, s 3m, w 9, p 54
Bonn, Joseph - Tobacconist, s 1m, w 16, p 168

115

Chapter 12

Slaveholders of Baltimore, 1840 & 1850

Bool, H. W. - Auctioneer, es $32,000, s 1f, w 10, p 74
Boone, Charles F. - 1m, w 9
Boone, Ruth - s 1m, w 3
Bose, William - Publisher-*Balto. Am.*, s 2f, w 10, p 56
Bosley, James H. - 1f, w 5
Bosley, Rebecca - es $10,000, s 2f, w 15, p 108
Bosley, William - s 1f, 1m, w 20
Boston, Esau ▲, s 1f, w 11
Boston, John B. ▲ - Hatter, es $4,000, s 1f, w 3, p 419
Boswell, James - Musical Instr. Maker, s 1f, 1m, w 3, p 419
Botteman, Thomas - s 1f, w 13
Bouldain, Owen - s 2f, w 8
Bouldin, A. J. ▲ - Surveyor B. Co. Records, es $5,000, s 1f, w 6, p 220
Bourne, George - Physician, s 2f, 1m, w 16, p 185
Bowden, George E. - Merchant, s 1f, 1m, w 11, p 194
Bowdle, Alexander - s 1f, w 6
Bowie, R. C. - Merchant, s 3f, 2m, w 10, p 101
Boyd, J. R. - s 1f, w 4
Boyd, Mary J. - es $7,000, s 1f, 1m, w 13, p 379
Boyer, Mary R. - s 1f, w 14, p 431
Bradford, A. - s 1f, w 12
Bradford, Charles H. - Physician, es $3,500, s 1m, w 6, p 250
Bradford, Jane - es $1,000, s 1f, 2m, w 6, p 253
Brady, Samuel - s 1f, w 4
Brannan, James M. - Clothier, s 2f, w 13, p 327
Brauns, M. S. - s 3f, w 14
Brea, Jacob - s 1f, w 9

Brenan, M. - s 1m, w 12
Brian, John G. - Hardware Dealer, es $9,000, s 1f, w 5, p 94
Brice, Judge - s 2f, w 11
Brice, M. A. - s 2f, w 10, p 105
Brick, George - s 1m, w 9
Briley, L. - s 1f, w 12
Brinks, Daniel B. - s 4f, 1m, w 12
Briscoe, Leah - s 1m, w 13
Briscoe, Mr. - s z1f, w 4
Briscoe, Susan - s 1m, w 16, p 167
Broadbent, William - Merchant, s 1f, 1m, w 10, p 63
Bromwell, Josiah - Clerk, s 1m, w 11, p 136
Brooks, William - Grocer, s 1f, w 8, p 439
Broom, Susan - s 1f, w 4
Broughton, James - Sailor, s 1f, w 3, p 311
Brown, Alfred - Dentist, s 1f, w 13, p 388
Brown, Alfred J. - s 1f, w 14
Brown, Henry G. - Hotel Keeper, es $2,500, s 3f, 1m, w 16, p 131
Brown, Kaufman - Clerk, s 1f, w 8, p 432
Brown, Louisa - s 1f, w 14
Brown, S. - s 1m, w 20
Brown, William T. - Bricklayer, s 1f, w 16, p 171
Browse, Ed - s 1f, w 17
Bruff, John W. ▲ - Merchant, s 1f, w 14, p 430
Bruff, Rachael R. - s 2f, w 14
Brundige, William - Grocer, s 2f, 1m, w 15, p 104
Brune, John W. - Merchant, s 1f,

Slaveholders of Baltimore, 1840 & 1850

w 11, p 148
Brunner, Daniel - Bookseller, s 1f, w 16, p 174
Bryson, Mr. - s 1f, w 3
Buchwalter, Abraham - Miller, es $6,000, s 1f, w 15, p 52
Buck, B. - Merchant, 1f, w 14, p 446
Buck, James M. - s 2f, 1m, w 18
Buck, John - Merchant, es $15,000, s 1f, w 4, p 87
Buck, William B. - Oyster Dealer, es $5,700, s 1f, w 4, p 87
Buckler, Dr. John - Physician, es $10,000, s 1m, w 10, p 106
Buckler, Dr. Thomas H. - Physician, s 1f, w 10, p 109
Buckley, R. S. - Sailor, s 1f, 1m, w 9, p 42
Buckmiller, Robert - Tanner, s 1f, w 11, p 206
Bull, E. - s 2f, 1m, w 12
Burns, Samuel - Lumber Merchant, s 1f, w 14, p 443
Burton, Robert H. - s 1f, w 18
Busey, Mrs. - s 1f, w 11
Bush, Joseph C. - s 1m, w 17
Butler, John - s 1f, w 15, p 58
Byers, Joseph H. - Lime Dealer, s 2f, 2m, w 16, p 157
Byrn, William - Merchant, s 1f, w 5, p 124
Byrn, William W. - Merchant, es $4,000, s 1f, w 15, p 51
Calloway, William ▲ - Plasterer, s 2f, 2m, w 8, p 455
Calvert, George - Fish Inspector, es $4,000, s 1f, w 8, p 441
Campbell, B. M. ▲ - s 16f, 19m, w 13
Campbell, George - s 1f, 2m, w 17
Campbell, Thomas W. - Clerk, s 1f, w 16, p 135
Canfield, J. C. - Merchant .. Jewelry, es $6,500, s 1m, w 10, p 57
Cann, Martha - s 1m, w 18
Cannon, J. B. - Auctioneer, s 1m, w 13, p 336
Carback, E. - Shoemaker, es $3,000, s 2f, w 20, p 284
Carmichael, W. - Inspector, s 1f, w 12, p 272
Carpenter, William C. - Merchant, s 1f, w 15, p 82
Carr, Joseph - Physician, es $5,000, s 2f, 1m, w 15, p 97
Carrol, Charles ▲ - s 4f, w 11
Carroll, Charles R. ▲ - s 5f, 3m, w 11, p 141
Carroll, Henry D. G. ▲ - s 1m, w 9
Carroll, Judith C. ▲ - s 3f, w 10, p 104
Carroll, T. K. - s 4f, 2m, w 11
Cate, Ammon - Restaurant, s 2m, w 13, p 334
Cator, Elizabeth ▲ - s 1f, 2m, w 15, p 104
Cator, Joseph - es $3,000, s 5f, 2m, w 15, p 108
Caughey, Michael ▲ - Clothier, s 2f, w 6, p 251
Caughy, Samuel - s 1f, w 5
Ceeland, Carey - s 1f, w 18
Chafee, Ms. - s 2f, 1m, w 12
Chalard, Ferderrayd E. - s 1m, w 13
Chalmers, James W. - Rope Maker, s 2f, w 8, p 440
Chamberlain, A. - s 1f, w 12

117

Chapter 12

Slaveholders of Baltimore, 1840 & 1850

Chaney, Floyd - Machinist, s 1f, w 15, p 50
Chaplain, James S. - Druggist, s 1m, w 13, p 388
Chapman, Allan - Merchant, es $10,000, s 1m, w 19, p 312
Chappell, John G. - Merchant, s 1m, w 15, p 52
Chenoweth, Benjamin - s 1m, w 7
Chenowith, Mary - s 1f, 1m, w 6, p 214
Cherbonier, Peter - French Teacher, s 2f, w 14, p 476
Chesley, Mrs. - s 1f, w 11
Chesney, Harriet - s 2f, 1m, w 8, p 439
Chesnut, William - s 1f, 2m, w 4
Childs, Brigadeer General - Soldier, es $8,000, s 1f, 2m, w 17, p 302
Childs, John D. - Merchant, es $4,000, s 1f, w 6, p 222
Childs, Samuel - Coach Maker, s 1m, w 5, p 135
Christian, Samuel W. - s 1m, w 17
Churchman, Martha - s 1f, w 15
Cinnamond, George R. - Conveyancer, es $2,500, s 2f, w 10, p 65
Claget, Eli - s 1f, w 4
Claget, William - s 1f, w 4
Claget, William - s 4f, w 4
Clagett, Mrs. M. - s 1f, w 11
Clarck, Charles - Pilot, es $2,000, s 2f, w 1, p 106
Clarck, Zack - Pilot, s 2f, 2m, w 1, p 11
Clarcke, E. M. - s 2f, 1m, w 20
Clarey, Aaron - s 1f, 1m, w 7

Clark Harriet - es $2,500, s 1f, w 4, p 19
Clark, John C. - s 1f, 1m, w 13
Clark, Mathew ▲ - s 1f, w 18, p 14
Clarke, George B. - Merchant, es $35,000, s 1f, w 15, p 47
Clarke, John A. - Boardinghouse Keeper, s 2f, 1m, w 10, p 112
Claypoole, John - Mariner, s 1f, w 6, p 186
Clayton, Samuel S. - Merchant, s 1f, w 15, p 112
Cleavland, Joseph C. - s 2f, w 3
Clemmens, Charles F. - s 1f, w 3
Clifford, Sylvester ▲ - Property Agent, es $1,500, s 1f, 1m, w 16, p 187
Cobb, Josiah - Grocer, es $20,000, s 1m, w 13, p 373
Cobb, Thomas M. - s 1f, w 13
Cochran, James E. - s 1f, w 6
Cochran, James E. - Oyster Dealer, s 1f, w 6, p 164
Cockey, Edward ▲ - s 1f, 2m, w 11
Cockey, John G. - Grocer, s 1f, w 16, p 163
Cockey, John P. - Physician, s 1f, 1m, w 4, p 32
Cockey, Joshua - Clerk, s 1f, w 11, p 115
Cockran, Thomas J. - Laborer, s 1f, w 2, p 181
Cockrill, R. - s 1f, w 2, p 278
Coffins, Charles E. - s 1f, w 2
Cole, A. G. - Merchant, s 2f, w 14, p 462
Cole, Cornelius H. - Livery Stable Keeper, s 1m, w 16, p 179

Slaveholders of Baltimore, 1840 & 1850

Cole, Elizabeth - s 2f, w 4
Cole, H. W. - Merchant Tailor, es $40,000, s 1f, w 4, p 88
Cole, Louis M. - Superintendent B+O R. R., es $500, s 1f, w 15, p 114
Cole, William P. ▲ - Hatter, es $5,000, s 2f, w 5, p 93
Coleman, D. - Grocer, s 1m, w 1, p 8
Coleman, William - Shipsmith, s 1f, w 3, p 385
Collins, J. E. - Hotel Keeper, s 1f, 2m, w 2, p 262
Collins, Sarah - s 3f, w 13, p 389
Colson, Eliza - s 1f, w 18
Colvin, Rachel - es $166,000, s 2f, 2m, w 3, p 425
Conine, W. C. - Broker, es $30,000, s 2f, w 10, p 84
Connor, John - s 2f, w 2
Conoway, R. - s 2f, w 2
Conrad, Emily - s 2f, 1m, w 18
Conrad, Emily - s 1m, w 18
Conrad, George M. - s 1f, 2m, w 4
Conway, Carvil - s 3f, w 4, p 30
Conway, John R. ▲ - Merchant, es $30,000, s 1f, 1m, w 15, p 83
Cook, Jacob - Bailiff, s 1f, w 12, p 290
Cook, Mrs. - s 1f, w 4
Cooper, Alexander - Druggist, w 7, p 269
Cooper, Edward O. - Sea Captain, es $2,500, s 2f, w 3, p 422
Cooper, James ▲, s 1f, 2m, w 9
Cooper, John - Tavern Keeper, s 1f, 1m, w 4, p 44
Corkran, Charles - s 1f, 1m, w 15

Corkran, William - Clerk, s 1f, w 15, p 79
Cornelius, Susan - s 1f, w 19, p 196
Corner, George W. - Merchant, es $5,000, p 357
Costello, Ann - s 1f, w 5
Cottman, James S. ▲ - s 2f, 1m, w 11
Cottrell, Clark - Waterer, s 1f, 4m, w 15, p 10
Coulbourn, Stephen D. - Commission Merchant, s 2f, w 13, p 371
Couley, C. - s 2f, w 10
Coulson, J. - s 1f, w 20, p 308
Councilman, Jacob - s 1m, w 14
Courtlan, James - Machinist, es $27,000, s 1m, w 4, p 86
Coward, Captain - s 1f, 2m, w 19
Cox, James G. - s 1f, 2m, w 19
Cox, Nathaniel - Lawyer, s 1f, w 19, p 184
Cox, Susannah - s 2f, w 15, p 197
Crane, Mrs. - s 1f, w 3
Crawford, Mary - s 1f, w 18
Creamer, David - Lumber Merchant, es $5,000, s 1f, 1m, w 8, p 388
Crey, Frederick - Paver, es $50,000, s 1m, w 8, p 369
Crichton, William ▲ - s 1f, w 11
Criss, M. - Dry Good Merchant, 1m, w 18, p 162
Cromwell, Thomas - s 1m, w 3
Cronmiller, Jacob - es $12,000, s 1m, w 18, p 59
Crook, Susan - s 1f, w 3
Crookshanks, John - Merchant, s 1f, w 15, p 104
Crosby, Joseph - Merchant, s 1m,

Chapter 12

Slaveholders of Baltimore, 1840 & 1850

w 14, p 425
Crosby, Samuel R. - Farmer, s 1m, w 14, p 425
Cross, Trueman - Cashier, s 1m, w 14, p 467
Crummer, Edward A. - Lime Dealer, s 1m, w 8, p 403
Cry, Henry - s 1f, w 8
Cunningham, Andrew - s 1f, w 7
Cunningham, B. A. - s 1f, w 13
Cunningham, Martha ▲ - s 2f, 1m, w 4
Curley, Henry - Builder, es $25,000, s 1f, w 11, p 145
Curley, James - s 1f, w 11
Curley, James W. - Hardware, s 1f, 1m, w 13, p 340
Cushony, John - s 1f, w 14
Dallam, F. J. - s 2f, w 11
Dallam, Mrs. - s 1f, w 11
Dalrymple, Alexander P. - Clerk, s 1f, 2m, w 15, p 49
Daniels, John D. - Brewer, s 2f, w 4, p 16
Darby, John - s 2f, w 4
Dare, Catharine - s 1f, w 15, p 80
Dare, Margaret - s 2f, w 15, p 50
Darling, Edward - s 5f, w 2
Dashields, Maria - s 1m, w 15, p 101
Dashields, Mary - s 2f, 2m, w 2
Davidson, S. A. - Physician, s 1f, w 9, p 40
Davis, Benjamin - s 1m, w 3
Davis, Charles S. - s 1f, 1m, w 4
Davis, James - s 1f, w 3
Davis, James C. - s 1f, w 3
Davis, Mrs. - s 1m, w 3
Davis, Robert - Druggist, s 1m, w 12, p 248
Davis, Robert C. - s 3m, w 9

Dawson, Cap - s 1f, w 3
Day, Mary - es $1,000, s 1f, w 8, p 365
Dean, George W. - Ship Joiner, s 1m, w 15, p 20
Dean, Rachael L. - s 1m, w 15
Delany, William - s 1f, w 19
Dell, George E. - s 1f, w 20
Delmast, A. - s 1m, w 5
Denison, Marcus - Merchant, es $50,000, s 1f, w 9, p 25
Denmead, Adam - Machinist, es $68,000, s 2f, 2m, w 8, p 452
Denning, John N. - Negro Buyer, s 1m, w 9, p 25
Deshields, W. L. - s 1m, w 2
Devalin, Hugh - Blacksmith, es $4,000, s 1f, w 5, p 125
Devere, William - Carpenter, s 2f, w 7, p 338
Devries, William - s 3f, 1m, w 12
Dickerson, William T. - s 1f, w 11
Dickerson, Zadock - Livery Stable Keeper, s 1m, w 16, p 170
Diffendeffer, Charles - Grocer, es $30,000, s 1f, w 4, p 44
Diffenderffer, John A. - Merchant, s 5f, 1m, w 9, p 55
Diffinderffer, Charles - 2f, w 4
Diggs, Richard H. ▲ - Ship Carpenter, s 1f, w 3, p 373
Dillahay, John - Merchant, s 1f, w 4, p 5
Doane, Mary ▲ - s 2f, w 11
Donovan, Joseph S. ▲ - Trading, es $8,000, s 3f, 7m, w 15, p 2
Dorbaker, William - Horse Dealer, s 1f, 1m, w 16, p 182
Dorman, Jane - s 1f, w 4, p 15
Dorsey, Allen - s 1f, w 18

Slaveholders of Baltimore, 1840 & 1850

Dorsey, Augustus - s 1f, w 5, p 139

Dorsey, Comfort W. ▲ - es $16,000, s 3f, 2m, w 10, p 111

Dorsey, Daniel - Proprietor, Hotel, s 1f, 1m, w 9, p 45

Dorsey, Edward H. ▲, s 5f, 1m, w 15, p 49

Dorsey, James L. - Merchant, s 1f, w 15, p 49

Dorsey, Judge - s 1f, w 11

Dorsey, Lorenzo - Clerk, s 1f, w 13, p 377

Dorsey, Mrs. E. H. - s 2f, w 10

Dorsey, Richard - s es $50,000, s 5f, 6m, w 11, w 153

Dorsey, Richard B. - Merchant, s 1f, w 11, p 196

Dowling, N. - es $4,000, s 1f, w 12, p 295

Downey, John - Merchant, es $4,000, s 1f, w 12, p 252

Doyle, Jane G. - s 1f, w 9, p 31

Drummond, Levin - Watchmaker, es $4,500, s 1f, w 4, p 34

Dryden, Joshua - Brickmaker, es $10,000, s 1f, w 19, p 142

Dryden, Samuel - Boot+Shoemaker, s 1f, w 13, p 372

Dubeldy, Elizabeth - s 1f, 18

Dugan, Frederick J. - Attorney At Law, s 2f, 1m, w 9, p 39

Duhurst, Mary - s 2f, w 10, p 74

Dukehear, V. - Manufacturer, s 1f, w 10, p 101

Dukeheart, Samuel - Clerk, s 1f, w 4, p 51

Dunbar, Dr. John R. - Physician, s 2f, 2m, w 13, p 382

Duncan, William - s 1m, w 18

Dunham, Thornton C. - Merchant, s 1f, w 14, p 418

Dunkel, John - s 1f, w 13

Dunn, James - Merchant, s 2f, 1m, w 16, p 169

Dunn, Rebie H. - 1m, w 19, p 144

Durborrow, Hammond - Merchant, s 1m, w 4, p 86

Durham, Lloyd - Grocer, es $2,000, s 1f, w 16, p 64

Dusenbury, S. B. - U. S. Army, s 3f, w 14, p 468

Dushane, John ▲ - Carpenter, es $50,000, s 2f, w 15, p 117

Dushane, N. G. - Carpenter, es $1,800, s 2f, w 20, p 245

Dutton, George R. - Lime Inspector, s 1f, w 3, p 322

Dutton, R. - Cabinet Maker, es $10,000, s 1f, w 2, p 234

Duvall, Aldridge - 2f, 1m, w 13

Duvall, Alfred - Machinist, s 1m, w 4, p 39

Duvall, C. - s 1m, w 18

Duvall, Caroline - s 1f, w 3

Duvall, Henry - Grocer, s 3f, 1m, w 15, p 98

Duvall, Mary - s 2f, w 14

Duvall, William B. ▲ - Merchant, es $8,000, s 2f, 1m, w 11, p 144

Eareckson, Robert - s 2f, w 4

Earhart, J. - s 1m, w 12

Edgerton, Charles - Goldsmith, s 1f, w 7, p 306

Edmonson, James - s 1f, 2m, w 17

Ehlen, J. H. ▲ - es $6,000, s 2f, w 12, p 271

Eichelberger, W. O. - s 2f, w 10

Elmore, James ▲ - Butcher, s 3f, w 1, p 112

121

Chapter 12

Slaveholders of Baltimore, 1840 & 1850

Elsey, Capt. A. - s 1f, w 11
Elzey, Letetia - s 2f, 1m, w 9, p 3
Embry, William H. - s 1f, w 11
Emery, John B. - Brickmaker, es $20,000, s 2f, 1m, w 16, p 179
Emery, Samuel G. - Merchant, es $5,000, s 1f, w 4, p 19
Emory, Ann W. - s 1f, w 11
Emory, Arthur ▲ - Merchant, es $45,000, s 3f, 1m, w 16, p 166
Emory, Daniel G. - Bank Officer, s 2f, w 11, p 136
Emory, W. J. - s 4f, 2m, w 10, p 65
Emory, William J. - s 1f, w 18
Erick, Mrs. - s 1f, w 4
Eschback, John - Paver, s 1f, w 11, p 190
Esender, James - s 1f, w 1
Estep, Henry - Brickmaker, s 3f, w 15, p 92
Etchberger, James - Sea Captain, es $1,800, s 2f, w 3, p 320
Etterman, Fred - Publican, es $6,000, s 1f, w 10, p 69
Ettings, S. E. - s 2f, w 11
Evans, George - s 1f, w 4
Evans, Mary - s 1f, w 14
Evans, Mary - s 1m, w 15, p 78
Evans, William - Plasterer, es $1,000, s 1f, w 7, p 334
Evans, William ▲ - Carpenter, s 1f, 1m, w 15, p 17
Evatt, Columbus - Locksmith, s 2f, w 13, p 362
Fahnestock, Sarah - s 1f, w 18
Fairbanks, William ▲ - s 1f, w 3
Fales, James - s 1f, w 3
Fant, Edward L. - Dry Goods Merchant, es $1,500, s 1f, w 13, p 385
Farnandis, Walter - es $50,000, s 2f, 1m, w 13, p 389
Farquharson, Cahrles - s 1f, w 3
Farrell, Sarah - s 1f, w 4, p 81
Fayward, Nehemiah P. - Stovemaker, s 1f, w 15, p 75
Federman, Miss - s 1f, w 11
Feinour, Cahrles - s 1f, w 3
Fell, Stephen - s 2f, 1m, w 8, p 445
Fenby, Samuel - es $30,000, s 1f, w 4, p 86
Fendall, Sarah E. - s 3f, w 13
Ferguson, David - Commission Agent, es $15,000, s 3f, w 12, p 324
Ferguson, Joshua ▲ - s 1f, w 4
Ferguson, Thomas - Merchant, es $60,000, s 1f, w 10, p 93
Finley, Catherine - s 1f, p 15
Fisher, Alexander - Merchant, es $20,000, s 1f, w 19, p 101
Fisher, Mary - es $10,000, s 1f, w 12, p 298
Fisher, William - Stock Broker, s 1m, w 10, p 56
Fitch, Dorcas - s 1f, w 6, p 208
Fitspatrick, Cecilia - es $15,000, s 1f, w 15, p 43
Flack, Rachael - 3f, w 14, p 461
Flack, Thomas J. ▲ - Spirit Dealer, s 1f, w 15, p 56
Flemings, James - s 3f, 1m, w 5
Ford, Henrietta B. - s 2f, w 18
Forrest, Captain - s 1f, w 4
Forrest, Morean ▲ - Physician, s 2f, 1m, w 14, p 467
Forster, Francis - Agent, s 1f, w 9, p 24
Forsyth, William - Clerk, s 1f, w

Slaveholders of Baltimore, 1840 & 1850

15, p 25
Forth, Samuel - s 1f, w 6
Fowell, Amelia - s 1f, w 2, p 207
Fowler, Benjamin - Tavern Keeper, s 1f, w 2, p 209
Fowler, Susan - s 1f, w 5, p 97
Fox, Luther - Tavern Keeper, es $10,000, s 3m, w 9, p 42
Frame, George - s 1f, w 3
Francke, Austin F. - Livery Stable Keeper, s 1f, 1m, w 15, p 53
Fraser, John - s 2f, 2m, w 16
Fraser, William R. - s 2f, w 15
Frazier, J. B. ▲ - s 2f, w 2
Frazier, James - s 2f, w 1
Frazier, L. - s 1m, w 2
Fremmea, Thomas H. - s 1m, w 3
Frey, Gauntlet - Shipping Master, s 1f, w 3, p 333
Fryer, Elijah S. - Gilder, s 1f, w 10, p 75
Fuller, Richard ▲ - Baptist Clergyman, s 2f, w 14, p 412
Furling, J. - s 1f, w 18
Gaggin, George S. - s 1m, w 15
Gale, George - s 1f, w 3
Gale, John - s 1f, w 3
Gale, Major - s 1f, w 5
Galt, Cyrus - s 1m, w 18
Gamble, Dr. - s 1m, w 14
Gambrill, Charles A. ▲ - s 1f, w 14
Gant, Rose - s 1f, w 3
Gardener, Elizabeth A. - s 1m, w 3
Gardener, William E. - Ship Builder, s 1f, w 2, p 246
Garnett, J. M. - Merchant, es $65,000, s 1f, 1m, w 19, p 229
Garrott, William - Commission Merchant, s 2f, w 16, p 179
Gaylor, Joseph - s 1f, w 1
Gealdhall, Thomas - s 1f, w 16
Gehrmann, Charles - Merchant, es $100,000, s 1m, w 10, p 100
Gelman, Charles - s 1m, w 13
Gelston, Hugh - Merchant, es $100,000, s 1f, 1m, w 10, p 106
George, S. - s 1f, w 12
Geshegan, Stewart - s 3f, 2m, w 15
Gethver, William - Clerk, s 1f, w 18, p 31
Gibney, Richard - Dentist, es $6,000, s 1m, w 10, p 72
Gibson, Dr. George ▲ - Physician, s 1m, w 11, p 144
Gibson, James - s 1m, w 1
Gidding, Mr. - s 2f, 3m, w 17
Giles, John R. - Confectioner, s 3m, w 10, p 69
Gill, J. M. - Joiner, es $8,670, s 2f, w 11, p 142
Gillingham, George - Grocer, es $3,000, s 1f, 1m, w 4, p 73
Gilmer, Charles S. - s 1f, w 11, p 150
Gilmor, Marian - es $37,000, s 1m, w 10, p 111
Gilmore, James - s 1f, w 4
Gittings, John S. ▲, s 1f, w 11
Glanville, John W. - Cabinet Maker, s 2f, w 16, p 120
Glass, Thomas - s 1f, w 2
Gleen, William - s 1f, 1m, w 18
Glenn, John - Lawyer, s 1m, w 13, p 388
Glenn, John - s 2f, 1m, w 13
Glenn, John - s 1f, w 18
Glenn, John B. - s 1f, w 3

123

Chapter 12

Slaveholders of Baltimore, 1840 & 1850

Glenn, William - s 1f, 1m, w 13
Gobright, Joseph - Coachman, s 1f, w 9, p 30
Goddard, Charles - Hotel Keeper, s 1f, 2m, w 14, p 469
Godwin, William - Grocer, s 1m, w 15, p 97
Golder, A. - Paperhanger, es $38,000, s 1f, w 13, p 341
Goldsmith, Eliza - es $25,000, s 1f, 1m, w 11, p 137
Good, Charles - s 1f, w 14
Gooding, Henry B. - s 1f, w 14
Goodwin, Eliza - s 1f, w 6
Goodwin, Penelope - es $50,000, s 3f, w 4, p 85
Goodwin, Penelope - s 1f, w 6
Gorden, J. W. - s 1f, w 14
Gordon, J. N. - Merchant, s 2f, 1m, w 10, p 64
Gordon, John H. - Wood Dealer, s 2f, 1m, w 15, p 56
Gorsuch, Jehu - s 1f, w 5
Gorsuch, Peregrine - Magistrate, es $2,000, s 1f, w 6, p 202
Gorsuch, Robert - Farmer, s 2f, 1m, w 6, p 220
Gorsuch, Robert - s 1f, 1m, w 12
Gorsuch, W. G. - 1m, w 12
Gorsuch, William - Stone Mason, s 1f, w 8, p 435
Gough, Harry - s 1f, w 6
Gould, Mary - s 3f, w 9, p 40
Gouldsmith, Elizabeth W. - es $6,000, s 2f, 1m, w 7, p 348
Gover, Gerard - s 1f, w 4, p 88
Gracen, John - Trader, s 1m, w 16, p 149
Graff, Dr. - s 1f, w 14
Grafton, Mark - es $26,000, s 1m, w 13, p 339

Grafton, Samuel H. s - Stove Dealer, s 1f, w 15, p 63
Graham, James - Merchant, s 1f, w 6, p 157
Graham, Matilda - s 3m, w 13, p 364
Graham, Robert - Merchant, es $6,000, s 2f, w 4, p 30
Graham, William - s 2f, 1m, w 3, p 408
Grant, Mrs. - s 1f, w 11
Gray, James - s 2f, 1m, w 15
Gray, John - Huckster, s 1m, w 3, p 335
Gray, W. - s 1f, w 9
Gray, William - s 1f, 2m, w 1
Greason, George - Carter, s 1m, w 16, p 135
Green, Charles B. - s 2f, w 5
Green, Cornelius - 1m, w 8
Green, Fanny - 1m, w 14
Green, Jacob - Merchant, s 1f, w 6, p 186
Gregg, Mrs. E. - s 2f, w 11
Grey, John - Hotel Keeper,, es $6,000, s 1f, 2m, w 10, p 94
Griffin, R. B. s - Merchant, s 1f, w 12, p 309
Griffiss, John - Lumber Merchant,, es $20,000, s 1m, w 4, p 33
Griffith, David - Sailor,, es $11,000, s 2f, 1m, w 15, p 119
Griffith, E. - s 1f, w 12
Griffith, F. - s 1f, w 18
Griffith, Henry - Tailor, s 1f, w 10, p 73
Griffith, Israel - Gry Goods Merchant, es $100,000, s 6f, 2m, w 13, p 382
Griffith, John - s 1f, 2m, w 4

Slaveholders of Baltimore, 1840 & 1850

Griffith, John - s 3f, w 15, p 78
Griffith, John s - s 2f, 1m, w 11
Griffith, Susan - s 2f, w 15, p 78
Griggs, James - es $10,000, s 2m, w 4, p 19
Grimes, Vincent - Sailor, es $1,000, s 1f, 1m, w 16, p 143
Grindall, John T. s - Clerk, s 2f, w 15, p 17
Gross, Lucretia - s 1m, w 16, p 167
Groverman, Anthony s - s 1f, w 4
Grubb, William - Morocco Dresser, s 1f, w 8, p 355
Guert, Mahola - s 1f, 2m, w 13
Gunby, M. - s 3f, w 1, p 73
Gunn, Ann M. - s 4f, w 13, p 362
Gurshier, G. M. - s 1f, w 19
Guy, William - Proprietor U. S. Hotel, s 2f, 4m, w 9, p 50
Guyther, Henry - Pilot, es $1,500, s 2f, w 4, p 59
Guyton, Beal - Merchant, s 1f, w 14, p 429
Guyton, John - Hotel Keeper, s 1f, 1m, w 5, p 113
Guyton, Miss A. - s 1f, w 18
Habbersett, Henry - Clerk, s 1f, 1m, w 8, p 398
Hackett, James - s 1f, w 13
Hackett, Mr. - s 1f, w 11
Hagan, John H. - Clerk, s 1f, w 16, p 158
Halbert, John - Shoemaker, s 1m, w 6, p 222
Hale, Colin - Merchant, s 1m, w 16, p 157
Hall, Elizabeth A. s - s 2f, w 9, p 1
Hall, Hester s - s 1f, w 3, p 366
Hall, Mrs. C. - s 1f, w 10
Hall, Nicholas - s 2f, w 4
Hall, R. H. - s 1f, w 13
Hall, Richard - 1m, w 3
Hall, Richard H. - Merchant, s 4f, 2m, w 11, p 147
Hall, Sarah s - s 6f, 2m, w 18, p 37
Hall, Susan - s 1f, w 3
Hall, Thomas J. - Merchant, es $35,000, s 2f, 1m, w 15, p 115
Hall, William - s 1f, w 18, p 126
Hambleton, P. - s 2f, w 2
Hambleton, T. E. - Merchant, es $20,000, s 1m, w 12, p 320
Hamill, Alexander - Miller, s 1f, w 8, p 451
Hammond, Charles - Tanner, es $20,000, s 2f, w 18, p 14
Hammond, Rezin - s 1f, 2m, w 17
Hanan, John - 3f, w 10
Hancock, Absolom - Collector, es $125,000, s 1f, w 3, p 417
Hardcastle, Marcus - Grocer, s 1f, w 7, p 284
Hardesty, Henry - s 1f, w 11, p 151
Hardesty, Richard S. s - Merchant, s 1f, w 14, p 425
Hardesty, Thomas - s 1f, w 18
Hardie, Robert - s 1f, w 3
Harman, George - s 1f, w 13
Harrington, James - Huckster, s 1m, w 17, p 243
Harris, Chapin A. - Dentist, s 1f, w 10, p 106
Harris, Elisa - 1m, w 15
Harris, Joseph - Gentleman, s 3f, w 14, p 448
Harris, Milkey - s 1f, 2m, w 16, p 180
Harris, Mr. - s 1f, w 4

Chapter 12

Slaveholders of Baltimore, 1840 & 1850

Harris, William S. - Broker, s 1f, 1m, w 2, p 182

Harrison, Benjamin - Dry Goods Dealer, s 2f, w 13, p 358

Harrison, John - Clerk, s 1f, w 13, p 358

Harrison, Mary s - s 2f, 1m, w 20, p 292

Harrison, N. - s 4f, 4m, w 18

Harrison, Robert - s 2f, 1m, w 3

Hart, Archibald - s 1f, w 14, p 439

Hart, Asa - Carpenter, es $5,000, s 1f, 3m, w 6, p 210

Hart, Mrs. - 1m, w 11

Hartman, James P. - s 2f, w 4

Harvey, Joshua - Merchant, s 1f, w 14, p 429

Harwood, Mrs. S. - s 1f, 1m, w 10

Haslehurst, H. T. R. - s 1f, w 10

Hasluo, Resin - Coachsmith, es $4,000, s 1m, w 10, p 102

Haslup, John - Coachsmith, s 1f, w 10, p 100

Hason, John - Wood Dealer, es $2,400, s 2f, w 4, p 87

Hatchson, Benjamin C. - 1m, w 2

Hathway, Mary A. - s 1f, 1m, w 14, p 467

Hawkins, John - es $6,000, s 2f, 2m, w 3, p 425

Hawkins, John W. - Grocer, s 1f, 1m, w 16, p 171

Hays, Sarah - s 1f, w 12

Hays, William - Butcher, s 1f, w 8, p 356

Hazlehurst, S. - s 1f, w 19

Hazlett, Manlope - s 1f, w 3

Heald, Belinda A. - 2m, w 14

Heald, William - Tanner, s 2f, w 6, p 235

Heath, Harlow W. - Teacher, es $18,000, s 1m, w 10, p 65

Heckrotte, William - Tavern Keeper, es $9,610, s 2f, 2m, w 15, p 56

Heginbotham, John - s 2f, w 4

Heiser, Henry - Merchant, s 2f, w 14, p 461

Henderson, James A. s - s 1f, w 9, p 26

Henderson, Mrs. S. - 1m, w 10

Henrix, Thomas - Merchant, s 1f, w 6, p 250

Herady, P. - s 1f, 1m, w 19

Hewett, A. K. - Bookeeper, s 1f, w 4, p 51

Hewitt, Elmer - Currier, es $34,000, s 1f, w 9, p 7

Hicks, J. - s 1f, w 12

Higgins, Edward - Confectioner, es $10,000, s 3f, 1m, w 15, p 1

Higgins, Thomas - Clerk, es $1,500, s 2f, w 4, p 26

High, Jane G. - s 1f, w 14

Hilland, Mrs. - s 1f, w 11

Hillon, William W. - 2m, w 7

Hines, Joseph - 1m, w 18

Hines, Joshua - s 1f, w 18

Hintze, F. E. B. - 2m, w 9

Hiss, Eliza G. - s 1f, w 4, p 12

Hissey, William - Shoemaker, es $1,000, s 1f, w 13, p 328

Hitch, Dr. - Physician, es $40,000, s 4f, 2m, w 19, p 228

Hoffman, S. Owings - Merchant, s 1f, 1m, w 11, p 153

Hoffman, Thomas C. - Clerk, s 1f, w 15, p 75

Hogg, James - Clerk, es $4,000, s 2f, w 4, p 87

Hogg, John - s 1f, w 12, p 245

Slaveholders of Baltimore, 1840 & 1850

Holbrook, Joseph - s 1f, w 4
Holden, Enoch P. - Baker, es $1,500, s 1f, w 4, p 30
Hollins, J. Smith - s 4f, w 9, p 39
Hollinsworth, Ann D. - es $1,000, s 2f, w 13, p 361
Holmes, Victor s - s 1f, w 5
Holt, George H. - Hatter, es $3,000, s 1f, w 16, p 187
Hoofnagle, Lydia - s 1f, w 15, p 12
Hooper, D. H. - Lawyer, s 2f, w 12, p 323
Hooper, E. s - s 3f, 2m, w 12
Hooper, James - Cabinet Maker, es $10,000, s 1f, w 6, p 216
Hooper, James - Grocer, es $20,000, s 1f, w 15, p 48
Hooper, James J. - Grocer, s 1f, 4m, w 18, p 39
Hooper, James Jr. - Merchant, s 1f, w 15, p 72
Hooper, John P. - Grocer, es $5,000, s 2f, 1m, w 15, p 48
Hooper, Thomas s - Merchant, es $15,000, s 2f, 1m, w 15, p 78
Hooper, William - s 1f, w 4, p 20
Hooper, William - Sailor, s 1f, w 16, p 139
Hooper, William C. - s 1f, w 4
Hoopier, Mrs. - s 1f, w 11
Hoover, F. - 1m, w 18
Hopkins, Robert - s 1f, w 6
Hopkins, Robert M. - Merchant, es $1,050, s 2f, w 6, p 224
Hopkins, Samuel - s 2f, w 11
Hopkins, W. - s 2f, w 4
Hopkins, William - s 1f, w 2
Hopper, Samuel W. - Dry Goods Merchant, s 1m, w 13, p 364
Horn, Benjamin - Manufacturer, es $16,000, s 1m, w 20, p 312
Horsell, M. - s 1f, w 18
Horwitz, J. - s 1f, 1m, w 12, p 325
Hoshall, Shadrack - Carpenter, s 1f, w 15, p 42
Hough, Mary G. - s 1f, w 11
House, William A. - es $10,000, s 2f, w 15, p 59
Houston, G. - s 1f, w 1
Howard, Charles s - Judge - Orphans Court, es $85,000, s 1m, w 11, p 211
Howard, Elenor - s 1f, w 14
Hubell, Pamelia - s 1f, w 13, p 378
Hudson, D. W. - s 1f, w 3
Huffington, William - Sea Captain, s 1m, w 3, p 289
Hugerford, Henry - s 1f, w 14
Hughes, Margaret S. - es $150,000, s 1m, w 10, p 103
Hungerford, S. - s 1f, 1m, w 19
Hunt, Henry - Tailor, s 1f, w 2, p 188
Hunt, Mr. - s 1f, w 4
Hunt, Prudence - s 1m, w 16, p 188
Hunter, Ann - s 1f, w 11
Hunter, Mary - s 1f, w 6
Hurt, Reverend William - s 1f, w 13
Hussey, A. R. - s 1f, w 12
Hutchinson, N. - s 3f, 3m, w 5
Hyde, Moses - Chandler, s 1f, w 8, p 390
Hyland, James C. - s 2f, 1m, w 10
Hyland, John - 1m, w 14
Ing, Edward? - s 1f, w 3, p 312
Inloes, J. S. - Physician, es $5,000, s 2f, w 2, p 246

Chapter 12

Slaveholders of Baltimore, 1840 & 1850

Inoloes, William - es $38,000, s 2f, 1m, w 3, p 416
Ireland, Edward s - s 1f, w 11
Irvin, Elisith - s 1f, w 10, p 61
Isaac, Richard s - Merchant, s 3f, w 16, p 179
Israel, Mrs. - 1m, w 3
Jackson, Charles M. - Bookkeeper, s 1f, w 15, p 109
Jackson, Francis - s 1f, w 19, p 189
Jackson, James M. - Grocer, s 2m, w 3, p 307
Jackson, Mary - s 1f, 3m, w 16
Jackson, Molly s - es $50,000, s 3f, 1m, w 10, p 104
Jacobs, Samuel s - Merchant, s 1f, w 15, p 71
James, Achsha - s 1f, w 13, p 355
James, Ann M. s - es $3,000, s 2f, w 3, p 378
James, E. - s 2f, w 2
James, George s - Coachmaker, es $3,500, s 1f, w 6, p 255
James, John - Coachmaker, es $5,000, s 1f, w 6, p 213
Jamison, C. C. - Cashier, es $10,000, s 3f, w 10, p 61
Jarrett, Asbury - Clothier, s 1f, w 4, p 40
Jarrett, Joshua - s 2f, w 12
Jeans, Mr. - s 1f, w 11
Jeffries, Margaret - s 1f, w 3
Jenkins, Ambrose - s 1f, w 11
Jenkins, Anthony H. - Cabinet Maker, s 1f, w 15, p 54
Jenkins, Austen s - s 4f, w 11
Jenkins, Courtney - 4f, w 11
Jenkins, Edward F. - s 1f, 1m, w 11
Jenkins, Eliza - s 1f, w 3
Jesson, J. - s 1f, w 18
Jessop, Priscilla - s 4f, w 6, p 230
Jessop, Priscilla - 1m, w 6
Jessup, Priscilla - 1m, w 6
Johns, Henry - s 1f, 1m, w 1
Johns, May - es $10,000, s 1f, w 8, p 441
Johnson, ? - s 1f, w 18
Johnson, Edward - s 1f, w 13
Johnson, Elizabeth - s 1f, 1m, w 4
Johnson, Nacey - 1m, w 15
Johnson, William H. s - Boatmaker, s 1m, w 5, p 90
Johnson, William s - s 1f, w 5
Johnson, William s - s 1f, w 6
Johnston, Christopher - Millwright, s 1f, w 8, p 402
Johnston, John - Waggoner, s 1f, w 8, p 371
Johnston, Richard - s 1f, w 7
Johnston, Thomas D. - s 3m, w 14
Jones, E. A. - s 1f, w 18
Jones, Edward - s 1f, w 14
Jones, Emily - s 1f, w 13, p 361
Jones, Harriet - s 1f, 1m, w 18
Jones, James - s 2f, 1m, w 9
Jones, James W. - s 1f, w 8
Jones, Levin - s 1f, w 15, p 46
Jones, M. - s 1f, w 12
Jones, Morcea - 1m, w 14
Jones, Nancy - 1m, w 13
Jones, Sarah A. s - s 1f, w 15, p 94
Jones, Stephen - s 1f, w 4
Jones, Susan - es $12,000, s 1f, w 4, p 43
Joseph, Joshua - 1m, w 8
Joy, S. P. - s 1f, w 20
Judick, Joseph - Lumber Mer-

Slaveholders of Baltimore, 1840 & 1850

chant, es $20,000, s 2f, 1m, w 12, p 290
Kane, Amelia S. - s 1f, w 15, p 69
Kane, George s - s 1f, w 4
Kane. Cap - s 1f, w 3
Kaughman, J. - 1m, w 19
Keach, Cyril - Tavern Keeper, s 2f, 2m, w 9, p 41
Keach, L. P. - Tavern Keeper, s 1m, w 5, p 91
Keborn, Eldridge G. - s 1f, 3m, w 18
Keen, John - s 1f, w 18
Keene, John s - s 1f, 2m, w 16
Keener, David - Agent - Copper Works, s 1f, w 13, p 387
Kelly, Caleb - Grocer, s 1f, w 16, p 186
Kelly, H. - s 1f, w 2
Kelly, Timothy - Tailor, es $48,000, s 2f, 1m, w 13, p 374
Kemp, Lewis - 1m, w 18
Kemp, Lewis - Merchant, es $20,000, s 3f, 1m, w 19, p 204
Kemp, Lewis G. - s 1f, w 14
Kenby, John R. - s 2m, w 14
Kennard, Mrs. - s 2f, 2m, w 19
Kennedy, William W. - Cabinet Maker, es $17,000, s 2f, w 15, p 84
Kernan, Peter - es $35,000, s 2f, w 15, p 72
Kettlewell, John - Merchant, s 1f, w 16, p 188
Kidd, Lydia - s 1f, w 10, p 96
Kimberly, Elizabeth - s 1f, 3m, w 8, p 451
Kimberly, Samuel - s 1f, w 8
King, Captain - s 1f, w 4
King, Caroline - es $12,000, s 2f, 2m, w 3, p 405
King, Henrietta - s 1f, w 16, p 162
King, William - 1m, w 1
Kingham, Elizabeth - 1m, w 4
KInsley, Barney - Glass Blower, es $100, s 1m, w 15, p 35
Kirby, John s - Tanner, es $30,000, s 2f, 1m, w 19, p 226
Kirkland, Alexander - Shipping Merchant, s 1m, w 14, p 456
Knighton, Thomas - Property Agent, s 2f, w 3, p 307
Knowles, William G. - Physician, s 1f, w 15, p 84
Koeppes, D. - s 2f, 1m, w 19
Kraft, M. - s 1f, w 18
Kramer, Samuel - Druggist, es $5,000, s 1f, w 15, p 156
Krebs, Henry W. - Beef And Pork Packer, s 1f, w 7, p 330
Kuster, Sarah W. - es $8,000, s 1f, w 15, p 115
Lafont, Mary - es $1,500, s 3f, w 4, p 31
Lambdin, Ann s - s 1f, w 4
Lambdin, J. M. - Merchant, s 1f, w 10, p 73
Lambdin, Mrs. - 3m, w 10
Lamden, Thomas - s 1f, w 15
Lanahan, William s - Confectioner, s 2f, w 16, p 163
Lane, Mr. - s 1f, w 3
Lane, Thomas A. - Sea Captain, es $3,000, s 2m, w 4, p 81
Laroque, Ed - Dentist, s 1f, w 10, p 64
Laroque, J. M. - Druggist, es $29,000, s 2f, w 10, p 74
Lassiter, William - s 1f, w 8
Latourner, Peter G. - s 1m, w 1
Laughlin, A. B. M. - s 2f, w 14

Chapter 12

Slaveholders of Baltimore, 1840 & 1850

Laurence, Mary - s 1f, w 3
Laurence, Richard - s 1f, w 3
Lavender, Benjamin A. - Lawyer, es $23,000, s 2f, w 13, p 341
Law, Sarah - s 2f, 2m, w 18, p 68
Lawrence, Richard - Ship Carpenter, s 1f, w 1, p 41
Leach, C. L. - s 2f, 4m, w 11
League, Thomas M. - es $30,000, s 1f, w 3, p 368
Leakin, George - s 1f, w 3
Leary, William D. s - s 1f, w 4
Leche, David - s 1f, w 13
Lecompte, Lloyd - Sailor, s 1f, w 15, p 40
Leddin, George - 1m, w 7
Lee, James H. - Shoe Factor, s 1f, w 14, p 410
Lee, Josiah - Banker, es $220,000, s 2f, 1m, w 10, p 107
Lee, Thomas s - Broker, s 2f, w 20, p 284
Leffler, George R. H. - Iron Founder, es $10,000, s 2f, w 16, p 185
Lefler, Daniel - Engineer, s 4f, w 17, p 259
Leitch, Ed - Merchant, s 2f, w 5, p 124
Leitch, John F. - Carpenter, s 1f, w 7, p 297
Lentz, L. H. - Seaman, s 1f, w 12, p 267
Levering, Clinton - s 1f, w 13
Levering, Eugene - Merchant, s 1f, w 15, p 111
Levering, Hannah - es $58,000, s 1f, w 15, p 90
Levering, Thomas W. s - Merchant, s 2f, 1m, w 16, p 160

Lewis, Allen T. - Merchant, s 2f, 1m, w 16, p 160
Lewis, John - 1m, w 7
Lewis, Joseph N. - s 1m, w 13
Lewis, L. - s 2f, w 12
Linsey, M. - 1m, w 18
Litig, Philip - Cashier of Bank, s 3f, 1m, w 3, p 321
Little, C. - es $10,000, s 2f, w 12, p 242
Loaney, William - s 1f, 1m, w 11, p 183
Lochman, George - s 1f, w 3
Logue, James - Merchant, es $15,000, s 1f, w 9, p 13
Long, Edward - s 1f, w 14
Long, H. R. s - Lawyer+Magistrate, es $2,000, s 3f, w 10, p 66
Long, Levi - s 1f, w 15, p 13
Long, Margaret - s 1f, w 5
Long, Matilda - s 1f, w 12
Long, Samuel - Shoemaker, s 2f, w 9, p 32
Love, Horace - s 5f, 1m, w 11
Lucas, Fielding Jr. - Bookseller, es $37,000, s 1m, w 10, p 57
Lucas, James - Printer, es $3,000, s 1f, w 5, p 132
Lucas, Samuel - Brewer, s 1f, w 15, p 53
Luckett, James H. - s 3f, w 11
Ludden, Lemeul - Hardwrae, es $11,250, s 1m, w 13, p 374
Lumsden, William O. - Physician, s 1f, w 15, p 28
Lusby, Charles W. - Clerk, s 1f, w 16, p 160
Lutz, John - 2m, w 9
Lyford, Margaret M. - s 1f, w 13, p 335

Slaveholders of Baltimore, 1840 & 1850

Lynch, Edward - s 1f, w 3
Lyon, M. C. - s 1f, 1m, w 19
Macauly, Mrs. - s 3f, 1m, w 11
Maccubbin, Ruth - s 1f, w 6
Mackall, Elizabeth - 3f, w 9
Mackelroy, John - s 1f, w 1
Mackensin, Thomas G. - s 1m, w 10
Mackewin, Dr. J. P. - 2m, w 10
Macneal, Andrew L. - s 1f, w 7
Mactumer, T. - Grocer, es $1,500, s 1f, w 17, p 266
Maddox, C. - s 1f, w 20
Maddox, Charles T. s - Postmaster, s 4f, 1m, w 10, p 58
Magness, Thomas - Hotel Keeper, es $5,000, s 1f, 3m, w 5, p 122
Magruder, John R. - s 2f, 2m, w 13
Maitland, B. - Merchant, s 4f, w 14, p 475
Malcolm, Janet B. - s 1f, w 10
Manly, John s - Blacksmith, s 2f, w 16, p 176
Manly, Stephen - Watchman, s 1m, w 17, p 232
Manning, Henry S. - Button Dealer, es $900, s 1f, w 15, p 67
Manro, R. - s 4f, 5m, w 20
Mansfield, William - s 1f, w 18
Manus, Dr. F. M. - 1m, w 13
Marden, Jesse - s 1f, w 9
Marellas, E. J. - s 1m, w 13
Maris, George - s 1f, 1m, w 10
Marrey, William R. - s 1f, w 13
Marriot, Richard W. - s 2f, w 13
Marriott, William H. - Lawyer, es $21,425, s 1f, 2m, w 13, p 389

Marshall, Sarah - s 2f, w 9, p 51
Martaige, S. L. - s 1f, 1m, w 2
Martha - s 1f, w 14
Martin, Buck - s 1f, w 7
Martin, George T. - Physician, s 2f, 1m, w 14, p 431
Martin, James - Cabinet Maker, s 1f, w 7, p 269
Martin, Thomas - 1m, w 4
Martin, Thomas M. - s 1f, w 14
Martin, William H. s - Post Office Clerk, s 1f, w 8, p 383
Mason, Anne - s 1f, 1m, w 16
Mason, Richard - 1m, w 3
Matlack, A. C. - s 2f, 1m, w 10
Mattingly, ? - s 1m, w 18
Maulsby, Jane - s 1f, w 6
May, Edward - Merchant, s 1f, w 12, p 254
Maynan, Mary - s 1f, 1m, w 12
Maynard, James - Currier, es $1,000, s 1f, w 8, p 396
Maynard, William - Carpenter, s 1f, w 15, p 52
McAllister, Jane - s 1f, w 10, p 57
McCall, Elizabeth - s 1f, w 14
McCambridge, Daniel - Tavern Keeper, s 1m, w 5, p 91
McCann, Anna - s 1f, w 4, p 23
McCann, William - s 6f, 1m, w 9
McCauley, James - s 1f, w 4
McClellan, Mary - es $4,500, s 1f, w 3, p 417
McClelland, Mr. - s 1f, 1m, w 11
McClenman, John McClusky - 20, s 2f
McComas, Isabella - s 1f, w 18, p 89
McConnell, John C. - Grocer, es $500, s 1f, 1m, w 15, p 58
McCormick, Ann - s 1f, w 18

Chapter 12

Slaveholders of Baltimore, 1840 & 1850

McCormick, Mrs. - s 1f, w 11
McCubbin, Nicholas - Tailor, s 1f, w 7, p 298
McDonald, John F. - es $30,000, s 1f, w 13, p 369
McDonnell, Samuel - s 5f, 4m, w 4
McDowell, R. - Carpet Dealer, es $5,000, s 1f, w 10, p 94
McDowell, T. - Bootmaker, es $1,000, s 1f, w 5, p 97
McElderry, Henry s - s 2m, w 6
McElderry, Hugh - Lumber Merchant, es $20,000, s 1f, 1m, w 10, p 58
McGeach, Mary - s 1f, w 4
McGinn, James R. - Clerk, s 1m, w 11, p 199
McGreevy, Hanah - es $3,000, s 1m, w 8, p 444
McHenry, Mrs. - s 1f, 1m, w 11
McIntosh, Caroline - s 1f, w 14
McKene, P. - s 1f, w 5
McKim, John s - es $182,000, s 2f, 3m, w 11, p 211
McLean, Arthur - Painter, s 1f, w 3, p 296
McMullen, John - s 1f, w 11, p 137
McMullen, John s - Cabinet Maker, s 1f, w 10, p 84
McNeal, James - Agent, s 1f, w 2, p 192
McNeal, Mrs. - s 1f, w 18
McNeil, James - Clerk, es $5,000, s 1m, w 3, p 357
McPhail, Mary - es $1,500, s 1f, w 10, p 66
McPherson, Samuel s - s 1m, w 1
McPherson, William - Physician, s 2f, 2m, w 12, p 324
McPherson, William - Inn Keeper, s 2f, 1m, w 18, p 136
McTavish, M. - s 1f, w 11
McTavish, Mary - s 1f, w 18
McTavish, Mrs. - s 1f, w 4
McTavish, William - 1m, w 4
McWhinney, Hester - s 1f, w 13, p 384
Meads, William - Gardener, es $10,000, s 2f, w 7, p 349
Medaman, John - s 1f, w 19
Medcalfe, William M. - Banker, s 2f, 1m, w 14, p 474
Meginness, Samuel - s 2f, 1m, w 15
Meixsell, John - Tobacconist, s 1f, w 12, p 259
Meltcher, Charles - Gardener, es $3,600, s 1f, w 7, p 439
Mercer, Ann - s 1f, w 4, p 54
Meredith, Jane - s 1f, w 3
Merrill, James H. - Gunsmith, s 1f, w 12, p 240
Merritt, William K. - Clerk, es $1,000, s 2f, w 10, p 108
Merryman, George s - s 2f, w 10
Miles, Samuel G. s - Grocer, s 1f, w 15, p 119
Millar, Daniel - s 1f, w 14
Millar, John - s 1f, w 14
Miller, Alexander - s 1f, 2m, w 13, p 368
Miller, Catherine - s 2f, w 4
Miller, Decatur H. s - Tobacco Merchant, s 1m, w 13, p 383
Miller, Dr. James H. - Physician, es $7,000, s 1m, w 13, p 339
Miller, Jacob - s 3f, 2m, w 18
Miller, Martha A. - s 1f, 1m, w 12
Miller, Mr. - s 1f, w 4
Miller, Sarah - s 1f, w 14, p 475

Slaveholders of Baltimore, 1840 & 1850

Millholland, R. D. - s 1f, w 1
Millikin, James - 1m, w 4
Mills, John G. - s 1f, w 15
Mills, Levin - Iron Furnace, s 2f, 1m, w 16, p 179
Mills, William P. - Tailor, s 1f, w 9, p 51
Miner, Mrs. - s 1f, w 6
Mister, Abraham - Merchant, es $4,500, s 2f, w 15, p 80
Mitchel, Jane - s 1f, w 7
Mitchell, Edward - Merchant, es $5,000, s 2m, w 4, p 34
Mitchell, James - s 1f, w 2
Mitchell, John s - Confectioner, s 1f, w 10, p 96
Moale, Randle - s 1f, w 11
Moffit, Robert - 2m, w 14
Monkur, John C. - s 1f, w 3
Monmonier, John s - s 1f, 1m, w 3
Moody, John B. - Tobacconist, s 1f, w 9, p 54
Moon, Michael - s 2m, w 3, p 423
Moore, Ed H. - s 1f, 1m, w 18
Moore, Elisabeth - s 1m, w 15, p 106
Moore, Nancy - 1m, w 14
Moore, William - s 3f, w 12
Moore, William H. - s 1f, w 1
Moran, Elisabeth - s 1f, w 15, p 75
Moran, J. J. - Physician, es $66,000, s 1f, 4m, w 3, p 356
Morehouse, Alanson - s 4f, 3m, w 3, p 422
Morgan, George W. - s 1f, 8m, w 9
Morgan, Ludwig - Carpenter, s 1f, 1m, w 6, p 205
Morris, Charles P. - Ship Carpenter, s 1f, w 3, p 372
Morris, Henry - Physician, s 1f, w 3, p 400
Morris, John B. s - Bank Officer, s 3f, 3m, w 11, p 144
Morris, Thomas C. - Ship Carpenter, s 1f, w 3, p 380
Morris, Thomas H. - s 1m, w 11
Morrison, E. - Grocer, s 1f, 1m, w 18, p 57
Mortimer, Henry H. - Clerk, s 1f, w 15, p 107
Morton, George C. - French Cousine, s 1m, w 12, p 291
Morton, Julia A. - es $7,500, s 1f, w 19, p 139
Mosher, Mrs. C. - s 1f, w 10
Mosley, Walter - s 1f, w 2
Muer, Mrs. - s 1f, w 11
Muir, James N. - Merchant, s 1f, w 15, p 115
Mullen, Philip - s 2f, w 9
Mullikin, Mary - s 1f, w 3
Munroe, John H. - Carpenter, s 1f, w 15, p 79
Murdock, Catharine - s 1m, w 13, p 330
Murphy, J. N. - Builder, s 1f, w 4, p 43
Murphy, Thomas - Printer, s 1f, w 5, p 122
Murray, Ann - es $3,000, s 1m, w 6, p 216
Musgrave, James - Tanner + Currier, s 1m, w 5, p 89
Myer, James - Grocer, es $6,000, s 2f, w 15, p 53
Myers, Charles - Butcher, es $7,000, s 1f, w 19, p 209
Myers, F. L. - s 2f, w 2
Myers, William - 1m, w 1

Chapter 12

Slaveholders of Baltimore, 1840 & 1850

Nabb, Ellen - s 1f, w 18
Neale, Francis - Merchant, s 3f, w 14, p 429
Nedall, Bernard - 1m, w 2
Nernetson, William - 1m, w 4
Nicholas, Wilson N. - es $25,000, s 1m, w 11, p 151
Nickerson, Pamelia A. - s 1f, w 13, p 350
Nicols, Jane - s 1f, w 4
Nicolson, Jacob C. - Merchant, es $300,000, s 5f, 3m, w 4, p 20
Ninde, James - Watchmaker, s 1f, w 9, p 35
Nixdorff, Mrs. A. - s 1f, w 18
Noble, James - Laborer, s 1f, w 2, p 242
Norris, John C. - Grocer, s 1f, w 16, p 163
Norris, John H. - Clerk, s 1f, w 16, p 163
Norris, William B. - Merchant, es $6,000, s 1f, 1m, w 15, p 68
Norris, William H. - Lawyer, es $80,500, s 2f, 1m, w 11, p 153
Norwood, Edward - s 1f, w 8
Norwood, Giles - Car Driver, s 1f, w 8, p 399
Nutter, Mary - s 1m, w 16, p 134
O'Brien, Martha - s 2f, w 15
O'Brien, Owen - s 2f, 2m, w 6
O'Brien, Owen - s 1m, w 9
O'Donnell, Dr. D. A. - Physician, s 2f, 3m, w 10, p 75
O'Neal, J. L. - s 1f, w 13
Ochenboe, F. - s 1f, w 19
Odesluys, Charles - Mercht, es $5,000, s 1f, w 3, p 421
Orem, John - Merchant Tailor, s 2f, w 14, p 425
Orndorff, Samuel ▲ - s 1f, w 14

Osborne, Garret - Plow, Maker, s 1f, w 15, p 18
Owen, Captain - s 1f, w 13
Owen, Isaac - s 1f, w 2
Owings, Dr. Thomas - s 2m, w 13
Owings, Samuel C. - Trader, s 4f, w 14, p 397
Oyborin, Ursula - s 1m, w 20, p 302
Paca, Julia - s 2f, w 14
Paine, Sarah - s 1f, w 18
Palmer, Joshua - s 1f, w 14
Pancoast, Joseph - Clerk, s 1m, w 13, p 349
Parker, Joshua H. - s 1f, w 15
Parr, David - China Dealer, es $5,000, s 1m, w 4, p 40
Parran, Caroline - s 1m, w 15, p 96
Parran, Hester - s 1m, w 16, p 130
Parran, John - s 1f, w 14
Parrish, L. - s 1f, w 2
Partridge, H. - s 1f, w 1, p 13
Patterson, Edward ▲ - Iron Merchant, es $125,000, s 4f, 1m, w 9, p 49
Patterson, John - 2f, 1m, w 9
Patterson, John H. - Physician, s 1f, 1m, w 11, p 19
Patterson, Sarah A. ▲ - s 1f, w 11, p 196
Patterson, William - Clerk, s 1f, w 15, p 79
Pattison, Charlotte H. - es $6,000, s 3f, w 15, p 83
Pattison, Ellen - s 2f, 1m, w 13
Pattison, Samuel - Merchant, s 2f, 1m, w 15, p 173
Peacock, Sarah - s 1f, 1m, w 6, p 214

Slaveholders of Baltimore, 1840 & 1850

Pearce, Stephen A. - Grocer, s 1f, 1m, w 4, p 66
Pearson, Andrew - Importer Of Furs, es $15,000, s 1f, w 13, p 379
Pearson, Joseph ▲ - Importer Of Furs, es $20,000, s 1m, w 13, p 380
Pease, Charlotte - s 2f, 2m, w 13, p 384
Peaver, Mrs. - s 1f, w 12
Peckocheck, A. - s 1f, w 5
Pendergest, Charles - s 1f, 1m, w 4
Pendexter, Henry - Merchant, es $4,000, s 2f, w 4, p 14
Pendleton, P. P. - Merchant, es $930, s 1f, 1m, w 11, p 150
Pendleton, Robert W. ▲ es $75,000, s 1f, 2m, w 13, p 388
Pentz, Henry B. - Butcher, s 1m, w 7, p 341
Perine, Thomas J. ▲ - Trader, s 1f, w 16, p 185
Perviance, Robert - s 3f, w 11
Peters, G. (Estate Of) - s 1m, w 11
Peters, Mrs. M. - s 1f, w 10
Peters, Sarah S. - es $50,000, s 1m, w 11, p 121
Peters, W. C. - Music Dealer, es $1,700, s 1f, w 20, p 279
Pherson, J. M. - s 3f, w 20
Philips, Solomon - s 1m, w 3
Pickerell, John F. - s 1f, w 11
Pickersgill, Mary - es $3,000, s 1f, w 4, p 17
Pickett, Mary - s 1f, w 4
Pinckney, Frederick - Sawyer, s 1f, w 13, p 356
Pindle, James ▲ - s 1f, w 3
Pirce, Augustus M. - s 1f, w 13
Pitt, Ann - es $15,000, s 2f, w 4, p 46
Pitt, Thomas J. - Druggist, es $2,000, s 1m, w 4, p 20
Placide, Henry S. - es $15,000, s 2f, 1m, w 4, p 49
Plummer, James H. - Printer, s 1f, w 15, p 51
Plummer, Robert - s 1m, w 14
Poe, Jacob - s 1f, 1m, w 18
Polk, James ▲ - Lawyer, s 1f, 1m, w 10, p 70
Pollett, Mrs. E. - s 3f, w 11
Pollitt, Elizabeth - s 2f, 1m, w 13, p 333
Pollitt, Mrs. - s 1f, w 13
Poole, William E. - Methodist Clergyman, s 1f, w 16, p 151
Porter, Mrs. - s 1f, 1m, w 4
Porter, Robert ▲ - Commission Merchant, s 1f, w 18, p 2
Potter, Elijah - Ship Wright, s 1f, w 7, p 306
Powder, A. - s 3f, w 12
Powell, Charles R. - Merchant, s 1f, w 9, p 24
Powell, Henry - Block Maker, s 1f, 1m, w 6, p 255
Pratt, Henry - Block Maker, s 1f, 1m, w 6, p 255
Pratt, Mrs. - s 1f, w 12
Pratt, Mrs. S. - s 1m, w 14
Pratt, Thomas - s 1m, w 3
Preston, William - Grocer, s 1f, w 14, p 455
Price, A. ▲ - s 1f, w 1
Price, John O. - s 1f, w 18
Price, William ▲ - s 1f, 2m, w 8
Prichard, Mrs. - s 1f, w 11
Pritchard, Elizabeth - s 1m, w 4

Chapter 12

Slaveholders of Baltimore, 1840 & 1850

Pugh, Eliza - s 1m, w 6
Pugh, James - Carpenter, s 1f, w 1, p 44
Purdue, Labari - s 1f, 1m, w 5
Purvis, James F. - Exchange Broker, es $40,000, s 2f, 1m, w 8, p 453
Pyle, Mary - s 1m, w 6
Quenels, Francis - s 1f, w 2
Quinlan, L. G. - 2f, 3m, w 12
Raborg, Christopher - s 2f, 1m, w 16
Raborg, Henrietta ▲ - s 1f, 1m, w 16
Ramsey, E. - s 2f, w 10
Ramsey, Mrs. - s 1f, w 4
Rattzell, Philip - s 3f, w 13
Rawlings, Ann E. - s 1f, w 15
Rawlings, Mary Ann - s 1f, 3m, w 13, p 362
Ray, Ann - s 1f, w 18
Raymo, Modest - s 1f, w 10
Raymond, Samuel W. - Merchant, s 1f, w 15, p 90
Reach, Stephen B. - s 1f, w 4
Reade, D. - s 1m, w 11
Ream, Joseph H. - Carpenter, es $165,000, s 2f, w 13, p 373
Rease, John L. - s 1f, w 15, p 8
Rease, Mr. - s 1m, w 11
Reasin, Robert W. - s 2f, w 8, p 432
Reckitt, Ann M. - s 1m, w 16, p 131
Redgrave, John B. - Lumber Inspector, s 1f, w 16, p 162
Redgrave, Samuel H. ▲ - Collector, es $8,000, s 1f, 2m, w 16, p 126
Reese, William - s 2f, w 15
Reiman, Alex - Merchant, s 1f, w 18, p 1
Rennick, William - s 1m, w 14
Rich, Arthur - Physician, es $18,000, s 1f, 1m, w 15, p 58
Richardson, B. C. ▲ - Clerk, es $2,000, s 2f, 1m, w 12, p236
Richardson, Edward J. - Agent Insurance Co., p 381
Richardson, Oliver - Waiter, s 1m, w 15, p 108
Richardson, Patience - s 1m, w 16, p 175
Richenberger, Joseph - Boot + Shoemaker, s 1m, w 15, p 6
Rider, Washington - Brickmaker, s 1f, w 15, p 104
Ridgely, David - s 1m, w 6
Ridgely, Lot - Merchant, s 1f, w 9, p 24
Ridgely, William H. - Merchant, s 1f, w 15, p 99
Rigney, J. F. - Clerk, es $3,000, s 1m, w 13, p 361
Ringgold, Mary - s 1f, w 15
Ringnose, John W. ▲ - s 3f, 1m, w 14
Ringold, Francis - s 1f, w 4
Ringold, Thomas - Laborer, s 1m, w 15, p 116
Rist, Sarah J. - s 1f, w 6
Rizzo, Samuel - s 3m, w 19
Roberts, Terry T. - s 2f, w 13
Robins, Henry R. - s 2f, w 16
Robinson, Mr. - s 2f, w 4
Robinson, William - s 1f, w 8
Roby, Townley B. - Tavern Keeper, s 1f, w 8, p 399
Roche, J. A. - s 1f, w 13
Rodenger, John - s 2f, w 14
Rodman, William - Manufactures pickles, es $12,000, s 3f, 1m,

Slaveholders of Baltimore, 1840 & 1850

w 13, p 362
Rogers, Charles - Framer, es $18,000, s 4f, 1m, w 7, p 348
Rogers, Francis - s 1f, w 4
Rogers, William - Hater, es $10,000, s 1f, w 9, p 44
Roney, John - Merchant, s 1m, w 6, p 192
Rose, George - Butcher, s 1m, w 17, p 281
Rose, Peter ▲ - Boatmaker, s 2f, w 5, p 92
Rose, Robert - s 1f, w 11
Rose, Robert - s 2m, w 13
Rose, Teresa - es $2,000, s 1f, w 17, p 281
Rose, William H. ▲ - Publican, s 2f, 3m, w 10, p 74
Ross, Benjamin B. - Merchant, es $40,000, s 6f, 1m, w 9, p 39
Ross, C. H. - s 2f, w 2
Ross, Sarah - es $10,000, s 1f, w 5, p 128
Rowles, Ann - s 1f, w 14
Rowles, Robert - s 1m, w 4
Royston, Joshua - Merchant, es $40,000, s 1f, w 15, p 115
Royston, Joshua T. - s 1f, w 18
Ruckle, Thomas C. - Portrait Painter, es $2,500, s 1f, w 13, p 337
Ruddach, Rebecca - es $6,500, s 1f, w 15, p 119
Rusk, Robert - s 2f, 2m, w 8
Rusk, Thomas J. - s 1f, 1m, w 1
Ruskell, Mrs. - s 1f, w 12
Russell, Ann - s 1m, w 15, p 48
Russell, G. - s 1f, 1m, w 12
Ruthall, Robert - s 1f, w 1
Rutler, Samuel S. - Tailor, s 1m, w 12, p 262

Ryan, J. - s 3f, 1m, w 11
Ryan, William H. - Merchant, s 1m, w 14, p 431
Sadler, Captain B. - s 1m, w 13
Sadtler, Henry - Sea Captain, s 2f, 1m, w 8, p 391
Sanders, Beverly C. - Merchant, s 1f, 1m, w 10, p 104
Sanders, Edward E. - Merchant, es $20,000, s 2f, w 4, p 43
Sanderson, H. S. - City Collecting, s 1f, w 5, p 130
Sanner, James - s 1f, w 2
Sarryston, W. R. - s 1f, w 12
Sauerwein, P. - s 1f, w 12
Savage, John - Mariner, s 1f, w 1, p 62
Schaeffer, George - s 1m, w 6
Schaeffer, John - Enginer, s 1f, w 15, p 5
Schanington, E. - s 1f, w 1
Schults, Louise - s 1m, w 15
Schunk, Ellen - s 1f, w 8
Schwartze, Edward - Physician, es $15,000, s 1m, w 15, p 75
Scott, F. - s 1m, w 20
Scott, Samuel - s 1f, w 1
Scott, Samuel - s 1f, w 11
Scott, T. Parkin - Lawyer, s 1f, w 10, p 60
Scribner, Sam - s 1f, w 18
Seth, William G. - s 1f, w 16
Seuter, Stephen - s 1f, w 15
Severd, J. W. - Pilot, es $1,800, s 2f, 1m, w 1
Seward, James - s 1f, w 1
Sewell, T. - s 6f, 4m, w 20
Sexton, John - Pile Driver, s 1f, w 1, p 63
Shamburg, William W. - Restaurant, es $10,000, s 3m, w 13, p

Chapter 12

Slaveholders of Baltimore, 1840 & 1850

373
Shane, Mathew - s 1m, w 5
Shanely, James - Teacher, s 1f, w 15, p 112
Share, Richard - s 1m, w 10
Shaw, Elias - s 1m, w 14
Shaw, William - s 4f, 1m, w 3
Shedden, Edward - s 1f, w 16
Sheil, Rachel - s 1m, w 4
Shephead, George - s 1f, w 13, p 337
Sherwood, B. - Tavern Keeper, s 1m, w 5, p 107
Sherwood, Richard P. ▲ - Publican, s 1f, 4m, w 10, p 90
Shipley, Daniel - Merchant - Tailor, s 2f, w 18, p 14
Shoats, Mary - s 1f, w 3
Shreck, Lucretia - Comb Store, s 2f, w 4, p 40
Shriver, J. S. - Agent - Steamboat, es $10,000, s 2f, 2m, w 12, p 233
Shuntz, W. D. - s 1f, w 20
Shutt, August P. - Chauncer, s 2f, 1m, w 10, p 85
Sides, Samuel - Tavern Keeper, s 2f, 1m, w 10, p 74
Simmonds, Samuel - s 1m, w 11
Simmons, J. - s 1m, w 12
Simmons, John - s 1m, w 17
Simms, Joseph - Stove Dealer, s 1f, w 15, p 110
Simpson, William - Engine Builder, s 2f, 1m, w 10, p 111
Singleton, William B. - Cotton Broker, es $1,000, s 1f, w 10, p 81
Sissel, Rebecca - s 1f, w 6
Sitter, Morris - s 1f, w 13
Skinner, A. P. - Clerk, s 1m, w 12, p 259
Skinner, Elizabeth - s 2f, w 14
Skinner, J. J. - Ship Builder, s 2f, w 15, p 94
Skinner, James A. ▲ - Ship Builder,s 2f, w 15, p 62
Skinner, Mrs. A. - s 1f, 1m, w 11
Skinner, William - Ship Carpenter, s 1f, w 15, p 43
Slater, George - Commission Merchant, s 1f, w 18, p 13
Slater, James ▲ - Salter, es $6,000, s 2m, w 3, p 381
Slater, Mary - s 1m, w 6, p 217
Slaughter, James M. - Commission Merchant, s 1f, w 18, p 45
Slayle, J. - Clerk, s 1f, w 12, p 243
Slingluff, Alston - s 1f, w 14
Slingluff, Charles D. - Merchant, s 2f, w 14, p 425
Sloan, Harriet - es $5,000, s 2f, w 15, p 66
Smith, Alexander - Merchant, s 3f, 1m, w 14, p 447
Smith, Charles - s 1f, w 1
Smith, Fanny - s 1f, w 3
Smith, George M. ▲ - s 1f, w 15
Smith, Jacob ▲ - s 1f, w 12
Smith, John A. - s 2f, w 3
Smith, Joseph - s 1m, w 20
Smith, Mrs. M. - s 1f, w 10
Smith, Nathan R. - Lawyer, es $23,000, s 1f, w 11, p 145
Smith, Peter - s 1f, w 4
Smith, Philip - Carpenter, s 1m, w 3, p 423
Smith, S. R. - s 1f, w 18
Smith, Samuel - s 1f, w 13
Smuthers, Rachael A. - s 1m, w

138

Slaveholders of Baltimore, 1840 & 1850

Snow, Frances - Sea Captain, s 1f, w 4, p 2

Snowden, Eliza - s 1f, w 13, p 383

Snyder, Eliza - es $1, s 1f, w 13, p 344

Solomon, Isaac - Soap+Candle Manufacturer, s 1f, w 6, p 261

Somerville, Mr. - s 1m, w 11

Spencer, Charlotte - es $6,000, s 1f, 2m, w 10, p 63

Spencer, Perrigrine - Ship Carpenter, s 1f, w 18, p 59

Spencer, S. C. - s 1f, w 18

Spencer, William - s 1f, w 13

Spenco, William W. - s 1m, w 10

Sperry, Peter - Merchant, s 1f, w 16, p 164

Spicer, Thomas Sr. - Clerk-District Court, es $9,000, s 1f, w 12, p 268

Spurrier, G. D. - s 1f, w 12

St. Clair, Ellen - s 1f, w 13

Stansbury, J. E. ▲ - Hack Agent, es $10,000, s 1f, 2m, w 2, p 252

Stansbury, James - Grocer, s 1m, w 2, p 189

Stansbury, John - s 1m, w 3

Stansbury, John - s 1f, w 4

Stansbury, N. - s 1f, w 5

Stansbury, Nathaniel - Collector, es $5,000, s 2f, 1m, w 6, p 219

Stansbury, Sarah - s 2f, w 10, p 104

Stanter, John - s 1f, 1m, w 13

Starr, Joseph - Hotel Keeper, s 2f, 3m, w 5, p 114

Startzman, Abraham - Tanner, es $2,500, s 1f, 2m, w 3, p 292

Stein, James T. - Professor of Language, s 3f, 4m, w 5, p 140

Stephens, John A. - Grocer, s 1f, w 15, p 104

Sterner, D. - s 3f, w 19

Steuart, James - Stone Cutter, s 1f, w 4, p 88

Steuart, Robert T. J. - Marble Cutter, es $11,000, s 3f, 1m, w 4, p 88

Steuart, William - s 1f, w 4

Stevens, Alexander - Builder, es $6,000, s 1f, 3m, w 4, p 26

Stevenson, Elizabeth ▲ - s 1m, w 6

Stevenson, O. P. - s 1f, w 12

Stevenson, Stephen - Boot + Shoemaker, s 1f, w 15, p 47

Stevenson, Uriah - s 1f, w 5

Stevenson, W. - Collector, es $3,000, s 2f, w 12, p 284

Steward, Mr. - s 1f, w 4

Stewart, Charles ▲ - Upholsterer, s 1f, w 7, p 269

Stewart, David - Clerk, s 2f, 1m, w 14, p 468

Stewart, E. - s 1f, w 12

Stewart, Ebeneser - Brickmaker, s 1f, w 16, p 172

Stewart, G. H. - s 1f, w 4

Stewart, Henry H. - s 2f, w 13, p 330

Stewart, John - s 2m, w 10

Stewart, Joseph B. - Huckster, es $1,000, s 1f, w 16, p 175

Stewart, William H. - Merchant, s 1f, w 15, p 67

Stine, Joseph - s 1f, w 14

Stineheart, John - s 1m, w 18

Stiner, Elizabeth - s 1f, w 14, p 429

Chapter 12

Slaveholders of Baltimore, 1840 & 1850

Stockdale, N. - s 2f, w 9
Stoddard, William - Tavern Keeper, s 1f, w 6, p 251
Stokes, Dr. William - Physician, s 1m, w 10, p 105
Stone, Samuel - s 2f, w 4
Stooper, Henry - s 1f, w 17
Storm, Samuel - s 1f, 1m, w 14
Story, Anna ▲ - s 2f, 1m, w 934
Stout, H. - es $13,000, s 2f, w 10, p 59
Street, Thomas - Bricklayer, s 18, w 18, p 9
Street, Thomas ▲ - Hotel Keeper, es $6,000, s 5f, 2m, w 5, p 95
Streeter, S. F. - Teacher, s 2f, w 10, p 97
Strong, Samuel - s 1m, w 14
Stuart, David - s 1m, w 3
Stuart, David - s 1f, 6m, w 4
Stuart, Dr. R. S. - Physician, es $12,000, s 3f, 2m, w 11, p 145
Stuart, George C. - s 1m, w 18
Stuart, George H. - Planter, es $100,000, s 4f, 2m, w 18, p 60
Stuart, Harriet - s 1f, w 3
Stump, Mary J. - s 2f, 1m, w 6
Stump, Mrs. - s 3f, w 20
Sturgeon, Edward G. ▲ - s 1f, w 15, p 100
Sullivan, J. - s 1m, w 18
Sullivan, John P. - Clothier, s 1m, w 15, p 112
Sullivan, Thomas H. - Leather Dealer, es $5,000, s 1f, w 4, p 5
Sultzer, Henry - Grocer, es $1,000, s 1f, w 3, p 359
Sumwalt, Thomas S. - Clerk, s 1f, w 15, p 107
Suter, Henry ▲ - Turner, s 1f, w 6, p 233
Sutherland, William - s 1m, w 2
Sutliff, Ann - s 1f, w 13
Sutton, Lewis Jr. - Merchant, s 2f, w 10, p 65
Swann, Horace D. ▲ - Merchant, s 2f, 2m, w 6, p 182
Swann, Mr. - s 1m, w 4
Swann, Thomas - s 1m, w 3
Swann, Thomas - Merchant, es $35,000, s 5f, 6m, w 11, p 153
Swiler, J. - s 2f, w 10, p 99
Sword, Alexander - Boat Builder, es $1,600, s 1f, w 3, p 406
Sword, William - Pilot, es $3,333, s 1f, w 3, p 385
Talbot, M. - s 1f, w 12
Talbot, P. - s 1m, w 14
Tall, Levin W. - Grocer, s 2f, 2m, w 15, p 52
Taneyhill, S. - Tailor, s 1f, w 10, p 81
Tarlton, Ann - es $1,200, s 1f, 1m, w 16, p 173
Tarlton, Ann - s 1f, w 18
Tarlton, Elisabeth - es $600, s 1f, w 16, p 157
Tarr, Wesley B. - Cabinet Maker, s 1m, w 10, p 85
Tatham, John - Merchant, s 3f, w 14, p 391
Taylor, Colonel Joseph P. - Colonel-U.S. Army, es $3,500, s 1f, w 10, p 70
Taylor, Daniel - s 1f, w 2
Taylor, Henry - s 1f, w 6
Taylor, R. Q. - Hatter, s 2f, w 10, p 102
Taylor, Samuel - s 1m, w 2
Taylor, Samuel - s 1f, w 2
Taylor, William S. ▲ - s 1f, w 16

Slaveholders of Baltimore, 1840 & 1850

Teackle, St. George W. - Lawyer, es $16,000, s 1f, 1m, w 10, p 60
Teal, Elisabeth - s 1f, w 15, p 47
Teller, Rebecca - s 1m, w 3, p 405
Tennant, Thomas - Stock Maker, es $9,586, s 1f, w 10, p 74
Thomas, C. K. - s 1f, w 18
Thomas, Catharine - s 1m, w 16, p 148
Thomas, David - s 1f, w 1
Thomas, Dr. J. Hanson - s 5f, 1m, w 11
Thomas, Elisa - s 1m, w 16
Thomas, Isabella - s 2f, 3m, w 2
Thomas, Jane - s 1m, w 19
Thomas, John A. ▲ - Ship Carpenter, es $1,600, s 1f, w 3, p 425
Thomas, L. R. - s 1f, w 2
Thomas, Mahala - s 1f, 1m, w 3
Thomas, Sterling - Butcher, es $5,000, s 1m, w 8, p 455
Thomas, William - s 1f, w 4
Thompson, Ann - s 2f, w 3
Thompson, Dr. - s 1f, w 4
Thompson, Henry A. - Merchant, es $5,200, s 1f, w 4, p 85
Thompson, John - s 1f, w 12
Thompson, John T. - Tailor, es $4,000, s 1m, w 9, p 26
Thompson, Mrs. - s 1f, w 11
Thompson, Nicholas - s 1f, w 16, p 177
Thrush, Nicholas - Sexton, s 1m, w 16, p 141
Thumbert, William H. - Clerk, s 1f, w 15, p 47
Thurston, P. - Proprietor - Hotel, s 3f, 3m, w 9, p 47
Tiernan, Gay R. - s 3f, 1m, w 11
Tilghman, Saint - s 1f, w 11
Todd, Mary - s 1m, w 6
Tomlinson, Frederick - Mate, s 1f, w 3, p 311
Toole, John - Clerk, s 1f, w 20, p 245
Torrance, Mary - es $10,000, s 1f, w 10, p 109
Townsend, Drusilla - s 1f, w 3
Townsend, Fidelia - s 1f, w 16, p 171
Townsend, Samuel ▲ - Clerk, s 2f, w 14, p 452
Toy, Mrs. E. A. - s 1f, w 10
Travers, D. D. - Mariner, s 1f, 1m, w 1, p 69
Travers, Deveraux - s 1f, w 3
Travers, Jeremiah T. - Grocer, s 1f, 1m, w 15, p 54
Travers, John - s 4f, w 15
Tripham, Littleton - s 1f, w 10
Trippe, May W. - es $25,000, s 1f, w 15, p 3
Trotton, Thomas ▲ - Store Keeper, es $5,000, s 2f, 1m, w 3, p 359
Trowbridge, L. - Carpenter, s 2f, w 12, p 299
Trust, Jacob - Fancy Goods, s 1m, w 13, p 337
Tuck, William - s 4f, 1m, w 20
Tucker, Captain - s 1m, w 6
Tucker, Gassaway ▲ - s 1f, w 3
Tucker, Joseph - Clothier, s 1f, w 10, p 67
Tull, J. J. - s 1f, w 18
Tulley, Elizabeth - s 1m, w 1
Tumblinson, William - Boat Builder, es $3,500, s 1f, w 15, p 75
Turerball, Evelina - s 4f, w 13

Chapter 12

Slaveholders of Baltimore, 1840 & 1850

Turner, Harry F. - Butcher, s 1f, w 7, p 341
Turner, J. M. - s 2f, 3m, w 1
Turner, Robert - s 1f, w 7
Turner, S. - s 1f, w 5
Turner, T. K. - Printer, es $600, s 1f, w 5, p 107
Turner, Thomas W. - Clerk, s 3f, 1m, w 16, p 171
Tweedy, Samuel A. - Carpenter, s 1f, w 16, p 174
Tyson, Harriet - s 1f, 1m, w 14
Tyttle, Jeremiah - s 2m, w 17
Underwood, Ann - s 2f, 2m, w 10, p 68
Unkle, Frederick - Machinist, s 1f, w 15, p 100
Uthoff, Ellen - s 1m, w 3
VanBibber, Lucreatta - s 1m, w 11
Vandeford, John - s 1m, w 3
VanNess, William J. - Grocer, es $440, s 1f, w 9, p 16
VanWick, J. C. - Collector, s 1f, 1m, w 18, p 13
Varden, Robert - Clerk, s 1f, w 6, p 234
Vernum, William K. - Carpenter, s 1f, w 13, p 327
Vickers, Joel - Flour Merchant, es $10,000, s 2f, 3m, w 15, p 67
Wafton, Elijah - s 1f, w 13
Waggerman, Mrs. - s 1f, 1m, w 11
Wagner, James V. - s 1f, w 4
Wales, Philip S. - Grower, s 1f, 1m, w 16, p 150
Walker, Hugh C. - Sea Captain, s 1f, w 3, p 424
Walker, Joshua ▲ - s 1f, w 4, p 56

Walker, Robert - s 1f, w 3
Wall, Joseph - Grocer, s 1f, w 18, p 69
Wallace, Anthony R. - Grocer, s 1f, 2m, w 15, p 80
Waller, C. R. - s 1m, w 12
Walls, C. R. - s 3f, 1m, w 12
Walsh, John - Hod Carrier, s 1f, w 3, p 402
Ward, Thomas M. - Silversmith, s 1f, w 15, p 73
Ward, Uriah - s 1f, w 18
Ward, William J. - Lawyer, s 1m, w 10, p 60
Ward, William ▲ - s 1f, w 10
Warfield, Daniel ▲ - Miller, es $8,000, s 1f, 1m, w 10, p 56
Warfield, H. - Merchant, s 2f, 1m, w 20, p 314
Watchman, John - Engineer, es $12,000, s 1f, 1m, w 15, p 17
Waters, Eleanor - s 2f, 1m, w 15, p 70
Waters, Elizabeth D. - s 1f, w 15, p 80
Waters, Francis - Physician, s 1f, 1m, w 12, p 325
Waters, R. - s 1f, w 12
Waters, R. T. - s 1f, w 2
Waters, Rebecca ▲ - es $2,000, s 1f, 3m, w 3, p 357
Waters, William C. ▲ - Merchant, s 1f, w 15, p 48
Wathington, Thomas - s 1m, w 18
Watkins, Elenor - s 1m, w 14
Watkins, J. W. ▲ - Bricklayer, es $5,000, s 1m, w 12, p 227
Watkins, John T. - Furniture Dealer, s 1f, w 9, p 32
Watkins, Nicholas E. - Wood

142

Slaveholders of Baltimore, 1840 & 1850

Importer, es $1,000, s 1f, w 4, p 46
Watkins, Thomas - s 2f, 1m, w 4
Watkins, Thomas - Dry Goods Merchant, es $9,000, s 3f, 1m, w 13, p 327
Watkins, Thomas - s 1f, 1m, w 14
Watkins, Thomas - s 1f, w 14
Watkins, William W. - Bank Clerk, s 1f, w 16, p 134
Watson, Mary A. - s 1f, w 18
Watts, Hester - s 1f, w 3
Watts, Susanna -, s 1f, 1m, w 6, p 195
Waugh, James B. ▲ - s 1m, w 14
Webb, Abner - es $40,000, s 2f, w 12, p 251
Webb, Charles Jr. - Tallow Handler, es $3,000, s 1f, 1m, w 6, p 219
Webb, George W. - Jeweller, es $10,000, s 1f, w 11, p 142
Webb, Milton - Grocer, s 1m, w 17, p 265
Webster, John L. - Physician, s 2f, 1m, w 11, p 144
Welch, J. B. ▲ - Commission Merchant, s 2f, 1m, w 3, p 292
Welch, Mary - s 1f, w 18
Welch, William - s 1f, w 12
Welling, J. W. - es $12,000, s 1m, w 18, p 13
Wells, Richard - Physician, s 1f, w 12, p 219
Wentz, Elizabeth - s 2f, w 2
Wesr, John T. ▲ - Clerk, s 1f, w 15, p 76
Whelam, Samuel - s 2f, w 18
Whelan, Thomas - es $70,000, s 1f, 1m, w 13, p 389
Whinford, Thomas - s 1f, w 1

White, Charles R. - s 3f, 1m, w 4
White, David - Collector, es $5,000, s 1f, w 19, p 165
White, Joseph - s 1f, w 20, p 280
White, William H. - Ship Joiner, s 1f, w 1, p 13
Whiteker, Thomas ▲ - es $8,000, s 1f, w 8, p 417
Whitely, Arthur - s 1f, w 18
Whitridge, Dr. John ▲ - Physician, es $3,000, s 2f, 2m, w 10, p 69
Whitridge, Horatio - s 1f, 1m, w 13
Wickersham, John ▲ - Lumber Merchant, es $29,000, s 1f, 3m, w 3, p 323
Wickes, John - Blacksmith, es $5,000, s 1f, w 4, p 17
Wier, Robert - Ship Chandler, s 1m, w 3, p 372
Wight, William J. - es $35,000, s 1m, w 15, p 3
Wilcox, T. S. ▲ - Boatmaker, s 1f, w 5, p 91
Wilcox, William L. - s 1f, w 5
Wilhelm, Ann E. - s 1f, w 3
Wilhelm, Wallace - s 1f, 1m, w 9
Wilkerson, James - Publican, s 2m, w 10, p 83
Willey, William - Clerk, s 2f, w 6, p 260
William, E. - s 2f, 1m, w 12
William, John ▲ - s 4f, w 11
Williams, Lydia - s 1m, w 15, p 90
Williams, Mary - s 1f, w 14
Williams, Nathaniel - s 1f, w 10
Williams, Percy - s 3f, 1m, w 14
Williams, Rachel A. - s 1m, w 16, p 121

Chapter 12

Slaveholders of Baltimore, 1840 & 1850

Williams, Sarah - s 1f, w 14
Williams, William - s 1f, w 7
Williamson, Ann - s 1f, w 14
Williamson, Charles A. - Merchant, es $50,000, s 3f, w 10, p 104
Williar, A. - s 2f, w 12
Willis, Henry N. - Merchant, s 1m, w 14, p 477
Wilmer, John W. - Merchant, s 1m, w 15, p 68
Wilmer, William H. - Farmer, s 5f, w 10, p 67
Wilson, Ann - s 1m, w 8, p 454
Wilson, Archibald - Shoemaker, s 1f, w 4, p 17
Wilson, B. H. - Iron Merchant, s 1f, w 11, p 116
Wilson, Henry R. - Merchant, s 1f, w 11, p 152
Wilson, Isabella - s 1m, w 7, p 320
Wilson, James - s 1f, w 4
Wilson, James - s 1f, w 10
Wilson, John - s 1m, w 10
Wilson, Joseph C. - Merchant, s 4f, 2m, w 10, p 109
Wilson, L. - s 1f, w 18
Wilson, Mr. - s 1f, 1m, w 4
Wilson, Mrs. - s 3f, w 18
Wilson, Thomas J. - Clerk, s 1f, w 16, p 179
Wilson, William - s 1f, w 4
Wilson, William - s 3m, w 7
Wimel, G. C. - Crier, City Court, es $6,000, s 1f, w 3, p 307
Winchester, Samuel - Broker, es $10,000, s 2f, w 10, p 106
Windsor, Jesse - s 1f, w 3
Wingate, George - Painter, s 2f, 2m, w 17, p 273

Winn, Christopher - Watchmaker, es $2,500, s 1f, w 13, p 327
Winn, William - s 1m, w 12
Withington, Henry - Merchant, s 1m, w 10, p 106
Witney, Georgeanna - s 1f, w 20
Wollet, Mr. - s 2f, 1m, w 4
Wood, William ▲ - Grocer, es $2,000, s 4f, w 15, p 72
Woodbury, Samuel - s 2f, w 17
Woodside, William - Merchant, es $15,000, s 1m, w 15, p 83
Woodward, Mrs. - s 1f, w 12
Woodward, Nick R. - Stable Keeper, es $10,000, s 1f, w 10, p 75
Woodward, S. - s 2f, w 18
Woodyear, Mrs. - s 2f, 1m, w 17
Worley, Joseph D. - Sadler, s 1f, w 15, p 79
Worthington, Abraham ▲ - Farmer, es $35,000, s 3f, 7m, w 7, p 348
Worthington, Thomas J. - s 3f, 3m, w 13
Worthington, William - s 1m, w 6
Wright, Dr. T. H. - Physician, es $15,000, s 2f, w 13, p 337
Wright, Edward - Preserves provisions, es $7,000, s 1f, w 15, p 57
Wright, W. H. D. C. - s 1f, 2m, w 11
Wright, William - s 1f, 1m, w 8
Wright, William T. - Clergyman, es $1,700, s 1f, 1m, w 8, p 254
Wyman, Samuel - Merchant, es $25,000, s 2f, w 11, p 187
Yeakly, Elizabeth - s 1m, w 18
Young, Alexander - Clerk, s 1f, 1m, w 14, p 430

Slaveholders of Baltimore, 1840 & 1850

Young, James - s 1f, w 3
Young, Joshua A. - Ship Joiner, s 1f, w 3, p 360
Zell, E. F. - Chair Maker, s 1f, w 12, p 319
Zell, Peter - s 1f, w 12

No. 1339 Levi Cohen   38 yrs 5¾

Nancy Cohen   30 y 13

Mary C Lewis   6 y 13

Mary Catherine Chase

On this 3d day of July A.D. 1863 before me George E daug-
low Clerk of the Superior Court of Baltimore City
personally appeared William A. Mason and made
oath on the Holy Evangely of Almighty God that
negro Mary Catherine Chase aged about 19 years about
8½ inches in height of a dark complexion has no visible
scars and is the same person that was manumitted by
Levi Chase by Deed dated February 7th 1849 and recorded
in Liber A.W.B. No. 77 folio 180 &c and was raised in Balti=
more City. Given under my hand and seal this 3d day
of July, 1863.
                                    Geo E Langston Clk

Wm A. Mason
  Witness

13
Baltimore County Applications for Certificates of Freedom

In 1806 an act of the General Assembly of Maryland required free Blacks to apply for documentation certifying their manumission or birth as a free person of color. Certificates of freedom (freedom papers) were usually acquired at the local county courts. Those applying had to provide a white witness willing to testify to the veracity of their statement. At the time of application a full description of the individual seeking the certificate was recorded by the clerk of the court. In the event that an applicant filed for a second certificate, on the grounds that he or she had lost the first, the filed description and return of the white witness assured the court that the second document was not likely to be used to aid in the escape of a slave.

Although thousands of Blacks were recorded in the files of Baltimore County between 1840 and 1864, only 468 offered the first and last names of former slaves. Twenty eight (denoted by a ♦) of the 468 names (6%) have the same surname as their former owner. Although this does not necessarily indicate kinship, it is possible to prove a relationship existed between slave and slaveholder in some instances. Through this record we occassionally uncover instances when free Blacks owned their own family members (for other examples of free Black ownership of slaves see the chapter on the slaveholder in the first essay of this book).

One excellent case in the applications for certificates of freedom is revealed in the record of Mary Catharine Chase. Her application, recorded in 1863, notes her manumission by Levi Chase in February of 1849. This places her date of birth as sometime in early 1844. A search of the Maryland census records of 1850, seventeen months after her manumission reveals that she is living with Levi and Nancy Chase. Both census and application for freedom records are shown here.

The following is an index of applications for certificates of freedom collected in Baltimore County between 1840-1864.

The index is organized as follows:

Surname and first name of ex-slave (applicant), age of slave at the time of application, manumitter's name, date when the slave was manumitted (dom), and date of application (doa).

Adams, Samuel, 30 - Micha Lloyd, dom 1/42, doa 12/42
Allen, Jerry, 35 - George W. Lamb, dom 6/42, doa 6/42
Amos, Harriet, 40 - Mary Fell, dom 3/57, doa 3/57

Chapter 13

Anderson, Lloyd, 25 - Benjamin F. Bennett, dom 6/53, doa 8/53
Anthony, James, 35 - Joshua Harvey, dom 4/42, doa 4/42
Anthony, Maria, 38 - John Buck Jr., dom 2/56, doa 2/56
Arthur, Richard, 30 - Emily McTavish, dom 1/52, doa 3/52
Augustus, Harriet, 38 - Marcellena McCann, dom 5/41, doa 5/41
Augustus, William Henry, 35 - Leonard G. Quinlan, dom 3/53, doa 4/53
Bailey, Mary - John N. Denning, dom 1/41, doa 12/57
Baker, Catherine, 5 - Samuel J. Jones, dom 5/52, doa 6/52
Baker, Eliza, 28 - Louisa Billups, dom 6/59, doa 6/59
Baker, John, 2 - Samuel J. Jones, dom 5/52, doa 6/52
Baker, John Henry - Edward B. Hardcastle, dom 9/52, doa 9/52
Baker, Matilda, 27 - Samuel J. Jones, dom 5/52, doa 6/52
Banton, Comfort, 38 - William P. Iddings, dom 4/45, doa 4/45
Bantum, Anne Maria, 30 - Washington River, dom 10/45, doa 10/45
Barton, George, 31 - Robert Gorsuch, dom 12/58, doa 12/58
Beirney, Francis, 27 - Carolina P. Wilson, dom 7/52, doa 1/53
Bell, Ellen, 29 - Francis A. Walter, dom 8/53, doa 8/53
Bennett, Abraham, 34 - Ann Hall, dom 6/49, doa 6/49
Bennett, Harry, 29 - Francis A. Walter, dom 7/42, doa 4/47
Berry, Matilda, 42 - Daniel Brisler, dom 6/44, doa 6/44
Bias, Charles, 24 - Galloway Cheston, dom 3/44, doa 12/44
Biays, Robert, 29 - John S. Skinner, dom 10/41, doa 10/41
Bishop, Jacob, 30 - Samuel W. Jacob, dom 1/43, doa 8/43
Blacke, Charlotte, 38 - Mary J. Ault, dom 2/57, doa 6/60
Blackstone, Teresa, 40 - Mary F. Wright, dom 9/56, doa 9/56
Blake, Henry, 30 - Susan Martin, dom 7/40, doa 7/46
Bolton, Thomas, 26 - Henry May, dom 4/52, doa 4/52
Boone, Delia, 45 - Sarah E. Chambers, dom 3/56, doa 1/57
Booth, Jim, 39 - Jacob Graff, dom 11/46, doa 11/46
Bordley, Margaret, 27 - Henry Brice, dom 4/40, doa 4/40
Bordley, Margaret, 27 - Henry Brice, dom 4/40, doa 4/40
Bower, Emily, 24 - Wiliam Hawkins, dom 10/58, doa 10/58
Bowser, Leah, 32 - John B. Pinney, dom 4/54, doa 4/54
Bowser, Milley, 1 - John B. Pinney, dom 5/54, doa 5/54
Bowyer, Ann, 18 - Nathan C. Brooks, dom 6/45, doa 6/45
Briscow, Thomas, 35 - Ursula McKeever, dom 7/50, doa 7/50
Brogden, Amos - William Woodward, dom 6/56, doa 6/56
Brook, James, 40 - James Heighe, dom 12/56, doa 12/56
Brooks, John, 34 - Jefferson Hough, dom 2/42, doa 2/42
Brooks, Perry, 29 - Aaron Fenton, dom 4/49, doa 6/49
Brooks, Sydney, 39 - dom 4/50, doa 4/50
Broom, Jesse - Samuel Chew, dom 4/53, doa 6/53
Brown, Charles Hale, 22 - John Ridgely, dom 8/46, doa 8/46

Baltimore County Applications for Certificates of Freedom

Brown, George W., 24 - J. V. Waters, dom 8/57, doa 8/57
Brown, Isaac, 30 - Francis J. Dallam, dom 2/43, doa 3/43
Brown, James, 31 - James Howard, dom 4/42, doa 12/42
Brown, Leah, 43 - W. H. Allen, dom 3/58, doa 3/58
Brown, Richard, 32 - Thomas ?, dom 3/40, doa 3/40
Brown, Sara A. - dom 2/57
Brown, Simon, 36 - James L. Donaldson, dom 3/52, doa 3/52
Brown, Susan, 24 - dom 6/57, doa 6/57
Brown, William, 24 - Dr. Amos Corbin, dom 3/55, doa 4/55
Bruce, Cecelia, 18 - dom 12/53, doa 2/54
Bryan, Elizabeth, 39 - Rebecca Gosnell, dom 10/46, doa 10/46
Buck, John, 37 - Clara S. March, dom 1/51, doa 5/61
Burgess, Eliza, 27 - Racheal Galloway, dom 4/51, doa 10/52
Burgess, Henry, 35 - Charlotte C. Harper, dom 11/41, doa 1/57
Butler, Jane, 37 - Sylvester J. Costigan, dom 4/50, doa 4/50
Butler, Maria, 32 - Eliuza B. G. Gordon, dom 3/54, doa 1/57
Campbell, Charity, 37 - dom 9/50, doa 9/50
Campbell, Ned, 39 - Elizabeth G. Scott, dom 10/42, doa 10/42
Campbell, Rachel, 41 - Elizabeth G. Scott, dom 10/42, doa 2/57
Campbell, William, 44 - Henry Carrol, dom 12/44, doa 12/44
Camper, Daniel, 21 - William Fisher, dom 6/59, doa 6/59
Camper, Henry, 27 - James Harrison, dom 6/40, doa 6/40
Cann, Hester, 42 - Nicholas J. Watkins, dom 4/58, doa 5/58
Carroll, Albert, 32 - Richard Albert, dom 10/59, doa 10/59
Carter, Deborah, 30 - Adam Denmead, dom 2/60, doa 2/60
Carter, henry H., 22 - Elijah Bailey, dom 6/55, doa 6/55
Carter, Mary, 29 - Sarah F. Law, dom 4/54, doa 5/60
Ceders, Patsy, 30 - George W. Core, dom 7/44, doa 7/44
Chase, Eliza, 22 - Hugh, Rolsory, dom 10/44, doa 10/44
Chase, Mary Catherine ♦, 19 - Levi Chase, dom 2/49, doa 7/63
Chase, William, 23 - William Reynolds, dom 4/41, doa 4/41
DeShields, George H., 39 - James U. Waters, dom 11/57, doa 11/57
Dixon, Sophia, 36 - Rev. Matthew Hamilton, dom 5/46, doa 5/46
Donaldson, Maria, 28 - Jane Dorsey, dom 5/45, doa 9/45
Dority, Samuel, 28 - Angelo Atkinson, dom 5/40, doa 5/40
Dorsey, Hanson, 48 - dom 4/55, doa 4/55
Dorsey, Louisa, 28 - James Hall, dom 9/45, doa 11/45
Dorsey, Maria ♦, 37 - Joshua Dorsey, dom 5/48, doa 5/48
Dorsey, Sally, 52 - John E. Willis, dom 8/59, doa 8/59
Dowden, Mary, 28 - dom 10/50, doa 10/50
Drummer, Charlotte, 27 - Joshua Dorsey, dom 10/51, doa 8/52
Duffin, Joseph, 41 - Aaron Clary, dom 4/48, doa 4/49
Dutton, Harriet, 33 - Elias Shaw, dom 10/43, doa 10/43

Chapter 13

Dyer, Nathan, 32 - H. Holt, dom 5/48, doa 5/48
Elsey, Wilmer J. - Joseph E. Muse, dom 12/57, doa 12/57
Elsey, Wilmer S. - Joseph E. Muse, dom 12/57, doa 12/57
Emory, Moses, 36 - Luther Fox, dom 1/54, doa 1/54
Ennis, Grace, 33 - Richard J. Dorsey, dom 1/55, doa 1/55
Fabbor, Jacob, 36 - Eliza Hohne, dom 5/42, doa 5/42
Fisher, William, 35 - James Hutchins, dom 7/46, doa 7/46
Fontaine, Ann ♦, 23 - Edward, Fontaine, dom 11/43, doa 11/43
Fontaine, Fender ♦, 21 - Edward Fontaine, dom 11/43, doa 11/43
Fontaine, Henrietta, 20 - Edward Fontaine, dom 11/43, doa 11/43
Ford, Louisa E., 27 - James W. Collins, dom 11/59, doa 2/60
Fountain, Samuel, 34 - Susan Wright, dom 12/58, doa 4/59
Franklin, John, 44 - Sarah B. Hall, dom 3/55, doa 3/55
Gaither, Elizabeth Ann, 14 - Ferdinand O. Chatan, dom 7/42, doa 7/42
Gaither, Violet, 44 - Ferdinand O. Chatan, dom 7/42, doa 7/42
Galloway, Sally, 35 - William F. Murdoch, dom 4/45, doa 6/45
Garner, Mary, 44 - Robert Hooper, dom 7/50, doa 10/56
Garner, Mary J., 16 - Robert Hooper, dom 7/50, doa 7/50
Garrett, Emily N., 38 - Gerard E. Morgan, dom 5/60, doa 11/60
Garrett, Thomas, 36 - Hy Brice, dom 9/40, doa 9/40
Gauntz, Phebe, 40 - Louisa S. Beatty, dom 4/60, doa 4/61
Gibson, Delia, 39 - David T. Mckim, dom 2/42, doa 2/42
Gibson, Eliza ♦, 32 - Gabriel Gibson, dom 11/41, doa 11/41
Gibson, Henry, 41 - David T. McKim, dom 2/42, doa 2/42
Gittings, Isaiah, 24 - Margaret Leakin, dom 3/53, doa 3/53
Gittings, Marshall F., 28 - Conduce Gatch, dom 11/54, doa 11/54
Golden, John, 28 - Jarvis Seward, dom 12/40, doa 12/41
Golding, Edward, 28 - Gidin B. Smith, dom 6/42, doa 9/42
Gooseberry, Julia, 28 - Rachel Sindall, dom 6/44, doa 6/44
Govans, Fanny, 39 - Mary M. Howard, dom 7/42, doa 7/42
Graves, Maria, 23 - Virginia Tenant, dom 8/43, doa 8/43
Gray, Amelia Jane, 18 - Rachel Green, dom 10/40, doa 12/40
Gray, James, 25 - Henrietta M. Frazier, dom 1/42, doa 1/42
Gray, Ruth, 43 - Rachel Green, dom 10/40, doa 12/40
Grayson, William, 40 - Henry W. Fitzhugh, dom 7/47, doa 11/47
Green, Ann, 34 - Robert J. Brent, dom 2/55, doa 2/55
Green, Anna, 36 - Robert J. Brent, dom 7/55, doa 9/61
Green, Diannah ♦, 45 - Jacob Green, dom 5/55, doa 5/55
Griffin, Laurinda, 30 - dom 5/41, doa 9/41
Grissam, Elijah, 34 - William Baker, dom 4/43, doa 4/43
Grooms, Othello, 30 - Joseph B. Townsend, doa 11/53
Gustus, Rebecca, 35 - Hezekiah Starr, dom 10/53, doa 10/53
Guy, Julia, 40 - James J. Hooper, dom 3/60, doa 3/60

Baltimore County Applications for Certificates of Freedom

Guy, Samuel, 27 - Shelly Cox, dom 10/48, doa 6/49
Guy, William, 29 - William Regris, dom 6/48, doa 6/49
Hall, Mary, 47 - Thomas Kelso, dom 3/60, doa 7/63
Hall, Nancy, 25 - Samuel T. Thompson, dom 5/40, doa 5/40
Hallan, Cecelia, 17 - Emily L. Harper, dom 5/45, doa 6/53
Hamilton, Rebecca, 7 - Caroline Mackall, dom 4/40, doa 4/40
Hamlett, James, 28 - Mary Brown, doa 10/50
Hammond, Andrew, 37 - George Spreckelson, dom 10/44, doa 10/44
Hammond, Edward, 38 - Patrick Lynch, dom 7/45, doa 1/46
Hammond, Felix, 30 - Edward Patterson, dom 2/60, doa 7/60
Hammond, Peter, 30 - Edward Patterson, dom 2/60, doa 7/60
Handy, Maria, 44 - dom 3/56, doa 3/56
Harris, Charles, 42 - Margaret C. Mills, dom 2/56, doa 2/56
Harris, Harriet C., 44 - Ann Browne, dom 11/58, doa 6/60
Harris, Henry, 35 - Samuel Childs, dom 8/51, doa 8/57
Harris, John, 29 - Mary Boyd, dom 4/55, doa 5/55
Harris, Luoisa, 34 - Patrick Gibson, dom 6/52
Harris, Sarah, 38 - George Poe Jr., dom 3/42, doa 8/48
Harvey, Martha, 19 - Mary Mercer, dom 10/53, doa 2/54
Hays, Laura, 16 - Charles Haysby, dom 9/40, doa 9/40
Heathfred, Delia, 41 - Oliver H. P. Cunningham, dom 8/45, doa 8/45
Henry, Maria, 32 - Peter Ayselott, dom 7/40, doa 7/40
Henson, James, 33 - Charles E. Phelps, dom 1/59, doa 2/60
Henson, Susan, 29 - Charles R. Jones, dom 8/51, doa 7/59
Hicks, Isaac - H. Fitzhugh, dom 4/46, doa 11/56
Hicks, Mary Ann, 26 - David, Herring, dom 9/43, doa 6/53
Hill, Davis, 36 - Emanuel Baltzell, dom 10/40, doa 10/40
Hill, Dick, 32 - Mary Green, dom 1/45, doa 2/45
Hill, James ◆, 56 - Charley Hill, dom 8/55, doa 8/55
Hilliday, Harriet, 37 - William Baker, dom 11/59, doa 12/59
Hilliday, Harriet, 37 - William Baker, dom 11/59, doa 12/59
Himes, George, 37 - Richard Cromwell, dom 2/44, doa 2/44
Hobbs, Mary, 18 - Galloway Cheston, dom 3/44, doa 8/45
Hogan, Sandy, 37 - Thomas Swann, dom 10/56, doa 10/58
Hollan, Dinah, 24 - Emily L. Harper, dom 5/45, doa 6/45
Holley, Harriet ◆, 26 - Augustus Holley, dom 5/56, doa 5/56
Holliday, Maria, 18 - Solomon Hillen, dom 3/56, doa 3/56
Holly, Delia, 35 - Hopewell Hebb, dom 9/41, doa 9/41
Howard, Ann, 25 - dom 5/49, doa 6/49
Howard, Cordelia, 34 - Benjamin Deford, dom 5/60, doa 5/60
Howard, George, 29 - Harry D. G. Carrol, dom 10/54, doa 10/54
Howard, Levy - dom 12/40, doa 12/40
Howard, Mary Ann, 35 - George W. Dobbin, dom 2/40, doa 2/40

Chapter 13

Hughes, Cornelius, 32 - Benjamin F. Bennett, dom 6/53, doa 4/55
Hughes, Singleton, 44 - John McCollum, dom 12/52, doa 12/53
Hull, Priscilla, 38 - Francis Rogers, dom 12/55, doa 12/55
Hynson, Albert, 30 - dom 10/47, doa 8/54
Hynson, Elizabeth, 18 - Hanna A. Brandt, dom 10/47, doa 6/57
Hynson, Phebe, 39 - Hanna A. Brandt, dom 10/47, doa 10/47
Jackson, Andrew, 41 - Gerard Gover, dom 5/60, doa 5/60
Jackson, Elias, 21 - Jane, dom Dorsey, doa 5/49
Jackson, Elizabeth, 18 - Alexander Dalrymple, dom 2/50, doa 6/56
Jackson, Elizabeth, 22 - Mary Jane Stewrad, dom 2/41, doa 2/41
Jackson, Emeline, 18 - Henry Schwartze, dom 10/43, doa 10/43
Jackson, Emeline, 36 - Betty Ann Carr, dom 9/53, doa 4/57
Jackson, Henry, 28 - Rebecca Waters, dom 8/59, doa 12/59
Jackson, Henry, 42 - Sarah F. Law, dom 12/50, doa 5/53
Jackson, Jane, 39 - James Young, dom 3/60, doa 3/60
Jackson, Mary Ellen, 21 - Mary Mercer, doa 10/53
Jackson, Priscilla, 36 - Jane Dorsey, dom 5/49, doa 5/49
Jackson, Thomas, 50 - Thomas Swann, dom 7/44, doa 8/44
James, Isaac, 32 - Patrick Gibson, dom 9/40, doa 9/40
Jason, George, 40 - E. W. Blanchard, dom 4/58, doa 4/58
Jenkins, Jacob, 35 - Mary Boyd, dom 1/46, doa 2/46
Jenkins, Jesse, 35 - Jacob Wolf, dom 12/54, doa 5/55
Johns, Charlotte, 33- doa 2/60
Johnson, Adaline, 21 - Richard Middleton, dom 34/49, doa 3/49
Johnson, David, 26 - Ann Eliza Cox, dom 10/45, doa 10/45
Johnson, Edward, 26 - Catherine Bealmer, dom 6/44, doa 6/44
Johnson, Eliza, 25 - Catharine Harris, dom 11/44, doa 11/44
Johnson, Eliza, 29 - Henry Burnside, dom 7/49, doa 7/49
Johnson, Eliza Jane, 39 - Mary Jane Sloan, dom 1/54, doa 5/60
Johnson, Eliza ♦, 27 - Adam Johnson, dom 11/40, doa 11/40
Johnson, Horace, 36 - Nicholas J. Watkins, dom 7/57, doa 7/57
Johnson, Jane Ellen ♦, 19 - Julia Johnson, dom 5/60, doa 8/60
Johnson, Jerry, 40 - Thomas Oliver, dom 3/40, doa 3/40
Johnson, Lavinia, 23 - Samuel Winchester, dom 10/55, doa 12/55
Johnson, Lucy, 40 - James Hooper, dom 1/42, doa 1/42
Johnson, Margaret, 20 - Ann Eliza Cox, dom 10/45, doa 10/45
Johnson, Mary Ann, 19 - Robert R. Hancock, dom 6/46, doa 7/46
Johnson, Nathan ♦, 29 - Harriet Johnson, dom 5/59, doa 5/59
Johnson, Peggy, 40 - James Mason, dom 7/43, doa 7/43
Johnson, Sophia, 31 - dom 8/44, doa 8/44
Johnson, Susan, 30 - Caroline Jane Bentz, dom 5/47, doa 5/47
Johnson, William, 36 - John Needles, dom 6/44, doa 6/44
Jones, Arthur, 25 - Nancy Lyons, dom 6/45, doa 1/46

Baltimore County Applications for Certificates of Freedom

Jones, Asbury, 32 - Robert Gilmer, dom 7/44, doa 7/44
Jones, Charles, 38 - John Smith, doa 7/52
Jones, Elijah, 23 - Cassandra Brookhart, dom 11/47, doa 2/48
Jones, Elizabeth, 27 - Joseph E. Clemm, dom 10/42, doa 4/44
Jones, Jack, 40 - Mary Fowler, dom 9/40, doa 9/40
Jones, Jones, 28 - Henry G. L. Carroll, dom 4/54, doa 4/54
Jones, Maria, 22 - Sarah F. Law, dom 1/54, doa 11/54
Jones, Phoebe, 38 - Hebb Fitzhugh, doa 9/54
Jones, Rosetta - Elizabeth Hall, dom 9/57, doa 9/57
Jones, Simon, 28 - Henry N. Hunt, dom 6/55, doa 6/55
Kennedy, Sarah, 36 - Patrick Lynch, dom 9/45, doa 9/56
Kenwood, Jane, 35 - Catharine Constable, dom 12/52, doa 1/62
King, Louisa, 25 - Caroline M. Green, dom 12/58, doa 1/59
King, Mickey, 65 - John B. Pinney, dom 5/54, doa 5/54
Lawson, Ellen, 30 - Mary E. Pigmen, dom 5/60, doa 3/62
Lecompt, Adeline, 29 - Thomas Hambleton, dom 2/59, doa 2/59
Lee, Charles, 37 - J. M. Duckett, dom 4/57, doa 4/57
Lee, James L., 25 - Dr. Ashton, doa 10/41
Lee, William, 22 - Asa Hart, dom 8/54, doa 8/54
Lembrey, Thomas, 39 - Andrew Flannigan, dom 7/43, doa 7/43
Lewell, Mary Jane, 29 - Isaac Denmead, dom 8/54, doa 8/54
Lewis, Emma, 36 - Eliza Kahne, dom 11/44, doa 11/44
Lewis, Joshua, 40 - John Anderson, dom 6/49, doa 6/49
Listen, John, 31 - Ann Hall, dom 6/49, doa 6/49
Lockerman, Fanny, 34 - Alexander Packie, dom 5/60, doa 2/63
Long, Sarah ♦, 26 - Elizabeth A. Long, dom 5/45, doa 5/45
Makah, Maria, 22 - Rachel Gross, dom 7/42, doa 7/42
Mallory, Henry, 38 - Thomas Swann, dom 10/46, doa 12/46
Marshall, Chesterfield, 35 - Eleanor P. Keene, dom 6/43, doa 5/46
Marshall, Eleanor, 32 - Elizabeth Philpot, dom 12/46, doa 12/46
Marshall, Hester, 37 - dom 4/50, doa 4/50
Marshall, Mellesley, 36 - Leonard Jarvis, dom 4/44, doa 6/44
Mathews, Daniel, 29 - Hanson Thomas, dom 1/53, doa 1/53
Matthews, Clinton, 18 - Ann R. Howard
Matthews, Samuel, 21 - Galloway Cheston, dom 12/44, doa 12/44
McDowell, Margaret, 52 - Eliza Kohne, dom 11/44, doa 11/44
McKinney, Harriet, 33 - Frederick A. Levering, dom 6/54, doa 6/54
McPherson, Alexander, 33 - James Jenkins, dom 12/42, doa 12/42
Meigs, Sophia, 27 - Catharine Key, doa 9/47
Milburn, Fanny, 33 - Milly Davage, dom 6/41, doa 6/41
Milburn, Harriet ♦ - Susan Milburn, dom 10/41, doa 3/49
Milburn, Shadrack, 38 - William R. Massey, dom 8/41, doa 8/44
Milligan, Hester Ann - Jane Adams, dom 2/53, doa 2/53

Chapter 13

Mitchell, Jacob ♦, 39 - James Mitchell, dom 5/60, doa 5/60
Mitchell, Samuel, 26 - Elizabeth Dare, dom 6/47, doa 6/47
Moore, Comfort ♦, 37 - Jacob M. Moore, dom 1/44
Moore, Peter ♦, 32 - Rebecca Moore, dom 7/40, doa 7/40
Moore, Sarah, 17 - William H. White, dom 9/56, doa 9/56
Morgan, Dolly, 22 - Francis W. Elder, dom 7/59, doa 7/59
Morris, John, 41 - Charles H. Birckhead, doa 5/50
Morris, William, 42 - Josiah Cable, dom 12/54, doa 3/55
Murray, David, 36 - Robert Riddle, dom 6/45, doa 7/45
Murray, Levi, 40 - John S. Tyson, dom 10/42, doa 10/42
Murray, Spencer, 31 - Jefferson Campbell, dom 7/43
Murry, William ♦, 44 - Rachel Murry, dom 1/47, doa 1/47
Myers, David, 43 - David T. McKim, dom 2/42, doa 2/42
Myers, Maria, 25 - Joshua Dryden, dom 1/56, doa 1/56
Myers, Samuel, 33 - Frederick Konig, dom 6/49, doa 6/69
Neal, Nelly, 35 - John B. Morris, dom 4/49, doa 4/49
Neil, Abraham, 31 - Jesse Slinghuff, doa 9/42
Neil, Thomas, 23 - Jesse Slinghuff, dom 9/42, doa 9/42
Neil, William, 27 - Jesse Slinghuff, dom 9/42, doa 9/42
Nicholas, Moses, 36 - Catherine F. Banning, dom 10/54, doa 10/54
Nickols, Ellen, 39 - Providence Gordon, doa 6/58
Nicols, Caroline, 25 - William B. Slack, dom 7/42, doa 7/42
Norris, Moses, 31 - Josias Pennington, dom 4/40, doa 4/40
Norris, Robert, 42 - Mary T. Thomas, dom 1/43, doa 6/43
O'Donnell, Henry T., 28 - John Meir, dom 1/42, doa 1/42
Ockerme, Thomas, 25 - David Stewart, dom 12/41, doa 1/42
Offord, Harriet ♦, 39 - Frederick Offord, dom 3/51, doa 3/52
Osier, Clara ♦, 38 - William Osier, dom 7/42, doa 7/42
Owens, Sophia, 36 - Tobias E. Stansbury, doa 4/45
Parker, Mary, 27 - Henry Leef, dom 1/41, doa 10/41
Parker, Susan, 44 - Benjamin F. Voss, dom 10/52, doa 10/52
Parker, Susannah, 21 - Nicholas Parker, dom 11/53, doa 11/53
Patterson, Rachel, 45 - John Needles, dom 3/58, doa 3/60
Phillips, Rosetta, 38 - John M. Orem, dom 11/59, doa 11/59
Pierce, Butler, 35 - John W. Buck, dom 4/55, doa 4/55
Pierce, Mary, 30 - John W. Buck, dom 4/55, doa 4/55
Pinkney, Henry, 47 - James McConnor, dom 10/52, doa 3/53
Pressgaes, Harriet Ann, 27 - William Hiss, dom 12/47, doa 9/55
Pressgaes, Rebecca - William Hiss, dom 11/47, doa 9/55
Pressgrove, Stephen, 40 - Davis Purvell, dom 7/46, doa 4/47
Preston, Maria, 36 - Joseph S. Donovan, dom 5/63, doa 5/63
Preston, Rose Ann, 36 - William Reese, dom 5/40, doa 2/54
Preston, Thomas, 19 - S. G. Wyman, dom 4/49, doa 4/49

Primbrook, Mary Jane, 29 - dom 3/54, doa 3/54
Proctor, Charles, 38 - Wiliam F. Pearce, dom 4/41, doa 4/41
Proctor, Samuel, 38 - William Pierce, dom 9/44, doa 9/44
Purviance, Christopher, 40 - William George eed, dom 5/58, doa 9/58
Reed, Charles, 37 - Elizabeth Webser, dom 6/56, doa 6/56
Reed, Thomas, 22 - Ann Brashaw, dom 9/42, doa 9/52
Rennolds, Harriet, 5 - Emily L. Harper, dom 3/56, doa 3/56
Reynolds, Ellen, 25 - Emily L. Harper, dom 2/60, doa 5/60
Rhodes, Abraham, 32 - Matthias Reuzinger, dom 9/43, doa 9/43
Richards, Sarah, A. - James Swan, dom 4/59, doa 4/59
Richarson, Hester, 22 - Cary A. Forman, dom 11/54, doa 9/58
Ricatds, Samuel, 40 - George Baughman, dom 8/45, doa 9/45
Ridgely, David, 35 - R. E. Heald, dom 12/59, doa 1/60
Riley, George W., 35 - Dorothy Mattingly, dom 5/55, doa 5/55
Roberts, Nathaniel, 27 - James Barroll, dom 9/43, doa 9/43
Roberts, Thomas, 35 - William Gray, dom 8/59, doa 8/59
Robinson, Mahala, 30 - C. Groverman, dom 9/47, doa 8/52
Rolins, Peter, 40 - Thomas Oliver, dom 3/40, doa 3/40
Rollins, Evett, 32 - John Heighe, dom 11/56, doa 12/56
Rollins, Jesse - John Heighe, dom 11/56, doa 12/56
Rose, Lewis, 30 - D. Sprigg, dom 8/56, doa 3/62
Royston, Rosannah, 32 - Margaret A. Dare, dom 2/48, doa 8/50
Rubens, Sally, 22 - Thomas P. Williams, dom 3/59, doa 3/59
Ruff, Philip, 28 - George King, dom 8/41, doa 9/41
Russell, George, 33 - Aquilla Talbot, dom 1/43, doa 3/43
Ruston, Rosetta, 31 - William J. Pearce', dom 11/40, doa 11/40
Sanders, George P., 28 - Hanna Canby, dom 6/52
Sanders, Mary Jane, 18 - Hanna Canby, dom 6/52
Saulsbury, Elisha, 37 - Jemima Ensor, doa 12/52
Scott, Candy, 35 - dom 3/42, doa 3/42
Scott, Emily, 24 - Hanna A. Brandt, dom 10/47, doa 10/47
Scott, Kitty, 42 - Rhetillah Bouche, dom 10/58, doa 12/58
Seymour, Julia Ann - Joseph F. Purvis, dom 7/56, doa 7/56
Shaw, Sophia, 35 - Pleasant Hunter, dom 7/47, doa 1/56
Silvester, Rhoda, 24 - Lydia Reynolds, dom 7/42, doa 3/47
Simpson, Mary Ann, 37 - Rachel H. Yongling, dom 5/60, doa 9/60
Slaughter, Phillis, 45 - Solomon Bowie, dom 2/58, doa 5/60
Smith, Ann E., 33 - Hammond Dugan, dom 10/58, doa 10/58
Smith, Anne, 36 - Mary Ann McClure, dom 4/43, doa 4/43
Smith, Benjamin, 33 - Zacheus O. Bond, dom 11/47, doa 1/48
Smith, David, 27 - Mary Evans, dom 1/46, doa 1/47
Smith, Dinah, 57 - Samuel Stevenson, dom 11/57, doa 11/57
Smith, Erme W., 27 - Samuel P. Smith, doa 2/45

Chapter 13

Smith, Henry, 24 - Jean Garrett, dom 9/40, doa 9/40
Smith, Henry, 47 - Mary Simmons, dom 10/51, doa 4/54
Smith, Julianna, 34 - Arthur Emory, dom 8/54, doa 8/54
Smith, Nancy, 36 - Edwrad Gray, dom 5/43, doa 5/43
Smith, Polly, 35 - Hugh Birckhead, dom 7/44, doa 7/44
Smith, Polly, 35 - Hugh Birckhead, dom 7/44, doa 7/44
Smith, Robert Jr. ♦, 39 - Robert Smith Sr., dom 8/47, doa 6/55
Smith, William Henry, 39 - dom 5/60, doa 5/60
Smith, William Henry, 39 - dom 5/60, doa 10/60
Smothers, Maria, 20 - Alexander W. Curtis, dom 12/52, doa 12/52
Snowden, Darius, 24 - Thomas Oliver, dom 3/40, doa 3/40
Spalding, Henrietta, 34 - Robert Leslie, dom 5/54, doa 5/54
Stephenson, Ace, 39 - Edward Hall, dom 4/44, doa 5/44
Stevenson, Milly, 35 - Rebecca Hicks, dom 12/45, doa 3/46
Steward, Reuben, 50 - Robert Ward, dom 8/40, doa 4/54
Stewart, Ann, 32 - Eleanor Bond, dom 11/41, doa 11/41
Stewart, Becky, 26 - William George Read, dom 3/58, doa 8/58
Stewart, Edward ♦, 40 - William Stewart(by will), dom 10/43, doa 10/43
Stewart, Enoch, 34 - James F. Purvis, dom 5/60, doa 9/60
Stewart, Julia, 38 - Galloway Chesten, dom 2/60, doa 2/60
Sullivan, Amelia, 41 - Juliana Williamson, dom 10/43, doa 11/43
Talbott, Beckey, 22 - Galloway Cheston, dom 3/44, doa 12/44
Tasquo, Joseph, 28 - Marianne R. Champayne, dom 6/43
Taylor, Abraham, 47 - Daniel Dail, dom 6/44, doa 6/44
Thomas, Emline, 37 - Sarah A. Beaty, dom 4/54, doa 4/54
Thomas, Henry, 44 - Samuel T. Emory, dom 5/51, doa 6/55
Thomas, James, 30 - Mary Dars, dom 12/56, doa 12/56
Thomas, John, 17 - Ann Hall, dom 8/51
Thomas, Maria, 28 - Thomas Corner, dom 10/52, doa 10/52
Thomas, Maria, 40 - George Myers Sr., dom 8/51, doa 5/53
Thomas, Richard, 33 - Ann Wilson, dom 10/48, doa 10/48
Thompson, James, 28 - Susan C. S. Carum, dom 10/52, doa 11/52
Thompson, James ♦, 21 - Willis Thompson, dom 7/54, doa 6/59
Thornton, Robert, 35 - Jacob Wolf, dom 12/54, doa 5/55
Tibbs, Bill, 35 - Lyde Goodwin, dom 2/40, doa 2/40
Tilghman, Harriet, 40 - Thomas Couser, dom 10/47, doa 10/47
Tilghman, Maria, 19 - Maurice Turpin, dom 11/43, doa 1/54
Tilghman, Nace, 52 - Mary Jenkins, dom 2/48, doa 4/57
Tilghman, William H., 20 - Maurice Turpin, dom 11/43, doa 1/54
Tillman, Mary ♦, 21 - Lucy Tillman, dom 6/40, doa 6/40
Trippe, Mary, 31 - Ms. H. Gordon, dom 8/42, doa 8/42
Tucker, Isaac - John Sumwalt, dom 12/45, doa 8/47
Tucker, Martha - John Sumwalt, dom 12/45, doa 8/47

Baltimore County Applications for Certificates of Freedom

Tucker, Mary Ann, 29 - David Hoffman, dom 1/41, doa 7/54
Turpin, Gertrude ♦, 30 - Maurice Turpin, dom 11/43, doa 11/43
Tyler, Basil, 26 - Hope H. Slatter, dom 7/48, doa 7/48
Walker, Hannah, 45 - Richard D. Hall, dom 9/56, doa 9/56
Walker, Mary, 29 - James P. Wilson, dom 10/47, doa 10/47
Wallis, Gerard, 32 - Edward Gorsuch, dom 10/48, doa 3/53
Wallis, Mary, 19 - John Hannan, dom 6/55, doa 6/55
Walter, Maria - John Sumwalt, dom 12/45, doa 8/57
Ward, Moses ♦, 38 - Mary Ward, dom 10/54, doa 10/54
Washington, Caroline, 30 - Timothy Stevens, dom 6/42, doa 6/42
Washington, Eliza, 43 - dom 3/53, doa 3/53
Waters, James ♦, 31 - Jane W. Waters, dom 4/52, doa 2/59
Watkins, Samuel, 26 - Jenny Johnston, dom 9/58, doa 9/58
Watts, Nelson, 35 - Margaret Dare, dom 11/43, doa 11/43
West, Henry, 27 - Jesse Slinghuff, dom 9/42
Wheeler, Mary, 34 - Samuel J. Donaldson, dom 1/42, doa 8/44
White, Cordelia A., 21 - Mary A. Hunt, dom 11/54, doa 11/54
Williams, Archibald, 27 - Elizabeth N. Rosler, dom 11/48, doa 12/48
Williams, Edward, 25 - Wiliam Riggin, dom 2/44, doa 3/44
Williams, James, 46 - Mary C. Lyon, dom 2/51, doa 3/56
Williams, Nancy, 49 - John W. Berry, dom 11/47, doa 1/49
Willis, William, 40 - Henry E. Bateman, dom 4/55, doa 7/55
Wilmer, Mary Ann, 43 - Caroline Ferguson, dom 5/61, doa 8/61
Wilson, Benjamin, 37 - William Scharf, dom 8/42
Wilson, Caroline, 30 - John D. Hooper, dom 1/54, doa 1/54
Wilson, Carvill, 35 - William Scharf, dom 8/42, doa 8/42
Wilson, Daniel, 35 - Racheal Galloway, dom 4/51, doa 10/52
Wilson, Esther, 33 - Racheal Galloway, dom 4/51, doa 10/52
Wilson, Esther, 43 - John Edmonson, dom 8/54, doa 1/55
Wilson, Hannah, 31 - James Hooper, dom 3/60, doa 3/60
Wilson, Harriet, 43 - G. S. Teackee Wallis, dom 12/46, doa 12/46
Wilson, Henry, 33 - Galloway Cheston, dom 11/58, doa 11/58
Wilson, Jacob, 34 - James Hooper, dom 11/46, doa 9/47
Wilson, James, 45 - G. S. Teackee Wallis, dom 12/46, doa 12/46
Wilson, Margaret, 39 - William Scharf, dom 8/42
Winchester, henry, 42 - Sophia V. Hook, dom 6/44, doa 5/45
Wood, Mary Elizabeth, 19 - Elizabeth G. Scott, dom 6/51, doa 4/62
Worthington, Jerry, 35 - George Slothower, dom 2/55, doa 2/55
Young, Harriott, 26 - John Werdebaugh, dom 11/41, doa 11/41

Reprinted with the kind permission of the *Flower of the Forest* - Black Genealogical Journal: Baltimore County Applications For Certificates of Freedom 1840 - 1864 v. 1, no. 8, 1989.

Chapter 13

The following is a cross index to applications for certificates of freedom for Baltimore County 1840-1864. This index was created by using information gleaned from the previous index of the same document. In this index, however, the manumitter is higlighted alphabetically, followed by the name of the manumitted slave.

The index is organized as follows:

Surname and first name of former slaveholder (manumitter), first and last name of manumitted slave.

Manumitter	Manumitted Slave
Adams, Jane	Hester Ann Milligan
Allen, W. H.	Leah Brown
Amos, Dr. Corbin	William Brown
Anderson, John	Joshua Lewis
Ashton, Dr.	James L. Lee
Atkinson, Angelo	Samuel Dority
Ault, Mary J.	Charlotte Blacke
Ayselott, Peter	Maria Henry
Bailey, Elijah	Henry H. Carter
Baker, William	Elijah Grissam
Baker, William	Harriet Holliday
Baltzell, Emanuel	Davis Hill
Banning, Catharine F.	Moses Nicholas
Barroll, James	Nathaniel Roberts
Bateman, Henry E.	William Willis
Baughman, George	Samuel Richards
Bealmear, Catharine	Edward Johnson
Beatty, Louisa S.	Phebe Gauntz
Beaty, Sarah A.	Emeline Thomas
Bennett, Benjamin F.	Lloyd Anderson
Bennett, Benjamin F.	Cornelius Hughes
Bentz, Caroline Jane	Susan JOhnson
Berry, John W.	Nancy Williams
Billups, Louisa	Eliza Baker
Birckhead, Charles Hugh	John Morris
Birckhead, Hugh	Polly Smith
Blanchard, E. W.	George Jason
Bond, Eleanor	Ann Stewart
Bond, Zacheus O.	Benjamin Smith
Bouche, Rhetillah	Kitty Scott
Bowie, Solomon	Phillis Slaughter

Baltimore County Applications for Certificates of Freedom

Manumitter	Manumitted Slave
Boyd, Mary	John Harris
Boyd, Mary	Jacob Jenkins
Bradshaw, Ann	Thomas Reed
Brandt, Hanna A.	Emily Scott
Brandt, Hannah A.	Phebe Hynson
Brent, Robert J.	Ann Green
Brent, Robert J.	Anna Green
Brice, Henry	Margaret Bordley
Brice, Hy	Thomas Garrett
Brisler, Daniel	Matilda Berry
Brookhart, Cassandra	Elijah Jones
Brooks, Nathan C.	Ann Bowyer
Brown, Mary	James Hamlett
Browne, Ann	Harriet Carroll Harris
Buck, John Jr.	Maria Anthony
Buck, John W.	Butler Pierce
Buck, John W.	Mary Pierce
Burnside, Henry	Eliza Johnson
Cable, Josiah	William Morris
Campbell, Jefferson	Spencer Murray
Canby, Hanna	George P. Sanders
Canby, Hanna	Mary Jane Sanders
Carr, Betty Ann	Emeline Jackson
Carroll, Harry D. G.	George Howard
Carroll, Henry	William Campbell
Carroll, Henry G. L.	Jones Jones
Carum, Susan C. S.	James Thompson
Chambers, Sarah E.	Delia Boone
Champayne, Marianne R.	Joseph Tasquo
Chase, Levi	Mary Catharine Chase
Chatan, Ferdinand O.	Elizabeth Ann Gaither
Cheston, Galloway	Charles Bias
Cheston, Galloway	Mary Hobbs
Cheston, Galloway	Samuel Matthews
Cheston, Galloway	Julia Stewart
Cheston, Galloway	Beckey Talbott
Cheston, Galloway	Henry Wilson
Chew, Samuel	Jesse Broom
Childs, Samuel	Henry Harris
Clary, Aaron	Joseph Duffin
Clemm, Joseph E.	Elizabeth Jones

Chapter 13

Manumitter	Manumitted Slave
Collins, James W.	Louisa E. Ford
Collins, James W.	Mary Ford
Constable, Catharine	Jane Kenword
Core, George W.	Patsy Ceders
Corner, Thomas	Maria Thomas
Costigan, Sylvester J.	Jane Butler
Couser, Thomas	Harriet Tilghman
Cox, Ann Eliza	David Johnson
Cox, Ann Eliza	Margaret Johnson
Cox, Shelly	Samuel Guy
Cromwell, Richard	George Himes
Cunningham, Oliver H. P.	Delia Heathfred
Curtis, Alexander W.	Maria Smothers
Dail, Daniel	Abraham Taylor
Dallam, Francis J.	Isaac Brown
Dalrymple, Alexander	Elizabeth Jackson
Dare, Elizabeth	Samuel Mitchell
Dare, Margaret	Nelson Watts
Dare, Margaret A.	Rosannah Royston
Dars, Mary	James Thomas
Davage, Milly	Fanny Milburn
Deford, Benjamin	Cordelia Howard
Denmead, Adam	Deborah Carter
Denmead, Isaac	Mary Jane Lewell
Denning, John N.	Mary Bailey
Dobbin, George W.	Mary Ann Howard
Donaldson, James L.	Simon Brown
Donaldson, Samuel J.	Mary Wheeler
Donovan, Joseph S.	Maria Preston
Dorsey, Jane	Maria Donaldson
Dorsey, Jane	Elias Jackson
Dorsey, Jane	Priscilla Jackson
Dorsey, Joshua	Maria Dorsey
Dorsey, Joshua	Charlotte Drummer
Dorsey, Richard J.	Grace Ennis
Dryden, Joshua	Maria Myers
Duckett, J. M.	Charles Lee
Dugan, Hammond	Ann E. Smith
Edmonson, John	Esther Wilson
Elder, Francis W.	Dolly Morgan
Emory, Arthur	Julianna Smith

Baltimore County Applications for Certificates of Freedom

Manumitter	Manumitted Slave
Emory, Samuel T.	Henry Thomas
Ensor, Jemima	Elisha Saulsbury
Evans, Mary	David Smith
Fell, Mary	Harriet Amos
Fenton, Aaron	Perry Brooks
Ferguson, Caroline	Mary Ann Wilmer
Fisher, William	Daniel Camper
Fitzhugh, H.	Isaac Hicks
Fitzhugh, Hebb	Phoebe Jones
Fitzhugh, Henry W.	William Grayson
Flannigan, Andrew	Thomas Lembrey
Fontaine, Edward	Ann Fontaine
Fontaine, Edward	Fender Fontaine
Fontaine, Edward	Henrietta Fontaine
Forman, Cary A.	Hester Richardson
Fowler, Mary	Jack Jones
Fox, Luther	Moses Emory
Frazier, Henrietta M.	James Gray
Galloway, Racheal	Eliza Burgess
Galloway, Racheal	Daniel Wilson
Galloway, Racheal	Esther Wilson
Garrett, Jean	Henry Smith
Gatch, Conduce	Marshall F. Gittings
Gibson, Gabriel	Eliza Gibson
Gibson, Patrick	Louisa Harris
Gibson, Patrick	Isaac James
Gilmer, Robert	Asbury Jones
Goodwin, Lyde	Bill Tibbs
Gordon, Eliza B. G.	Maria Butler
Gordon, Ms. H.	Mary Trippe
Gordon, Providence	Ellen Nickols
Gorsuch, Edward	Gerard Wallis
Gorsuch, Robert	George Barton
Gosnell, Rebecca	Elizabeth Bryan
Gover, Gerard	Andrew Jackson
Graff, Jacob	Jim Booth
Gray, Edward	Nancy Smith
Gray, William	Thomas Roberts
Green, Caroline M.	Louisa King
Green, Jacob	Diannah Green
Green, Mary	Dick Hill

Chapter 13

Manumitter	Manumitted Slave
Green, Rachel	Amelia Jane Gray
Green, Rachel	Ruth Gray
Gross, Rachel	Maria Makah
Groverman, C.	Mahala Robinson
Hall, Ann	Abraham Bennett
Hall, Ann	John Listen
Hall, Ann	John Thomas
Hall, Edward	Ace Stephenson
Hall, Elizabeth	Rosetta Jones
Hall, James	Louisa Dorsey
Hall, Richard D.	Hannah Walker
Hall, Sarah B.	John Franklin
Hambleton, Ann	Ellen Lecompt
Hambleton, Thomas	Adeline Lecompt
Hamilton, Rev. Matthew	Sophia Dixon
Hancock, Robert R.	Mary Ann Johnson
Hannan, John	Mary Wallis
Hardcastle, Edward B.	John Henry Baker
Harper, Charlotte C.	Henry Burgess
Harper, Emily L.	Cecelia Hallan
Harper, Emily L.	Dinah Hollan
Harper, Emily L.	Harriet Rennolds
Harper, Emily L.	Ellen Reynolds
Harris, C. H.	Dianna Smith
Harris, Catharine	Eliza Johnson
Harrison, James	Henry Camper
Hart Asa	William Lee
Harvey, Joshua	James Anthony
Hawkins, William	Emily Bower
Haysby, Charles	Laura Hays
Heald, R. E.	David Ridgely
Hebb, Hopewell	Delia Holly
Heighe, John	Jesse Rollins
Heighe, John	Evett Rollins
Herring, David	Mary Ann Hicks
Hicks, Rebecca	Milly Stevenson
Hill, Charley	James Hill
Hillen, Solomon	Maria Holliday
Hiss, William	Harriet Ann Pressgaes
Hiss, William	Rebecca Pressgaes
Hiss, William	Sarah J. Pressgaes

Baltimore County Applications for Certificates of Freedom

Manumitter	Manumitted Slave
Hoffman, David	Mary Ann Turner
Hohne, Eliza	Jacob Fabbor
Holley, Augustus	Harriet Holley
Holt, George H.	Nathan Dyer
Hook, Sophia V.	Henry Winchester
Hooper, James	Lucy Johnson
Hooper, James	Hannah Wilson
Hooper, James	Jacob Wilson
Hooper, James J.	Julia Guy
Hooper, John D.	Caroline Wilson
Hooper, Robert	Mary Garner
Hooper, Robert	Mary J. Garner
Hough, Jefferson	John Brooks
Howard, Ann R.	Clinton Matthews
Howard, James	James Brown
Howard, Mary M.	Fanny Govans
Hunt, Henry N.	Simon JOnes
Hunt, Mary A.	Cordelia A. White
Hunter, Pleasant	Sophia Shaw
Hutchins, James	William Fisher
Iddings, William P.	Comfort Banton
Jarvis, Leonard	Mellesley Marshall
Jenkins, James	Alexander McPherson
Jenkins, Mary	Nace Tilghman
Johnson, Adam	Eliza Johnson
Johnson, Harriet	Nathan Johnson
Johnson, Julia	Jane Ellen Johnson
Johnston, Jenny	Samuel Watkins
Jones, Charles R.	Susan Henson
Jones, Samuel J.	Catherine Baker
Jones, Samuel J.	John Baker
Jones, Samuel J.	John Baker
Kahne, Eliza	Emma Lewis
Keene, Eleanor P.	Chesterfield Marshall
Kelso, Thomas	Mary Hall
Key, Catharine	Sophia Meigs
King, George	Philip Ruff
Kohne, Eliza	Margaret McDowell
Konig, Frederick	Samuel Myers
Lamb. George W.	Jerry Allen
Law, Sarah F.	Mary Carter

Chapter 13

Manumitter	Manumitted Slave
Law, Sarah F.	Henry Jackson
Law, Sarah F.	Maria Jones
Leakin, Margaret	Isaiah Gittings
Lee, Lydia	Harry Bennett
Leef, Henry	Mary Parker
Leslie, Robert	Henrietta Spalding
Levering, Frederick A.	Harriet McKinney
Lloyd, Micha	Samuel Adams
Long, Elizabeth A.	Sarah Long
Lynch, Patrick	Edward Hammond
Lynch, Patrick	Sarah Kennedy
Lyon, Mary C.	James Williams
Lyons, Nancy	Arthur Jones
Mackall, Caroline	Rebecca Hamilton
March, Clara S.	John Buck
Martin, Susan	Henry Blake
Mason, James	Peggy Johnson
Massey, William R.	Shadrack Milburn
Mattingly, Dorothy	George W. Riley
May, Henry	Thomas Bolton
McCann, Marcellus	Harriet Augustus
McClure, Mary Ann	Anne Smith
McCollum, John	Singleton Hughes
McConnor, James	Henry Pinkney
McKeever, Ursula	Thomas Briscow
McKim, David T.	Delia Gibson
McKim, David T.	Henry Gibson
McKim, David T.	David Myers
McTavish, Emily	Richard Arthur
Meir, John	Henry T. O'Donnell
Mercer, Mary	Martha Harvey
Mercer, Mary	Mary Ellen Jackson
Middleton, Richard	Adaline Johnson
Milburn, Susan	Harriet Milburn
Mills, Margaret C.	Charles Harris
Mitchell, James	Jacob Mitchell
Moore, Jacob M.	Comfort Moore
Moore, Rebecca	Peter Moore
Morgan, Gerard E.	Emily N. Garrett
Morris, John B.	Nelly Neal
Mudoch, William F.	Sally Galloway

Baltimore County Applications for Certificates of Freedom

Manumitter	Manumitted Slave
Murry, Rachel	William Murry
Muse, Joseph E.	Wilmer J. Elsey
Muse, Joseph E.	Wilmer S. Elsey
Myers, George Sr.	Maria Thomas
Needles, John	William Johnson
Needles, John	Rachel Patterson
Offord, Frederick	Harriet Offord
Oliver, Thomas	Jerry Johnson
Oliver, Thomas	Peter Rollins
Oliver, Thomas	Darius Snowden
Orem, John M.	Rosetta Phillips
Osier, William	Clara Osier
Packie, Alexander	Fanny Lockerman
Parker, Nicholas	Susannah Parker
Patterson, Edward	Felix Hammond
Patterson, Edward	Peter Hammond
Pearce, William F.	Charles Proctor
Pearce, William J.	Rosetta Ruston
Pennington, Josias	Moses Norris
Phelps, Charles E.	James Henson
Philpot, Elizabeth	Eleanor Marshall
Pierce, William	Samuel Proctor
Pigmen, Mary E.	Ellen Lawson
Pinney, John B.	Leah Bowser
Pinney, John B.	Milley Bowser
Pinney, John B.	Mickey King
Poe, George Jr.	Sarah Harris
Purvell, Davis	Stephen Pressgrove
Purvis, James F.	Enoch Stewart
Purvis, Joseph F.	Julia Ann Seymour
Quinlan, Leonard G.	William Henry Augustus
Read, William George	Becky Stewart
Read, William George	Christopher Purviance
Reese, William	Rose Ann Preston
Regris, William	William Guy
Reuzinger, Matthias	Abraham Rhodes
Reynolds, Lydia	Rhoda Silvester
Reynolds, William	William Chase
Riddle, Robert	David Murray
Ridgely, John	Charles Hale Brown
Riggin, William	Edward Williams

Chapter 13

Manumitter	Manumitted Slave
River, Washington	Anne Maria Bantum
Rogers, Francis	Priscilla Hull
Rolosory, Hugh	Eliza Chase
Rosler, Elizabeth N.	Archibald Williams
Scharf, William	Benjamin Wilson
Scharf, William	Carvill Wilson
Scharf, William	Margaret Wilson
Schwartze, Henry	Emeline Jackson
Scott, Elizabeth G.	Rachel Campbell
Scott, Elizabeth G.	Mary Elizabeth Wood
Seward, Jarvis	John Golden
Shaw, Elias	Harriet Dutton
Simmons, Mary	Henry Smith
Sindall, Rachel	Julia Gooseberry
Skinner, Charles S.	Robert Biays
Slack, William B.	Caroline Nichols
Slatter, Hope H.	Basil Tyler
Slinghuff, Jesse	Abraham Neil
Slinghuff, Jesse	Thomas Neil
Slinghuff, Jesse	William Neil
Slinghuff, Jesse	Henry West
Sloan, Mary Jane	Eliza Jane Johnson
Slothower, George	Jerry Worthington
Smith, Gidin B.	Edward Golding
Smith, John	Charles Jones
Smith, Robert Sr.	Robert Smith Jr.
Smith, Samuel P.	Erme W. Smith
Smith, Samuel W.	Jacob Bishop
Spreckelson, George A. V.	Andrew Hammond
Sprigg, D.	Lewis Rose
Stansbury, Tobias E.	Sophia Owens
Starr, Hezekiah	Rebecca Gustus
Stevens, Timothy	Caroline Washington
Stevenson, Samuel	Dinah Smith
Stewart, David	Thomas Ockerme
Stewart, William Will Of	Edward Stewart
Stewrad, Mary Jane	Elizabeth Jackson
Sumwalt, John	Isaac Tucker
Sumwalt, John	Martha Tucker
Sumwalt, John	Maria Walter
Swan, James	Sarah A. Richards

Baltimore County Applications for Certificates of Freedom

Manumitter	Manumitted Slave
Swann, Thomas	Sandy Hogan
Swann, Thomas	Thomas Jackson
Swann, Thomas	Hnery Mallory
Talbot, Aquilla	George Russell
Tenant, Virginia	Maria Graves
Thomas, Hanson	Daniel Mathews
Thomas, Mary T.	Robert Norris
Thompson, Samuel T.	Mary Hall
Thompson, Willis	James Thompson
Tillman, Lucy	Mary Tillman
Townsend, Joseph B.	Othello Grooms
Turpin, Maurice	Maria Tilghman
Turpin, Maurice	William H. Tilghman
Turpin, Maurice	Gertrude Turpin
Tyson, John S.	Levi Murray
Tyson, Richard W.	Albert Carroll
Voss, Benjamin F.	Susan Parker
Wallis, G. S. Teackee	James Wilson
Wallis, Teackee	Harriet Wilson
Walter, Francis A.	Ellen Bell
Ward, Mary	Moses Ward
Ward, Robert	Reuben Steward
Waters, J. V.	George W. Brown
Waters, James U.	George H. DeShields
Waters, Jane W.	James Waters
Waters, Rebecca	henry Jackson
Watkins, Nicholas J.	Hester Cann
Watkins, Nicholas J.	Horace Johnson
Webster, Elizabeth	Charles Reed
Werdebaugh, John	Harriott Young
White, William H.	Sarah Moore
Williams, Thomas P.	Sally Rubens
Williamson, Juliana	Amelia Sullivan
Willis, John E.	Sally Dorsey
Wilson, Anna	Richard Thomas
Wilson, Caroline P.	Frances Beirney
Wilson, Henrietta B.	William Henry Smith
Wilson, James P.	Mary Walker
Winchester, Samuel	Lavinia Johnson
Wolf, Jacob	Jesse Jenkins
Wolf, Jacob	Robert Thornton

Chapter 13

Manumitter	Manumitted Slave
Woodward, William	Amos Brogden
Wright, Mary F.	Teresa Blackstone
Wright, Mary F.	Teresa Blackstone
Wright, Susan	Samuel Fountain
Wyman, S. G.	Thomas Preston
Yongling, Rachel H.	Mary Ann Simpson
Young, James	Jane Jackson

14
Maryland Colonization Society Gleanings from the Baltimore Sun

Throughout the 1840's and 1850's a number of articles on colonization appeared in the "local matters" section of the *Baltimore Sun*. The text of this material provides detailed information on functions of the Maryland Colonization Society. The great majority of articles announced passenger arrivals and departures on the ships and barques employed by the Society. This material provides excellent insight into particulars such as religious ceremonies, ship building, departure locations and colonization statistics.

The following is a list of abstracts of colonization articles that appeared in the *Sun* from September, 1847 through December, 1860. The heading under which the material appeared is recorded below. The date and page of the item is noted, followed by a brief synopsis of the material provided therein.

Departure Of Emigrants From Liberia 9/3/47-2
Liberia Packet "Captain Goodmanson" to leave Wilson's wharf this morning. Religious services will be performed by Rev. Mr. Payne of Bethel church.

The Liberia Packet 8/3/48-2
Liberian Packet to be sent out on the fall trip as early as September 10, if ship arrives on time.

The Liberian Emigrants 9/6/48-2
Liberian Packet to sail on fourth voyage from Wilson's wharf, Fells' Point. The number of emigrants is to be small. Most of the emigrants are from Washington city.

Sailing Of The Liberia Packet 2/26/49-2
Liberia Packet, "Captain Goodmanson" with 62 manumitted slaves aboard leaves for the African Republic. (Lengthy article.)

Colonization 3/21/49-2
Vessel to be dispatched on or about April 20th. Vessel will take on more than 270 emigrants at Savannah.

Chapter 14

Liberia Packet 7/6/49-2
The Packet will sail for Liberia about the first of August.

Sailing Of The Liberia Packet 8/2/49-2
Liberian Packet, "Captain Goodmanson." Twenty-five emigrants (10 from Maryland and 15 from North Carolina) were on board. Departure of vessel was delayed for fear that a fugitive had slipped on board. (Lengthy article.)

The Liberia Packet 8/3/49-2
Friends of the Colonization Society purchased the freedom of Thomas Gross and family who sailed on the Packet of August the second.

For Liberia 12/21/50-1
Barque Liberia Packet... Captain Howe will sail from Baltimore to Liberia (Monrovia) this morning with more than seventy emigrants. Five states are represented by the passengers. A number of passengers of the cabin are also traveling on the Barque. (Many of them are named.)

For Liberia 3/19/51-2
A large number of respectful colored men and their families are preparing to depart for Liberia. Most of them are from the southern section of the city.

For Liberia 4/30/51-1
A large number of emigrants will leave from Baltimore on the Liberia Packet about the first of June. Many will be from Virginia. Thesed emigrants, who will form a new settlement at Bassa Cove, will be taking a steam engine with them.

Colonization Movement 6/14/51-1
Jacob Moore (a colored preacher, physician, and divine) delivered a lecture to the free negroes at Snow Hill, Maryland. His hopes were to induce them to go with him to Liberia.

Colonization Cause 7/29/51-1
Rev. John Says, agent for the Maryland Colonization Society, presented the cause of colonization at the Caroline Street Methodist Episcopal church. His subject revolved around a verse in the book of Genesis "Send me away, that I may go unto my own people."

Maryland Colonization Gleanings from the Baltimore Sun

Emigrants For Liberia 11/1/51-1
This morning the vessel "Morgan Dix" sailed with 145 emigrants on board. Most of the emigrants were manumitted slaves from Virginia and North Carolina.

Emigrants Sailed 11/3/51-4
The Barque "Morgan Dix" sailed with 145 emigrants on board. Most of the emigrants were manumitted slaves from Virginia and North Carolina.

May Expedition To Liberia 4/19/52-1
The "Ralph Cross," recently purchased by the Chesapeake and Liberia Trading Company, will disembark from baltimore with emigrants from New York on May 1st. The vessel will take on fifty additional emigrants in Hampton Roads

Liberian Emigrants 5/3/52-1
The Barque "Ralph Cross" sailed with 95 emigrants from Baltimore. Five states were represented, including 20 from Maryland. The barque will also pick up 70 emigrants from Norfolk. Most of the emigrants from the slave states are manumitted slaves. Bishop Payne and 5 or 6 missionaries also sailed with the emigrants.

Colored Emigration 5/25/52-4
A meeting is to be held at St. James Church (North and Saratoga St.) to discuss the propriety of holding a convention. The convention would discuss the expediency of emigrating to Liberia.

The Colonization Cause 5/27/52-4
At a meeting held in the St. James Colored Protestant Episcopal Church on the 25th, the colored community has decided to hold a convention to discuss the importance of emigrating to Liberia.

For Liberia 11/10/52-1
The barque "Joseph Maxwell" is taking on cargo for Monrovia. The vessel will sail to Wilmington, N. C. to pick up 150 emigrants. The barque "Shirley" will leave port on two weeks with Maryland emigrants. At The same time the "Linda Stewart" will leave Norfolk with 200 emigrants. (Lengthy article.)

For Liberia 11/29/52-1
The barque "Shirley" (built by Messrs. Perry and Brigham) left

Chapter 14

for Liberia on her maiden voyage with 50 emigrants and a number of missionaries. (Names of the ship's construction workers are given.)

Missionaries For Liberia 12/1/52-1
Rev. Mr. Scott, Bishop of the Methodist Episcopal Church and other missionaries traveling on the barque "Shirley" for Liberia. Miss Freeman of Rev. B. S. Killen's congregation is to assist Bishop Payne's wife in general missionary duties.

For Liberia 3/26/53-1
The Chesapeake and LIberia Trading Company chartered the ship "Banshee" from Messrs. Hugh Jenkins and Co. for a voyage to Monrovia, Bossa, and Cape Palmas. Most Marylanders from among the several hundred emigrants wiil land at Cape Palmas.

Expedition For Liberia 10/19/54-1
The ship "Euphrasia" will leave this port the first of November for Liberia. She will be carrying more than 200 emigrants from 5 states. She is a large ship, 8, 000 bbls capacity. The "Estella" is to sail from New York with emigrants on the 25th.

Bound For Africa 12/7/54-1
The barque "Shirley," owned by Mr. G. W. Hall, will leave this port on a trading voyage to Africa. A few emigrants will also leave on the vessel.

For Liberia 10/25/55-1
A number of emigrants will leave on the barque "Cora" bound for Monrovia and other ports. Captain Moore will be in command.

Departure Of The Liberia Expedition 11/2/55-1
The barque "Cora" sailed with 64 emigrants yesterday morning. Seven of the emigrants were emancipated by Mrs. E. L. Young of Prince George's County. The other five from Maryland were a free family by the name of Hardy.

Maryland State Colonization Society 1/5/56-4
Rev. John Seys, traveling agent of the Society for 6 years, has resigned his post and will be moving to Ohio.

The Colonization Ship "Mary Caroline Stevens" 11/26/56-1
Built by the well known Baltimore shipbuilders Abrams and

Ashcroft, the ship was constucted as a result of a gift of $36,000 willed by the late Col. John Stevens of Talbot County. (This lengthy article describes the ship and its method of construction in detail.)

Arrival For Liberia 4/16/57-1
The ship "Mary Caroline Stevens," returning from the coast of Africa has reached Hampton Roads, Virginia. The ship will sail again about the first of May.

The Colonization Ship 5/18/57-1
The shop "Mary Caroline Stevens" will sail today for Liberia with about 185 emigrants. This is the second voyage of the ship. (Lengthy article.)

The Ship Mary C. Stevens 5/27/51-1
The ship M. C. Stevens was detained due to inclement weather. She is expected to be hauled into the stream and sail as soon as clearance is issued from the custom's house. (This is a lengthy article indicating the names and ages of dozens of emigrants leaving on the vessel for Africa.)

For Africa 5/29/57-1
The new schooner "President Benson," named after the president of Liberia, is about to sail for Monrovia. She belongs to Mr Hall of this city and will be used for the coasting trade in Liberia.

For Liberia 10/28/57-1
The packet ship "Mary Caroline Stevens" will sail with a large number of emigrants from this port next Saturday. (Several of their manumitters are named in this article.)

For Liberia 11/3/57-1
The ship "Mary Caroline Stevens" will sail today. Among the emigrants on board are 30 former slaves freed by Mrs. Riggen of this city.

The Colonization Ship "Mary Caroline Stevens" 1/27/58-1
The packet ship "Mary Caroline Stevens" was reported off of Cape St Ann Shoals on Decenber 16th. She was about two days sail from Monrovia at that time.

Maryland State Colonization Society 1/29/58-1
The Society assembled on Wednesday for the election of officers.

Chapter 14

(Elected officers are named.)

Maryland State Colonization Society 2/1/58-1
The report of the board of managers of the Maryland State Colonization Society has been made. *(Particulars of the report are indicated in this lengthy article.)*

The Legislature And The Colonization Cause 2/2/58-1
The managers of the Maryland State Colonization Society have sent an adress to the Maryland State Legislature giving a statement of the Society's condition. *(Particulars of the address are indicated in this article.)*

For Western Africa 4/22/58-1
The ship "Mary Caroline Stevens" will sail from Baltimore about the first of May with 100 emigrants.

Sailing Of The Liberia Packet 5/3/58-1
The Packet ship "Mary Caroline Stevens" sailed saturday from Manikin's wharf. The ship had 120 passengers, most of them manumitted slaves from Virginia. Religious services were conducted by Rev. Mr. Seys.

Emigrants For Africa 11/2/58-1
The ship "Mary Caroline Stevens" will sail for Liberia Tomorrow with 60 emigrants and 19 cabin passengers, Among the freight will be the necessary materials for the establishment of the first newspaper in Africa, the Lone Star. A meeting was held in the Bethel Church on Saratoga Street last night. *(Particulars of the meeting are given.)*

Sailing Of The Mary C. Stevens 11/3/58-4
The ship "Mary Caroline Stevens" will leave today with emigrants from 7 states on board. *(A number of cabin passengers are named.)*

The Maryland State Colonization Society 2/1/59-1
The general election of the officers of the Maryland State Colonization Society took place yesterday. *(The newly elected officers are named, as well as the offices they fill.)*

Going To Africa 4/25/59-1
Two hundred colored persons, one of the largest groups in

several years have made arrangements to emigrate. It is hoped they will leave on the ship "Mary Caroline Stevens" sometime in May. Among those going are 50 liberated slaves formerly belonging to the late John McDonogh of New Orleans.

Sailing Of The Liberia Packet 5/12/59-1
The Liberia Packet "Mary Caroline Stevens" will sail today with about 150 passengers including three colored Presbyterian ministers.

The Liberia Packet 5/31/59-1
The "Mary Caroline Stevens" sailed yesterday with 150 passengers. (Article names the three colored minister passengers as well as officials who gave farewell addresses before the departure of the ship.)

For Africa 11/1/59-4
The ship "Mary Caroline Stevens" will sail today with emigrants and missionaries for the west coast of Africa.

Arrival Of The Colonization Ship 3/6/60-1
The colonization ship "Mary Caroline Stevens" arrived yesterday from Cape Moubt, west coast of Africa. She was on passage of thirty five days to the Cape. She reports that the schooner "James Hall" of this port has been sold at Monrovia.

Sailing Of The Ship Mary Caroline Stevens 4/20/60-1
The ship "Mary Caroline Stevens" will leave port today for the Republic of Liberia. George Tucker (of Philadelphia) and his two daughters are on board. Mr. Tucker, who is an excellent cabinet maker will carry his tools with him. It is said he purchased his own freedom as well as the freedom of his daughters.

Departure Of The Ship Mary Caroline Stevens 8/21/60-1
The ship "Mary Caroline Stevens" left anchorage at quarantine saturday for Liberia. Passengers were taken down saturday morning by the steam tug "Lioness."

Arrivals Of The Colonization Ship 8/21/60-1
The colonization ship "Mary Caroline Stevens" arrived yesterday after a passage of 34 days from the west coast of Africa.

Sailing Of African Emigrants 11/5/60-1

Chapter 14

On friday the ship "Mary Caroline Stevens" left for Liberia with 80 emigrants from a total of 8 states. Religious services were performed on board.

The Cause Of Colonization In Liberia 12/11/60-1
The whole number of emigrants sent to Liberia by the American Colonization Society and its' auxiliaries since its inception has been 10, 545. (The receipts of the Society are detailed in this lengthy article. Also detailed is the trip of the "Mary C. Stevens." During the November sailing 3 Africans captured from a slaver were returned to Africa.)

Reprinted here with the kind permission of the *Flower of the Forest* - Black Genealogical Journal: Maryland Colonization Society Gleanings from the Sun Newspaper v. 1, no. 9, 1990.

15
The Baltimore Census of 1830: The Free Black Population

The following is an index of the Black Population in the 1830 census of Baltimore. The compilization of this index presented a number of problems for the author. The handwriting styles of the various enumerators, along with numerous misspellings of names were tremendous obstacles to overcome. A number of pages in the document were nearly illegible due to a number of enumerators' failure to "dip the pen" sufficiently before transcribing the names. All researchers aim for 100% accuracy. Publishers as well as researchers, however, will admit that a 95% rate of accuracy is acceptable in difficult documents. The following document was so difficult to work with that the author would find a 90% rate of accuracy acceptable. The reader should be advised that misspellings have been retained in an attempt to duplicate the document with as much accuracy as possible. Names like Henery (Henry) and Barnebas (Barnabas) are transcribed as they were found in the original.

A sample entry of the document is as follows:

Anderson, Barnebas - w 12, p 510.

A translation of the entry is as follows:

Barnebas Anderson is the head of house in the twelfth ward of Baltimore city in 1830. His household's residents are recorded on page 510 of the twelfth ward of the city.

Baltimore Census of 1830 - Free Blacks

Abraham, Dobson - w 2, p 78
Abrahams, Pabloe - w 3, p 154
Adams, Adam - w 3, p 154
Adams, Charles - w 11, p 430
Adams, Hilery - w 3, p 105
Adams, James - w 3, p 159
Adams, James - w 9, p 326
Adams, Mary - w 10, p 369
Adison, Ellen - w 10, p 380
Aiken, Samuel - w 2, p 46
Aires, Andrew - w 9, p 327

Airs, Thomas - w 12, p 450
Alby, Levey - w 10, p 354
Alender, Turer - w 10, p 392
Alin, Rachel - w 2, p 84
Allen, Amos - w 11, p 403
Allen, Thomas - w 10, p 384
Allen, William - w 5, p 224
Allin, Amy - w 2, p 50
Almer, Milky - w 2, p 46
Ambrose, Henry - w 3, p 133
Amby, Benjamin - w 2, p 52

Chapter 15

Baltimore Census of 1830 - Free Blacks

Amby, Isaac - w 2, p 60
Amos, Hetty - w 3, p 134
Amos, Rachael - w 3, p 135
Anan, Mary - w 12, p 457
Anderson, Barnebas - w 12, p 510
Anderson, Charles - w 4, p 177
Anderson, Elijah - w 2, p 87
Anderson, Eliza - w 12, p 514
Anderson, Henry - w 2, p 87
Anderson, Henry - w 8, p 295
Anderson, James - w 12, p 494
Anderson, Joseph - w 12, p 502
Anderson, Maria - w 3, p 111
Anderson, Matthias - w 11, p 424
Anderson, Samuel - w 1, p 16
Anderson, Stephen - w 12, p 514
Anderson, Thomas - w 4, p 183
Anderson, Thomas - w 10, p 358
Andrews, Rachael - w 12, p 504
Applobery, William - w 8, p 304
Arien, Eliza - w 12, p 475
Armistead, Lucinda - w 4, p 190
Armstead, William - w 12, p 515
Armstrong, Isaac - w 12, p 514
Armstrong, John - w 12, p 514
Armstrong, Major - w 9, p 338
Asburn, Lewis - w 11, p 436
Ash, Peter - w 5, p 232
Asker, Rus. - w 9, p 344
Askins, Isaac - w 12, p 518
Augustus, Matilda - w 6, p 260
Ayres, John - w 3, p 154
Backons, Rosina - w 12, p 474
Bacon, Benjamin - w 12, p 502
Bacon, Edward - w 12, p 510
Bacon, William - w 11, p 410
Badger, Elisha - w 9, p 326
Badger, Ivory - w 11, p 403
Badger, Jarett - w 12, p 517
Badger, Richard - w 11, p 403
Bagden, Joshua - w 12, p 507

Bailey, Draper - w 3, p 107
Bailey, John - w 11, p 403
Bailey, Lewis - w 10, p 361
Bailey, Nancy - w 11, p 404
Bailey, Phillis - w 10, p 361
Bailey, Susan - w 5, p 220
Bailies, James - w 12, p 479
Baily, Darky - w 12, p 474
Baily, Isaac - w 12, p 520
Balden, Joseph - w 12, p 513
Baley, Isaac - w 9, p 345
Baley, Samuel - w 2, p 78
Ballman, Mariah - w 10, p 363
Banks, Benjamin - w 1, p 17
Banks, Leo - w 2, p 75
Banning, Jacob - w 12, p 517
Banton, Richard - w 5, p 230
Barcroft, Rolla - w 2, p 67
Barker, Adam - w 4, p 183
Barker, Basil - w 8, p 314
Barnes, Ann - w 4, p 213
Barnes, Charles - w 8, p 307
Barnes, David - w 3, p 125
Barnet, Philip - w 12, p 516
Barnet, Susana - w 2, p 85
Barnett, Benjamin - w 11, p 414
Barnett, Henry - w 3, p 139
Barnett, John - w 3, p 110
Barnett, William - w 1, p 17
Barney, Ceaser - w 2, p 86
Barney, James - w 11, p 441
Barney, William - w 9, p 345
Barns, Fanny - w 12, p 507
Barns, Patience - w 1, p 10
Barraway, Abraham - w 10, p 396
Barry, Jacob - w 2, p 59
Barton, Charles - w 2, p 81
Barton, Henry - w 12, p 499
Barton, James - w 12, p 499
Barton, Nathaniel - w 1, p 12
Bassett, Harry - w 4, p 179

The Baltimore Census of 1830: The Free Black Population

Baltimore Census of 1830 - Free Blacks

Bateman, Edward - w 3, p 152
Bates, Rachal - w 11, p 436
Battes, Thomas - w 10, p 351
Baum, Samuel - w 12, p 493
Bayley, Elizabeth - w 4, p 195
Bazill, Harry - w 3, p 112
Bean, William - w 12, p 489
Beasly, Samuel - w 12, p 463
Beatty, Mary - w 8, p 317
Becker, Rachael - w 3, p 133
Becks, Catherine - w 12, p 494
Behoc, Moses - w 11, p 403
Bell, Eliza - w 12, p 487
Benedict, Christian - w 11, p 421
Bennett, Peter - w 3, p 139
Bennett, Stephen - w 3, p 153
Benson, Edward - w 3, p 142
Benson, John - w 2, p 87
Benson, John - w 3, p 155
Benson, Nancy - w 3, p 127
Benson, Perry - w 9, p 337
Benson, Peter - w 1, p 22
Benson, Rachel - w 10, p 382
Benson, Robert - w 10, p 364
Berry, Dina - w 3, p 135
Berry, Harriet - w 9, p 330
Berry, James - w 11, p 440
Berry, John - w 3, p 125
Berry, William - w 8, p 293
Berryman, Sarah - w 4, p 171
Bias, Stephen - w 2, p 86
Billingsly, Henry - w 12, p 463
Bishop, Perry - w 10, p 395
Blackston, Elizabeth - w 4, p 195
Bladford, Fanny - w 4, p 168
Blake, Cater - w 12, p 504
Blake, Danniel - w 2, p 81
Blake, George - w 8, p 319
Blake, Isaac - w 1, p 10
Blake, Jacob - w 3, p 152
Blake, James - w 3, p 153

Blake, Jane - w 2, p 57
Blake, Levin - w 2, p 61
Blake, Moses - w 12, p 463
Blake, Vincent - w 4, p 189
Bogon, Sarah - w 2, p 66
Bohen, Andrew - w 12, p 498
Boice, Benjamin - w 12, p 482
Boister, David - w 3, p 139
Boling, William - w 3, p 99
Bon, Aquilla - w 12, p 446
Bond, Chillas - w 3, p 159
Bond, Levi - w 9, p 340
Bond, Robert - w 2, p 37
Bond, Sandles - w 8, p 293
Bond, Washington - w 3, p 132
Bone, Solomon - w 8, p 307
Bonnapart, John - w 8, p 316
Boom, Benjamin - w 12, p 489
Boon, John - w 5, p 228
Boon, Joshua - w 2, p 78
Booth, Elijah - w 12, p 487
Booth, Joshua - w 2, p 57
Booth, Paul - w 10, p 354
Booth, William - w 12, p 452
Booze, John - w 2, p 82
Bordly, Anthony - w 12, p 492
Borin, Henry - w 8, p 313
Boston, Abraham - w 6, p 259
Boston, Charles - w 12, p 521
Boston, Daniel - w 2, p 55
Boston, Daniel - w 9, p 344
Boston, Daniel - w 8, p 306
Boston, George - w 9, p 336
Boston, George - w 12, p 494
Boston, John - w 11, p 424
Boston, Mary - w 2, p 38
Boston, Peter - w 9, p 344
Boston, Robert - w 8, p 302
Botehlor, Richard? - w 10, p 361
Boundry, Perry - w 8, p 313
Bowan, Jane - w 10, p 364

Chapter 15

Baltimore Census of 1830 - Free Blacks

Bowden, Benjamin - w 8, p 312
Bowen, Harris - w 10, p 386
Bowen, John - w 3, p 152
Bowen, Josiah - w 11, p 430
Bowey, David - w 2, p 74
Bowley, Gabriel - w 9, p 342
Bowling, John - w 9, p 344
Bowman, George - w 3, p 135
Bowser, Henry - w 2, p 59
Bowser, Robert - w 6, p 247
Boyd, Emily - w 12, p 510
Boyer, Henry - w 12, p 485
Boyer, Tobias - w 11, p 408
Boyer, William - w 2, p 85
Boyerman, Jacob - w 3, p 150
Boyne, Abraham - w 11, p 437
Bradford, Fanny - w 3, p 155
Bradford, Richard - w 3, p 156
Bradkins, W. - w 8, p 292
Bradley, Samuel - w 11, p 435
Bragton, William - w 10, p 356
Branson, Samuel - w 3, p 137
Brawder, John - w 12, p 448
Bretton, Henry - w 12, p 490
Briady, Henry - w 10, p 361
Brian, Sylva - w 5, p 225
Brice, Philip - w 12, p 481
Brice, Susana - w 3, p 142
Bridge, Henry - w 3, p 157
Bridge, Rebeca - w 4, p 170
Brighton, Rebecca - w 12, p 455
Brigs, Mary - w 2, p 85
Brisco, Joseph - w 8, p 302
Briscoe, Nathan - w 2, p 61
Brisker, Jacob - w 4, p 169
Brockdel, David - w 12, p 493
Broclon, William - w 11, p 412
Brogden, Elisha - w 12, p 471
Brook, Sarah - w 12, p 445
Brooks, Benjamin - w 9, p 340
Brooks, Elizabeth - w 3, p 139

Brooks, George - w 2, p 65
Brooks, John - w 9, p 337
Brooks, Nathan - w 4, p 213
Brooks, Richard - w 4, p 171
Brown, Anna - w 3, p 141
Brown, Buster - w 12, p 493
Brown, Charles - w 8, p 293
Brown, Charles - w 1, p 16
Brown, Charles - w 8, p 312
Brown, Charles - w 12, p 463
Brown, Charlotte - w 11, p 403
Brown, David - w 12, p 498
Brown, Edward - w 2, p 90
Brown, Edwin - w 12, p 500
Brown, Elisha - w 12, p 502
Brown, Elizabeth - w 3, p 113
Brown, Elizabeth - w 3, p 125
Brown, Fanny - w 8, p 291
Brown, Francis - w 4, p 195
Brown, George - w 8, p 306
Brown, Greenberry ? - w 10, p 387
Brown, Henry - w 4, p 190
Brown, Henry - w 12, p 454
Brown, Hester - w 10, p 361
Brown, Holly - w 8, p 315
Brown, Jacob - w 3, p 112
Brown, Jacob - w 11, p 406
Brown, Jacob - w 12, p 448
Brown, Jacob - w 12, p 474
Brown, James - w 2, p 86
Brown, James - w 3, p 127
Brown, James - w 4, p 171
Brown, James - w 10, p 371
Brown, James - w 12, p 479
Brown, James - w 12, p 515
Brown, Jane - w 12, p 477
Brown, Jerremia - w 10, p 357
Brown, John - w 8, p 312
Brown, John - w 12, p 450
Brown, John F. - w 8, p 294
Brown, John H. - w 9, p 306

The Baltimore Census of 1830: The Free Black Population

Baltimore Census of 1830 - Free Blacks

Brown, Joseph - w 3, p 125
Brown, Joshua - w 11, p 410
Brown, Joshua - w 12, p 502
Brown, Julia - w 9, p 336
Brown, Lucy - w 2, p 40
Brown, Lucy C. - w 4, p 170
Brown, Minory - w 2, p 60
Brown, Moses - w 12, p 473
Brown, Nathaniel - w 4, p 209
Brown, Othello - w 5, p 239
Brown, Perry - w 2, p 76
Brown, Perry - w 3, p 123
Brown, Perry - w 8, p 312
Brown, Peter - w 11, p 406
Brown, Peter - w 11, p 441
Brown, Philip - w 3, p 139
Brown, Phinney - w 12, p 489
Brown, Rachael - w 12, p 502
Brown, Reuben - w 3, p 133
Brown, Richard - w 3, p 119
Brown, Roseta - w 8, p 318
Brown, Rusan - w 10, p 367
Brown, Ruth - w 1, p 30
Brown, Sally - w 11, p 422
Brown, Samuel - w 12, p 522
Brown, Solomon - w 7, p 271
Brown, Stephen - w 3, p 132
Brown, Thomas - w 2, p 66
Brown, Thomas - w 2, p 75
Brown, Violet - w 2, p 42
Brown, William - w 10, p 369
Bruce, Peter - w 3, p 109
Bryan, Levin - w 3, p 133
Bryant, Solomon - w 2, p 79
Brydant, Sam? - w 8, p 320
Bryson, Peter - w 8, p 320
Buck, James - w 2, p 62
Bull, Abraham - w 10, p 354
Bullen, Frederick - w 12, p 445
Buly, Cirus - w 2, p 76
Bups, Simus - w 12, p 502

Burgess, Alexander - w 3, p 123
Burget, Henney - w 10, p 385
Burgoin, Augustus - w 2, p 66
Burk, Clement - w 3, p 133
Burk, David - w 1, p 11
Burk, Henry - w 2, p 78
Burk, Thomas - w 1, p 21
Burk, Thomas Jr. - w 1, p 22
Burley, Isaac - w 3, p 115
Burly, Perry - w 8, p 313
Burn, Mathew - w 8, p 313
Burris, James - w 8, p 298
Burt, Julias - w 4, p 206
Burton, Nace - w 2, p 71
Buster, Susan - w 12, p 486
Butchmon, Mily - w 8, p 294
Butler, Ann - w 4, p 214
Butler, Basil - w 9, p 343
Butler, Benjamin - w 10, p 382
Butler, Clemson - w 9, p 325
Butler, Elisabeth - w 11, p 434
Butler, George - w 2, p 90
Butler, Henry - w 3, p 132
Butler, Joseph - w 12, p 477
Butler, Josiah - w 12, p 506
Butler, Mathew - w 10, p 361
Butler, Minto - w 12, p 510
Butler, Richard - w 3, p 134
Butler, Samuel - w 2, p 79
Butler, Widow - w 10, p 377
Butter, Peter - w 2, p 52
Byais, Alford - w 10, p 363
Byall, Isaac - w 9, p 347
Cabaro, Joseph - w 10, p 372
Caby, Elijah - w 10, p 359
Cagen, William - w 2, p 50
Cain, Elenor - w 2, p 85
Caldwell, George - w 3, p 160
Caldwell, Perry - w 9, p 344
Caldwell, William - w 3, p 146
Calhoon, Peter - w 12, p 492

Chapter 15

Baltimore Census of 1830 - Free Blacks

Camper, Levin - w 3, p 138
Camper, Moses - w 8, p 319
Camphor, Stephen - w 11, p 404
Campkine, Solomon - w 4, p 170
Canada, Robb - w 4, p 202
Cane, Nancy - w 8, p 295
Canibell, Caleb - w 8, p 307
Cantell, Joseph - w 11, p 437
Canuis, George - w 11, p 432
Carden, William - w 12, p 487
Carey, Joseph - w 5, p 232
Carey, Richard - w 11, p 404
Carl, Bernard - w 1, p 20
Carmack, Elizabeth - w 3, p 148
Carpenter, Catherine - w 10, p 385
Carr, Ellen - w 9, p 346
Carroll, James - w 12, p 511
Carrol, John - w 2, p 80
Carrol, John - w 12, p 500
Carrol, Lucy - w 12, p 507
Carroll, Peter - w 9, p 346
Carroll, Peter - w 12, p 479
Carroll, Toney - w 4, p 211
Carson, Sarah - w 9, p 345
Carter, Abertrige - w 2, p 92
Carter, George - w 10, p 358
Carter, Joseph - w 12, p 502
Carter, Philemon - w 4, p 206
Carter, Richard - w 12, p 523
Carter, Samuel - w 10, p 361
Cary, Ellenor - w 2, p 71
Cassaway, George - w 8, p 307
Castle, Samuel - w 12, p 489
Castle, William - w 4, p 173
Cator, Rebecca - w 12, p 506
Cator, Richard Sr. - w 4, p 174
Ceney, Ann - w 2, p 84
Chace, Richard - w 10, p 373
Chains, Jacob - w 3, p 158
Chalk, Mordecai - w 1, p 5
Chambers, Benjamin - w 11, p 403

Chambers, Deby - w 10, p 351
Chambers, Henry - w 12, p 501
Chambers, Hetty - w 4, p 208
Chambers, Isaac - w 2, p 85
Chambers, Isaiah - w 4, p 215
Chambers, James - w 7, p 269
Chambers, Joshua - w 12, p 481
Chambers, Lucy - w 11, p 413
Chambers, Perry - w 3, p 141
Chambers, Silas - w 3, p 141
Chambers, Susan - w 11, p 406
Chambers, William - w 10, p 362
Chambers, Zeicle - w 12, p 502
Chaplin, David - w 12, p 514
Chapman, Isaac - w 9, p 342
Chapman, Jeremiah - w 6, p 262
Chappel, Richard - w 4, p 215
Charles, Elizabeth - w 11, p 433
Charles, Mary - w 12, p 445
Charlston, Charles - w 2, p 42
Chase, Bazil - w 3, p 138
Chase, Ennals - w 2, p 54
Chase, Henry - w 2, p 78
Chase, John - w 3, p 136
Chase, Margaret - w 10, p 372
Chase, Samuel - w 2, p 63
Chaves, Moses - w 8, p 319
Chery, Rebecca - w 12, p 497
Chester, Stanley - w 1, p 16
Chester, Stephen - w 2, p 66
Chew, John - w 11, p 402
Chew, Thomas - w 11, p 405
Chisley, Eliza - w 3, p 136
Christmas, James - w 3, p 158
Christy, Gabrel - w 3, p 123
Christy, George - w 3, p 112
Chubs, Anthony - w 12, p 472
Chunks, George - w 3, p 138
Church, Martha - w 9, p 330
Clark, Hannah - w 3, p 145
Clark, James - w 2, p 84

The Baltimore Census of 1830: The Free Black Population

Baltimore Census of 1830 - Free Blacks

Clark, Nancy - w 9, p 344
Clark, Rachael - w 12, p 503
Clark, Sampson - w 11, p 401
Clayton, Pompey - w 2, p 41
Clement, Ebby - w 9, p 336
Clemmon, Peter - w 2, p 70
Clifin, Thomas - w 2, p 74
Cloper, Lewis - w 10, p 392
Clopper, Ann - w 10, p 362
Coages, Samuel - w 8, p 312
Coale, James - w 10, p 362
Coale, Nancy - w 10, p 395
Coats, Jeremiah - w 3, p 139
Coats, Mathias - w 10, p 372
Coats, William - w 2, p 70
Coby, Archibald - w 11, p 421
Cockey, Cato - w 3, p 151
Cockey, Ellen - w 4, p 210
Cohwell, Jerry - w 8, p 312
Coker, Abner - w 3, p 147
Colbert, Leonard - w 1, p 22
Colburn, Lear - w 1, p 22
Cole, Deby - w 12, p 453
Cole, Diana - w 2, p 59
Cole, Philip - w 8, p 295
Cole, Phosby - w 3, p 125
Cole, Prince - w 12, p 488
Cole, Sarah - w 3, p 153
Coleman, John - w 11, p 407
Coleman, Sarah - w 10, p 361
Colle, Heger? - w 8, p 290
Colliner, William - w 10, p 387
Collins, Ellen - w 10, p 361
Collins, Harriet - w 2, p 57
Collins, John - w 12, - w p, p 513
Colman, Adam - w 8, p 312
Colvin, Charles - w 12, p 470
Colvin, Ennals - w 2, p 52
Colvin, Thomas - w 2, p 56
Comegys, Philip - w 12, p 513
Comodore, Richard - w 12, p 502

Comodore, Richard - w 10, p 361
Coney, Lloyd - w 11, p 407
Coney, William - w 1, p 10
Conklin, Mary - w 12, p 460
Conleway, Eliza - w 8, p 297
Cook, Andrew - w 12, p 458
Cook, Charles - w 11, p 414
Cook, Delia - w 11, p 424
Cook, Dinah - w 11, p 403
Cook, Henry - w 4, p 204
Cook, Mark - w 10, p 385
Cook, Nathan - w 12, p 502
Cook, Precil - w 8, p 295
Cook, Thomas - w 12, p 470
Cook, Thomas - w 12, p 499
Cook, William - w 3, p 127
Cooley, Robert - w 3, p 139
Cooly, Warick ? - w 10, p 394
Cooper, Benjamin - w 3, p 131
Cooper, Benjamin - w 3, p 138
Cooper, Benjamin - w 8, p 312
Cooper, Hannah - w 2, p 84
Cooper, Henry - w 12, p 523
Cooper, Isaac - w 12, p 470
Cooper, James - w 1, p 11
Cooper, Perry - w 3, p 123
Cooper, Richard - w 1, p 12
Cooper, Thomas - w 1, p 10
Cooper, Thomas - w 2, p 46
Cooper, Thomas - w 3, p 113
Cooper, William - w 4, p 186
Copper, Isaac - w 3, p 115
Cornish, Edward - w 2, p 68
Cornish, Jacob - w 1, p 18
Corrhes, Jenac - w 8, p 313
Corrnack, Joel - w 3, p 116
Cotter, Milly - w 10, p 362
Cotton, Daniel - w 12, p 447
Coulson, Jane - w 8, p 307
Coursey, Ann - w 12, p 449
Coursey, Edward - w 8, p 291

Chapter 15

Baltimore Census of 1830 - Free Blacks

Coursey, George - w 12, p 465
Coursey, Wilson - w 12, p 500
Cox, Benjamin - w 12, p 453
Cox, Charlotte - w 3, p 133
Cox, Thomas - w 2, p 88
Coxton, Sarah - w 4, p 170
Craig, George - w 2, p 61
Crawford, Rachel - w 10, p 364
Crawford, William - w 12, p 504
Crayerafit, Sarah - w 10, p 367
Creek, Richard - w 4, p 193
Creighton, James - w 1, p 8
Crew, Edward - w 12, p 477
Cristman, Calart - w 8, p 298
Cromwell, Gabriel - w 4, p 180
Cromwell, George - w 11, p 403
Cromwell, Mary Ann - w 5, p 236
Crook, Moses - w 4, p 213
Cross, John - w 12, p 511
Crowart, Perry - w 6, p 263
Crummel, Caleb - w 8, p 290
Crunk, Ceaser - w 5, p 231
Cuff, John - w 2, p 51
Cumford, Cumford - w 10, p 392
Cummings, John - w 8, p 307
Cummins, James - w 2, p 76
Cure, Daniel - w 12, p 481
Cure, Rachael - w 12, p 492
Curnes, William - w 8, p 299
Curry, John - w 2, p 79
Curry, Rachael - w 3, p 105
Curtis, Clement - w 9, p 338
Curtis, Henry - w 10, p 361
Curtis, Richard - w 5, p 225
Dailey, Richard - w 10, p 361
Dalph, Basil - w 3, p 119
Dansbury, Wrightson - w 12, p 516
Darby, Myer - w 10, p 395
Darling, Mary - w 11, p 419
Dask, Francis - w 12, p 523
Dauden, Michael - w 1, p 6

Daugenfield, David - w 3, p 154
Davidge, John - w 12, p 463
Davis, Ann - w 8, p 313
Davis, Betsy - w 11, p 406
Davis, Elizabeth - w 7, p 284
Davis, Fanny - w 10, p 371
Davis, Francis - w 2, p 81
Davis, Francis - w 5, p 220
Davis, Isabela - w 10, p 350
Davis, Jacob - w 3, p 155
Davis, James - w 1, p 17
Davis, John - w 2, p 52
Davis, Joseph - w 3, p 137
Davis, Lewis - w 10, p 364
Davis, Maria - w 4, p 185
Davis, Robert - w 8, p 291
Davis, Samuel - w 2, p 79
Davis, William - w 1, p 5
Davis, William - w 9, p 347
Davis, William - w 11, p 405
Dawes, Fanney - w 10, p 362
Dawkins, Robert - w 11, p 405
Dawson, Henny - w 2, p 71
Deaver, James - w 3, p 132
Deboughy, Joseph - w 3, p 118
DeHaire, Magdalen - w 12, p 444
Delas, David - w 12, p 507
Denby, John - w 3, p 155
Denby, Richard - w 3, p 107
Denison, Sam - w 8, p 307
Denney, Rady - w 10, p 363
Dennis, Peter - w 4, p 195
Denny, Henry - w 9, p 339
Denny, Samuel - w 3, p 119
Depen, Nicholas - w 12, p 513
Detter, Joseph - w 2, p 63
Devine, Amy - w 3, p 157
Dickenson, Dan - w 8, p 306
Dickerson, Richard - w 3, p 132
Dickerson, Richard - w 8, p 312
Dickinson, James - w 8, p 307

The Baltimore Census of 1830: The Free Black Population

Baltimore Census of 1830 - Free Blacks

Dickinson, Maria - w 7, p 279
Dickinson, William - w 2, p 72
Dickson, Henry - w 12, p 502
Dickson, James - w 4, p 203
Dickson, Mary - w 11, p 404
Dickson, Phillis - w 2, p 61
Dickson, Samuel - w 4, p 203
Dickson, Wesley - w 11, p 421
Diggs, Charles - w 12, p 447
Diggs, George - w 12, p 520
Diggs, James - w 12, p 495
Diggs, William - w 12, p 507
Dillin, Sarah - w 2, p 65
Dinkey, Ann - w 8, p 292
Distance, Hetty - w 12, p 445
Distance, William - w 11, p 411
Distence, Josias - w 3, p 157
Divincare, Darby? - w 10, p 373
Divine, Rosana - w 2, p 57
Dixson, James - w 3, p 145
Dixson, James - w 3, p 145
Dixson, Perry - w 3, p 152
Dixson, Perry - w 3, p 156
Dixson, Valentine - w 3, p 129
Dode, Peter - w 5, p 230
Doiles, Peter - w 8, p 316
Doldin, Robert - w 5, p 224
Dompson, Sam - w 8, p 321
Donaldson, Dianna - w 3, p 125
Done, John - w 3, p 158
Donge, John - w 3, p 132
Donnell, James - w 4, p 185
Dorkins, Diana - w 2, p 75
Dorsey, Ben - w 12, p 518
Dorsey, Charles - w 11, p 404
Dorsey, Daniel - w 2, p 69
Dorsey, Edward - w 3, p 123
Dorsey, Emory - w 8, p 295
Dorsey, Grace - w 3, p 145
Dorsey, Henry - w 9, p 335
Dorsey, Henry - w 12, p 506

Dorsey, Isaac - w 2, p 77
Dorsey, James - w 2, p 74
Dorsey, Lucinda - w 4, p 186
Dorsey, Martha - w 12, p 520
Dorsey, Mary - w 9, p 336
Dorsey, Norris - w 3, p 153
Dorsey, Robert - w 3, p 124
Dorsey, Susan - w 9, p 339
Dorsley, Domingo - w 1, p 20
Dosson, John Joseph - w 5, p 239
Douglas, Casper - w 12, p 490
Douglass, George - w 8, p 320
Douglass, Maria - w 12, p 457
Douglass, Thomas - w 11, p 427
Douglass, William - w 8, p 319
Douton, Lydia - w 7, p 275
Dowden, Levi - w 3, p 135
Dowden, Nicholas - w 3, p 153
Dowden, Solomon - w 3, p 132
Dowdon, Perry - w 8, p 312
Downey, Robert - w 2, p 88
Downing, John - w 11, p 432
Draper, Garretson - w 4, p 196
Draper, Reland - w 3, p 121
Drummer, Elizabeth - w 2, p 76
Drummon, Perry - w 12, p 489
Drummond, Evan - w 9, p 343
Ducker, Peter - w 10, p 350
Duckett, Francis - w 11, p 424
Duckmond, Fanny - w 7, p 271
Duffy, Abraham - w 1, p 30
Dukhard, Peter - w 10, p 364
Dunbar, Charles - w 11, p 430
Dunbrook, Henry - w 2, p 47
Dunmore, Jacob - w 12, p 446
Dunn, Charles - w 3, p 146
Dunn, George W. - w 8, p 313
Dunn, Susana - w 8, p 313
Durand, Benjamin - w 4, p 170
Durham, Julia - w 4, p 205
Dyer, Martha - w 2, p 67

Chapter 15

Baltimore Census of 1830 - Free Blacks

Dyne, Ney - w 11, p 401
Ears, Henry - w 4, p 211
Ebram, Thomas - w 8, p 313
Eddicks, Jarnett - w 11, p 401
Edmondson, Francis - w 5, p 232
Edward, Nathan - w 2, p 77
Edwards, John - w 12, p 498
Edwards, Nicholas - w 2, p 43
Edwards, William - w 10, p 371
Effort, Henry - w 11, p 408
Elberd, Leters - w 8, p 313
Ellen, Sarah - w 1, p 5
Elliot, Samuel - w 12, p 493
Elliott, David - w 2, p 78
Elliott, William - w 2, p 71
Ellis, Elizabeth - w 3, p 132
Ellis, James - w 2, p 50
Ellison, Nathan - w 1, p 30
Ellison, Thomas - w 2, p 88
Elsbury, Charles - w 2, p 51
Elsey, Robert - w 2, p 809
Emonerson, Charlotte - w 3, p 128
Emory, Richard - w 4, p 182
Enderson, Harris - w 8, p 319
Ennals, John - w 2, p 62
Ennals, William - w 2, p 71
Ennis, Benjamin - w 8, p 307
Ennis, Jane - w 2, p 84
Ennis, William - w 12, p 504
Ermy, John - w 12, p 507
Ervine, Peter - w 10, p 382
Euza, Jane - w 3, p 124
Evans, James - w 3, p 132
Evans, James - w 3, p 155
Evans, Nathan - w 12, p 446
Everett, Joseph - w 3, p 156
Farrell, Absolem - w 3, p 147
Farrell, Louis - w 3, p 143
Fartrow, William - w 11, p 404
Featis, Joseph - w 8, p 317
Fernandiz, John - w 2, p 40

Feushet, John - w 12, p 448
Field, Anna - w 9, p 342
Finder, James - w 9, p 342
Fingles, Matilda - w 2, p 89
Fisher, Becker - w 12, p 510
Fisher, Levin - w 3, p 141
Fisher, Sarah - w 12, p 463
Fisher, Tobias - w 11, p 427
Flamee, Nancy - w 4, p 169
Fleetwood, Benjamin - w 10, p 364
Fleetwood, Thomas - w 3, p 124
Flood, Lilly - w 3, p 142
Foot, Bazil - w 3, p 137
Foot, Easter - w 12, p 501
Foot, Rachel - w 4, p 184
Ford, Caroline - w 1, p 12
Ford, Washington - w 10, p 358
Ford, William - w 3, p 131
Foreman, Milly - w 2, p 82
Foreman, Stephen - w 10, p 361
Fortune, John - w 2, p 61
Forty, Harriet - w 10, p 391
Forty, Henry - w 10, p 391
Forty, John - w 3, p 135
Foster, Perry - w 12, p 501
Foulam, Richard - w 8, p 319
Fowler, Easter - w 11, p 430
Fowler, Leonard - w 8, p 295
Fox, Campton - w 3, p 132
Frances, John - w 12, p 445
Francis, George - w 10, p 373
Francis, Mary M. - w 10, p 358
Francis, Perry - w 12, p 517
Francisco, Camilia - w 2, p 74
Francois, Mary - w 11, p 439
Franklin, Thomas - w 11, p 402
Free, Charles - w 11, p 402
Freeman, Henry - w 3, p 133
Freeman, Hesther - w 2, p 70
Freeman, Isaac - w 11, p 405
Freeman, Nancy - w 3, p 133

The Baltimore Census of 1830: The Free Black Population

Baltimore Census of 1830 - Free Blacks

Freeman, Samuel - w 12, p 510
Freeman, Sophia - w 8, p 296
French, Lucretia - w 9, p 344
Frisbey, George - w 8, p 307
Frisby, Charles - w 3, p 132
Frisby, Emanuel - w 3, p 139
Frisby, Richard - w 5, p 225
Frisby, Terry - w 5, p 225
Fullard, Widow - w 10, p 352
Fuller, Clare - w 12, p 518
Fuller, Thomas - w 10, p 354
Gage, Dina - w 7, p 269
Gale, Isaac - w 2, p 69
Gale, John - w 1, p 6
Gale, Joseph - w 1, p 5
Gallin, John - w 11, p 402
Gamble, Peter - w 12, p 486
Gannard, James - w 1, p 26
Gannon, Nelly - w 11, p 401
Gansey, Joseph - w 4, p 211
Gardener, Christopher - w 6, p 249
Gardner, Benjamin - w 12, p 489
Garnet, Michael - w 10, p 375
Garrat, Debora - w 10, p 373
Garreson, Honor - w 12, p 448
Garret, John - w 12, p 512
Garret, William - w 3, p 146
Garretson, Freeborn - w 2, p 40
Garretson, Wesley - w 4, p 212
Garrett, Richard - w 12, p 455
Garrison, Ralph - w 3, p 152
Gaser, Catherine - w 12, p 512
George, Franklin - w 8, p 296
Gibbs, Jacob - w 3, p 135
Gibbs, Nancy - w 12, p 484
Gibson, Affa - w 3, p 107
Gibson, Basil - w 11, p 431
Gibson, David - w 11, p 408
Gibson, Delila - w 4, p 186
Gibson, Jacob - w 11, p 419
Gibson, Joseph - w 10, p 374

Gibson, Philip - w 3, p 135
Gibson, Pompey - w 1, p 10
Gibson, Richard - w 12, p 452
Gibson, Robert - w 11, p 405
Gibson, Sam - w 8, p 313
Gibson, William - w 11, p 438
Gibson, William - w 12, p 453
Gids, William - w 2, p 62
Gilbert, Asbury - w 2, p 37
Gilbert, Peter - w 10, p 357
Gilbert, William - w 2, p 70
Giles, Gray - w 11, p 403
Gilles, Ann - w 10, p 361
Gilyard, Nicholas - w 4, p 213
Gist, Jacob - w 2, p 54
Gland, Milly - w 11, p 436
Goaden, Thomas - w 10, p 370
Gocen, Joline - w 3, p 132
Gocen, Peter - w 3, p 132
Godman, Pudy - w 12, p 474
Going, James - w 3, p 137
Golden, William - w 12, p 452
Goldsborough, Charles - w 2, p 64
Goldsborough, Richard - w 1, p 10
Goldsborough, Robert - w 1, p 18
Goldsbury, Perry - w 2, p 78
Good, Richard - w 2, p 56
Gott, Priscilla - w 2, p 42
Gough, Frances A. - w 3, p 134
Gough, Richard - w 1, p 11
Gough, Samuel - w 11, p 438
Gould, John - w 12, p 473
Gould, Robert - w 12, p 495
Goulding, Jerry - w 11, p 430
Gounds, Hanna - w 8, p 307
Govan, Daniel - w 3, p 131
Grace, Samuel - w 9, p 340
Grace, William - w 12, p 493
Grain, Rebecca - w 5, p 222
Gran, Rebeca? - w 8, p 303
Grandison, Charles - w 3, p 135

Chapter 15

Baltimore Census of 1830 - Free Blacks

Granger, Stephen - w 3, p 144
Grant, Charles - w 12, p 497
Grant, Rabaca ? - w 8, p 315
Grant, Thomas - w 3, p 154
Granwood, Ellen - w 12, p 492
Grasell, John - w 8, p 320
Grason, Elizabeth - w 4, p 180
Gratefull, John - w 10, p 370
Graut, Charles - w 3, p 152
Graves, Barney - w 12, p 474
Graves, David - w 12, p 486
Graw, Sarah - w 3, p 123
Gray, David - w 11, p 405
Gray, James - w 10, p 394
Gray, Jerry - w 12, p 474
Gray, John - w 10, p 370
Gray, Levin - w 3, p 123
Gray, Rachel - w 4, p 195
Gray, Richard - w 12, p 520
Gray, Robert - w 2, p 57
Gray, Samuel - w 11, p 407
Gray, Sarah - w 9, p 346
Gray, William - w 8, p 317
Greaner, Jacob - w 11, p 418
Green, Cassandra - w 4, p 193
Green, Charles - w 2, p 74
Green, Heslip - w 12, p 513
Green, John - w 2, p 77
Green, Nanky - w 12, p 489
Green, Richard - w 7, p 269
Green, Sophia - w 1, p 5
Green, Thomas - w 7, p 281
Green, Tritto - w 10, p 392
Green, William - w 10, p 396
Greenfield, Darcus - w 2, p 46
Greenwood, Henry - w 11, p 406
Greenwood, Isaac - w 8, p 294
Greenwood, Perregrin - w 2, p 56
Greenwood, Richard - w 8, p 307
Grice, Hezekiah - w 3, p 154
Gridon, Benjamin - w 2, p 85

Griffin, Alexander - w 11, p 406
Griffin, Calem - w 8, p 319
Griffin, Cuffi - w 10, p 395
Griffin, George - w 3, p 132
Griffin, Henry - w 11, p 402
Griffin, Jacob - w 2, p 62
Griffin, Maria - w 9, p 326
Griffin, Susan - w 11, p 429
Griffin, William - w 8, p 299
Griffith, Henney - w 10, p 363
Griffith, Peter - w 11, p 429
Griffith, Susan - w 4, p 179
Grimes, Fielding - w 12, p 492
Groom, Emery - w 3, p 137
Groome, Thomas - w 10, p 363
Grooms, Nathan - w 4, p 215
Grooms, William - w 12, p 502
Gross, Benjamin - w 12, p 474
Gross, Clarissa - w 2, p 85
Gross, Cornelius - w 12, p 502
Gross, Henry - w 8, p 292
Gross, James - w 8, p 291
Gross, Philip - w 8, p 290
Gross, Rachael - w 12, p 452
Groves, Henry - w 3, p 140
Groves, Mary - w 3, p 153
Grumage, Thomas - w 3, p 154
Gruner, Richard - w 3, p 144
Guilliard, Charlotte - w 11, p 429
Gustis, Abraham - w 2, p 86
Gustis, Vinson - w 2, p 63
Gwin, James - w 3, p 112
Gwinn, Charles - w 3, p 136
Gwinn, William - w 3, p 159
Hacket, Charles - w 3, p 137
Hacket, John - w 2, p 87
Hacket, Philip - w 3, p 141
Hackett, George A. - w 6, p 261
Hackney, Marey ? - w 10, p 380
Hagar, Cito ? - w 11, p 405
Hains, Thomas - w 12, p 512

The Baltimore Census of 1830: The Free Black Population

Baltimore Census of 1830 - Free Blacks

Hake, Frisby - w 6, p 260
Haldan, James - w 10, p 356
Hale, Edward - w 12, p 480
Hale, Jacob - w 12, p 455
Hale, John - w 12, p 445
Hale, Levin - w 12, p 456
Haley, Alexander - w 2, p 62
Hall, Aaron - w 12, p 500
Hall, Aaron - w 12, p 512
Hall, Amos - w 11, p 438
Hall, Ann Carlos - w 3, p 110
Hall, Arthur - w 3, p 109
Hall, Charles - w 12, p 503
Hall, Edward - w 2, p 86
Hall, Eliza - w 12, p 487
Hall, Francis - w 12, p 510
Hall, Grace - w 2, p 55
Hall, James - w 12, p 473
Hall, John - w 11, p 403
Hall, John - w 11, p 429
Hall, Joseph - w 4, p 199
Hall, Kitty - w 6, p 262
Hall, Mordecai - w 1, p 5
Hall, Moses - w 12, p 512
Hall, Pattie - w 10, p 361
Hall, Sarah - w 2, p 83
Hall, Thomas - w 1, p 29
Hall, Thomas - w 4, p 183
Hall, William - w 12, p 522
Hamilton, Sara - w 8, p 319
Hammer, Jacob - w 2, p 79
Hammon, John - w 12, p 480
Hammond, George - w 2, p 71
Hammond, James - w 11, p 440
Hampleton, Patrick - w 11, p 426
Hance, William - w 3, p 138
Handensay, Fred? - w 8, p 314
Handy, Ephriam - w 4, p 210
Handy, Priestman - w 1, p 8
Hannoser, Southern - w 3, p 157
Hanson, Abigal - w 3, p 133

Hanson, Crasey - w 8, p 292
Hanson, David - w 7, p 271
Hanson, James - w 8, p 312
Hanson, Phoebe - w 12, p 474
Hardcastle, Ann A. - w 4, p 170
Harden, Bazil - w 3, p 133
Harden, Jacob - w 4, p 211
Harden, James - w 3, p 110
Harden, John W. - w 12, p 489
Harden, John? - w 10, p 356
Harden, Lucy - w 12, p 486
Harden, Mathew - w 12, p 489
Harden, Phipitt ? - w 11, p 406
Harden, Thomas - w 3, p 153
Hardin, R. - w 7, p 269
Hardy, Abraham - w 3, p 120
Hardy, Fanny - w 11, p 405
Hardy, Kitty - w 11, p 405
Hardy, Samuel - w 12, p 497
Harman, Stephen - w 3, p 151
Harmon, Paul - w 2, p 71
Harper, Jane - w 2, p 86
Harrand, Mathew? - w 9, p 338
Harrard, Henry - w 2, p 61
Harris, Ann - w 12, p 463
Harris, Caesar - w 12, p 513
Harris, Cecelia - w 3, p 136
Harris, Danniel - w 2, p 42
Harris, Edward - w 2, p 77
Harris, George - w 3, p 143
Harris, Harriott - w 3, p 154
Harris, Henry - w 11, p 405
Harris, Indianna - w 3, p 139
Harris, Jacob - w 10, p 371
Harris, Jacob - w 11, p 403
Harris, James - w 11, p 404
Harris, James - w 11, p 417
Harris, John - w 11, p 412
Harris, Joseph - w 3, p 154
Harris, Lucretia - w 11, p 436
Harris, Martin - w 4, p 187

Chapter 15

Baltimore Census of 1830 - Free Blacks

Harris, N. - w 6, p 259
Harris, Nelson - w 1, p 6
Harris, Rachael - w 12, p 499
Harris, Robert - w 3, p 125
Harris, Stephen - w 3, p 153
Harris, Theodore - w 3, p 125
Harris, Thomas - w 10, p 360
Harris, Tiny - w 12, p 502
Harris, William - w 1, p 14
Harrison, Charles - w 5, p 239
Harrison, John - w 10, p 364
Harrison, Joseph - w 10, p 386
Harrison, Phillip - w 2, p 58
Harrison, Will - w 8, p 291
Harrison, William - w 8, p 293
Harrod, Elijah - w 11, p 408
Harrod, William - w 12, p 505
Haward, Edward ? - w 10, p 361
Hawkings, Benjamin - w 8, p 297
Hawkins, Fredrick - w 2, p 77
Hawkins, James - w 11, p 401
Hawkins, James - w 12, p 493
Hawkins, Mr. - w 11, p 403
Hawkins, Peter - w 11, p 408
Hawkins, Stephen - w 3, p 132
Hays, Cato - w 10, p 364
Hayward, Isaac - w 2, p 63
Hayward, Rachel - w 5, p 234
Heaby, Ann - w 8, p 295
Heath, Lucy - w 9, p 345
Heath, Mark - w 8, p 307
Hebrews, William - w 1, p 11
Hedges, Charles - w 3, p 134
Heiser, Jacob - w 2, p 92
Hemsley, Henry - w 3, p 122
Henderson, John - w 12, p 485
Henry, Charlottee - w 2, p 60
Henry, James - w 6, p 260
Henson, David - w 7, p 269
Henson, Emory - w 5, p 240
Henson, Jacob - w 10, p 387

Henson, James - w 3, p 128
Henson, James - w 5, p 225
Henson, James - w 10, p 381
Henson, John - w 7, p 268
Henson, Rachael - w 3, p 132
Herbert, Elizabeth - w 3, p 135
Hewit, Daniel - w 12, p 471
Hickey, E. - w 7, p 268
Hicks, Emanuel - w 9, p 341
High, James - w 5, p 239
Higins, Jeremiah - w 12, p 489
Hilburn, Samuel - w 11, p 438
Hill, Ann - w 12, p 504
Hill, Charles - w 3, p 139
Hill, Easter - w 11, p 402
Hill, Edward - w 2, p 64
Hill, Henrietta - w 3, p 128
Hill, James - w 12, p 500
Hill, Joshua - w 3, p 112
Hill, Sarah - w 3, p 151
Hill, Susana - w 8, p 319
Hill, Thomas - w 9, p 339
Hillirt, Thomas - w 11, p 436
Hills, Margaret - w 2, p 86
Hinson, Joseph - w 2, p 88
Hinson, Joseph - w 3, p 133
Hinson, Joshua - w 10, p 350
Hinson, Nace - w 11, p 408
Hinson, Patty - w 2, p 80
Hinson, Sally - w 10, p 369
Hithe, Hester - w 2, p 52
Hoeard, William - w 3, p 154
Holaday, Rachel - w 10, p 362
Holaday, Richard - w 2, p 59
Hold, Peter - w 10, p 393
Holiday, James - w 2, p 65
Holland, Denby - w 9, p 347
Holland, Frank - w 6, p 260
Holland, Henry - w 12, p 502
Holland, James - w 2, p 48
Holland, Milly - w 11, p 403

The Baltimore Census of 1830: The Free Black Population

Baltimore Census of 1830 - Free Blacks

Hollang, Philip - w 8, p 295
Holliday, Benjamin - w 12, p 447
Hollins, Joseph - w 12, p 497
Hollins, Walter - w 8, p 316
Hollis, David - w 3, p 132
Hollowday, Ann - w 4, p 192
Hollowday, Barney - w 4, p 211
Hollowday, James - w 4, p 197
Hood, Ruth - w 11, p 438
Hooker, Tobias - w 3, p 134
Hooper, Harriott - w 4, p 183
Hooper, Isaac - w 3, p 137
Hooper, Jacob - w 9, p 347
Hooper, Stephen - w 11, p 401
Horace, Hannah - w 3, p 146
Horsey, James - w 2, p 80
Horval, Dennis - w 12, p 513
How, Robert - w 2, p 83
How, William - w 2, p 59
Howard, Charles - w 12, p 513
Howard, Chloe - w 6, p 259
Howard, Edward - w 8, p 301
Howard, Emanuel - w 9, p 346
Howard, George - w 2, p 72
Howard, James - w 4, p 192
Howard, James - w 10, p 357
Howard, James - w 12, p 499
Howard, Lucky - w 12, p 474
Howard, Mary - w 11, p 403
Howard, Milky - w 4, p 211
Howard, Nicholas - w 3, p 135
Howard, Philip - w 5, p 240
Howard, Rachael - w 12, p 487
Howard, Samuel - w 4, p 183
Howard, Samuel - w 10, p 361
Howard, Samuel - w 12, p 497
Howard, Sarah - w 12, p 485
Howard, Susan - w 11, p 406
Howden, Harris - w 12, p 518
Howe, Samuel - w 1, p 13
Hudson, William - w 1, p 16

Huges, Janes - w 8, p 296
Hughe, Simon - w 1, p 20
Hughes, Jesse - w 3, p 99
Hughes, Sophia - w 3, p 112
Hughs, Jonas - w 1, p 10
Hull, Elizabeth - w 2, p 54
Hunt, John - w 8, p 307
Hurst, Shedrick - w 10, p 373
Hutchens, Samuel - w 12, p 522
Hutchins, Alexander - w 3, p 136
Hutchins, Isaac - w 3, p 157
Hutchinson, Joseph - w 10, p 358
Hutchson, Mary - w 3, p 129
Ingroin, William - w 12, p 504
Inloes, Samuel - w 12, p 496
Inpy, Jacob - w 2, p 56
Ireland, Harriet - w 10, p 353
Irorn, David - w 2, p 93
Irvin, Edward - w 3, p 142
Isaacs, Farro - w 5, p 226
Jackson, Abraham - w 11, p 404
Jackson, Agnes - w 10, p 377
Jackson, Ann - w 4, p 211
Jackson, Delila - w 2, p 83
Jackson, Dianna - w 2, p 64
Jackson, Dorcas - w 9, p 332
Jackson, Fredrick - w 3, p 134
Jackson, James - w 1, p 16
Jackson, James - w 11, p 405
Jackson, James - w 12, p 481
Jackson, Joseph - w 3, p 148
Jackson, Martha - w 9, p 346
Jackson, Mary - w 12, p 473
Jackson, Nace - w 11, p 401
Jackson, Ra?leus - w 12, p 510
Jackson, Sarah - w 9, p 338
Jackson, Teny - w 2, p 51
Jackson, Thomas - w 12, p 500
Jackson, Widow - w 10, p 382
Jackson, William - w 2, p 54
Jackson, William - w 11, p 401

Chapter 15

Baltimore Census of 1830 - Free Blacks

Jacobs, Elias - w 10, p 363
Jacobs, Nathan - w 12, p 472
Jake, Frederick - w 10, p 355
Jamarson, George - w 8, p 293
James, Mary - w 3, p 104
James, Peter - w 2, p 70
James, Robert - w 12, p 453
James, Samuel - w 11, p 437
Janey, Anthony - w 8, p 295
Janny, Munday - w 12, p 523
Jaro, Blade - w 10, p 354
Jarvis, Ormon - w 8, p 313
Jefferis, Mingo - w 3, p 123
Jefferson, Isaac - w 4, p 192
Jefferson, Philip - w 10, p 369
Jenkins, Ellen - w 12, p 455
Jenkins, George - w 3, p 157
Jenkins, Margaret - w 3, p 112
Jenkins, Rebeca - w 10, p 358
Jenkins, Samuel - w 2, p 63
Jenkins, William - w 3, p 134
Jenney, Theresa - w 4, p 179
Jennings, Thomas - w 12, p 507
Jerome, George - w 11, p 402
Johndire, Arren ? - w 8, p 313
Johns, William - w 1, p 21
Johnson, Caleb - w 12, p 460
Johnson, Dan - w 8, p 315
Johnson, Eli - w 10, p 361
Johnson, Francis - w 3, p 132
Johnson, Francis - w 12, p 513
Johnson, George P. - w 12, p 451
Johnson, Harriot - w 12, p 450
Johnson, Henry - w 1, p 13
Johnson, Henry - w 5, p 236
Johnson, Isaac - w 8, p 300
Johnson, Isaac - w 12, p 448
Johnson, Jacob - w 5, p 225
Johnson, James - w 12, p 515
Johnson, Job - w 12, p 471
Johnson, John - w 10, p 361

Johnson, Joseph - w 9, p 339
Johnson, Joseph - w 10, p 357
Johnson, Kitty - w 9, p 343
Johnson, Mary - w 3, p 158
Johnson, Mary - w 12, p 493
Johnson, Math ? - w 8, p 312
Johnson, Matthias - w 1, p 4
Johnson, Michael - w 8, p 319
Johnson, Milky - w 3, p 133
Johnson, Moses - w 9, p 339
Johnson, Phoebe - w 12, p 521
Johnson, Rachael - w 3, p 158
Johnson, Rachael - w 12, p 508
Johnson, Rachel - w 3, p 139
Johnson, Rachel - w 3, p 139
Johnson, Rebecca - w 3, p 131
Johnson, Richard - w 3, p 133
Johnson, Richard - w 12, p 472
Johnson, Richard - w 12, p 477
Johnson, Robert - w 5, p 240
Johnson, Robert - w 9, p 344
Johnson, Robert - w 12, p 460
Johnson, Samuel - w 9, p 344
Johnson, Samuel - w 12, p 517
Johnson, Severn - w 12, p 513
Johnson, Solomon - w 12, p 495
Johnson, Solomon - w 12, p 510
Johnson, Sophia - w 3, p 159
Johnson, Stephen - w 12, p 484
Johnson, Susan - w 7, p 269
Johnson, Thomas - w 12, p 492
Johnson, William - w 4, p 214
Johnson, William - w 9, p 345
Johnson, William - w 12, p 473
Johnson, James - w 4, p 174
Johnson, Mary - w 7, p 269
Johnston, C. - w 10, p 390
Johnston, Cary - w 11, p 407
Johnston, Cator - w 2, p 84
Johnston, Charles - w 2, p 56
Johnston, Charles - w 2, p 61

Baltimore Census of 1830 - Free Blacks

Johnston, Charles - w 10, p 385
Johnston, Charlote - w 11, p 424
Johnston, E. - w 19, p 390
Johnston, Eli - w 11, p 424
Johnston, Elizabeth - w 3, p 143
Johnston, Emmanuel - w 2, p 67
Johnston, George - w 3, p 120
Johnston, Gustus - w 11, p 437
Johnston, Hardesty - w 2, p 67
Johnston, Henney - w 10, p 374
Johnston, Henry - w 3, p 141
Johnston, James - w 2, p 63
Johnston, James - w 11, p 439
Johnston, Jerry - w 11, p 424
Johnston, John - w 2, p 74
Johnston, John - w 3, p 155
Johnston, John - w 10, p 370
Johnston, Mary - w 2, p 79
Johnston, Mary - w 11, p 401
Johnston, Moses - w 4, p 177
Johnston, Nathan - w 2, p 64
Johnston, Nicholas - w 2, p 61
Johnston, Peter - w 2, p 78
Johnston, Peter - w 11, p 402
Johnston, Rachal - w 11, p 432
Johnston, Risden - w 2, p 58
Johnston, Ruth - w 10, p 359
Johnston, Samuel - w 4, p 171
Johnston, Samuel - w 10, p 385
Johnston, Silvy - w 2, p 50
Johnston, Thomas - w 10, p 363
Johnston, Thomas - w 11, p 424
Johnston, William - w 2, p 63
Johnston, William - w 11, p 410
Jones, (not indicated) - w 12, p 473
Jones, Adam - w 12, p 522
Jones, Amos - w 3, p 133
Jones, Andrew - w 3, p 136
Jones, Benjamin - w 3, p 124
Jones, Benjamin - w 3, p 157
Jones, Betty - w 3, p 112

Jones, Capius - w 3, p 124
Jones, Charles - w 5, p 232
Jones, Charlotta - w 12, p 503
Jones, David - w 12, p 494
Jones, Ely - w 2, p 67
Jones, Francis - w 5, p 231
Jones, Francis - w 11, p 427
Jones, Francis Jr. - w 5, p 231
Jones, George - w 8, p 300
Jones, George - w 11, p 402
Jones, Gracey - w 2, p 47
Jones, Gracy - w 8, p 321
Jones, Henrry - w 2, p 63
Jones, Henry - w 3, p 141
Jones, Isaac - w 11, p 401
Jones, Isaac - w 11, p 401
Jones, Iseral - w 3, p 137
Jones, Jacob - w 3, p 145
Jones, Jacob - w 4, p 171
Jones, Jacob - w 11, p 410
Jones, James - w 12, p 502
Jones, Jonas - w 8, p 298
Jones, Joseph - w 3, p 124
Jones, Joseph - w 10, p 392
Jones, Lewis - w 1, p 30
Jones, Martha - w 11, p 429
Jones, Richard - w 1, p 16
Jones, Richard - w 12, p 518
Jones, Robert - w 1, p 18
Jones, Robert - w 3, p 128
Jones, Samuel - w 10, p 372
Jones, Sarah - w 4, p 167
Jones, Steven - w 10, p 382
Jones, Thomas - w 1, p 14
Jones, Thomas - w 2, p 91
Jones, Thomas - w 11, p 437
Jones, Veney - w 10, p 363
Jones, W. S. - w 8, p 296
Jones, William - w 10, p 383
Jorden, John - w 3, p 135
Josse, Anthony - w 2, p 81

Chapter 15

Baltimore Census of 1830 - Free Blacks

Julious, Massy - w 2, p 69
Kant, Charles - w 10, p 387
Keener, Peter - w 11, p 417
Kelly, Andrew - w 11, p 440
Kelly, William - w 11, p 406
Kelso, Philip - w 12, p 514
Kennard, Nicholas - w 2, p 79
Kennard, William - w 2, p 85
Kent, Isaac - w 2, p 77
Kent, Samuel - w 2, p 78
Kent, William - w 2, p 78
Kerral, William - w 10, p 384
Kerz, William - w 8, p 313
Kestely, Hesther - w 2, p 63
Keys, John - w 2, p 77
Keys, John - w 8, p 290
Keys, Thomas - w 3, p 141
Kier, samuel - w 9, p 346
Kill, David - w 9, p 346
King, Arthur - w 12, p 489
King, Joseph - w 10, p 374
King, Thomas - w 3, p 155
Kist, Rachel - w 2, p 52
Kubree, S. B. ? - w 10, p 375
Labrera, Solomon - w 2, p 64
Lancaster, Evan - w 4, p 214
Landa, John - w 10, p 373
Langford, Charity - w 2, p 85
Lard, Richard - w 3, p 124
Larkins, Peter - w 3, p 136
Laurence - w 8, p 294
Law, James - w 10, p 376
Lawson, Charles - w 2, p 37
Lawson, Isaac - w 12, p 505
Lawson, Solomon - w 12, p 505
Le, Jacob - w 3, p 133
Lea, Ceaser - w 7, p 279
Lea, John - w 12, p 481
Lea, Philip - w 12, p 471
LeCourt, Adolph - w 5, p 239
Ledgewith, Rebecca - w 12, p 451

Ledgwig, Thomas - w 12, p 451
Lee, Daniel - w 12, p 506
Lee, Elizabeth - w 2, p 40
Lee, Jacob - w 1, p 8
Lee, Levin - w 3, p 153
Lee, Philip - w 11, p 401
Lee, Rachael - w 3, p 142
Lee, Rebecca - w 10, p 354
Lee, Samuel - w 3, p 135
Lee, Samuel - w 10, p 362
Lee, Spencer - w 3, p 125
Lems, Elizabeth? - w 6, p 260
Lemus, Charles - w 3, p 109
Leorance, John? - w 11, p 439
Leport, Eli - w 10, p 375
Lernarae, Al - w 3, p 113
Lernon, Susan - w 3, p 103
Levy, Sarah - w 3, p 131
Levy, Sarah - w 3, p 159
Lewis, Andrew - w 12, p 506
Lewis, Catherine - w 12, p 510
Lewis, Elisabeth - w 10, p 355
Lewis, James - w 11, p 412
Lewis, John - w 2, p 63
Lewis, John - w 6, p 256
Lewis, John - w 10, p 374
Lewis, M. - w 10, p 372
Lewis, Mary - w 2, p 46
Lewis, Richard - w 2, p 87
Lewis, Sally - w 9, p 329
Lewis, Edward - w 12, p 493
Lexey, Selvia - w 4, p 179
Lilly, Peter - w 3, p 133
Limas, Brudame - w 10, p 367
Lindenberger, J. H. - w 10, p 396
Lingan, Eliza - w 12, p 450
Linsey, David - w 3, p 132
Little, Adam - w 12, p 474
Livingston, William - w 11, p 411
Lloyd, Edward - w 2, p 50
Lloyd, John - w 9, p 337

The Baltimore Census of 1830: The Free Black Population

Baltimore Census of 1830 - Free Blacks

Lochman, Fanny - w 10, p 361
Lock, Alexander - w 10, p 369
Lock, John - w 2, p 64
Lockerman, Daniel - w 3, p 141
Lockerman, David - w 2, p 77
Locknet, Bates - w 10, p 373
Locks, Stephen - w 2, p 63
Log, Jane? - w 4, p 186
Logan, Moses - w 7, p 270
Lomax, David - w 2, p 53
Lomax, David - w 2, p 67
Lomax, David - w 2, p 73
London, James P. - w 4, p 180
Long, Caty - w 10, p 382
Lucas, James - w 12, p 506
Lucas, Thomas - w 2, p 78
Lucey, Eliza Ann - w 12, p 482
Luden, Flora - w 3, p 144
Lurdin, Jacob? - w 8, p 307
Lusby, Mary - w 6, p 261
Lynch, John - w 11, p 438
Lynch, Moses - w 6, p 260
Mackey, Aaron - w 12, p 459
Madden, George - w 12, p 499
Madden, Rachel - w 2, p 77
Madden, Samuel - w 12, p 446
Maddis, Spencer - w 9, p 344
Maddox, William - w 11, p 407
Mae, Shandy Mrs, - w 10, p 373
Magruder, Francis - w 3, p 154
Maguigan, James? - w 5, p 240
Mahur, E. ? - w 10, p 390
Maker, Minta - w 11, p 403
Malsbury, Abraham - w 2, p 87
Mana, Jesse - w 3, p 137
Mance, Jesse - w 10, p 350
Maneso, George? - w 10, p 372
Manis, Sep ? - w 12, p 459
Manos, Ed - w 12, p 454
Marey, Lester? - w 10, p 352
Marshall, George - w 11, p 437

Marshall, John - w 4, p 187
Martin, Ennels - w 1, p 12
Martin, Francis - w 1, p 12
Martin, Henry - w 9, p 342
Martin, Joshua - w 12, p 465
Martin, Mary - w 5, p 232
Martin, Nancy - w 12, p 478
Martin, Philis - w 3, p 132
Martin, Saly - w 8, p 292
Martin, William - w 2, p 85
Masain, John - w 10, p 382
Masfield, John - w 9, p 326
Masica, Trona ? - w 10, p 363
Mason, A lex - w 9, p 347
Mason, Isaac - w 3, p 138
Mason, John - w 12, p 518
Mason, Nancy - w 12, p 465
Mathewes, Mrs. ? - w 10, p 371
Mathews, Carter - w 12, p 471
Mathews, Charlotte - w 3, p 122
Mathews, Heny - w 12, p 493
Mathews, James - w 12, p 455
Mathews, Joseph - w 12, p 477
Mathews, Joshua - w 12, p 446
Mathews, Michael - w 3, p 156
Mathews, Richard - w 12, p 477
Mathews, Richard - w 12, p 481
Mathias, Richard - w 10, p 356
Mathias, Richard - w 10, p 363
Mathias, Rose - w 10, p 371
Mattax, Ann - w 3, p 107
Mattee, Alexander - w 2, p 64
Matthews, Elizabeth - w 11, p 427
Matthews, Samuel - w 11, p 402
Matthews, Sasarus - w 11, p 406
Matthews, William - w 11, p 429
Maxfield, Isaac - w 12, p 463
Maxwell, Samuel - w 6, p 257
Maybury, Mark - w 12, p 503
MCay, Robert - w 10, p 367
McCabe, Elizabeth - w 7, p 278

Chapter 15

Baltimore Census of 1830 - Free Blacks

McComas, Richard - w 3, p 135
McCubbin, Jerry - w 12, p 500
McDaniel, Nancy - w 8, p 312
McDonald, Jane - w 3, p 133
McDowney, Henry - w 2, p 78
McFarles, Edward - w 3, p 136
McGill, Sarah - w 12, p 507
McGruder, Adam - w 12, p 512
McHenry, Henry - w 11, p 402
McQuay, Richard - w 3, p 155
Meads, Harriet - w 6, p 259
Meads, Stephen - w 2, p 71
Medley, George - w 2, p 84
Meredeth, Nancy - w 11, p 439
Merson, Peter? - w 10, p 358
Middleton, Ann - w 2, p 86
Mifry, John - w 2, p 63
Milagan, Henry - w 3, p 124
Milburn, Phillip - w 2, p 66
Miles, Laransa - w 10, p 358
Miles, York - w 12, p 467
Miller, Harriet - w 9, p 343
Miller, Henney - w 10, p 377
Miller, Henry - w 3, p 124
Miller, James - w 7, p 270
Miller, James - w 11, p 403
Miller, James - w 11, p 403
Miller, John - w 3, p 160
Miller, Margaret - w 5, p 225
Miller, Mary - w 11, p 436
Mills, Elisa - w 11, p 437
Mills, Ellenore - w 3, p 148
Mills, John - w 12, p 489
Mitchel, Ann E. - w 12, p 515
Mitchel, Clay - w 12, p 474
Mitchel, James - w 2, p 72
Mitchel, Samuel - w 3, p 103
Mitchele, Cloe - w 11, p 412
Mitchell, Elijah - w 1, p 16
Mitchell, George - w 1, p 16
Mitchell, Mary - w 5, p 236

Mitchell, Priscilla - w 4, p 186
Mitchell, Robert - w 5, p 231
Mitchell, William - w 11, p 402
Mocket, A. W. - w 10, p 358
Mohon, Peter - w 2, p 77
Moles, John - w 2, p 85
Montgomery, Amos - w 2, p 77
Montgomery, John - w 2, p 88
Montgomery, Martin - w 2, p 59
Montgomery, Milly - w 2, p 59
Montgomery, Nathan - w 2, p 42
Montgomery, Nathaniel - w 1, p 24
Mooney, Joshua - w 3, p 113
Moore, Abraham - w 10, p 357
Moore, Daniel - w 11, p 406
Moore, George - w 3, p 138
Moore, Hamlet - w 2, p 64
Moore, James - w 11, p 437
Moore, Maria - w 5, p 225
Moore, Mary - w 12, p 512
Moore, Moses? - w 10, p 352
Moore, Peter - w 11, p 403
Moore, Sarah - w 10, p 381
Moore, William - w 2, p 81
Morden, Henny? - w 10, p 358
Morgan, Mary - w 5, p 232
Morris, Linda - w 10, p 362
Morris, Perry - w 10, p 350
Morris, Stephen - w 3, p 155
Morrison, Henry - w 12, p 472
Morrison, James - w 3, p 134
Morrison, John - w 3, p 158
Morrison, Rebecca - w 12, p 485
Morsall, Peter - w 8, p 295
Mosck, Phillip - w 2, p 54
Mosebury, Hannah - w 12, p 473
Moss, Cynthia - w 2, p 73
Moutoin, Eliza? - w 7, p 286
Mullen, William - w 3, p 157
Mullikin, Adam - w 2, p 63
Murphy, Moses - w 7, p 286

The Baltimore Census of 1830: The Free Black Population

Baltimore Census of 1830 - Free Blacks

Murphy, William - w 11, p 424
Murray, Aaron - w 4, p 186
Murry, Alexander - w 3, p 110
Murry, David - w 2, p 70
Murry, George - w 3, p 138
Murry, Jacob - w 2, p 59
Murry, Jane - w 7, p 284
Murry, Marey? - w 10, p 387
Murry, Robert - w 3, p 148
Murry, Samuel - w 12, p 474
Murry, William - w 10, p 396
Myers, Daniel - w 2, p 70
Myers, Edward - w 8, p 320
Myers, Henrietta - w 3, p 103
Myers, Jeremiah - w 12, p 517
Myers, Jeremiah - w 2, p 79
Myers, Nathan - w 3, p 125
Myers, Perry - w 8, p 313
Myers, Pricila - w 10, p 387
Myers, Robbert - w 2, p 67
Narren, Adam? - w 9, p 328
Nathan, William - w 3, p 125
Nathen, Daniel - w 10, p 364
Neal, Frances - w 8, p 292
Neal, John - w 1, p 4
Neal, John - w 2, p 56
Neal, John - w 10, p 383
Neal, Richard - w 8, p 306
Neale, (not indicated) - w 11, p 402
Needles, John - w 10, p 396
Neilson, Jacob - w 12, p 489
Neilson, William - w 2, p 78
Nelson, Matha - w 5, p 232
Nelson, Sarah - w 3, p 133
Newbern, John - w 2, p 84
Newel, Ellen - w 12, p 452
Newman, Jacob - w 12, p 502
Newman, Moses - w 4, p 171
Newton, Peace? - w 8, p 291
Nichols, Charles - w 11, p 407
Nichols, Flora - w 3, p 136

Nichols, George - w 11, p 410
Nichols, Jerremiah - w 2, p 61
Nichols, John - w 3, p 139
Nichols, Joseph - w 11, p 438
Nichols, Milly - w 11, p 407
Nicholson, Henry - w 4, p 214
Nordan, Lea - w 10, p 361
Norice, Jacob - w 8, p 306
Norris, Eliza - w 8, p 321
Norris, Epharam - w 10, p 370
Norris, Julia - w 4, p 208
Norris, Nas? - w 8, p 320
Norris, Patty - w 9, p 331
Norris, Richard - w 7, p 271
Nulton, Marg - w 3, p 111
Nutter, Mildred - w 8, p 320
Offer, John - w 2, p 65
Ogle, Samuel - w 3, p 147
Oliver, Henrietta - w 3, p 135
Oliver, James - w 12, p 510
Oliver, Sarah - w 10, p 375
Oliver, William - w 3, p 159
Olliver, Noah - w 2, p 62
Oram, Tobias - w 2, p 50
Oram, Tobias - w 11, p 437
Owens, Joshua - w 3, p 135
Owings, Bazil - w 12, p 490
Owings, Richard - w 12, p 489
Oxford, George - w 2, p 77
Page, Sirus - w 2, p 79
Paine, Spencer - w 1, p 9
Palmer, James - w 12, p 472
Parker, Charles - w 12, p 480
Parker, Eliza - w 8, p 319
Parker, Ellen - w 12, p 477
Parker, James - w 12, p 474
Parker, Jesse - w 3, p 160
Parker, Levy - w 2, p 66
Parker, Mary - w 12, p 482
Parker, Nicholaus - w 10, p 355
Parker, Samuel - w 10, p 358

Chapter 15

Baltimore Census of 1830 - Free Blacks

Parks, George - w 10, p 361
Parks, Lloyd - w 11, p 437
Parks, Peter - w 1, p 4
Parks, William - w 10, p 364
Parley, John - w 12, p 517
Parraway, Nicholas - w 8, p 295
Parrott, Debby - w 9, p 346
Parvil, Thomis - w 10, p 396
Pascall, Peter - w 3, p 137
Patale, Mrs. - w 10, p 373
Patterson, Adam - w 11, p 402
Patterson, Daniel - w 1, p 4
Patterson, Joshua - w 2, p 66
Patterson, William - w 12, p 481
Paunelia, Rebecca? - w 4, p 184
Paytner, Vachel - w 4, p 211
Pea, James - w 2, p 56
Peach, Samuel - w 9, p 339
Pearson, Caroline - w 11, p 432
Peck, David - w 2, p 62
Peck, John - w 4, p 215
Peck, Kitty - w 9, p 345
Peck, Lackin - w 7, p 272
Peck, Leven - w 8, p 313
Peck, Nat - w 6, p 260
Peck, Thomas - w 4, p 213
Peet, Adam? - w 4, p 204
Pelasio, Victorine - w 2, p 40
Pembleton, John - w 11, p 404
Pendel, Mary - w 12, p 474
Pennington, John - w 1, p 7
Pennington, Julia - w 12, p 485
Perch, William - w 10, p 395
Perkins, Charlotte - w 12, p 463
Perry, Francis - w 1, p 9
Perry, John - w 12, p 486
Perry, Magor - w 2, p 56
Peter, Noel - w 9, p 330
Peters, Hetty - w 4, p 171
Peters, John - w 10, p 361
Peters, Sophia - w 10, p 370

Peters, Thomas - w 2, p 74
Peterson, Elijah - w 1, p 30
Peterson, John - w 2, p 54
Philips, Lewis - w 4, p 185
Phillips, Brister - w 2, p 61
Phillips, Charles - w 2, p 69
Phillips, Charles - w 2, p 78
Phillips, Isaac - w 12, p 463
Phillips, James - w 2, p 75
Phillips, James - w 2, p 79
Phillips, Perry - w 2, p 66
Phillips, Perry - w 2, p 79
Phipps, Ann - w 11, p 432
Piers, George - w 2, p 66
Pimpleton, John - w 10, p 395
Pines, Joseph? - w 8, p 296
Pinkney, Robert - w 3, p 124
Pinkney, William - w 7, p 271
Pinkny, Dennis - w 12, p 518
Pion, George? - 9, p 344
Piper, Peter - w 3, p 112
Pitt, Samuel - w 3, p 157
Plasind, Edward - w 10, p 394
Plater, John - w 12, p 483
Plyman, John - w 9, p 335
Pock, Davey - w 8, p 307
Pogue, Abraham - w 10, p 375
Porter, Jacob - w 10, p 370
Posey, Stephen - w 12, p 507
Poston, George - w 11, p 436
Powel, Jane - w 12, p 473
Powell, Ellen - w 11, p 406
Powell, Ellis - w 9, p 337
Powell, Emanuel - w 3, p 135
Powell, Hace? - w 4, p 208
Pratt, John - w 5, p 232
Pratt, Truman - w 12, p 471
Presco, James - w 4, p 189
Preston, Milly - w 2, p 70
Preston, Peter - w 10, p 363
Price, David - w 7, p 286

Baltimore Census of 1830 - Free Blacks

Price, Elisabeth - w 11, p 420
Price, Maria - w 10, p 357
Price, Nathan - w 3, p 145
Price, Sarah - w 10, p 360
Price, Thomas - w 10, p 386
Price, William - w 3, p 156
Primrose, George - w 12, p 523
Primrose, Greenbury - w 3, p 136
Prout, Arthur - w 11, p 406
Prout, Charity - w 12, p 506
Prout, John - w 10, p 396
Prout, Phillis - w 2, p 51
Prout, William - w 9, p 344
Prout, William B. - w 11, p 407
Pully, Edward - w 3, p 129
Purviance, Abraham - w 4, p 214
Purviance, Samuel - w 3, p 148
Pyner, Samuel - w 10, p 394
Queen, Anthony - w 9, p 347
Queen, Robert - w 2, p 48
Queen, S. - w 8, p 306
Quin, Bennet - w 11, p 402
Quin, Hiser? - w 8, p 291
Quin, John - w 8, p 291
Quin, William - w 12, p 473
Quinn, Edward - w 9, p 340
Quinn, John - w 4, p 169
Quinton, James - w 11, p 402
Rabicon, Richard - w 10, p 372
Ragan, Samuel - w 11, p 431
Ralph, Benjamin - w 2, p 57
Ramsey, Elizabeth - w 3, p 155
Randal, Jacob - w 12, p 482
Randels, Nelly - w 12, p 452
Rause, Peggy - w 10, p 394
Ray, Benjamin - w 12, p 452
Ray, James - w 10, p 363
Ray, Parky - w 12, p 449
Reaves, William - w 3, p 118
Reed, Felix - w 11, p 408
Reed, Thomas - w 11, p 408

Reeds, James - w 8, p 290
Reese, George - w 2, p 50
Reister, Abraham - w 3, p 111
Reuben, Hetty - w 11, p 437
Richards, Abraham - w 11, p 431
Richards, James - w 1, p 29
Richardson, Benjamin - w 1, p 11
Richardson, Ellen - w 1, p 13
Richardson, Henry - w 4, p 208
Richardson, James - w 5, p 222
Richardson, Jesse - w 1, p 10
Richardson, John - w 2, p 60
Richardson, Patience - w 12, p 449
Richardson, Phillip - w 2, p 60
Richardson, William - w 12, p 510
Ridgaway, Henry - w 5, p 240
Ridgeley, Pompey - w 11, p 401
Ridgely, Loyed? - w 7, p 270
Ridgely, Sidney - w 12, p 504
Ridgeway, Perry - w 4, p 193
Ridgley, Charlotte - w 3, p 131
Right, James - w 2, p 57
Riley, Jonathan - w 4, p 186
Ringgold, Hezekiah - w 3, p 103
Ringgold, Jesse - w 9, p 338
Ringgold, Mary - w 11, p 410
Ringgold, Moses - w 9, p 330
Ringold, Benjamin - w 7, p 286
Ringold, Jacob - w 7, p 269
Ringold, Thomas - w 10, p 387
Rishab, Riston ? - w 10, p 367
Roach, York - w 2, p 86
Roads, Elijah - w 10, p 367
Roath, Edward - w 10, p 352
Robenson, Henry - w 12, p 495
Roberts, Cheeserman - w 3, p 123
Roberts, David - w 9, p 325
Roberts, George - w 12, p 455
Roberts, James - w 11, p 431
Roberts, John - w 9, p 344
Roberts, Julia - w 5, p 225

Chapter 15

Baltimore Census of 1830 - Free Blacks

Roberts, Nelson - w 3, p 137
Roberts, Philip - w 3, p 140
Roberts, Philip - w 3, p 155
Robins, Thomas - w 3, p 125
Robinson, Christina - w 2, p 54
Robinson, E. - w 6, p 259
Robinson, Edward - w 2, p 55
Robinson, Hannah - w 9, p 346
Robinson, Henry - w 4, p 193
Robinson, James - w 12, p 485
Robinson, John - w 2, p 53
Robinson, Joseph - w 4, p 186
Robinson, Kitty - w 11, p 406
Robinson, Leon - w 3, p 107
Robinson, Sarah - w 7, p 269
Robinson, Seiver ? - w 11, p 403
Robinson, Zachariah - w 2, p 66
Robonson, Peter - w 11, p 404
Rock, Catherine - w 4, p 178
Rock, William - w 10, p 395
Rockberry, Sarah? - w 8, p 294
Roden, Henry - w 1, p 11
Rodgers, David - w 2, p 85
Rodgers, Elijah - w 12, p 480
Rogers, Andrew - w 3, p 125
Romane, John E. - w 12, p 472
Ross, Benn - w 10, p 395
Ross, Lace - w 12, p 477
Ross, Sarah - w 9, p 346
Ross, William - w 12, p 497
Rosune, Daniel - w 3, p 155
Rowles, Isaac - w 1, p 4
Ruff, George - w 4, p 183
Ruff, Nelly - w 3, p 157
Ruitt, William - w 2, p 46
Rupele, Leonard ? - w 12, p 452
Rupell, Charlotte - w 3, p 124
Rupier, Harriet - w 7, p 276
Rusell, Barber ? - w 8, p 320
Rydout, Davey - w 8, p 307
Sadler, Emory - w 12, p 504

Sailes, A . - w 7, p 270
Sailos, Nathaniel - w 8, p 293
Sale, Ruth - w 1, p 6
Sales, Nicholas - w 3, p 123
Salter, Joseph - w 4, p 168
Salter, Samuel - w 12, p 498
Sampson, James - w 12, p 474
Sampson, Walter - w 9, p 331
Samson, Jacob - w 8, p 315
Sanders, Elisabeth - w 10, p 373
Sanders, Henney ? - w 10, p 392
Sanders, Jarret - w 2, p 62
Sanders, Maria - w 12, p 472
Sanders, Mary - w 12, p 498
Sanders, Thomas - w 2, p 65
Sanley, Levin - w 11, p 437
Saucer, John - w 1, p 16
Savery, Samuel - w 12, p 463
Savoy, Basil - w 9, p 346
Savoy, Richard - w 4, p 181
Sawyer, David - w 2, p 72
Scheller, Sinder - w 12, p 512
Scott, Charlotte - w 11, p 403
Scott, Francis - w 7, p 270
Scott, Francis - w 12, p 493
Scott, Hancy - w 1, p 6
Scott, Isaac - w 2, p 46
Scott, John - w 2, p 64
Scott, Littleton - w 6, p 256
Scott, Martha - w 3, p 128
Scott, Nathan - w 5, p 230
Scott, Patrick - w 11, p 403
Scott, Philip - w 3, p 148
Scott, Rachael - w 12, p 445
Scott, Robert - w 2, p 50
Scott, Robert - w 3, p 156
Scott, Samuel - w 3, p 122
Scott, Sophia - w 9, p 344
Scott, Stephen - w 12, p 512
Scott, Thomas - w 12, p 520
Scott, Widow - w 10, p 360

The Baltimore Census of 1830: The Free Black Population

Baltimore Census of 1830 - Free Blacks

Scott, William - w 8, p 307
Scott, William - w 10, p 358
Scott, Margaret - w 9, p 340
Scroner, Isaac - w 9, p 346
Seany, Benjamin - w 3, p 115
Sears, William - w 3, p 139
Seaver, Lewis - w 11, p 436
Segar, Benedick - w 4, p 171
Selvy, Robert - w 2, p 56
Sewal, Thomas - w 10, p 364
Sewel, William - w 12, p 514
Sewell, Simon - w 11, p 436
Shale, George - w 9, p 342
Shark, James - w 2, p 51
Sharp, Henry - w 2, p 56
Sharp, Henry - w 2, p 68
Sharp, Henry - w 4, p 188
Sharper, Zachariah - w 4, p 190
Sheaf, Henry - w 3, p 132
Sheaf, Joseph - w 3, p 153
Sheaves, William - w 3, p 125
Sheppard, B. - w 7, p 286
Sheppard, William - w 4, p 181
Sherrick, John F. - w 9, p 338
Shipley, Peter - w 12, p 463
Shipper, Charles - w 2, p 72
Shoder, Thomas - w 8, p 307
Shooter, Hanna - w 8, p 312
Shorter, Charles - w 2, p 80
Shorter, Richard - w 11, p 432
Shrivers, Widow ? - w 10, p 377
Shupping, Priscilla - w 4, p 182
Sickinson, Joseph - w 8, p 313
Sillet, Peter ? - w 11, p 430
Silvester, Moses - w 12, p 499
Simas, Betsy ? - w 11, p 406
Simmon, John - w 8, p 302
Simmons, Ann - w 1, p 16
Simms, Joseph - w 3, p 135
Simpson, Agnes - w 11, p 407
Simpson, Hughy - w 3, p 155

Simpson, Ruth - w 11, p 404
Sims, Henry - w 1, p 6
Sims, John - w 12, p 481
Sims, Nancy - w 12, p 522
Sims, Zacary - w 8, p 317
Singleton, Fela - w 5, p 226
Skinner, Benson - w 4, p 170
Skinner, Henry - w 11, p 402
Skinner, Thomas - w 9, p 344
Sly, Jane - w 12, p 472
Smaley, Amelia G. - w 11, p 432
Small, George - w 12, p 514
Small, Leon - w 3, p 110
Small, Moses - w 7, p 286
Small, Sigh - w 12, p 523
Smallwood, David - w 12, p 448
Smallwood, Hannah - w 12, p 504
Smallwood, Richard - w 3, p 119
Smiley, George - w 3, p 152
Smith, Abraham - w 3, p 132
Smith, Ann - w 3, p 119
Smith, Ann - w 7, p 284
Smith, Benjamin - w 9, p 336
Smith, Benjamin - w 11, p 402
Smith, Dianna - w 3, p 133
Smith, Edward - w 3, p 139
Smith, Edward - w 10, p 370
Smith, Edward - w 10, p 371
Smith, Hanah - w 10, p 350
Smith, Hannah - w 4, p 189
Smith, Henry - w 1, p 10
Smith, Henry - w 2, p 56
Smith, Henry? - w 7, p 286
Smith, Isaac - w 12, p 472
Smith, Jacob - w 6, p 246
Smith, James - w 1, p 5
Smith, James - w 2, p 81
Smith, Jane ? - w 12, p 510
Smith, John - w 2, p 63
Smith, John - w 3, p 135
Smith, Joseph - w 3, p 141

Chapter 15

Baltimore Census of 1830 - Free Blacks

Smith, Joseph - w 10, p 372
Smith, Joseph - w 12, p 479
Smith, Lady - w 8, p 307
Smith, Louisa - w 3, p 136
Smith, Mary - w 2, p 37
Smith, Mary - w 6, p 262
Smith, Mary - w 10, p 358
Smith, Nathan - w 2, p 82
Smith, Nathan - w 3, p 133
Smith, Perry - w 3, p 153
Smith, Perry - w 12, p 479
Smith, Peter - w 6, p 263
Smith, Rebecca - w 3, p 132
Smith, Richard - w 12, p 492
Smith, Sally - w 12, p 449
Smith, Samuel - w 12, p 496
Smith, Solomon - w 4, p 171
Smith, Sophia - w 12, p 453
Smith, Temperance - w 3, p 107
Smith, Thomas - w 8, p 290
Smith, Torey - w 2, p 53
Smith, William - w 9, p 327
Smith, William - w 11, p 436
Smith, Jane - w 7, p 269
Sneese, Arthur - w 4, p 214
Snow, Patty - w 12, p 481
Snowden, Peter - w 12, p 465
Sodis, Saras? - w 8, p 293
Soller, Charles - w 8, p 300
Sollers, Abraham - w 6, p 262
Sollers, Jane - w 12, p 472
Sourden, William - w 12, p 510
Sparr, John - w 12, p 463
Speaks, Reuben - w 11, p 410
Spencer, Philip - w 8, p 306
Spinyard, Richard - w 3, p 155
Sport, J. K. ? - w 8, p 306
Sprigg, Anthony - w 12, p 477
Sprigg, Margaret - w 7, p 270
Spriggs, George - w 4, p 179
Spriggs, Thomas - w 4, p 184

Sprigs, Jolin - w 8, p 313
Sprigs, Mariah - w 2, p 43
Stafford, Eliza Sim - w 2, p 47
Staira, Mary Ann - w 12, p 444
Stanley, Adam - w 8, p 291
Stansberry, Barbary? - w 10, p 356
Stansberry, Betsy - w 8, p 292
Stansbury, Abraham - w 11, p 410
Stansbury, Charlotte - w 7, p 284
Stansbury, George - w 11, p 410
Stansbury, Moses - w 12, p 489
Stansbury, T. ? - w 4, p 206
Stephens, Benjamin - w 2, p 80
Stephens, Sebbleton - w 12, p 461
Stephenson, Anna - w 9, p 338
Stephenson, Melville - w 9, p 327
Sterem, Ann ? - w 8, p 321
Sterling, Peter - w 3, p 133
Sterrett, Nancy - w 9, p 343
Sterrett, Ralph - w 9, p 343
Steuart, Charles - w 4, p 182
Steuart, Thomas - w 12, p 465
Steven, Diana - w 8, p 307
Stevenson, Jane? - w 8, p 306
Stevenson, John - w 10, p 382
Stevenson, Joshua - w 3, p 135
Stevenson, Shedrick - w 10, p 373
Stew, Julia - w 4, p 209
Steward, Elijah - w 12, p 449
Steward, George - w 8, p 312
Steward, Godfrey - w 12, p 447
Steward, Isaac - w 12, p 489
Steward, Stephen - w 12, p 515
Stewart, Clory - w 2, p 89
Stewart, Daniel - w 3, p 110
Stewart, Fanny - w 11, p 402
Stewart, William - w 3, p 135
Stewart, William - w 9, p 343
Stewrad, Edward - w 10, p 362
Stewrad, Sarah - w 10, p 368
Stewrat, Mitchel - w 1, p 17

The Baltimore Census of 1830: The Free Black Population

Baltimore Census of 1830 - Free Blacks

Stiles, Fredrick - w 3, p 137
Stite, Abram? - w 8, p 312
Stocks, Charles - w 7, p 276
Stokes, Robert - w 3, p 155
Studely, William - w 3, p 122
Stullely, Jane - w 3, p 159
Sularene, Sam? - w 8, p 290
Sumervill, Elizabeth - w 2, p 74
Sunas, William? - w 11, p 404
Sutton, Abraham - w 3, p 153
Sutton, Richard - w 12, p 484
Swan, Charity - w 12, p 458
Talbot, Benjamin - w 2, p 50
Talbot, Edward - w 3, p 137
Talbot, Perry - w 2, p 69
Tally, James - w 10, p 361
Tartar, John H. - w 12, p 463
Taylor, Bazil - w 3, p 153
Taylor, Dorcas - w 2, p 41
Taylor, Isaac - w 2, p 64
Taylor, Jacob - w 4, p 183
Taylor, James - w 2, p 61
Taylor, John - w 4, p 171
Taylor, Margaret - w 3, p 107
Taylor, William - w 3, p 112
Ted, Richard - w 12, p 448
Tele, Hannah - w 12, p 474
Tellowson, Mansry - w 12, p 522
Tellowson, Perry - w 123, p 521
Terivenor, William - w 9, p 345
Thomas, Adam - w 8, p 296
Thomas, Andrew - w 4, p 190
Thomas, Ann - w 3, p 150
Thomas, Benjamin - w 2, p 85
Thomas, Caesar - w 12, p 502
Thomas, David - w 12, p 486
Thomas, David - w 12, p 502
Thomas, Elizabeth - w 2, p 74
Thomas, Garretson - w 11, p 402
Thomas, George - w 2, p 62
Thomas, George - w 2, p 87
Thomas, Gustavus - w 12, p 474
Thomas, Handy - w 3, p 138
Thomas, Harriot - w 12, p 467
Thomas, Jacob - w 12, p 456
Thomas, Jacob - w 12, p 501
Thomas, John - w 7, p 269
Thomas, Joseph - w 2, p 50
Thomas, Kitty - w 2, p 71
Thomas, Mariah - w 2, p 78
Thomas, Mary - w 7, p 269
Thomas, Morris - w 11, p 429
Thomas, Neal - w 3, p 142
Thomas, Perry - w 3, p 154
Thomas, Phillip - w 2, p 53
Thomas, Rachael - w 3, p 158
Thomas, Rachael - w 6, p 249
Thomas, Richard - w 1, p 9
Thomas, Richard - w 12, p 449
Thomas, Samuel - w 11, p 419
Thomas, Sandy - w 12, p 508
Thomas, Seth - w 1, p 12
Thomas, Stephen - w 1, p 9
Thomas, Thomas - w 4, p 198
Thomas, William - w 2, p 82
Thompson, Andrew - w 2, p 50
Thompson, Cator - w 4, p 211
Thompson, Ceasar - w 2, p 74
Thompson, Edward - w 2, p 79
Thompson, Jacob - w 9, p 346
Thompson, Michael - w 5, p 225
Thompson, Pompy - w 11, p 424
Thompson, Richard - w 1, p 16
Thompson, Samuel - w 2, p 39
Thompson, Tempe? - w 9, p 344
Thompson, Thomas - w 12, p 484
Thompson, William - w 4, p 190
Thomson, Lewis - w 9, p 339
Thomson, Peter - w 8, p 313
Thomson, Willis - w 3, p 124
Thornton, John - w 10, p 367
Tilghman, Hester - w 3, p 109

Chapter 15

Baltimore Census of 1830 - Free Blacks

Tilghman, Robert - w 2, p 50
Tillham, Perry - w 3, p 150
Tilyard, Benjamin - w 4, p 213
Toany, Stephen - w 12, p 510
Todd, Sarah - w 4, p 194
Toes, Thomas - w 12, p 501
Tolbert, Murry - w 7, p 270
Toogood, Charles - w 11, p 429
Toogood, Jacob - w 11, p 409
Toogood, John - w 11, p 427
Toogood, William - w 12, p 512
Topen, Benjamin - w 3, p 152
Topkin, Charles - w 12, p 446
Travers, Abraham - w 12, p 485
Traverse, Abraham - w 11, p 411
Travis, Hester - w 9, p 342
Travors, Nancy ? - w 11, p 402
Trip, Emily - w 10, p 363
Tripp, John - w 2, p 81
Tross, Hickson - w 12, p 521
Trury, William ? - w 11, p 404
Trusty, Aaron - w 10, p 374
Trusty, Jonathan - w 2, p 40
Trusty, Perry - w 12, p 447
Trusty, Samuel - w 3, p 158
Tucker, Abraham - w 1, p 13
Tue, Samuel - w 3, p 147
Turner, James - w 8, p 321
Turner, John - w 12, p 449
Turner, Joseph - w 3, p 132
Turner, Mary - w 12, p 456
Twogood, Nancy - w 12, p 504
Uncles, Isaac - w 12, p 501
Vails, Levin - w 2, p 52
Valdon, Harriet - w 5, p 237
Valentine, Johannah - w 12, p 477
Varlow, Edith - w 12, p 502
Vattier, Benjamin D. - w 4, p 189
Vendon, Isaac - w 8, p 295
Vequin, Nancy - w 5, p 222
Victoire, Mary A. - w 11, p 417

Victor, Barber - w 5, p 235
Waldon, Sam - w 8, p 312
Wales, Doratha - w 4, p 204
Wales, Jeremiah - w 3, p 135
Walker, James - w 2, p 85
Walker, Joseph - w 2, p 66
Walker, Rob - w 8, p 294
Walker, Robert - w 1, p 17
Walker, Saly - w 8, p 313
Wallace, Charles - w 3, p 107
Wallace, Francis - w 12, p 512
Wallace, Isaac - w 12, p 511
Wallace, Major - w 3, p 135
Wallace, Rebecca - w 12, p 494
Wallis, Charles - w 10, p 373
Wallis, Lydia - w 10, p 364
Walsh, Peter - w 2, p 59
Walter, Benjamin - w 10, p 363
Walter, Charles - w 11, p 431
Walton, Harrison - w 11, p 437
Ward, Robert - w 2, p 38
Ward, Stephen - w 2, p 56
Ward, Wiliam - w 11, p 405
Warner, Eliza - w 12, p 517
Warner, Garrison - w 8, p 313
Warner, James - w 4, p 170
Warson, Peter - w 12, p 522
Washington, George - w 11, p 413
Washington, John - w 3, p 141
Washington, Widow - w 10, p 374
Waters, Benjamin - w 4, p 205
Waters, Edward - w 3, p 159
Waters, Elisa - w 11, p 420
Waters, Hager - w 4, p 196
Waters, Harriot - w 12, p 497
Waters, Jacob - w 2, p 93
Waters, Joshua - w 2, p 59
Waters, Mary - w 3, p 132
Waters, Priestman - w 2, p 60
Watkins, George - w 12, p 471
Watkins, John - w 3, p 111

The Baltimore Census of 1830: The Free Black Population

Baltimore Census of 1830 - Free Blacks

Watkins, John - w 11, p 421
Watkins, John - w 12, p 497
Watkins, Lilly - w 2, p 47
Watkins, Lucretia - w 12, p 484
Watkins, Thomas - w 4, p 183
Watkins, William - w 11, p 407
Watkins, William - w 11, p 439
Wats, Rachel - w 2, p 52
Watson, John - w 10, p 385
Watts, Isaac - w 10, p 383
Weaver, Lorence - w 12, p 474
Webb, Isaac - w 11, p 408
Webb, William - w 12, p 453
Webb, Winten - w 2, p 76
Webber, Isaac - w 10, p 352
Webster, David - w 12, p 497
Webster, James - w 12, p 497
Webster, Lydia - w 3, p 154
Webster, William - w 12, p 510
Weeks, George - w 10, p 372
Wells, Lewis - w 11, p 425
Wells, Maria - w 3, p 110
Wells, Nelson - w 8, p 303
Wells, Rachel - w 10, p 382
Wells, Richard - w 10, p 361
Welsh, Thomas - w 12, p 463
Wenny, (not indicated) - w 12, p 485
West, Charles - w 10, p 358
West, Francis - w 3, p 138
West, John - w 1, p 10
West, Milly - w 11, p 439
Weston, Mary - w 10, p 363
Wheatley, Levin - w 2, p 69
Wheatley, Lydia - w 2, p 74
Wheeler, B. - w 10, p 382
Wheeler, Isaac - w 4, p 210
Wheeler, William - w 12, p 504
Whelan, John - w 10, p 392
White, Adam - w 1, p 6
White, Charlotte - w 1, p 21

White, Henney - w 10, p 363
White, James - w 3, p 157
White, Job - w 1, p 12
White, Mrs. J. - w 8, p 317
Whitington, William - w 2, p 59
Wiggin, Isaac - w 8, p 294
Wiley, Murray - w 4, p 171
Wilkins, Joseph - w 12, p 506
Wilkinson, David - w 12, p 488
Wilks, George - w 12, p 452
Wilks, Letitia - w 3, p 119
William, Anthony - w 8, p 300
William, Benjamin - w 10, p 394
William, David - w 8, p 292
William, Ellen - w 8, p 298
William, Samuel - w 10, p 364
William, Steven - w 8, p 307
Williams, Ann - w 1, p 9
Williams, Ann - w 2, p 72
Williams, Benjamin - w 1, p 16
Williams, Cassandra - w 3, p 135
Williams, Charles - w 8, p 319
Williams, Charles - w 12, p 510
Williams, Charles - w 12, p 511
Williams, Ephraim - w 2, p 77
Williams, Ezekiel - w 2, p 79
Williams, George - w 2, p 81
Williams, Greenbury - w 5, p 232
Williams, Harry - w 3, p 131
Williams, Henry - w 12, p 459
Williams, Hester - w 2, p 37
Williams, Hester - w 11, p 406
Williams, James - w 10, p 382
Williams, James - w 10, p 392
Williams, Jeffrey - w 11, p 401
Williams, Jeffry - w 2, p 52
Williams, John - w 2, p 57
Williams, John - w 10, p 392
Williams, John - w 11, p 401
Williams, John - w 11, p 402
Williams, Joseph - w 2, p 63

Chapter 15

Baltimore Census of 1830 - Free Blacks

Williams, Joseph - w 4, p 215
Williams, Lewis - w 12, p 460
Williams, Lucy - w 12, p 452
Williams, Lydia - w 2, p 81
Williams, Martha - w 1, p 23
Williams, Mary - w 4, p 213
Williams, Mary - w 12, p 474
Williams, Mater - w 2, p 77
Williams, Nathaniel - w 2, p 76
Williams, Nathaniel - w 4, p 171
Williams, Nelly - w 11, p 401
Williams, Pembuck - w 1, p 4
Williams, Perry - w 1, p 17
Williams, Peter - w 11, p 406
Williams, Philip - w 10, p 391
Williams, Philip - w 11, p 427
Williams, Prince - w 12, p 452
Williams, Rachael - w 12, p 504
Williams, Richard - w 12, p 474
Williams, Richard - w 12, p 489
Williams, Richard - w 12, p 508
Williams, Samuel - w 1, p 11
Williams, Samuel - w 3, p 160
Williams, Samuel - w 10, p 369
Williams, Sarah - w 4, p 214
Williams, Sinah - w 11, p 438
Williams, Spindele - w 3, p 134
Williams, Thomas - w 1, p 23
Williams, Thomas - w 11, p 403
Williams, William - w 1, p 5
Williams, William - w 9, p 346
Williams, William - w 10, p 364
Williamson, Edward - w 2, p 58
Williamson, Thomas - w 1, p 17
Willis, Lydia - w 10, p 382
Willmore, Michael - w 3, p 141
Wills, Nathaniel - w 11, p 406
Willson, R. - w 7, p 276
Wilmer, Perry - w 3, p 158
Wilmer, William - w 3, p 138
Wilson, Abraham - w 3, p 160

Wilson, Abraham - w 4, p 171
Wilson, Andrew - w 1, p 13
Wilson, Ann - w 12, p 485
Wilson, Baynard - w 2, p 86
Wilson, Benjamin - w 10, p 382
Wilson, Carvel - w 3, p 138
Wilson, Catherine - w 10, p 375
Wilson, Comfort - w 3, p 153
Wilson, Elizabeth - w 2, p 57
Wilson, Ephraim - w 2, p 74
Wilson, Francis - w 9, p 343
Wilson, George - w 2, p 91
Wilson, Isaac - w 2, p 78
Wilson, James - w 2, p 64
Wilson, John - w 2, p 39
Wilson, Joseph - w 12, p 454
Wilson, Joseph N. - w 10, p 387
Wilson, Lloyd - w 3, p 119
Wilson, Peter - w 2, p 78
Wilson, Peter - w 8, p 312
Wilson, Rachel - w 5, p 240
Wilson, Samuel - w 11, p 410
Wilson, Tower - w 2, p 84
Wilson, William - w 10, p 354
Wilson, William - w 12, p 490
Winder, Lucy - w 10, p 377
Wireman, Samuel - w 3, p 150
Wise, Nancy - w 12, p 452
Wollin, Susan - w 12, p 445
Wood, Henrietta - w 4, p 188
Wood, William - w 4, p 213
Woodfield, Rebecca - w 11, p 406
Woodlin, Fredrack - w 12, p 481
Woods, Betsey ? - w 11, p 427
Woodyear, Garret - w 3, p 156
Woodyear, Jefferson - w 12, p 451
Woodyear, Mary - w 12, p 452
Woolen, Eliza - w 12, p 502
Woolford, Jacob - w 2, p 66
Woolford, Maria - w 9, p 344
World, Henry - w 8, p 312

206

The Baltimore Census of 1830: The Free Black Population

Baltimore Census of 1830 - Free Blacks

Worthington, Absalom F. - w 24
Wright, Benjamin - w 3, p 136
Wright, Chadrick - w 4, p 211
Wright, Dorsey - w 3, p 133
Wright, Edward - w 3, p 140
Wright, Emory - w 7, p 269
Wright, Mary - w 12, p 453
Wright, Nancy - w 11, p 407
Wright, Robert - w 12, p 452
Wright, Samuel - w 5, p 241
Wry, John - w 4, p 167
Yates, Sandy - w 3, p 123
Yeats, Perry - w 12, p 502

Yonker, Edward - w 3, p 159
Young, Abigal - w 3, p 136
Young, Charlotte - w 12, p 452
Young, Jacob - w 3, p 133
Young, Jane - w 2, p 85
Young, Joseph - w 4, p 211
Young, Joseph - w 11, p 402
Young, Marian - w 8, p 301
Young, Martha - w 8, p 301
Young, Perry - w 10, p 358
Young, Rachael - w 1, p 12
Young, Saley - w 10, p 392

16
The Baltimore City Directory of 1831: The Free Black Population

The following is a compilation of the Black populace from the city directory of 1831. The Black population was indicated in the directory by an unusual mark to the left of the name. The mark resembles a dagger or a cross. Although the names are listed by surname they are often found to be out of strict natural order. This document is valuable as a source for the occupations and geographic locations of Black people in the city of Baltimore. When used in conjunction with the Federal Population Census of 1830 (see previous index) it provides excellent historical and genealogical information for the researcher. The following is a sample entry in the list:

Adams, James - whitewasher, 26 South Charles

The record translates: James Adams is a whitewasher whose residence is at 26 South Charles street, Baltimore, in the year 1831.

Index to the Free Black Population

Adams, Adam - Cordwainer, Orleans St.
Adams, Henry - Granby St.
Adams, James - Whitewasher, 26 South Charles
Adams, James - Upholsterer, Chaisty's Alley
Adams, John - Blacksmith, Park Lane
Adams, John - 80 East St.
Adams, John - Laborer, 1 Sharp
Addison, Ellen - Washer, 83 Liberty St.
Aitkin, Samuel - Laborer, Apple Alley
Alford, Jane - Laundress, Bond St.
Allen, Caeser - Peace Alley
Allen, Mary - Eden

Allen, Sarah - Laundress, Argyle Alley
Allen, Solomon - Oilman, Howard St.
Allen, William - Tallow Chandler, Forrest
Allice, Amey - Laundress, Argyle Alley
Allison, Betsy - Terrapin Hill
Ambrose, Rachel - Laundress, German
Amley, Harry - Wilk St.
Amley, T. - Sawyer, Wilk St.
Amos, Betsy - Potter St.
Amos, Charlotte - Laundress, East St.
Amos, Rachel - Whitewasher, Potter

Chapter 16

Index to the Free Black Population

Anderson, Abraham - Porter, 74 N. Howard St.
Anderson, Ann - Laundress, Sarah Ann
Anderson, Betsy - Laundress, Happy Alley
Anderson, Cesar - Drayman, 10 Ross St.
Anderson, Charles - 26 Second St.
Anderson, Charles - Whitewasher, Potter
Anderson, Elijah - Laborer, Little Hamstead St.
Anderson, G. - Potter St.
Anderson, Henry - Brass Founder, Necessity Alley
Anderson, John - Forrest St.
Anderson, Matthias - Laborer, Saratoga
Anderson, Solomon - Brickmaker, Bottle Alley
Anderson, Stanly - Laborer, Caroline St.
Anthony, Rachel - Douglass St.
Appleberry, William - Laborer, Little Hughes St.
Armisted, Lydia - Laundress, Burgundy Alley
Armstrong, Isaac - Bricklayer, Ann
Armstrong, Isley - Brickmaker, Park
Armstrong, Mrs. Mary - Garden St.
Arthur, Mary - Necessity Alley
Ash, Peter - Alley (unnamed)
Askins, Christ - Laborer, Busy Alley
Audorun, Mary Jane - Nurse, 64 N. Front St.
Bacon, William - Waiter, Carpenter's Alley
Badger, Elisha - Porter, Dutch Alley
Badger, Francis - Blacksmith, Har Avenue
Badger, Jarret - Porter, Eutaw St.
Bailey, D. - Laborer, Wilk
Bailey, D. - Laborer, Wilk
Bailey, Elizabeth - Laundress, Potter
Bailey, Isaac - Drayman, Honey Alley
Bailey, John - Hill St.
Bailey, John - Hill St.
Bailey, Joseph - Stevedore, E. Falls Avenue
Bailey, Perry - Caulker, Guilford's Alley
Bailey, Perry - Caulker, Guilford's Alley
Bailey, Richard - Carpenter, Bottle Alley
Bailey, Samuel - Caulker, Happy Alley
Baily, Darkey - Laundress, Pierce
Baily, Lucy - Laundress, Lerew's Alley
Baily, Phillis - washer, Lerew's Alley
Ballard, Robert - Laborer, Alley (unnamed)
Banning, Charles - Porter, Cross St.
Banning, Jacob - Porter, S. Eutaw
Bantum, Susan - Washer, Forrest St.
Barcroft, Rolla - Seaman, Bank St.
Barker, Bazil - Cordwainer, Alley (unnamed)
Barker, David - Short St.
Barker, Mrs. Eliza - Short St.

The Baltimore City Directory of 1831: The Free Black Population

Index to the Free Black Population

Barker, Nathan - Waiter, Hammond's Alley
Barnes, Anna - Happy Alley
Barnes, David - Porter, Potter St.
Barnes, Francis - German St.
Barnes, Patience - Wolf St.
Barnes, William - Caulker, 14 W. Fleet St.
Barnet, Susan - Washer, alley (unnamed)
Barney, Caesar - Sawyer, Eden St.
Barney, Harriet - 122 Wolf St.
Barney, James - Laborer, Saratoga St.
Barney, John - Stevedore, Salisbury Alley
Barney, Perry - Ship Carpenter, Caroline
Barney, Philip - Carter, Eutaw St.
Barney, William - Brickmoulder, Light St.
Barton, Benjamin - Sawyer, 60 N. Gay St.
Bateman, Edward - Drayman, Canal St.
Batton, James - Laborer, 6 Tyson St.
Bedinton, Brice - Laborer, Lexington St.
Beehoe, Lymas - Drayman, Asbury Lane
Beekus, Rachel - Washer, East St.
Beems, William - Boot & Shoemaker, 35 N. Liberty St.
Bell, Ann - 4 Ruxton St.
Bender, Henrietta - Washer, Green St.
Bennet, Rachel - Washer, Pratt St.
Bennett, Hy - Laborer, Guilford's Alley
Bennett, Peter - Carpenter, Forrest St.
Benson, Edward - Sawyer, Low St.
Benson, Henry - Waterman, Pearce Alley
Benson, John - Waiter, Short St.
Benson, John - Stevedore, S. Market St.
Benson, Nancy - washer, Front St.
Beo, Thomas - Laborer, Asbury Lane
Berry, Deborah - 80 Ensor St.
Berry, Harriet - Uhler's Alley
Berry, John - Mariner, Low St.
Berry, Mrs. Elizabeth - Sharp
Berry, Patsy - Whitewasher, Low St.
Berx, Susan - Washer, Green St.
Betts, Adam - Barber, Forest St.
Bias, Alfred - Drayman, Franklin St.
Bias, James - Laborer, Lerew's Alley
Bias, John - Porter, Leadenhall St.
Billingsly, Henry - Hack Driver, Carpenter's Alley
Birchman, Abel - Laborer, Alley (unnamed)
Birckhead, Mrs. Hannah - 20 N. Sharp St.
Bishop, Perry - Carter, Welcome Alley
Bishop, Rozden - N. Sharp St.
Black, Bethesda - Washer, Davis St.
Black, William - Laborer, Mulberry St.
Blackston, William - Waterman, French Alley
Blackston, William - Laborer, Potter St.
Blair, Hesther - Washer, Granby

Chapter 16

Index to the Free Black Population

Blake, Cato - Drayman, Rock St.
Blake, D. - Drayman, Bounty Lane
Blake, Frisby - laborer, Davis St.
Blake, Gotleb - Laborer, Greenwich St.
Blake, Harrison - Laborer, Fayette St.
Blake, Levin - laborer, Spring St.
Blake, Peyton - Waiter, Exeter St.
Blake, Winsor - Porter, Exeter St.
Boardley, Anthony - Laborer, Baltimore St.
Boaz, Benjamin - Sarah Ann
Bodeley, Anthony - Porter, Fayette St.
Bodely, Perry - Laborer, Wagon Alley
Bonaparte, John - Hair Dresser, Saratoga St.
Bond, Aquilla - 3 Stirling St.
Bond, Aquilla - Laborer, St. Mary's St.
Bond, Charles - Hughes St.
Bond, Levi - Brickmaker, Welcome Alley
Bond, Rachel - Jefferson St.
Bond, Sandy - Carter, William St.
Bond, Stephen - Porter, Exeter St.
Bond, Stephen - Waiter, Sharp St.
Bond, Washington - laborer, Long Lane
Boon, Benjamin - Carter, Run Alley
Boon, Benjamin - Laborer, Lerew's Alley
Boon, John - Sawyer, Salisbury St.
Boon, John - laborer, Busy Alley
Boon, Nelson - Brickmaker, Sugar Alley
Boon, Resin - Blacksmith, Lane (unnamed)
Boose, John - Stevedore, Little Hamstead St.
Booth, Edward - Sawyer, Tyson St.
Booth, Joshua - Caulker, Fleet St.
Boston, Abraham - Coachman, Davis St.
Boston, Charles - Laborer, Biddle Alley
Boston, Daniel - Waiter, Charles St.
Boston, Daniel - Boarding House, 123 Bond St.
Boston, Daniel - Carter, Busy Alley
Boston, George - Pratt St.
Boston, George - Blacksmith, Conway St.
Boston, John - Laborer, Wagon Alley
Boston, Lucy - washer, Chasty's Alley
Boston, Margaret - Ruxton St.
Boston, Robert - Laborer, 111 Camden St.
Bouldin, James - Carter, Happy Alley
Bowen, Charles - Laborer, Camden St.
Bowen, Clara - Lerew's Alley
Bowen, John - Drayman, Canal St.
Bowen, Samuel - Tanner, Chamberlain Alley
Bowers, Horace - Drayman, Hamilton
Bowie, David - Scourer, Strawberry Alley
Bowie, Solomon - Carter, Hill St.
Bowlin, William - Scowman, Bishop's Alley
Bowman, Sarah - Laundress, Wilk

The Baltimore City Directory of 1831: The Free Black Population

Index to the Free Black Population

Bowser, Benjamin - Guilford's St. Alley

Bowser, Henry - Sawyer, Spring St.

Bowser, Jerry - Sawyer, 8 Tyson St.

Bowser, Moses - Mulberry St.

Bowser, Robert - Boarding House, 51 South St.

Bowyer, William - Laborer, Spring St.

Boyce, Roger - Sawyer, Centre St.

Braddock, Jerry - Laborer, Sharp St.

Bradford, Isaac - Seaman, Aisquith St.

Bradford, Richard - Laborer, Short St.

Bradley, Samuel - Chesnut Alley

Brady, Milly - Laundress, German St.

Brewer, Letty - washer, Bottle Alley

Briant, Fanny - Laundress, Caroline St.

Brice, Kinsey - Laborer, Short Alley

Brice, Philip - Drayman, Sarah Ann

Bridge, Henry - Laborer, 1 Forest

Bridge, Rebecca - Washer, Holliday St.

Bridge, Rebecca - Washer, President St.

Briggs, Mary - Alley (unnamed)

Bright, Sarah - Washer, Lerew's Alley

Brighton, Henry - Drayman, Pine St.

Brightwell, Rebecca - Hoffman St.

Briscoe, Betsy - 4 Ruxton St.

Briscoe, Jacob - Laborer, Bishop's Alley

Briscoe, Joseph - Sawyer, Conway St.

Briscoe, Nathan - laborer, Bank St.

Brister, Jenny - Washer, Caroline St.

Bristow, David - Porter, Forest St.

Bristow, Susan - Laundress, Pearl St.

Brittenton, Mary - Strawberry Alley

Brogden, Elijah - Carman, Pierce St.

Brogden, Joshua - Laborer, Cove St.

Brogden, William - Sawyer, Pratt St.

Brogden, William - Carter, Lerew's Alley

Brogden, Zachariah - Hack Driver, Chesnut Alley

Brooks, Betsy - Washer, Forest St.

Brooks, George - Sawyer, Strawberry Alley

Brooks, Henry - Welcome Alley

Brooks, Jenny - Washer, Strawberry Alley

Brooks, John - Carpenter, Conway St.

Brooks, Robert - Caulker, 110 Bond St.

Broom, Benjamin - S. Charles St.

Brooze, Peter - Coachman, Salisbury Alley

Broughton, John - Porter, Pine St.

Brown, Abraham - Laborer, Low St.

Brown, Anderson - Carter, Pratt

Chapter 16

Index to the Free Black Population

Brown, Andrew - Sailor, 50 Park St.
Brown, Ann - Aisquith St.
Brown, Bristol - Wagoner, Park Lane
Brown, Caleb - Drayman, South Lane
Brown, Catherine - Washer, Chaisty's Alley
Brown, Charles - Sawyer, 34 Happy Alley
Brown, Charles - Laborer, Guilford's Alley
Brown, Charlotte - Washer, Conway
Brown, David - Hostler, Park Lane
Brown, Edward - Baker, Holland St.
Brown, Edwin - Harford Avenue
Brown, Elijah - Asbury Lane
Brown, Elizabeth - Grocer, Bayard St.
Brown, Flora - 91 Ensor St.
Brown, Frisby - Peace Alley
Brown, George - Ship Carpenter, Hill St.
Brown, Greenbury - Laborer, Sharp St.
Brown, Hager - Ensor St.
Brown, Henry - Porter, Preston St.
Brown, Henry - Washer, Potter St.
Brown, Henry - Porter, Sterling St.
Brown, Henry - Drayman, Baltimore St.
Brown, Hetty - Washer, Joy Alley
Brown, Jacob - Peace Alley
Brown, Jacob - Laborer, Salisbury St.
Brown, James - Laborer, Wagon Alley
Brown, James - Laborer, Jew's Alley
Brown, James - Fisherman, Fort Road
Brown, Jane - Washer, Saratoga St.
Brown, Jerry - Blacksmith, Centre St.
Brown, John - Sawyer, 13 Happy Alley
Brown, John - Laborer, Cross St.
Brown, John F. - Stevedore, 12 Gun Battery
Brown, Joseph - Blacksmith, Conway St.
Brown, Joshua - Carter, Pratt St.
Brown, Joshua - Porter, Carpenter's Alley
Brown, Laborer - Laborer, Baltimore St.
Brown, Leah - Sugar Alley
Brown, Lydia - French St.
Brown, Maria - Washer, Biddle Alley
Brown, Maria - Washer, Alley (unnamed)
Brown, Nancy - Peace Alley
Brown, Perry - Blacksmith, Strawberry Alley
Brown, Perry - Gardener, E. Canal
Brown, Pheney - Washer, Run Alley
Brown, Philip - Waiter, Hull's Lane
Brown, Rachael - Asbury Lane
Brown, Reuben - Carriage Driver, Aisquith St.
Brown, Ruth - Washer, 4 happy Alley
Brown, Sally - Washer, Eutaw St.

The Baltimore City Directory of 1831: The Free Black Population

Index to the Free Black Population

Brown, Sally - Alice Anna
Brown, Samuel - Waiter, Mulberry St.
Brown, Stephen - Laborer, 4 Happy Alley
Brown, Stephen - Carter, Forest St.
Brown, Sukey - Washer, Peace Alley
Brown, Thomas - Drayman, Strawberry Alley
Brown, Thomas - Quarrier, Guilford's Alley
Brown, Thomas - Laborer, Conway St.
Brown, Ted - Laborer, City Bounds
Brown, William - Laborer, Lerew's Alley
Brown, William - Laborer, Sharp St.
Bryan, Abraham - Drayman, Moore's Lane
Bryan, Isaac - Porter, Stable Alley
Bryan, Levin - Sawyer, East St.
Bryan, Sylvia - Washer, 34 N. Frederick St.
Bryson, Peter - Blacksmith, French Alley
Buck, James - Laborer, Wilk St.
Buck, James - Oyster Seller, 55 Water St.
Budd, Julius - Laborer, Pine St.
Budd, Julius - Whitewasher, Ensor St.
Buley, Silas - Laborer, Apple Alley
Bullen, Frederick - Hair Dresser, Pratt And Eutaw
Buois, John - Laborer, 21 Ruxton St.
Burgess, Alex - Coachman, 7 Potter St.
Burgoine, Gustine - Gardener, 86 Caroline St.
Burke, Clement - Teacher, East St.
Burke, Henry - Stevedore, Caroline St.
Burke, Milly - Washer, Eager Alley
Burke, Thomas - Caulker, 8 Happy Alley
Burke, Thomas - Stevedore, 9 Happy Alley
Burley, Isaac - Laborer, Temple
Busick, James - Laborer, Strawberry Alley
Butler, Abraham - Bank and Strawberry Alley
Butler, Ann - Washer, Harford Avenue
Butler, Basil - Cook, Hill St.
Butler, Charles - Laborer, Long Lane
Butler, E. - Hack Driver, German Lane
Butler, Elizabeth - Washer, Ross St.
Butler, Francis - Waiter, 15 Ruxton St.
Butler, George - Holland St.
Butler, Henry - Washer, Necessity Alley
Butler, Henry - Brickmaker, German
Butler, Josiah - Oak Cooper, German St.
Butler, Minty - Washer, Bottle Alley
Butler, Mrs. Rachel - Calvert St.
Butler, Nathaniel - Laborer, Lerew's Alley

215

Chapter 16

Index to the Free Black Population

Butler, Peter - 34 Fleet St.
Butler, Peter - Laborer, 32 Fleet St.
Byall, Isaac - Brickmaker, Charles St.
Cager, Ann - Washer, Spring St.
Cager, James - Wolf St.
Cager, Plato - Brickmaker, Richmond St.
Cagey, John - Little Hamstead
Caldwell, Delia - Washer, Mulberry St.
Caldwell, Ennis - Laborer, Argyle Alley
Caldwell, George - Sawyer, Harford Avenue
Caldwell, Margaret - Washer, Strawberry Alley
Caldwell, Perry - Brickmaker, Busy Alley
Caldwell, Perry - Sawyer, Guilford's Alley
Caldwell, Thomas - Strawberry Alley
Caldwell, William - Hack Driver, N. Gay St.
Calhoun, Peter - Drayman, Run Alley
Campbell, Charles - Brickmaker, Eden St.
Camper, Andrew - Leadenhall St.
Camper, Charles - Stevedore, Short St.
Camper, Moses - Sawyer, South Lane
Canvas, George - Waiter, New St.
Carey, Peter - Laborer, Pratt St.
Carmack, Jehu - Carter, 80 Ensor St.
Carmack, Joel - Porter, Painter's Court

Carr, Mrs. Ellen - Montgomery St.
Carr, Purnell - Sawyer, Argyle Alley
Carr, Rachel - Wilk St.
Carrol, Lucy - Green St.
Carroll, C. - Washer, Doctor's Lane
Carroll, Caesar - Porter, Sarah Ann
Carroll, John - Mariner, Strawberry Alley
Carroll, Peter - Laborer, Montgomery
Carroll, William - Shop Keeper, 3 Park St.
Carson, James - Long Alley
Carson, Samuel - Farmer, Run Alley
Carter, Job - Asbury Lane
Carter, Philemon - York Road
Carter, Samuel - Sawyer, Lerew's Alley
Cassell, William - Barber, 57 Wagon Alley
Ceney, Benjamin - Laborer, Salisbury St.
Ceney, Nancy - Little Hamstead
Chamberlain, Joshua - Drayman, Saratoga St.
Chambers, Benjamin - Laborer, Wolf's Alley
Chambers, Charity - Washer, Dutch Alley
Chambers, Edward - Waiter, Ensor St.
Chambers, Ezekiel - Mariner, Columbia St.
Chambers, Hager - Centre St.
Chambers, Josiah - Sailor, Love St.
Chambers, Perry - Laborer, Salis-

The Baltimore City Directory of 1831: The Free Black Population

Index to the Free Black Population

bury St.
Chambers, Susan - Eutaw St.
Chapman, David - Drayman, Leadenhall St.
Chapman, Isaac - Laborer, S. Charles St.
Chapman, Jeremiah - Blacksmith, Pratt St.
Chappell, Richard - Stevedore, Old Harford Road
Charles, Charles - Huckster, Wagon Alley
Charles, Theodore - Laborer, Spring St.
Chase, Basil - Drayman, Hull's Lane
Chase, John - Cooper, Forest St.
Chase, Mary - Cinway St.
Chase, Patty - Saratoga St.
Chase, Richard - Cordwainer, Wagon Alley
Chase, Samuel - Sawyer, 65 Strawberry Alley
Chase, Samuel W. - Teacher, Spring St.
Cherry, Rebecca - Park Lane
Chester, Stanly - Wagoner, 22 Strawberry Alley
Chester, Stanly - Sawyer, 41 Happy Alley
Chew, John - Nightman, S. Charles
Chew, Judy - Stirling St.
Chew, Samuel - Sawyer, Low St.
Chew, Thomas - Nightman, Peace Alley
Chrisby, Rose - Kipp's Row
Christal, G. H. - Laborer, Salisbury St.
Christian, Charles - Waiter, Biddle Alley

Christmas, Caleb - Caulker, William St.
Christmas, James - Caulker, Ensor St.
Chubb, Anthony - Waiter, Pine St.
Clark, Jerry - Sawyer, Strawberry Alley
Clark, Rachel - Washer, German St.
Clark, Robinson - 76 N. High St.
Clark, Sampson - Brickmaker, S. End Eutaw
Clayton, Pompey - Strawberry Alley
Clements, ? - Doctress, Conway St.
Clinton, Tom - Rag Man, Strawberry Alley
Coates, H. - Laborer, Wagon Alley
Coates, James - Laborer, 58 Park St.
Coates, Jeremiah - Sawyer, 101 East St.
Coby, Elijah - Laborer, Mulberry St.
Cockey, Cato - Laborer, Holland St.
Cockey, Ellen - Washer, Harford Avenue
Coe, Sarah - Huckster, Short St.
Coge, Simon - Grain Measurer, Guilford's Alley
Coker, Abner - Otter, Low St.
Coker, Joseph - 1 Forest St.
Cole, Debora - Washer, Chaisty's Alley
Cole, Diana - 14 W. Fleet St.
Cole, Maris - Washer, Starr Alley
Cole, Philip - Brickmaker, Cross St.
Cole, Prince - Whitewasher, Pearl St.

217

Chapter 16

Index to the Free Black Population

Coleby, Ann - Washer, Busy Alley
Coleman, Adam - Sawyer, Guilford's Alley
Coleman, Josiah - Lerew's Alley
Coleman, Levin - Sawyer, Happy Alley
Colick, Samuel - 3 Kipp's Alley
Collins, John - Brickmaker, Fort Road
Collins, Nanny - Lerew's Alley
Collins, William - Cooper, Liberty St.
Commodore, Richard - Drayman, Chesnut Alley
Congo, Eli - Peace Alley
Cook, Andrew - Laborer, Pennsylvania Av.
Cook, Delia - Old Clothes Dealer, Kimmell's Alley
Cook, Diana - Huckster, Conway St.
Cook, Henry - Waiter, 34 N. Frederick St.
Cook, Mackenzie - Laborer, N. Sharp St.
Cook, Thomas - Barber, Franklin St.
Cook, Thomas - Pratt St.
Cooper, Benjamin - Sawyer, Aisquith St.
Cooper, Henry - Drayman, Eutaw St.
Cooper, Jacob - Carter, Sugar Alley
Cooper, James - Caulker, Happy Alley
Cooper, James - Drayman, Peace Alley
Cooper, Joseph - Laborer, Happy Alley
Cooper, Nancy - Alley (unnamed)
Cooper, Perry - Laborer, Homespun Alley
Cooper, Perry - Laborer, Strawberry St.
Cooper, Robert - Caulker, Happy Alley
Cooper, Samuel - Caulker, Wolf St.
Cooper, Thomas - Drayman, Lloyd St.
Cooper, William - Caulker, Happy Alley
Copper, Sarah - Washer, Temple St.
Copplin, Joseph - Laborer, Wagon Alley
Cornish, Edward - Sawyer, Bank St.
Cornish, George - Sawyer, Guilford's Alley
Cornish, Jacob - Sawyer, Argyle Alley
Corporal, Abraham - Guilford's Alley
Corporal, Benjamin - Guilford's Alley
Cothey, Anne - Washer, German St.
Cotton, Daniel - Sawyer, Biddle Alley
Coursey, Edward - Rope Maker, Gould's Slaughterhouse
Cowley, Robert - Teacher, Hull's Lane
Cozens, Isaac - Carter, Stirling St.
Craw, Catherine - Washer, 6 Happy Alley
Crawford, William - Laborer, Cove St.
Craycroft, Sarah - Mantua Maker, 74 N. Liberty St.

The Baltimore City Directory of 1831: The Free Black Population

Index to the Free Black Population

Creek, Richard - Stevedore, Exeter St.
Crew, Edward - Sawyer, Peace Alley
Crisp, John - Laborer, Bath St.
Cromwell, Edward - Cordwainer, Peach Alley
Cromwell, Gabriel - Barber, Low St.
Cromwell, George - Shoemaker, Conway St.
Cromwell, Joseph - Laborer, German Lane
Cromwell, Mary Ann - Salisbury Alley
Cromwell, Richard - Conway St.
Crough, Mary - Happy Alley
Crowner, ? - Porter, Liberty St.
Croxall, John - Cook Shop, 22 Lombard St.
Crumwell, G. - Boot & Shoemaker, 86 W. Pratt St.
Culbert, Samuel - Howard St.
Culley, Harriet - Washer, 30 W. Fleet St.
Cummins, James - Laborer, Apple Alley
Cummins, John - Mariner, Strawberry Alley
Curry, John - Caroline St.
Curtis, Abednego - Harford Avenue
Curtis, Adam - Laborer, Starr Alley
Curtis, Clement - Barre St.
Curtis, Darkey - Washer, German Lane
Curtis, Henry - Lerew's Alley
Curtis, Perry - Carter, Park Lane
Curtis, William - Sawyer, Little Hamstead

Dangerfield, David - Douglass St.
Dansbury, Rightson - Laborer, S. Eutaw St.
Dappy, Priscilla - Washer, Sharp St.
Darby, Major - Pratt St.
Dary, Samuel - Hack Driver, Union St.
Dask, Francis - Carpenter, German St.
Davidge, Amos - Waiter, Chestnut Alley
Davis and Sanders - Whitewashers, Front St.
Davis, Betsey - Water St.
Davis, Betsey - Washer, Peace Alley
Davis, Catherine - Washer, Eden St.
Davis, Eliza - Ruxton St.
Davis, Fanny - Washer, 56 Park St.
Davis, Francis - Porter, Bounty Lane
Davis, Francis - 58 N. Gay St.
Davis, Jacob - Laborer, Short St.
Davis, James - Laborer, 34 Happy Alley
Davis, James - Drayman, Saratoga St.
Davis, John - Seaman, 15 Happy Alley
Davis, John - Shoemaker, 50 Fleet St.
Davis, Joseph - Laborer, Happy Alley
Davis, Lewis - Drayman, Mulberry St.
Davis, Mrs. - York Avenue
Davis, Robert - Sawyer, William St.

Chapter 16

Index to the Free Black Population

Davis, Samuel - Gardener, Caroline St.
Davis, Susan - Biddle Alley
Davis, William - Sawyer, Welcome Alley
Davis, William - Carter, Charles
Dawden, Adam - Laborer, Forest St.
Dawson, Thomas - Ship Carpenter, Wilk St.
Day, Cato - Caulker, 48 Happy Aley
Day, Robert - Dealer, Chaisty's Alley
Deakins, Julia - Washer, W. Pratt St.
Delany, Joseph - Sawyer, Spring St.
Delany, Michael - Mill Stone Maker, Ross St.
Denny, Samuel - Laborer, Necessity Alley
Derrick, William - Gardener, Fisherman
Devertier, Mary - Cook, Wagon Alley
Dickerson, Nathan - Leadenhall St.
Dickerson, Perry - Scowman, Short St.
Dickerson, Phillis - Washer, Bank St.
Dickerson, Richard - Forest St.
Dickerson, William - Laborer, Spring St.
Dickson, James - Hack Driver, Gay St.
Dickson, Perry - Hack Driver, Low St.
Diggs, George - Whitewasher, Eutaw St.
Diggs, William - Drayman, Cove St.
Distance, William - Mariner, Canal St.
Ditto, Joseph - Mariner, 24 Wilk St.
Dixon, Daniel - Drayman, Chrales St.
Dixon, Harry - Sawyer, Asbury lane
Dixon, Mary - Washer, Peace Alley
Dixon, Samuel - Hack Driver, Hillen St.
Dixon, Valentine - Laborer, Potter St.
Dixon, William - Drayman, Hill St.
Dobson, Greenbury - Granby St.
Dode, Peter - Clothing Store, 28 E. Pratt St.
Doekins, Robert - Brickmaker, Busy Alley
Doldin, Robert - Waiter, 42 N. Frederick St.
Donnell, Washington - Granby St.
Dorkins, Charles - Waiter, Sharp St.
Dorling, Patty - Washer, East St.
Dorrile, Mathew - Laborer, French Alley
Dorsey, Abbey - Chestnut Alley
Dorsey, Aminta - Saratoga St.
Dorsey, Cresy - Washer, German Lane
Dorsey, Henry - Laborer, German St.
Dorsey, Henry - Laborer, Chapel Alley
Dorsey, Isaac - Strawberry Alley
Dorsey, James - Hack Driver, Caroline St.
Dorsey, Lucinda - Huckster,

The Baltimore City Directory of 1831: The Free Black Population

Index to the Free Black Population

Addison St.
Dorsey, Perry - Guilford's Alley
Dorsey, Susan - Washer, Sharp St.
Douglass, George - Drayman, 32 Light St.
Douglass, Samuel - Porter, Pine St.
Douglass, Thomas - Drayman, Eager Alley
Douglass, William - Blacksmith, French Alley
Dove, Adam - Laborer, Bank St.
Dowden, Sole - Sawyer, Forest St.
Dowlan, Isaac - Drayman, Doctor's Lane
Downs, James - Waiter, Potter St.
Downs, Julia - 13 Ruxton St.
Dowsley, Robert - Laborer, Holland St.
Doyle, Richard - Eager Alley
Draper, Ryland - Teacher, Long Alley
Drewitt, Susan - Washer, 24 Lexington St.
Drummer, Evan - Brickmaker, Hill St.
Drummond, Perry - Waiter, Run Alley
Duff, Basil - Halfmoon Alley
Dukehart, Peter L. - Pleasant St.
Dunaho, Thomas - Silver Plater, 6 Block St.
Dunbar, Charles - Chamberlain Alley
Dunlap, Diana - Bound St.
Dunn, Charles - Gay St.
Duppins, Phoebe - Washer, Broad Alley
Durham, Rachel - Forest St.
Dyer, Martha - Eden St.
Ebert, Siddy - Laundress, Guilford's Alley
Edex, Jarrett - Hack Driver, Howard St.
Edmondson, Francis - Laborer, Alley (unnamed)
Edmondson, William - Laborer, Argyle Alley
Efford, Hy - Brickmaker, Bottle Alley
Elliott, Samuel - Porter, Baltimore St.
Elliott, William - Laborer, 9 Lancaster St.
Ellis, Jacob - Laborer, 18 E. Baltimore St.
Ellitt, David - 34 Fleet St.
Ellsberry, Charles - Mariner, Lancaster St.
Emory, Chloe - Jews Alley
Ennals, Jacob - Laborer, Cove St.
Ennals, William - Caulker, Spring St.
Ennerstairs, Mrs. Mary - Paca St.
Ennis, Benjamin - Lumber Wagoner, Little Hughes St.
Ennis, Harriet - Washer, 30 N. Frederick St.
Ennis, William - German St.
Evans, Henrietta - Washer, 114 Bond St.
Evans, James - Porter, Short St.
Evans, James - Laborer, Forest St.
Fell, Hannah - Washer, Pierce St.
Ferguson, Benjamin - Laborer, Hill St.
Ferrell, Absalom - Low St.
Fisher, Eliza - Washer, 125 Bond St.
Fisher, Sally - Washer, Chestnut Alley
Fisher, Tobias - Eager Alley

Chapter 16

Index to the Free Black Population

Fisher, York - Greenwich St.
Flamer, Nancy - Washer, Bishop's Alley
Fleetwood, Benjamin - Sailor, Mulberry St.
Fleetwood, Thomas - Ship Carpenter, Apple Alley
Flood, Lydia - Washer, Low St.
Foot, Basil - Sawyer, Hull's Lane
Foot, Hester - Asbury Lane
Foot, Rachel - Washer, Mechanic's St.
Ford, Benjamin - Grocer, 30 Lombard St.
Ford, Thomas - Laborer, St. Paul St.
Ford, Washington - Ostler, Lerew's Alley
Ford, William - Shoemaker, Potter St.
Ford, William - Cordwainer, Forest St.
Fortie, George - Cordwainer, Inloe's Alley
Fortie, Henry - Drayman, Lane
Fortie, Jacob - Laborer, Park St.
Fortie, John - Teacher, Asbury St.
Fortune, John - Laborer, Spring St.
Foster, Perry - Asbury Lane
Fowler, Leonard - Fort Road
Fowler, Peter - Chamberlain's Alley
Fowler, Rachel - Washer, N. Howard
Fox, Hamilton - Sawyer, Forest St.
Francis, Adelaide - Nurse, 22 Potter St.
Francis, John - Seaman, Bank St.
Francis, Perry - Laborer, Eutaw St.

Francis, Thomas - Laborer, Conway St.
Frank; and, Winny [[??]] - Howard St.
Freeman, Hester - Washer, 42 N. Frederick St.
Freeman, Isaac - Laborer, Howard St.
Freeman, Peter - Sarah Ann
Freeman, Samuel - Laborer, Howard St.
Freeman, Stephen - Long Alley
French, Elizabeth - Busy Alley
Frfeeman, Samuel - Blacksmith, Eutaw St.
Frisby, Charles - Brickmaker, Forest St.
Frisby, George - Salisbury St.
Frisby, Manuel - Laborer, Hawk St.
Frisby, Perry - Laborer, Bottle Alley
Fuller, Thomas - Carter, Hamilton St.
Gable, Henry - Fishman, Cross St.
Gaither, Catherine - Scott St.
Galamoon, Joseph - Mariner, Caroline St.
Gale, Isaac - Hack Driver, Shakespeare St.
Gale, Phoebe - Washer, Shakespeare St.
Gannon, Betsy - Washer, Conway St.
Gannon, Michael - Wagon Alley
Gannon, Washington - Sawyer, Homespun Alley
Gansey, Joseph - Laborer, Eden St.
Gant, Henry - Alley (unnamed)
Gantt, Joshua - Laborer, Chaisty's

The Baltimore City Directory of 1831: The Free Black Population

Index to the Free Black Population

Alley
Gardner, Benjamin - Seaman, Forest St.
Garrett, William - Porter, Bank Lane
Garrison, Wiley - Hack Driver, York Avenue
Gassaway, George - Laborer, S. Charles
Gaswell, David G. - Porter, Park St.
Gibbs, Nancy - Scott St.
Gibson, Basil - Drayman, Long Alley
Gibson, Hester - Washer, Strawberry Alley
Gibson, Philip - Hack Driver, Potter St.
Gibson, Richard - Centre St.
Gibson, Robert - Laborer, Peace Alley
Gibson, Samuel - Sawyer, Guilford's Alley
Gibson, Sewell - Laborer, Lerew's Alley
Gilbert, Joshua - Laborer, Centre St.
Gilbert, Paco - Laborer, Centre St.
Giles, Grace - Conway St.
Giles, Jane - Washer, Lerew's Alley
Giles, Phoebe - Happy Alley
Gilliard, Charlotte - Chamberlain Alley
Gilliard, Nicholas - Blacksmith, Harford Avenue
Gilliard, Susan - Harford Avenue
Glover, Ann - Washer, 56 Park St.
Goans, James - Carter, Forest St.
Godman, Prudence - Washer, Pierce St.
Goff, Ann - Washer, Forest St.
Golder, Robert - Grocer, Howard St.
Goldin, Charles - Blacksmith, 15 Happy Alley
Goldsberry, Charles - Woodsawyer, 148 Bond St.
Goldsborough, Hnery - Sawyer, Argyle Alley
Goldsborough, Richard - Ship Carpenter, Wolf St.
Goodwin, Charles - Carter, Johnson St.
Goodwin, Thomas - Laborer, Park St.
Gooldin, Geoffrey - Drayman, Douglass St.
Gooseberry, Joseph - Laborer, 40 Happy Alley
Gordon, Benajmin - Sawyer, Low St.
Gordon, Joseph - Cooper, Mulberry St.
Gott, Priscilla - Washer, Shakespeare St.
Gough, Deborah - Washer, Wagon Alley
Gould, John - Laborer, Mulberry St.
Gould, Richard - Woodsawyer, Eden St.
Gould, Richard - Laborer, Carpenter's Alley
Gould, Robert - Laborer, Rock St.
Goy, Francis - Laborer, Richmond St.
Grace, James - Laborer, Happy Alley
Grace, William - Fayette St.
Graham, Henry - Porter, Pine St.
Grand, Charles - Park Lane

Chapter 16

Index to the Free Black Population

Granger, Stephen - Laborer, Potter St.
Grant, Charles - Canal St.
Grant, Nancy - Armistead Lane
Graves, George E. - Canal St.
Graves, Henry - Laborer, French Alley
Gray, Caesar - Sawyer, Potter St.
Gray, David - Drayman, Camden St.
Gray, David - Drayman, Peace Alley
Gray, Deborah - Apple Alley
Gray, Fanny - Spring St.
Gray, Henry - Alley (unnamed)
Gray, James - Laborer, 111 Camden St.
Gray, Jerry - Brickmaker, Pierce St.
Gray, Joseph - Cordwainer, 21 Ruxton St.
Gray, Levin - Laborer, Alley (unnamed)
Gray, Sarah - Montgomery St.
Green Jenny - Washer, Peace Alley
Green, Anne - Washer, Moore's Lane
Green, Charles - Laborer, Caroline St.
Green, Charlotte - Washer, Peace Alley
Green, David - Laborer, Potter St.
Green, David - Packer, Welcome Alley
Green, David - Laborer, 11 Happy Alley
Green, John - Sawyer, Forest St.
Green, Richard - Porter, Potter St.
Green, Richard - Porter, Hamilton St.
Green, Sophia - 76 Argyle Alley
Green, Thomas - Hair Dresser, 4 Light St.
Green, Thomas - Hair Dresser, Bank Lane
Green, Vincent - Laborer, Lerew's Alley
Green, William - Laborer, Montgomery St.
Greener, Rebecca - Washer, Dutch Alley
Greenwood, Eleanor - Washer, Fayette St.
Greenwood, Henry - Drayman, Howard St.
Greenwood, Isaac - Fort Road
Greenwood, Perry - Sawyer, 10 Thames St.
Greenwood, Peter - Laborer, Guilford's Alley
Greenwood, Samuel - Drayman, Fayette St.
Grice, Hezekiah - Dealer In Ice, Aisquith St.
Griffin, Alex - Sexton, S. Of Bottle Alley
Griffin, Barney - Lombard St.
Griffin, Cuffy - Porter, Welcome Alley
Griffin, Henry - Comb Alley
Griffin, Henry - Laborer, Chappel Alley
Griffin, Hetty - Washer, German St.
Griffin, Margaret - Washer, 36 N. Frederick St.
Griffin, Mary - Eden St.
Griffin, Peter - Laborer, Lerew's Alley
Griffin, Ruth - Spring St.
Griffin, Single - Carter, Strawber-

224

The Baltimore City Directory of 1831: The Free Black Population

Index to the Free Black Population

ry Alley
Griffin, Susan - Lerew's Alley
Griffin, Susan - Canal St.
Griffith, William - Brickmaker, Sugar Alley
Grimes, John - Carter, Park Lane
Grisson, Samuel - Laborer, Mechanics's St.
Groom, Billy - W. Pratt St.
Groom, Tobias - Laborer, College Alley
Grooms, Diana - Short St.
Grooms, Emery - Forest St.
Grooms, Mrs. Little - Hughes St.
Gross, Abraham - Drayman, Howard St.
Gross, Abraham - Brickmaker, Charles St.
Gross, Benjamin - Drayman, Pierce St.
Gross, Charles - St Paul's St.
Gross, Henry - Drayman, Cross St.
Gross, Joseph - Laborer, Necessity Alley
Gross, Philip - Ropemaker, Cross St.
Gross, Polly - Washer, Lerew's Alley
Gross, Rachel - Short St.
Gross, Rachel - Washer, 82 French St.
Gross, Samuel - Sawyer, Welcome Alley
Gross, Leonard - 4 Ruxton Lane
Grows, Henry - Sawyer, 11 Douglass St.
Grows, Jacob - Sawyer, 11 Douglass St.
Guest, Margaret - Fleet St.
Gustive, John - Cordwainer, 3 Forest St.
Gustus, Matilda - Washer, Davis St.
Gustus, Winsen - Caulker, Wilk St.
Guy, Samuel - Howard St.
Gwynn, James - Laborer, Salisbury St.
Gwynn, London - Sawyer, Doctor's Lane
Gwynn, William - Laborer, Ensor St.
Hacket, Charles - Drayman, 14 Forest St.
Hacket, George A. - Keeper of Livery Stable, Bath St.
Hacket, Philip - Laborer, Low St.
Hacket, Robert - Biddle Alley
Hall, Aaron - Brickmaker, Scott St.
Hall, Adam - Park Lane
Hall, Arthur - Drayman, Bounty Lane
Hall, Charles - Laborer, German St.
Hall, Charles - Drayman, Lerew's Alley
Hall, Edward - Porter, Chapel Alley
Hall, Ellen - S. Howard
Hall, Francis - Laborer, Cove St.
Hall, Francis - Sailor, Low St.
Hall, Jacob - Fayette St.
Hall, Jacob - Waiter, Mechanic's St.
Hall, Jane - Washer, 80 French St.
Hall, John - Tanner, East St.
Hall, John - Drayman, Pearl St.
Hall, Joseph - Blacksmith, Beuren St.
Hall, Maria - Washer, E den St.
Hall, Moses - Carpenter, Scott St.

Chapter 16

Index to the Free Black Population

Hall, Mrs. - 18 Salisbury St.
Hall, Patty - Washer, Lerew's Alley
Hall, Sarah - Washer, Alley (unnamed)
Hall, William - Porter, Biddle St.
Hammond, George - Eden St.
Hammond, Paul - Sawyer, Eden St.
Hammond, Savage - Monument St.
Hammond, Southey - Monument St.
Handy, Ishmael - Harford Avenue
Handy, James - Laborer, Guilford's Alley
Handy, Priestman - 52 Happy Alley
Hanson, Emory - Laborer, Concord St.
Hanson, James - Sawyer, Guilford's Alley
Hanson, John - Run Alley
Hanson, Joseph - Drayman, East St.
Harden, Ann - Bottle Alley
Harden, George - Carpenter, Potter St.
Harden, Harriet - Spring St.
Harden, James - Waiter, Gay St.
Harden, Leah - Alley (unnamed)
Harden, Lucy - Huckster, Pearl St.
Harden, Mathew - Laborer, Run Alley
Harden, Rachel - Washer, Centre St.
Harden, Thomas - Blacksmith, Short St.
Harding, John - Drayman, Lerew's Alley
Harding, Philip - Sawyer, Peace Alley
Hare, Abraham - Waiter, 11 N. Exeter St.
Hare, Andrew - Waiter, Potter St.
Hare, Samuel - Washington Lane
Harris, Archibald - Laborer, Union St.
Harris, Benjamin - 13 S. Howard St.
Harris, Cecelia - Washer, Douglass St.
Harris, Edward - Ship Carpenter, Strawberry Alley
Harris, George - Blacksmith, Necessity Alley
Harris, Indiana - College Alley
Harris, Jacob - Sailor, Conway St.
Harris, Jacob - Laborer, Light St.
Harris, Jesse - Sawyer, Spring St.
Harris, John - Laborer, Rock St.
Harris, Joseph - Carter, Orleans St.
Harris, Leon - Gardener, Baltimore St.
Harris, Letetia - Washer, 10 Ross St.
Harris, Matilda - Peace Alley
Harris, Rosetta - 3 Kipp's Alley
Harris, Stephen - Short St.
Harris, William - Asbury Lane
Harrison, Dolly - Lexington St.
Harrison, Louisa - Lexington St.
Harrison, Nicholas - Laborer, Davis St.
Harrison, William - Blacksmith, Light St.
Harriwood, William - Chappel Alley
Harrod, Joseph - Exeter St.
Harrody, William - Sawyer, Baltimore St.

The Baltimore City Directory of 1831: The Free Black Population

Index to the Free Black Population

Hart, Shadrack - Laborer, Wagon Alley
Hasler, John - Butcher, Halfmoon Alley
Hawkins, Frederick - Sawyer, Hammond's Alley
Hawkins, James - Howard St.
Hawkins, Peter - Eutaw St.
Hays, Cato - Little Pleasant St.
Hayward, Isaac - Fisherman, Strawberry Alley
Hayward, Rachel - Huckster, Poter St.
Haywrad, Edward - Porter, Lerew's Alley
Hazard, Henry - Seaman, Spring St.
Hazard, John - Blacksmith, Bank Lane
Hazard, Matthew - Laborer, Barre St.
Haze, John - Laborer, Bishop's Alley
Haze, Timothy - Scowman, Happy Alley
Heath, Lucy - Washer, Honey Alley
Hensley, Henny - Washer, Hawk St.
Henson, Jacob - Laborer, Dutch Alley
Henson, James - 30 N. Frederick St.
Henson, James - Drayman, East St.
Henson, Mary - Washer, Sharp St.
Hewes, James - Carter, Terrapin Hill
Hewins, Edward - Laborer, Low St.
Hicks, Emanuel - Laborer, Barre St.
Hicks, Erasmus - Waiter, Centre St.
Hicks, Milly - Washer, St. Paul St.
Hiland, Lazarus - Alley (unnamed)
Hill, Charles - Porter, Painter's Court
Hill, Edward - Laborer, Apple Alley
Hill, H. J. - Cabinet Maker, 64 N. Howard St.
Hill, Henrietta - Washer, East St.
Hill, James - Wagoner, Baltimore St.
Hill, Joshua - Laborer, Salisbury St.
Hill, Samuel - Drayman, Pierce St.
Hill, Sarah - Washer, Holland St.
Hill, Susan - Washer, French Alley
Hill, Thomas - Carter, Homespun Alley
Hillary, Ambrose - Hair Dresser, East St.
Hiner, Jacob - Victualler, E. Canal St.
Hiner, Samuel - Victualler, Pitt St.
Hinson, David - Porter, St Paul St.
Hinson, Joseph - Sawyer, Eden St.
Hithe, Samuel - N. High St.
Hodges, Maria - Salisbury St.
Holland, Denby - Sawyer, Cross St.
Holland, Dinah - Peace Alley
Holland, Dinah - Huckster, Howard St.
Holland, Henry - Cordwainer, German St.
Holland, James - Laborer, Conway St.
Holland, Joseph - Sawyer, Park Lane

227

Chapter 16

Index to the Free Black Population

Holland, Philip - Shingle Shaver, William St.
Holland, Sikey - Mariner, Davis St.
Holliday, Barney - Long Lane
Holliday, Benjamin - Drayman, Biddle Alley
Holliday, Harriet - Bond St.
Holliday, James - Carter, Ensor St.
Holliday, nanny - Biddle Alley
Holliday, Richard - Stevedore, Hammond's Alley
Hollingsworth, Abraham - Drayman, 42 N. Frederick St.
Hollis, David - Laborer, Forest St.
Holly, George - Bottle Alley
Holmes, Thomas - Laborer, Exeter St.
Holt, George - Waterman, Potter St.
Holton, Jarvis - Laborer, Lerew's Alley
Homas, John - Laborer, Peach Alley
Hooper, Isaac - Mechanic's St.
Hooper, Sarah - Washer, 26 S. Charles St.
Hopkins, Cato - Laborer, Salisbury St.
Hotchcock, Elizabeth - Alley (unnamed)
Howard, Carlos - Gardener, Saratoga St.
Howard, Chloe - Washer, Davis St.
Howard, Emanuel - Montgomery St.
Howard, Isaac - Laborer, Halfmoon Alley
Howard, James - Hack Driver, Centre St.
Howard, Nicholas - Porter, Potter St.
Howard, Samuel - Drayman, Mechanic's St.
Howard, Samuel - Lerew's Alley
Howard, Samuel - Washington Lane
Howard, Susan - Peace Alley
Howard, Waite - Howard St.
Howard, William - Hack Driver, Short St.
Howell, Samuel - Laborer, 124 Wolf St.
Hubbard, Charles - Laborer, Potter St.
Hubbell, Samuel - Teacher, 146 S. Sharp St.
Hubley, Benjamin - Hamilton St.
Hudson, ? - Caulker, 66 Wolf St.
Hughes, James - E. Baltimore St.
Hughes, John - Sarah Ann St.
Hughes, Simon - Argyle Alley
Hutchins, Ann Maria - Peace Alley
Hutchins, James - Drayman, Bank Lane
Hutchins, Mrs. Mary - Potter St.
Hutchins, Samuel - Porter, Pierce St.
Hutchinson, Joseph - Lerew's Alley
Imey, Michael - Waiter, N. Gay St.
Impey, Comfort - Washer, Homespun Alley
Impey, Jacob - Laborer, Strawberry Alley
Inloes, Charlotte - Washer, Cross St.
Inloes, Samuel - Drayman, Pierce St.
Inloes, Thomas - Cooper, Eager Alley

The Baltimore City Directory of 1831: The Free Black Population

Index to the Free Black Population

Irby, Mrs. Ann - Cross St.
Ireland, Jesse - Newspaper Carrier, Forest St.
Ireland, Louisa - Low St.
Ireland, Milly - Washer, Potter St.
Ireland, William - Howard St.
Isaacs, Pharoah - Sawyer, Gay St.
Jackson, Diana - Apple Alley
Jackson, Elijah - Laborer, Wagon Alley
Jackson, George - Laborer, Howard St.
Jackson, Harry - Peace Alley
Jackson, Henry - Laborer, Alley (unnamed)
Jackson, James - Porter, Peace Alley
Jackson, John - Carter, Ann St.
Jackson, Joseph - Laborer, 94 Ensor St.
Jackson, Juliet - Washer, Biddle Alley
Jackson, Mary - Fleet St.
Jackson, Murray - Drayman, Mulberry St.
Jackson, Nace - Howard St.
Jackson, Sarah - Washer, Barre St.
Jackson, Shadrack - Sawyer, Douglass St.
Jackson, Stephen - Wagoner, Alley (unnamed)
Jackson, Susan - Washer, 145 Sharp St.
Jackson, Thomas - Laborer, Baltimore St.
Jackson, Thomas - Howard St.
Jackson, Thomas - Montgomery St.
Jackson, Uriah - Carpenter, Conway St.
Jackson, William - Sawyer, Dutch Alley
Jackson, William - Sawyer, Homespun Alley
Jackson, Willis - Hamilton St.
Jacob, Elias - Painter, Mulberry St.
Jacobs, Nathan - Laborer, Pine St.
Jacobs, Nathan - Laborer, German Lane
Jakes, Frederick - Waiter + Boot Cleaner, 7 S. Calvert St.
James, Edward - Carter, Barre St.
James, Maria - Washer, Pierce St.
James, Nancy - Gough St.
James, Samuel - Moore's Lane
James, Robert - Laborer, Chaisty's Alley
Jamison, George - Laborer, Charles St.
Janer, Anthony - Fort Road
Janey, Monday - Measurer, Eutaw St.
Jefferson, Diana - Potter St.
Jefferson, Philip - Carter, Sharp St.
Jefferson, Thomas - Porter, Pearl St.
Jenkins, B. - Shopkeeper, Lerew's Alley
Jenkins, Frisby - Laborer, Hill St.
Jenkins, George - Roller At Press, Potter St.
Jenkins, Jacob - Drayman, Hoffman St.
Jenkins, James - Laborer, Union St.
Jenkins, Josias - Fruit Shop, W. Pratt St.
Jenkins, Samuel - Laborer, 2 Strawberry Alley

Chapter 16

Index to the Free Black Population

Jennings, Thomsa - Laborer, German St.
Jervis, Thomas - Laborer, Long Alley
Jilcoat, Jerry - Laborer, Howard St.
Johns, Moses - Oysterman, Sharp St.
Johns, Mrs. Martha - Eager Alley
Johnson, Aaron - Guilford Alley
Johnson, Amey - Washer, Happy Alley
Johnson, Ann - Huckster, French St.
Johnson, Ann - Washer, Caroline St.
Johnson, Cassy - Washer, 115 Camden St.
Johnson, Cassy - Washer, Peace Alley
Johnson, Charles - Caulker, 25 Wilk St.
Johnson, Daniel - Carter, Hill St.
Johnson, Dorcas - Washer, Cypress Alley
Johnson, Eli - Drayman, Wagon Alley
Johnson, Eli - Drayman, Eutaw St.
Johnson, Emanuel - Scourer, Caroline St.
Johnson, Francis - Laborer, Hill St.
Johnson, Francis - Laborer, Forest St.
Johnson, George - Laborer, Biddle Alley
Johnson, George - Drayman, German St.
Johnson, George - Cordwainer, N. Exeter St.
Johnson, George W. - Aisquith St.
Johnson, Grace - Bottle Alley
Johnson, Grace - Argyle Alley
Johnson, Hardester - Stevedore, Spring St.
Johnson, Henney - Huckster, Low St.
Johnson, Henry - Seaman, Addison St.
Johnson, Jacob - Harford Avenue
Johnson, Jake - Alley (unnamed)
Johnson, James - Cordwainer, East St.
Johnson, James - Sawyer, Strawberry Alley
Johnson, James - Laborer, Short St.
Johnson, James - Boot & Shoemaker, 2 W. Fayette St.
Johnson, James - Elbow lane
Johnson, Job - Laborer, Chatsworth St.
Johnson, John - Hairdresser, Franklin St.
Johnson, John - Laborer, Lerew's Alley
Johnson, John - Park St.
Johnson, John - Laborer, Johnson St.
Johnson, John - Barber, Little Pleasant St.
Johnson, John W. - Waiter, Saratoga St.
Johnson, Jonathan - Carter, East St.
Johnson, Joseph - Fort Road
Johnson, Joshua - Laborer, Dutch Alley
Johnson, Julianna - Spring St.
Johnson, Lucy - Washer, Liberty St.

The Baltimore City Directory of 1831: The Free Black Population

Index to the Free Black Population

Johnson, Lucy - 55 Happy Alley
Johnson, M. - Douglass St.
Johnson, Magdaline - Washer, Chestnut Alley
Johnson, Margaret - Salisbury St.
Johnson, Martha - Washer, Honey Alley
Johnson, Mary - Homespun Alley
Johnson, Mary Ann - S. Cove St.
Johnson, Michael - Waterman, French Alley
Johnson, Molly - Washer, Hamilton St.
Johnson, Moses - Waterman, Hill St.
Johnson, Moses - Front St.
Johnson, Mrs. Susan - Hamilton St.
Johnson, Nancy - Park Lane
Johnson, Nathan - Laborer, 165 Wilk St.
Johnson, Nathaniel - Laborer, Happy Alley
Johnson, Peggy - Chamberlain Alley
Johnson, Peter - Laborer, Strawberry Alley
Johnson, Rachel - Ensor St.
Johnson, Ralph - Porter, South Lane
Johnson, Richard - Sawyer, Pine St.
Johnson, Richard - Waiter, East St.
Johnson, Richard - Laborer, Peach Alley
Johnson, Robert - Drayman, Park Lane
Johnson, Robert - Carter, Concord St.
Johnson, Sally - Whitewasher, 43 Wilk St.
Johnson, Samuel - Lane (unnamed)
Johnson, Samuel - Laborer, Sharp St.
Johnson, Samuel - Drayman, Park Lane
Johnson, Samuel - Ropemaker, Sugar Alley
Johnson, Samuel - Apple Alley
Johnson, Sarah - Washer, Alley (unnamed)
Johnson, Solomon - Cordwainer, Rock St.
Johnson, Sylvia - Argyle Alley
Johnson, Tenant - Saratoga St.
Johnson, Thomas - Laborer, Wagon Alley
Johnson, Thomas - Park Lane
Johnson, Thomas P. - Grocer, Lombard St.
Johnson, William - Mariner, Strawberry Alley
Johnson, William - Carpenter, Alley (unnamed)
Johnson, William - Plasterer, 13 Ross St.
Johnson, William - Laborer, Howard St.
Jones, Amelia - Alley (unnamed)
Jones, Amos - Laborer, East St.
Jones, Andrew - Gardener, Douglass St.
Jones, Ann - Pearl St.
Jones, Charles - Porter, Short Alley
Jones, Clement - Gay St.
Jones, David - Drayman, Fayette St.
Jones, Eli - Mariner, Caroline St.
Jones, Frances - Washer, Granby

Chapter 16

Index to the Free Black Population

Jones, Francis - Laborer, Alley (unnamed)
Jones, Henney - Washer, Low St.
Jones, Isaac - Hoeard St.
Jones, Isaac - Drayman, Howard St.
Jones, Israel - Caulker, Forest St.
Jones, Jacob - Carter, Carpenter's Alley
Jones, James - Asbury Lane
Jones, James - Caulker, Sharp St.
Jones, Joseph - Laborer, Peace Alley
Jones, Lucretia - Washer, Peace Alley
Jones, Matilda - Washer, Cove St.
Jones, Peter - Laborer, Bishop's Alley
Jones, Robert - Laborer, Argyle Alley
Jones, Robert - Turner, East St.
Jones, Sally - Huckster, Ensor St.
Jones, Stephen - Drayman, Dutch Alley
Jones, Thomas - Sugar Alley
Jones, Thomas - Laborer, Spring St.
Jones, William - Waiter, Cove St.
Jones, Williamson - Laborer, 111 Camden St.
Jones, Alice - Short St.
Jones, Benjamin - Potter St.
Jones, John - Caulker, Granby St.
Jordan, John - Cabinet Maker, Potter St.
Joyce, Lambert - German St.
Kain, Debonshire - Strawberry Alley
Kain, Ellen - Alley (unnamed)
Kane, George - Laborer, Lerew's Alley
Keener, Peter - Porter, Kimmel's Alley
Kell, David - Montgomery St.
Kelly, C. - Sawyer, Happy Alley
Kemp, Henry - Laborer, Strawberry Alley
Kennard, William - Bayard St.
Kent, William - Mariner, Strawberry Alley
Kew, John - Wagoner, Park Lane
Key, Thomas - Wagoner, Pierce St.
Keys, Daniel - Laborer, Strawberry Alley
Keys, Francis - Brickmaker, Pierce St.
Keys, John - Carter, Light St.
Keys, Mary Ann - Potter St.
Keys, Widge - Alley (unnamed)
Kiar, Daniel - Hair Dresser, Montgomery St.
Kidle, Hester - Strawberry Alley
King, Joseph - Waiter, Park St.
King, Thomas - Carpenter, Alley (unnamed)
Knight, Robert - Carter, 29 Union St.
Knox, Ann - Oyster Woman, 18 Happy Alley
Konig, Hager - 113 Camden St.
Lampert, Cornish - Porter, Biddle St.
Lancaster, Evan - Laborer, Short Alley
Lancaster, William - Laborer, German St.
Landsdale, Kitty - Little Pleasant St.
Landsey, Watt - Laborer, Carpenter's Alley
Langly, George - Waiter, Biddle

The Baltimore City Directory of 1831: The Free Black Population

Index to the Free Black Population

Lard, Richard - Porter, 21 Potter St.
Larkins, ? - Ensor St.
Lawrence, A. - Sawyer, Argyle Alley
Lawrence, John - Stevedore, 1 Dugan's Wharf
Lawson, Isaac - Baltimore St.
Le Brun, Mary - Mantua Maker, Bond St.
Lebark, Eli - Hack Driver, 40 Park St.
Lecture, Lewis - Laborer, Davis St.
Lee, Charles - Carter, Conway St.
Lee, Charles - Homespun Alley
Lee, Daniel - Laborer, German St.
Lee, Jacob - Douglass St.
Lee, Jane - Washer, Jew's Alley
Lee, Lemeul - Drayman, Short St.
Lee, Philip - Porter, Howard St.
Lee, Philip - Laborer, Pierce St.
Lee, Rachel - Washer, Low St.
Lee, Samuel - Porter, Saratoga St.
Lee, Spencer - Carter + Wood Yard, Potter St.
Lemmon, William - Laborer, Bishop's Alley
Levin, Philip - Caulker, 3 Wolf St.
Lewis, Andrew - Blacksmith, German St.
Lewis, Charles - Laborer, Bottle Alley
Lewis, Emanuel - Porter, Fayette St.
Lewis, John - Toy Alley
Lewis, M. - Washer, Harford Avenue
Lewis, Matilda - Washer, Wagon Alley
Lewis, Richard - Laborer, 4 Forest St.
Lewis, Wesley - Waiter, German Lane
Lilly, Peter - Laborer, Chamberlain Alley
Limers, John - Laborer, Sharp St.
Lindsey, David - Laborer, Halfmoon Alley
Linnet, Peter - Laborer, Douglass St.
Livingston, William - Teacher, Howard St.
Lloyd, Edward - Aegyle Alley
Lloyd, Henry - Eager Alley
Lloyd, William - Forest St.
Lockerman, Daniel - Low St.
Lockerman, Fanny - Joy Alley
Lockett, William - Blacksmith, Spring St.
Locks, Sandy - Sharp St.
Lomax, David - Caulker, S. Caroline St.
Lomax, David - Caulker, 110 Bond St.
Lorder, John - Baker, Potter St.
Lott, Jonathan - Carter, Apple Alley
Lovedy, Hester - Forest St.
Lucas, James - Laborer, German St.
Lymers, Charles - 4 Salisbury Alley
Lymers, Susan - Peace Alley
Lymers, William - Peace Alley
Lynch, Dolly - Washer, Davis St.
Mackall, Mintey - Conway St.
Mackall, Samuel - Sailor, Howard St.
Maddox, Lazarus - Porter, Park Lane
Maddox, Nancy - Huckster, Low

Chapter 16

Index to the Free Black Population

Magruder, Adam - Scott St.
Mainus, Scipio - Greenwich St.
Mann, Issac - Porter, Comb Alley
Marese, Catherine - N. Front St.
Mars, Perry - Carman, Grant St.
Marshall, George - Laborer, Moore's Lane
Marshall, John - Whitewasher, French St.
Marshall, Solomon - Laborer, Spring St.
Martin, Ennals - Laborer, Wilk St.
Martin, Henry - Cook Shop, Hawk St.
Martin, Henry - Carter, Eutaw St.
Martin, Henry - Porter, Inloes Alley
Martin, John - Grocer, 78 S. Howard St.
Martin, Joshua - Carter, Chatsworth St.
Martin, William - Laborer, Spring St.
Mason, Caleb - Carter, Charles St.
Mason, Isaac - East St.
Mason, James - Porter, Dutch Alley
Mason, John - Laborer, Eutaw St.
Mass, Polly - Washer, Jefferson St.
Mattees, Betsy - Happy Alley
Matthews, Cato - Laborer, Pierce St.
Matthews, Charles - Lerew's Alley
Matthews, Dinah - Washer, 11 Saratoga St.
Matthews, James - Trunk Maker, Lerew's Alley
Matthews, Julia - Old York Road
Matthews, Michael - Short St.
Matthews, Richard - Pleasant St.
Matthews, Samuel - Laborer, Run Alley
Matthews, William - Drayman, Eager Alley
Mattox, William - Laborer, 111 Camden St.
Maulick, C. - Washer, Bottle Alley
Maxfield, John - Laborer, 26 S. Charles St.
Maxwell, Samuel - Sawyer, North St.
Maybury, Mark - Laborer, German St.
Maynard, Charles - Barber, 81 Liberty St.
McClo, Peter - Park St.
McCoy, James - Laborer, Mechanic's St.
McCoy, Robert - Waiter, Sharp St.
McDaniel, Nancy - Guilford's Alley
McDonald, Jane - Huckster, East St.
McFarlan, William - Caulker, Apple Alley
McGill, Sarah - Washer, Germanb St.
McQuay, Richard - Sailor, Short Alley
Meads, Jane - Washer, Chaisty's Alley
Meads, Stephen - Sailor, Spring St.
Meads, Zachariah - Porter, Centre St.
Medley, George - Little Hampstead St.
Meeds, Jesse - Laborer, Saratoga St.
Meeds, Sarah - Run Alley
Mercer, Eliza - Caroline St.
Merrika, Moses - College Alley

The Baltimore City Directory of 1831: The Free Black Population

Index to the Free Black Population

Merryman, Betsy - Washer, Fleet St.
Merton, Gabriel - Carter, Happy Alley
Middleton, A. - Eden St.
Milburn, Levi - Sarah Ann St.
Miller, Dick - Laborer, Hill St.
Miller, H. - Laborer, Water St.
Miller, James - Laborer, Mulberry St.
Miller, James - Laborer, Guilford's Alley
Miller, Lloyd - Conway St.
Miller, Margaret - Washer, 36 N. Frederick St.
Miller, Peter - Drayman, Hill St.
Miller, Peter - Laborer, 56 N. Exeter St.
Millington, Kitty - Park Lane
Mills, John - Sawyer, Scott St.
Mills, Nelly - Washer+Waiter, 82 Ensor St.
Mills, York - Boot Black, Franklin St.
Mingo, James - Laborer, Happy Alley
Mingo, Sarah - Scott St.
Mitchell, Aminta - 56 Happy Alley
Mitchell, Clara - Washer, Pierce St.
Mitchell, Elisha - Sawyer, Alice Anna St.
Mitchell, James - Dutch Alley
Mitchell, James - Caulker, Spring St.
Mitchell, John - Caulker, Apple Alley
Mitchell, Robert - Ell Alley
Mitchell, Samuel - Blacksmith, Bishop's Alley
Moales, Charles - Carter, Potter St.
Moales, John - Laborer, Strawberry Alley
Mohor, Peter - Carter, Strawberry Alley
Mollison, Henry - Laborer, Pine St.
Monk, Philip - Caulker, Fleet St.
Montgomery, Martin - Caulker, Spring St.
Montgomery, Nathaniel - Alice Anna St.
Montgomery, Nathaniel - Laborer, Wilk St.
Montgomery, Rachel - E. Canal St.
Montgomery, Rosetta - Spring St.
Mooney, Joshua - Drayman, Lloyd St.
Moore, Abraham - Waiter, Centre St.
Moore, Abraham - Shopkeeper, Park St.
Moore, Cyrus - Porter, Eutaw St.
Moore, George - Waiter, Hill's Lane
Moore, George - Welcome Alley
Moore, Hamlet - Sawyer, Caroline St.
Moore, Hannah - Argyle Alley
Moore, Henrietta - Washer, Conway St.
Moore, Jane - Apple Alley
Moore, Maria - Washer, Cathederal St.
Moore, Mary - Scott St.
Moore, Matthew - Mariner, Happy Alley
Moore, Matthew - Laborer, N. Frederick St.
Moore, Peter - Elbow Lane
Moore, Richard - Laborer, Happy

235

Chapter 16

Index to the Free Black Population

Moore, William - Laborer, Caroline St.
Morris, John - Tanner, Ensor St.
Morris, Stephen - Laborer, Short St.
Morrison, Barbara - Pearl St.
Morrison, Patience - Scott St.
Morsell, Peter - Johnson St.
Moss, Cynthia - Caroline St.
Mouldem, Eliza - Washer, Balderson St.
Mucket, Michael - Mulberry St.
Mundowny, Henry - Mariner, Strawberry Alley
Murphy, Harry - Laborer, Lerew's Alley
Murphy, Moses - Laborer, Bank Lane
Murphy, Nicholas - Laborer, Long Alley
Murphy, William - Laborer, Kimmel's Alley
Murray, Aaron - Barber, Addison St.
Murray, Alexander - Waiter, 20 Salisbury St.
Murray, David - Laborer, Spring St.
Murray, Deborah - Washer, Strawberry Alley
Murray, George - Laborer, Forest St.
Murray, Jacob - Laborer, Hammond's Alley
Murray, John - Laborer, Hancock St.
Murray, Mrs. Nancy - Water St.
Murray, Parish - Laborer, Happy Alley
Murray, Perry - Laborer, Ruxton St.
Murray, Samuel - Brick Moulder, Pierce St.
Murray, Sylvia - Washer, Forest St.
Murray, William - Laborer, Wolf's Alley
Myers, Henrietta - Bishop's Alley
Myers, Henry - Blacksmith, Liberty St.
Myers, Jerry - Dutch Alley
Myers, John - Drayman, Bounty Lane
Myers, Maria - Spring St.
Myers, Mary - Washer, Garden St.
Myers, Nathaniel - Drayman, Potter St.
Myers, Rachel - 24 Lombard St.
Myers, Richard - Laborer, St. Mary's St.
Myers, Robert - Carter, Apple Alley
Nail, Mary - Whitewasher, Mulberry St.
Nailor, Jacob - Sawyer, French St.
Nathans, Daniel - Waiter, Mulberry St.
Naylor, Nathan - Salisbury St.
Naylor, Samuel - Guilford's Alley
Neal, Richard - Drayman, Charles St.
Neal, Thomas - Drayman, Peace Alley
Neale, John - Carter, Argyle Alley
Needs, Joseph - Laborer, German St.
Neilson, Perry - Orleans St.
Neilson, William - Blacksmith, Strawberry Alley
Nelson, Jacob - Run Alley
Netter, Dennis - Welcome Alley

Index to the Free Black Population

Nettles, John - Brick Moulder, Hill St.
Newall, Nelly - Washer, Chaisty Alley
Newbern, ? - Sawyer, Spring St.
Newett, Daniel - Drayman, Pierce St.
Newman, Jacob - Asbury Lane
Newton, Isaac - Warren St.
Nicholas, Mary - Washer, Biddle St.
Nicholls, Elizabeth - Garden St.
Nicholls, Henry - St. Mary's St.
Nicholls, John - Barber, Hull's Lane
Nichols, Henry - Harford Avenue
Nichols, Jeremiah - Stevedore, Bank St.
Nichols, Margaret - Washer, Hawk St.
Nicholson, Adam - Waiter, Pierce St.
Nicholson, George - Porter, Carpenter's Alley
Nicholson, John - Caulker, Starr Alley
Nickerson, Nancy - Douglass St.
Noel, John - Hairdresser, 7 + 28 N. Howard St.
Noel, Linda - Huckster, Wagon Alley
Norris, Hannah - Washer, German St.
Norris, Jacob - Little Hughes St.
Norris, Nimrod - Laborer, Ensor St.
Norris, Priscilla - Washer, Pratt St.
Norris, Richard - Waiter, 5 Salisbury Alley
Norris, Robert - Whitewasher, Wine Alley
Norton, Sarah - Washer, Montgomery St.
Nunan, Moses - Laborer, Grant St.
Ogle, Samuel - Sawyer, Low St.
Oliver, Henrietta - Barber, Potter St.
Oliver, James - Sawyer, Cove St.
Oliver, William - Laborer, Ensor St.
Osborne, D. - Brickmaker, Ensor St.
Osborne, Lewis - Drayman, Chesnut Alley
Owens, Fanny - Washer, Eden St.
Owens, Richard - Run Alley
Oxford, John - Laborer, Strawberry Alley
Page, Cyrus - Caroline St.
Paidler, Vaiche - Sawyer, York Avenue
Palmer, James - Laborer, Pierce St.
Paraway, Isabella - Conway St.
Paraway, John - Laborer, Wolf's Alley
Parker, Ellen - Moore's Lane
Parker, Ellen - Washer, Pearl St.
Parker, James - Laborer, Pierce St.
Parker, John - Laborer, Sarah Ann St.
Parker, Nicholas - Sawyer, Park St.
Parker, Polly - Washer, Sarah Ann St.
Parker, Samuel - Laborer, Park St.
Parker, Sophia - Washer, Ruxton St.
Parks, Lloyd - Moore's Lane

Chapter 16

Index to the Free Black Population

Parks, Peter - Sawyer, Argyle Alley
Parks, William - Little Pleasant St.
Parraway, Absalom - Hill St.
Parrott, Betsey - Leadenhall St.
Parsons, Matilda - Douglass St.
Patterson, Adam - Homespun Alley
Patterson, Daniel - Laborer, Argyle Alley
Patterson, Joshua - Laborer, 69 Caroline St.
Peach, Samuel - Homespun Alley
Peach, William - Welcome Alley
Peacock, Mary - St. Mary's St.
Peaker, Stephen - Porter, 72 French St.
Peck, Catherine - Carpet Waever, Honey Alley
Peck, Henry - Laborer, Columbia St.
Peck, Levin - Laborer, Guilford's Alley
Peck, Nathaniel - Whitewasher, Bath St.
Peel, John - Sawyer, Lerew's Alley
Peel, Richard - St. Mary's St.
Pemberton, John - Montgomery St.
Pemberton, John - Musician, 103 S. Eutaw St.
Pennington, Julia A. - Washer, Pearl St.
Pepper, Peter - Laborer, Salisbury St.
Peters, John - Laborer, Lerew's Alley
Peters, Mary - 34 S. Charles St.
Peters, Peter - Huckster, Wagon Alley
Peters, Sophia - Park St.
Peters, Thomas - Carter, Strawberry Alley
Peterson, Henny - Washer, Potter St.
Peterson, John - Strawberry Alley
Pevins, Charles - Fisherman, Johnson St.
Phillips, B. - Stevedore, Bank St.
Phillips, Charles - Laborer, Eden St.
Phillips, Isaac - Carter, Chestnut Alley
Phillips, James - Laborer, Spring St.
Phillips, James - Carter, Spring St.
Phillips, Lewis - Porter, 78 French St.
Phillips, Perry - Hack Driver, Caroline St.
Phipps, Ann - New St.
Pier, Ann - Huckster, 22 Strawberry Alley
Pierson, Elizabeth - 62 Happy Alley
Pindell, Mary - Washer, Pierce St.
Piner, Samuel - Sawyer, Barre St.
Pinkney, Dennis - 3 Kipp's Alley
Pitt, Samuel - Porter, 2 Stirling St.
Plyman, John - Hairdresser, 53 Camden St.
Polk, David - Cordwainer, Hill St.
Posey, Stephen - Laborer, Chestnut Alley
Poulson, Elizabeth - Sharp St.
Poulson, George - Eutaw St.
Powell, Ann - Washer, Peace Alley
Powell, Harry - Drayman, Ensor St.
Powell, James - Huckster, Potter

The Baltimore City Directory of 1831: The Free Black Population

Index to the Free Black Population

Powell, Jane - Washer, Mulberry St.
Powell, Phillis - Washer, Conway St.
Powell, Thomas - Sawyer, Hill St.
Powers, Charles - Sawyer, Douglass St.
Pratt, John - Laborer, Alley (unnamed)
Pratt, Trueman - Laborer, Pierce St.
Presgrove, James - Wagoner, N. Exeter St.
Preston, Milly - Washer, Douglass St.
Preston, Peter - Little Pleasant St.
Price, David - Laborer, Water St.
Price, Jacob - Sarah Ann St.
Price, John - Welcome Alley
Price, Nathan - Blacksmith, 79 N. Gay St.
Price, Thomas S. - White Washer, McClellan's Alley
Price, William - White Washer, Bath St.
Priestman, John - Laborer, Wilk St.
Prigg, Letitia - Washer, 4 Tyson St.
Primrose, Greenbury - Forest St.
Procton, John - Stone Mason, Garden St.
Proctor, Charlotte - Washer, Forest St.
Prout, Alfred - Carter, German St.
Prout, Edward - Blacksmith, Argyle Alley
Prout, John J. - Oil Dealer, Hill St.
Prout, Mrs. Charity - German St.
Prout, Philis - Alice Anna
Prout, Polly - Washer, Peace Alley
Prout, Rebecca - 79 Liberty St.
Prout, William - Drayman, Busy Alley
Prout, William - Laborer, Starr Alley
Prout, William B. - Shoemaker, 119 Camden St.
Pulley, Edward - Porter, East St.
Purviance, Samuel - Carter, 82 Ensor St.
Queen, Harriet - Washer, Frederick St.
Queen, John - Laborer, Montgomery St.
Queen, Sibby - Washer, Charles St.
Queen, Sophia - President St.
Queen, Stephen - Clothes Dealer, Hill St.
Queen, Thomas - Hairdresser, 17 Light St. Wharf
Quinn, Michael - Charles St.
Quinn, William - Drayman, Mulberry St.
Quinton, ? - Barre St.
Quinton, James - Howard St.
Ragans, Simon - Laborer, Long Alley
Ray, Benjamin - Laborer, Union St.
Reed, James - Laborer, Ferry Road
Reed, Polly - Alley (unnamed)
Reed, Richard - Carter, Bottle Alley
Reed, Thomas - Carter, Bottle Alley
Reese, George - Laborer, Argyle Alley
Reester, Abraham - Carter, Bishop's Alley

Chapter 16

Index to the Free Black Population

Reynolds, John - Mariner, Spring St.
Rhodes, Elijah - Nightman, Saratoga St.
Rice, Emory - Laborer, Long Alley
Rice, Shields - Ship Carpenter, Caroline St.
Richard, Jacob - Boot Black, 20 N. Gay St.
Richard, Thompson - Caulker, Wolf St.
Richards, Jesse - Terrapin Hill
Richards, Nicholas - Greenwich St.
Richards, Solomon - Blacksmith, Hillen
Richardson + Carey - Grocers, 93 W. Pratt St.
Richardson + London - Dyers + Scourers, 44 N. Frederick St.
Richardson, Abraham - Sawyer, Long Alley
Richardson, Caroline - Washer, College Alley
Richardson, Ellen - Shop Keeper, Washington St.
Richardson, Rachel - Washer, Bottle Alley
Richardson, William - Barber, Howard St.
Richardson, William - Centre St.
Riley, Harriet - Alley (unnamed)
Riley, Lee - Carpenter, Lerew's Alley
Riley, Warwick - Drayman, 111 Camden St.
Ringfield, Dorcas - Strawberry Alley
Ringgold, Benjamin - Laborer, Grant St.
Ringgold, Hezekiah - Blacksmith, Bishop's Alley
Ringgold, Jacob - Hamilton St.
Ringgold, Joseph - Laborer, Conway St.
Ringgold, Moses - Laborer, Short Alley
Ringgold, Thomas - Liberty St.
Ringgold, Thomas - Hill St.
Ringgold, Thomas - Laborer, Cross St.
Ringgold, Thomas - Waiter, Howard St.
Roberts, Charity - Washer, Carpenter's Alley
Roberts, Charles - Laborer, Eden St.
Roberts, David - German Lane
Roberts, George - Sawyer, Hoffman St.
Roberts, James - Long Alley
Roberts, Maria - Cook, Comb Alley
Roberts, Nelson - Waiter, Forest St.
Robinson Joseph - Laborer, 75 French St.
Robinson, Ann - Washer, Davis St.
Robinson, Charles - Block St.
Robinson, Edward - Sailor, 97 Bond St.
Robinson, Eli - Laborer, Bishop's Alley
Robinson, George - Hack Driver, Caroline St.
Robinson, Henry - Asbury Lane
Robinson, James - Laborer, French Alley
Robinson, Levin - Sailor, Bishop's Alley
Robinson, Lewis - Howard St.
Robinson, Lydia - Concord St.
Robinson, Mary - Saratoga St.
Robinson, Mary - Washer, 2 Kipp's

The Baltimore City Directory of 1831: The Free Black Population

Index to the Free Black Population

Robinson, Peter - Peace Alley
Robinson, Willey - Mechanic's St.
Robinson, Willey - Washer, 115 Camden St.
Robinson, Zillah - Bishop's Alley
Rocks, Peter - Tanner, Bell Alley
Rogers, Andrew - Laborer, East St.
Rogers, Rice - Drayman, Alley (unnamed)
Roman, John - Drayman, Run Alley
Ross, Daniel - Laborer, Welcome Alley
Ross, Nace - Laborer, Hill St.
Roxbury, Sarah - Bloomsbury Farm
Russell, Clement - Kimmell's Alley
Russell, John - Paper Hanger, Sharp St.
Sadler, Emory - German St.
Sales, Aaron - Drayman, 18 Ross St.
Salter, Joseph - Mariner, 67 Albermarle St.
Sampson, James - Sawyer, Pierce St.
Sampson, Mary - South Lane
Sanders, Jarret - Laborer, Caroline St.
Sanders, Thomas - 22 Strawberry Alley
Sanders, William - Conway St.
Savoy, Basil - Montgomery St.
Savoy, Dennis - Howard St.
Savoy, Richard C. - Waiter, 18 Gay St.
Savoy, Samuel - Chestnut Alley
Sawyer, David - Caroline St.
Scott, Dinah - Washer, N. Howard St.
Scott, Frances - Washer, Calvert St.
Scott, John - Sawyer, Lerew's Alley
Scott, John - Mariner, Caroline St.
Scott, Joseph - Wagoner, Fort Road
Scott, Littleton - Sexton, Afr. Church, E. Saratoga St.
Scott, Margaret - Busy Alley
Scott, Margaret - Washer, Peace Alley
Scott, Martha - East St.
Scott, Philip - Porter, Ensor St.
Scott, Robert - Carter, Argyle Alley
Scott, Thomas - Carter, Bottle Alley
Scotti, Robert - Sawyer, Jefferson St.
Scottin, Wealthy - 3 Stirling St.
Scottin, William - Hairdresser, 22 1/2 Charles St.
Scrivener, Isaac - Laborer, Cross St.
Scrivener, William - Cross St.
Seagrove, Clara - Alley (unnamed)
Sears, William - Waiter, Forest St.
Seaton, Flora - Washer, Potter St.
Sedars, Charles - Howard St.
Sedgwick, Baker - Union Alley
Sephus, William - Bishop's Alley
Sergick, Mary - Charles St.
Sewell, Thomas - Laborer, Chapel Alley
Sewell, William - Porter, Elbow Lane
Sheaf, Harry - Mariner, Halfmoon Alley
Sheaf, Joseph - Drayman, Short St.

Chapter 16

Index to the Free Black Population

Sheppard, Benjamin - Porter, Grant St.
Shipley, Peter - Carter, Chestnut Alley
Shirac, Jean Francois - Barre St.
Shorter, Charles - Caulker, Spring St.
Shorter, Lucy - Washer, Lombard St.
Shorter, Richard - Sawyer, Pierce St.
Silver, Alexander - Hairdresser, S. Gay St.
Skyler, Benson - President St.
Skyler, Henry - Montgomery St.
Sly, Jane - Washer, Pine St.
Small, Moses - Bank Lane
Smallwood, David - Drayman, Biddle Alley
Smallwood, Levin - Brickmaker, Short St.
Smallwood, Levin - 3 Salisbury Alley
Smiley, George - Gardener, Aisquith St.
Smith, Abraham - Carter, Forest St.
Smith, Aquilla - Farmer, Forest St.
Smith, Benjamin - Carter, Howard St.
Smith, David - Waiter, Cathederal St.
Smith, Dianna - Huckster, East St.
Smith, Edward - Moore's Lane
Smith, Edward - Laborer, Wagon Alley
Smith, Henny - Washer, Wilk St.
Smith, Hy? - Calico Printer, Potter St.
Smith, Isaac - Laborer, Chatsworth St.
Smith, James - Sawyer, Argyle Alley
Smith, James - Woodsawyer, Caroline St.
Smith, James - Laborer, Holliday St.
Smith, Jane - Washer, Centre St.
Smith, John - Weaver, Ann St.
Smith, John - Laborer, Potter St.
Smith, John - Nightman, Lerew's Alley
Smith, John - Laborer, German St.
Smith, Joseph - Gardener, Low St.
Smith, Joseph - Carter, Saratoga St.
Smith, Joshua - Drayman, Wagon Alley
Smith, Levin - Waiter, Hill St.
Smith, Mary - Washer, Strawberry Alley
Smith, Mrs. Lydia - Hill St.
Smith, Nancy - Washer, German Lane
Smith, Nathan - Carter, Bond St.
Smith, Nathaniel - Waiter, East St.
Smith, Perry - Carter, Saratoga St.
Smith, Perry - Porter, Short St.
Smith, Peter M. - Porter, Bath St.
Smith, Richard - Carter, Park Lane
Smith, Samuel - Drayman, Saratoga St.
Smith, Sarah - Washer, Biddle Alley
Smith, Sylvia - College Alley
Smith, T. - Whitewasher, 16 Fleet St.

The Baltimore City Directory of 1831: The Free Black Population

Index to the Free Black Population

Smith, Temperance - Washer, Water St.
Smith, Thomas - Laborer, Ferry Road
Smith, William - Strawberry Alley
Smith, William - Drayman, Saratoga St.
Smothers, Fusby - Porter, Peace Alley
Smothers, Harry - Laborer, Peace Alley
Sneed, Arthur - Laborer, Harford Avenue
Snowden, Peter - Chatsworth St.
Snowden, Thomas - Laborer, German St.
Soarden, William - Laborer, Bottle Alley
Sollers, Abraham - Carter, Run Alley
Sollers, Charles - Labor, Sugar Alley
Sorcer, John - Caulker, 13 Wolf St.
Sorden, William - Laborer, Cove St.
Spaniard, Peter - Gardener, 114 Bond St.
Sparrow, John - Chestnut Alley
Sparrow, Thomas - Lerew's Alley
Speaks, Reuben - Carpenter's Alley
Spencer, Philip - Homespun Alley
Spineyard, Richard - Short Alley
Sprigg, Richard - Waiter, 37 N. Liberty St.
Sprigg, Thomas - Laborer, Mechanic's St.
Spriggs, Anthony - Peach Alley
Spriggs, John - Peach Alley
Spriggs, John - Guilford's Alley
Spriggs, Stephen - Lancaster St.

Stanford, Aaron - Ship Carpenter, Wolf St.
Stanley, Adam - Charles St.
Stanley, Levin - Laborer, Moore's Lane
Stansbury, Abraham - Brickmaker, Carpenter's Alley
Stansbury, Barbara - Lerew's Alley
Stansbury, George - Carpenter's Alley
Stansbury, Moses - Laborer, Fayette St.
Stansbury, Samuel - Drayman, Water St.
Stanton, Matilda - Strawberry Alley
Sterett, Nancy - 147 Sharp St.
Sterett, Ralph - Drayman, Welcome Alley
Sterling, Peter - Porter, East St.
Stevens, Benjamin - Drayman, Spring St.
Stevens, Joseph - Laborer, Wagon Alley
Stevens, Rachel - Barre St.
Stevenson, David - Laborer, Alley (unnamed)
Stevenson, David - Boatman, Spring St.
Stevenson, Davy - Howard St.
Stevenson, Diana - Washer, Lee St.
Stevenson, John - S. Eutaw St.
Stevenson, John - Huckster, Ruxton St.
Stevenson, Joshua - Bricklayer, Potter St.
Stevenson, Milbury - Boatman, Spring St.
Stevenson, Nancy - Washer, S.

243

Chapter 16

Index to the Free Black Population

Charles
Stevenson, Shadrack - Carpenter, Wagon Alley
Stewart, Allen - Waiter, Centre St.
Stewart, Daniel - Salisbury Alley
Stewart, Edward - Porter, Inloes Alley
Stewart, Ellen - Union Alley
Stewart, George - Laborer, Guilford's Alley
Stewart, Godfrey - Necessity Alley
Stewart, Isaac - Run Alley
Stewart, John - Drayman, Hill St.
Stewart, Luke - Laborer, Forest St.
Stewart, Mitchell - Caulker, Starr Alley
Stewart, Rezin - Sawyer, Honey Alley
Stewart, Sarah - Milk Seller, 26 1-2 Lexington St.
Stewart, Stephen - Laborer, Burgundy Alley
Stewart, Thomas - Chesnut Alley
Stiles, Abraham - Sailore, Lane (unnamed)
Stiles, Milly - Laundress, Potter St.
Stoud, Chloe - Eden St.
Sullivan, Daniel - Porter, College Alley
Sullivan, R. William - Laborer, Strawberry Alley
Sullivan, Samuel - Laborer, Ferry Road
Summerfield, John - Laborer, Mulberry St.
Summerville, David - Stevedore, Wolf St.
Sutton, Abraham - Baker, Short St.
Sutton, Richard - Gardener, Saratoga St.
Syroe, Samuel - Laborer, Happy Alley
Talbot, B. - Carpenter, Argyle Alley
Talbot, Perry - Brickmaker, Eden St.
Tally, James - Laborer, Lerew's Alley
Tartar, Henry - Porter, Bottle Alley
Taylor, Basil - Laborer, Short St.
Taylor, H. - Washer, Eden St.
Taylor, Henry - Laborer, Forest St.
Taylor, Isaiah - Stevedore, Apple Alley
Taylor, John - Sailor, Spring St.
Taylor, Margaret - Washer, Jew's Alley
Taylor, Sophia - Mechanic's St.
Thomas, Adam - Sawyer, Happy Alley
Thomas, Andrew - Exeter St.
Thomas, August - Baker, Pierce St.
Thomas, Benjamin - Laborer, Strawberry Alley
Thomas, Cesar - Carter, Asbury Lane
Thomas, Charlotte - Eden St.
Thomas, David - Drayman, Run Alley
Thomas, David - Laborer, Asbury lane
Thomas, Dinah - Wolf St.
Thomas, Elizabeth - Washer, Caroline St.
Thomas, George - Laborer, Union Alley
Thomas, Handy - Sawyer, 5 Forest

The Baltimore City Directory of 1831: The Free Black Population

Index to the Free Black Population

Thomas, Harriet - Doctress, Cove St.
Thomas, Hazel - Drayman, Asbury Lane
Thomas, Henny - Washer, Low St.
Thomas, Horace - Laborer, Strawberry Alley
Thomas, J. - Gardener, Pennsylvania Av.
Thomas, Jacob - Drayman, Asbury Lane
Thomas, John - Laborer, Centre St.
Thomas, John - Carter, Lerew's Alley
Thomas, John - Baker, New St.
Thomas, John - Drayman, 72 French St.
Thomas, Joseph - Ship Carpenter, Argyle Alley
Thomas, Mary - Caroline St.
Thomas, Mary - Washer, Centre St.
Thomas, Mary - Washer, Lerew's Alley
Thomas, Perry - Laborer, Pennsylvania Av.
Thomas, Philip - Stevedore, Wilk St.
Thomas, Rachel Ann - Dutch Alley
Thomas, Richard - Laborer, Pennsylvania Av.
Thomas, Richard - Carter, Pratt St.
Thomas, Sib - Drayman, Biddle Alley
Thomas, William - Laborer, Lerew's Alley
Thompson, Caleb - Laborer, Spring St.
Thompson, Cesar - Caulker, Strawberry Alley
Thompson, Cyrus - Homespun Alley
Thompson, Edward - Hack Driver, Caroline St.
Thompson, Isaac - Laborer, Park Lane
Thompson, Jacob - Sawyer, Montgomery St.
Thompson, James - Laborer, Park Lane
Thompson, Michael - Laborer, 30 N. Frederick St.
Thompson, Mrs. Mary - Washer, Park St.
Thompson, Noah - Laborer, Alley (unnamed)
Thompson, Peter - Laborer, Park Lane
Thompson, Pompey - Laborer, Kimmel's Alley
Thompson, Samuel - Laborer, Apple Alley
Thompson, Seth - Laborer, Wilk St.
Thompson, Shadrack - Laborer, 78 Howard St.
Todd, Sally - 23 Potter St.
Toller, John H. - Cartman, Chesnut Alley
Tolson, William - Waiter, 1 Dugan St.
Toogood, Ann - Washer, German St.
Toogood, Charles - Chamberlain Alley
Toogood, Jacob - Porter, Pratt St.
Toogood, Jame - Eager Alley
Toomay, Hy - Confectioner, 14 Forest St.

Chapter 16

Index to the Free Black Population

Toomey, Caroline - Little Pleasant St.
Toppin, Charles - Drayman, Biddle Alley
Toppin, Henry - Porter, Exeter St.
Toukes, Harry - Cordwainer, Hawk St.
Toy, Anthony - Sawyer, Happy Alley
Toy, Elozabeth - Necessity Alley
Travers, Abraham - Carter, Pearl St.
Travers, Edward - Porter, Howard St.
Travers, Mary - Terrapin Hill
Travers, Nancy - Homespun Alley
Tripp, Emeline - Washer, Little Pleasant St.
Tripp, John - Laborer, Boubty Lane
Tripp, Nancy - Washer, Hull's Lane
Trusty, Jonathan - Stevedore, Apple Alley
Trusty, Perry - Drayman, Biddle Alley
Trusty, Samuel - Sawyer, Ensor St.
Tucker, Silkey - Washer, 42 N. Frederick St.
Tue, Nelly - Washer, Harford Avenue
Turner, Joseph - Sawyer, Forest St.
Turner, Polly - Pennsylvania Av.
Turner, William - Laborer, Sugar Alley
Tuttle, William - Exeter St.
Tynes, Joseph - Porter, German St.
Uncles, Isaac - Blacksmith, Asbury Lane
Valentine, Archibald - Blacksmith, 36 N. Frederick St.
Valentine, Joanna - Washer, Peace Alley
Vanard, James - Button Maker, Wagon Alley
Vest, Anthony - Laborer, Little Pleasant St.
Vezey, Cassey - Washer, Sterling St.
Walton, Benjamin - Brickmaker, Forest St.
Walton, Benjamin - Sawyer, Little Pleasant St.
Walton, Charles - Sawyer, Long Alley
Walton, Isaac - Sawyer, Little Pleasant St.
Ward, Esther - N. Exeter St.
Ward, Robert - Laborer, Block St.
Ward, Stephen - Laborer, 70 Caroline St.
Warfield, Reuben - Rope Maker, Strawberry Alley
Warner, Ellen - Washer, Hill St.
Warner, Garrison - Caulker, Guilford's Alley
Warner, James - Caulker, President St.
Warren, Adam - Laborer, German St.
Warwick, Charlotte - Starr Alley
Washington, Ruth - Cook Shop, 29 Marsh Market Sp.
Waters, Edward - Carter, Ensor St.
Waters, Hetty - Washer, 30 N. Frederick St.
Waters, Jacob - Blacksmith, Harford Avenue

The Baltimore City Directory of 1831: The Free Black Population

Index to the Free Black Population

Watkins, George - Laborer, Pierce St.
Watkins, Isaac - Sarah Ann St.
Watkins, Jane - Biddle Alley
Watkins, John - Laborer, Salisbury St.
Watkins, Jonathan - Sarah Ann St.
Watkins, William - Sawyer, Baltimore St.
Watkins, William - Boot+ Shoemaker, 113 Camden St.
Watson, Hetty - Fayette St.
Watson, John - 5 N. Liberty St.
Watson, Peter - Laborer, Peace Alley
Watters, John - Dutch Alley
Watts, Alexander - Busy Alley
Watts, Jerry - Porter, Potter St.
Watts, Rachel - Argyle Alley
Weals, Levin - Apple Alley
Weaver, Moses - Carpenter, Short Alley
Webster, David - Laborer, Saratogha St.
Webster, Isaac - Sawyer, Welcome Alley
Webster, William - Cove St.
Wells, Charles - Laborer, Saratoga St.
Wells, Dr. Lewis - Doctor, Wagon Alley
Wells, Jesse - Waiter, Hamilton St.
Wells, Letitia - Washer, Peace Alley
Wells, Mrs. Rachel - Dutch Alley
Wells, Nathaniel - Carter, Peace Alley
Wells, Nelson - Drayman, Charles St.
Wells, Solomon - Laborer, 56 N. Exeter St.
Welmore, Perry - Sawyer, Ensor St.
Welsh, Peter - Caulker, Strawberry Alley
Welsh, Thomas - Laborer, Union St.
Wesley, Ann - St. Paul's St.
Wesley, John - Barber, Gay St.
West, Eliza - Fleet St.
West, Francis - Hull's Lane
West, John - Laborer, Terrapin Hill
Wheatley, Levin - Mariner, Eden St.
Wheatley, Lydia - Strawberry Alley
Wheeler, Allen - Laborer, German St.
Wheeler, Archibald - Waiter, Dutch Alley
Wheeler, John - Carter, Howard St.
Wheeler, Rosanna - Salisbury St.
Whipper, Isaac - 7 Tyson St.
White, Henry - Boot Black, Long Alley
White, Jacob - Laborer, Franklin St.
White, Job - Caulker, Starr Alley
White, Reuben - Sawyer, Howard St.
Whittington, Jane - Washer, Strawberry Alley
Wiliams, John - Stevedpre, 17 Happy Alley
Williams, Ann - Sarah Ann St.
Williams, Ann - Washer, Happy Alley
Williams, Ann - Washer, Caroline

Chapter 16

Index to the Free Black Population

Williams, Anthony - Porter, Sugar Alley
Williams, Benjamin - Homespun Alley
Williams, Benjamin - Eutaw St.
Williams, Catherine - Huckster, Potter St.
Williams, Daniel - Sharp St.
Williams, David - Laborer, Homespun Alley
Williams, Easter - Washer, Philpot St.
Williams, Elizabeth - Potter St.
Williams, Emanuel - Mariner, Spring St.
Williams, Ephraim - Sawyer, Strawberry Alley
Williams, Fanny - Scott St.
Williams, Frisby - Hairdresser, 18 Water St.
Williams, George - Mariner, Caroline St.
Williams, Greenbury - Happy Alley
Williams, Henry - Brickmaker, Greenwich St.
Williams, Hesther - Laundress, Howard St.
Williams, Hnery - Blacksmith, 11 Douglass St.
Williams, J. - Laborer, Howard St.
Williams, James - Laborer, Apple Alley
Williams, Jeffry - Sawyer, Argyle Alley
Williams, John - Laborer, Pierce St.
Williams, John - Brickmaker, Howard St.
Williams, John - Brickmaker, Peace Alley
Williams, John - Laborer, Conway St.
Williams, John - Laborer, Strawberry Alley
Williams, Joseph - Laborer, Strawberry Alley
Williams, Joseph - Laborer, Bank Lane
Williams, Lucy - Intelligence Office, Homespun Alley
Williams, M. - Waiter, East St.
Williams, Maria - Cook, Saratoga St.
Williams, Mrs. Ellen - Armistead Lane
Williams, Nathan - Drayman, Granby St.
Williams, Palto - Laborer, Strawberry Alley
Williams, Pembrook - Ship Carpenter, 95 Ann St.
Williams, Philip - Howard St.
Williams, Prince - Laborer, 29 Union St.
Williams, Rachel - Washer, Howard St.
Williams, Rebecca - Washer, Harford Avenue
Williams, Rebecca - Washer, Greenwich St.
Williams, Richard - Dairyman, Pierce St.
Williams, Richard - Whitewasher, Conway St.
Williams, Ruth - 2 Kipp's Alley
Williams, Samuel - Waiter, Pleasant St.
Williams, Sibby - Peace Alley
Williams, Spinyard - Carter, Potter St.

The Baltimore City Directory of 1831: The Free Black Population

Index to the Free Black Population

Williams, Splinter - Carter, East St.
Williams, Stephen - Brickmaker, Little Hughes St.
Williams, Thomas - Laborer, Howard St.
Williams, William - Laborer, 12 Gun Battery
Williams, William - Laborer, Low St.
Williams, William - Sailor, Mulberry St.
Williams, William - Porter, Sharp St.
Williams, George - Dyer, 6 Forest St.
Williamson, Charles - Brickmaker, Saratoga St.
Wilmore, Michael - Laborer, Low St.
Wilmore, Samuel - Waiter, Gay St.
Wilson, Abraham - Harford Avenue
Wilson, Abraham - Blacksmith, Concord St.
Wilson, Abraham - Sailor, Granby St.
Wilson, Aminta - Laundress, Guilford's Alley
Wilson, Anthony - Laborer, 12 Potter St.
Wilson, Benjamin - Porter, Dutch Alley
Wilson, Carville - Short Alley
Wilson, Comfort B. - Laundress, Aisquith St.
Wilson, Ephraim - Laborer, Strawberry Alley
Wilson, Francis - Hill St.
Wilson, James - Laborer, Park St.
Wilson, James - Drayman, Sarah Ann St.
Wilson, John - Drayman, Howard St.
Wilson, Joseph - Grocer, Sharp St.
Wilson, Lloyd - Necessity Alley
Wilson, Margaret - Laundress, Garden St.
Wilson, Nancy - Long Lane
Wilson, Reynard - Laborer, Eden St.
Wilson, Rosetta - Laundress, Calvert St.
Wilson, Samuel - Waiter, Forest St.
Wilson, Samuel - Laborer, Guilford's Alley
Wilson, Samuel - Waiter, Carpenter's Alley
Wilson, Tarr - Laborer, Spring St.
Wilson, Thomas - Brickmaker, Barre St.
Wilson, William - Sawyer, 10 Thames St.
Wilson, William - Laborer, Lerew's Alley
Winder, Louisa - Washer, 31 E. Liberty St.
Winson, Isaac - Measurer, Johnson St.
Winson, Thomas - Porter, Homespun Alley
Woodlin, Elisha - Pratt St. Road
Woodyard, Polly - Washer, Union St.
Woodyear, Jefferson - Wagoner, Union St.
Worrell, Henry - Laborer, Guilford's Alley
Worthington, Eliza - Scott St.
Worthington, John - Laborer, Douglass St.

Chapter 16

Index to the Free Black Population

Worthington, John P. - Porter, Eutaw St.
Wren, ? - Wilk St.
Wright, Dorsey - Laborer, East St.
Wright, Edward - Drayman, Bank Lane
Wright, Emory - Laborer, Centre St.
Wright, Mary - Chaisty's Alley
Wright, Samuel - Brickmaker, Hull's Lane
Wright, Shadrack - Doctor's Lane
Wright, Tom - Brickmaker, Guilford's Alley
Wright, William - Laborer, Homespun Alley
Yates, Perry - Drayman, Pratt St. Road
Yates, Sandy - Necessity Alley
Young, Abigail - Porter St.
Young, Benjamin - Brickmaker, Conway St.
Young, Jacob - Whitewasher, Douglass St.
Young, John - Laborer, Mulberry St.
Young, Joseph - Blacksmith, Howard St.
Young, Joseph - Laborer, Cove St.
Young, Joseph - Laborer, Short Alley
Young, Lloyd - Drayman, Wagon Alley
Young, Mrs. Louisa - Little Hampstead
Young, Rachel - Star Alley
Young, Richard - Alley (unnamed)

17
Black Property Holders of Baltimore City, 1850

An analysis of the free black property holders of Baltimore in the 1850 census reveals an abscence of real estate holdings for that community in wards 10, 11, 12, 14, and 18.

Of the 15 wards in which real estate holdings are evident ward 3 (27 black property holders) and ward 6 (also 27 property holders) are the clear leaders.

Showing a distant second is ward 15 with 8 real estate holders, the remaining wards are as follows:

Ward	4	6
Ward	5	6
Ward	7	5
Ward	1	4
Ward	16	3
Ward	9	3
Ward	8	2
Ward	13	2
Ward	2	1
Ward	19	1
Ward	20	1
Ward	17	1

The wards with real estate holders possessing $2,000 or more in property are:

Ward	4	$4,300	and	$3,000 and $2,000
Ward	3	$11,000	and	$11,000
Ward	5	$4,000	and	$2,800
Ward	6	$2,500	and	$2,000
Ward	15	$3,000	and	$3,000
Ward	1	$2,500		
Ward	7	$40,000		
Ward	9	$3,000		

In the third ward a number of black families living on Bethel and Dallas street owned property:

Chapter 17

David Lecompt, a 40-year-old Sailor, owned $500 worth of real estate while residing at 58 Dallas. **Allen Chase**, a 50-year-old laborer, owned $500 worth of real estate while residing just down the street At 70 Dallas.

In the next block **Daniel Chapman**, a 54-year-old carter, owned $800 worth of real estate at 141 Dallas. Several doors away **James Morris**, a 54-year-old ship carpenter, also held $800 in real estate.

In the same neighborhood a number of black families living on Bethel Street near Bank Street owned real estate.

Joseph Chaplin, a 30-year-old caulker, and **Enoch Cummins**, a 40-year-old stevedore, each owned $600 worth of real estate.

Also on Bethel **Adam Thomas**, a 50-year-old sawyer, owned $600 worth of real estate while 31-year-old brickmaker **Edward Gatch** owned $700 worth of real estate. Just down the street on Bethel **Jonathan Trusty**, a 53-year-old stevedore held $600 worth of real estate.

Daniel Myers, living at 80 Bank Street in ward three, was a 58-year-old Sailor with $1,200 worth of real estate. One of the largest black real estate holders also resided in the third ward of the city. His name was **William H. Green**, a 50-year-old physician known as a Thomsonian Doctor (a doctor who utilized herbal medicine in his practice). Dr. Green resided at 93 Wolf Street and owned $11,000 worth of real estate.

Sixteen more black families held real estate in the third ward. More than $35,000 worth of real estate was owned by these families in the third ward.

Sharing the distiction as the ward with the largest number of black real estate holders was ward six, also with twenty seven. Real estate holders were to be found on Forest Street as well as Douglass, East, Jefferson, North Canal, Short and others.

A number of real estate owners resided in the first two blocks of Forest Street. **John Green**, a 50-year-old sawyer residing at 19 Forest Street, owned $1,000 worth of property. His next door neighbor **John H. Green**, a 33-year-old waiter residing at 17 Forest, owned $500 worth of real estate.

0**Charles Smith** of 12 Forest Street and **Nathaniel Smith** of 6 Forest Street, both drayman, owned $500 and $300 worth of real estate respectively.

James N. Williams, a sawyer at 48 Forest, and **James Young**, a coachman at 42 Forest, both owned $400 worth of real estate. Their neighbor **Israel Jones**, a 50-year-old caulker living at 58 Forest Street, owned $800 worth of real estate.

John Fortie, a 63-year-old teacher residing at 45 Jefferson Street, held the distinction of having the most real estate in ward six with

$2,500 worth of real estate.

A number of blacks on East Street in the sixth ward owned property. Among them were **Frances Carmack** at 77 east Street with $500 worth of real estate. Next door neighbor **Moses Clayton**, a 50-year-old carpenter at 79 East Street, owned $1,000 in real estate.

Frederick Wilson, a 45-year-old trader residing at 73 east Street, owned $1,000 worth of real estate. At 87 East Street **Spencer Waters**, a 50-year-old carter, owned $2,000 worth of real estate.

Andrew D. Jones, a 50-year-old bottler and wine refiner, had $1,500 worth of real estate while residing at 28 Douglass Street in the sixth ward. **Levin Lee**, a 62-year-old preacher residing at 34 Short Street, held $738 worth of real estate.

The total value of real estate owned by Black families in the sixth ward was $30,788.

Although wards three and six shared the largest numbers of real estate owners a number of wealthy owners resided in other parts of the city.

Samuel Hiner, a 59-year-old butcher residing at 186 E, Fayette Street, owned $40,000 worth of real estate. Reverend **John R. V. Morgan**, pastor of the Ebenezer African Church on S. Howard Street in ward 15, held $3,000 worth of real estate.

John Gordon, a 44-year-old cabinet maker residing in ward 5, held $5,000 worth of real estate.

These real estate holdings are indicated by the value of the dollar in 1850 of course. The buying power of the dollar today is approximately 18 - 20 times that of the buying power of the dollar in 1850 (of course the cost of living has risen accordingly). Therefore if someone owned $3,000 worth of real estate in 1850 that would represent approximately $50,000 - $60,000 today. It is easy to see how wealthy several of these black families were. Samuel Hiner, the butcher on Fayette Street, would today have real estate valued at approximately $700,000 - $800,000.

Although carters and drayman head the list of real estate owners in the Black community of Baltimore in 1850, a number of occupations are represented. Those occupations cover a wide spectrum of unskilled, semi skilled, and skilled occupations. The occupations represented are:

Barber	7
Blacksmith	1
Bottler	1
Brickmaker	5
Butcher	1
Cabinet Maker	1
Carpenter	1

Chapter 17

Carter	11
Caulker	6
Clergyman	1
Clothier	1
Coachman	3
Confectioner	1
Drayman	8
Gardener	1
Hack Driver	2
Hackman	1
Hay Merchant	1
Huckster	1
Laborer	3
Musician	2
Physician	2
Porter	3
Preacher	1
Sailmaker	1
Sailor	3
Sawyer	3
Ship Carpenter	1
Shoemaker	1
Stevedore	5
Steward	1
Stone Cutter	1
Storekeeper	1
Teacher	1
Trader	2
Victualler	1
Wagoner	1
Waiter	3

It is important to note that all addresses indicated above are the pre 1886 adresses. In 1886 the vast majority of addresses in the city of Baltimore were changed. In order to locate the post 1886 addresses that match those addresses indicated above one must use a 1887 city directory. The directory printed a list of all the old and new addresses city wide.

The 1850 Federal Population Census noted the real estate holdings of all free people. Personal estate was not listed until the 1860 census. Real estate as listed in this index would have represented such items as houses or property. Personal estate indicated in the 1860 census would have represented such items as furniture, gold watches, carriages, etc.

The following index lists a number of free African Americans in

Black Property Holders of Baltimore City, 1850

Baltimore that held property (real estate) in the year 1850.

This list, while representative of those holdings, is not 100% complete. Studies of other documents of the time (for example city tax assesment work books) will provide estate holders not indicated in the census records.

The index is organized as follows:

Surname and first name of real estate holder, age, occupation, estate holdings, ward, and page number.

The pages used in this index are the boldly stamped page numbers in the upper right hand corner of the document.

Each stamped page represents that page as well as the unstamped page immediately following. Therefore 244A would indicate the page that is actually stamped 244, while 244B would indicate the unstamped page following 244.

A sample entry would read as follows:

Anderson, Jacob - 50, barber, $3,000, w 15, p 93b

The translation of this material notes that Jacob Anderson, a 50-year-old barber residing in ward 15 of Baltimore in 1850 holds $3,000 worth of real estate. This information is recorded on page 93b of the census record for that ward.

Black Property Holders - 1850

Anderson, Jacob - Barber, $3,000, w 15, p 93b

Badger, Jarret - Drayman, $600, w 16, p 143a

Bailey, John B. - Barber, $500, w 5, p 93a

Bateman, Edward - Drayman, $700, w 7, p 342?

Baugh, Charles A. - Barber, $800, w 3, p 310a

Bishop, John H. - Sailor, $700, w 3, p 382a

Blake, Cato - Stone Cutter, $500, w 19, p 151a

Bowen, Ephraim - Drayman, $300, w 6, p 178b

Brown, Robert - Caulker, $800, w 1, p 23b

Brown, William - Brickmaker, $300, w 3, p 331a

Burk, Thomas - Caulker, $800, w 3, p 398b

Butler, George - Hack Driver, $1,000, w 2, p 237a

Caldwell, William - Hackman, $500, w 6, p 223b

Carmack, Frances - $500, w 6, p 245b

Chapell, Richard - Stevedore, $300, w 8, p 453a

Chapter 17

Black Property Holders - 1850

Chaplin, Joseph - Caulker, $600, w 3, p 374a

Chapman, Daniel - Carter, $800, w 3, p 330b

Chase, Allen - Laborer, $500, w 3, p 344b

Clark, Lewis - Musician, $800, w 13, p 366a

Clayton, Moses - Carpenter, $1,000, w 6, p 245b

Cooper, Thomas - Caulker, $500, w 1, p 35a

Cromwell, Garretson - Waiter, $600, w 17, p 291a

Cummins, Enoch - Stevedore, $600, w 3, p 374a

Davis, Francis - Sailmaker, $750, w 9, p 30b

Dessin, Henry - Confectioner, $3,000, w 4, p 18a

Dickinson, James - Victualler, $500, w 6, p 239b

Dode, Peter - Clothier, $3,000, w 9, p 21a

Elliott, Samuel - Carter, $4,300, w 4, p 51a

Ellman, George - Drayman, $300, w 3, p 351b

Fortie, Henry - Drayman, $500, w 6, p 245a

Fortie, John - Teacher, $2,500, w 6, p 245a

Gannon, Washington - Carter, $800, w 16, p 133b

Gant, Otho T. - Hay Merchant, $2,000, w 20, p 240b

Gatch, Edward - Brickmaker, $700, w 3, p 381b

Gibson, James - Stevedore, $300, w 3, p 309a

Gilliard, Nicholas - Blacksmith, $300, w 6, p 229b

Gordon, John - Cabinet Maker, $4,000, w 5, p 118a

Govens, Daniel - Storekeeper, $2,800, w 5, p 114b

Green Thomas - Barber, $1,000, w 9, p 47a

Green, John - Sawyer, $1,000, w 6, p 242a

Green, John H. - Waiter, $500, w 6, p 238b

Green, William H. - Physician, $11,000, w 3, p 398b

Hall, Sarah - $700, w 7, p 349a

Harris, Moses - Carpenter, $400, w 3, p 343a

Hernan, Jacob - Wagoner, $600, w 3, p 348a

Hiner, Samuel - Butcher, $40,000, w 7, p 305a

Howard, Joshua - Carter, $700, w 4, p 51a

Hoytt, Adam - Carter, $600, w 3, p 343a

Hubbard, George W. - Carter, $300, w 6, p 243b

Hyman, John - Barber, $1,400, w 15, p 82a

Jackson, Randal - Carter, $500, w 3, p 344a

Jefferson, Stephen - Coachman, $1,000, w 15, p 113a

Johnson, Carlos - Physician, $500, w 15, p 117a

Johnson, George - Shoemaker, $550, w 6, p 207b

Jones, Andrew D. - Bottler, $1,500, w 6, p 246a

Jones, Clementine - $500, w 6, p 208b

Jones, Israel - Caulker, $800, w 6,

Black Property Holders - 1850

p 244b
Jones, Thomas - Stevedore, $600, w 3, p 374a
Keith, Daniel - Caulker, $800, w 1, p 24b
LeCompt, David - Sailor, $500, w 3, p 344a
Lee, Levin - Preacher, $738, w 6, p 177a
Lemon, James - Carter, $500, w 4, p 51a
Loumoine, Louisa - $990, w 3, p 330a
Matthews, Thomas - Coachman, $550, w 6, p 201b
McFarland, Edward - Drayman, $300, w 3, p 403b
Morgan, John R. V. - Clergyman, $3,000, w 15, p 100a
Morris, James - Ship Carpenter, $800, w 3, p 330b
Murray, Robert - Barber, $11,000, w 3, p 343a
Murray, Robert - Musician, $500, w 5, p 94b
Myers, Daniel - Sailor, $1,200, w 3, p 330a
Myers, Edward - Hackman, $1,000, w 6, p 247b
Newall, Joseph - Porter, $300, w 5, p 146b
Noerton, Patrick - Carter, $700, w 6, p 244a
Pindel, Matthew - Brickmaker, $100, w 16, p 130b
Price, David - Laborer, $500, w 15, p 5a
Ridgaway, Henry - Trader, $500, w 15, p 5a
Ross, Robert - Huckster, $2,000, w 4, p 1b

Sears, William T. - Gardener, $500, w 6, p 238a
Simms, Charles - Waiter, $500, w 6, p 245b
Smith, Charles - Drayman, $500, w 6, p 243a
Smith, Levina - $600, w 7, p 329b
Smith, Nathaniel - Drayman, $300, w 6, p 243a
St. James, William - Barber, $2,500, w 1, p 37a
Stump, Aquilla - Brickamker, $150, w 7, p 346b
Thomas, Adam - Sawyer, $600, w 8, p 374a
Thompson, Cornelius - Porter, $500, w 13, p 366a
Thompson, Edward J. - Hack Driver, $300, w 3, p 311b
Trusty, Jonathan - Stevedore, $600, w 3, p 381b
Waters, Spencer - Carter, $2,000, w 6, p 245a
White, Arthur - Porter, $100, w 15, p 91b
Williams, Benjamin - Carter, $500, w 4, p 51a
Williams, Henry - Steward, $700, w 3, p 377a
Williams, James N. - Sawyer, $400, w 6, p 244a
Wilson, Frederick - Trader, $1,000, w 6, p 245b
Winsey, William - Brickmaker, $1,000, w 5, p 138a
York, John - Laborer, $600, w 3, p 353b
Young, James - Coachman, $400, w 6, p 244a

Chapter 17

Reprinted with the kind permission of the *Flower of the Forest - Black Genealogical Journal*: The Black Real Estate Holders of Baltimore - 1850 v. 1, no. 9, 1991.

18
Black Real Estate and Personal Estate Holders in the Census of 1860

The following is an index to Black real estate and personal estate holders located in the population census of Baltimore, Maryland in 1860.

The index is organized as follows:

Surname and first name of property holder, occupation, personal estate (pe) and real estate (re) holdings, ward of residence (w), page number (p) in the population census schedule. Not all of the previous categories of information are available in every case.

Black Estate Holders - 1860

Acier, Edward - Cigar Maker, pe $300, w 20, p 133
Adams, Alexander - pe $160, w 14, p 63
Adams, Alfred - Laborer, pe $30, w 8, p 564
Adams, Charles - Day Laborer, pe $100, w 2, p 96
Adams, George W. - Shoemaker, pe $800, w 6, p 225
Adams, Helmisty? - Waiter, pe $40, w 11, p 64
Adams, Henny - Washerwoman, pe $90, w 14, p 54
Adams, James H. - Porter-R. R. Co., pe $300, w 11, p 132
Adams, James P. - Barber, pe $75, w 11, p 129
Adams, John - Porter, pe $200, w 17, p 4
Adams, John B. - Porter, pe $25, w 20, p 84
Adams, Matilda - Washerwoman, pe $20, w 11, p 153
Adams, Nathan - Laborer, pe $25, w 16, p 106
Adams, Robert - Teamster, pe $40, w 14, p 62
Adams, Samuel - Whitewasher, pe $30, w 8, p 263
Adams, Sarah - Washerwoman, pe $50, w 11, p 99
Addison, John - Carter, pe $50, w 14, p 16
Addison, Mary - Washerwoman, pe $30, w 11, p 60
Adlechel, Phoeby - re $100, w 12, p 167
Agustus, Der? - Laborer, pe $10, w 17, p 45
Aires, Charles - Seaman, pe $50, w 16, p 59
Akum, John - Drayman, pe $20, w 17, p 24
Alchom, Rebecca - pe $50, w 16, p 69
Alchom, Terry - Carter, pe $75, w 16, p 68
Aldridge, William - Laborer, pe $30, w 20, p 125

259

Chapter 18

Black Estate Holders - 1860

Aleses?, Nancy - pe $50, re $600, w 17, p 258
Alexander, Nelson - Laborer, pe $25, w 8, p 294
Allan, Ann - Washerwoman, pe $20, w 8, p 339
Allen, Alexander - Day Laborer, pe $200, re $600, w 2, p 61
Allen, Amos - Brickmaker, pe $50, w 16, p 68
Allen, Charles - Shoemaker, pe $600, w 15, p 298
Allen, James - Speculator, pe $100, w 3, p 355
Allen, Mary - Washerwoman, pe $30, w 13, p 3472
Alridge, Alfred - Whitewasher, pe $40, w 18, p 426
Amos, Maria - Washerwoman, pe $50, w 8, p 284
Anderson, Abram - Laborer, pe $25, w 18, p 375
Anderson, Dennis - Drayman, pe $100, w 7, p 360
Anderson, Dorkis - Washerwoman, pe $10, w 20, p 74
Anderson, Hebby - Washerwoman, pe $20, w 8, p 294
Anderson, Isaiah - Laborer, pe $40, w 14, p 93
Anderson, Israel - Laborer, pe $50, w 14, p 55
Anderson, John - Drayman, pe $50, w 8, p 294
Anderson, John - Hack Driver, pe $20, w 11, p 128
Anderson, John - Brickmaker, pe $25, w 17, p 202
Anderson, Josiah - Carter, pe $10, w 17, p 176
Anderson, Milla - pe $45, w 18, p 433
Anderson, Robert - Wagon Driver, pe $40, w 20, p 102
Anderson, Samuel - Caulker, pe $15, w 17, p 232
Anderson, Solomon - Baker, pe $30, w 11, p 164
Anderson, Stephen - Farm Laborer, pe $200, w 6, p 73
Anthony, John - Day Laborer, pe $100, w 2, p 79
Anthony, Levi - pe $20, w 20, p 84
Appleby, William - Brickmaker, pe $100, w 16, p 167
Archer, Rebecca - pe $15, w 17, p 184
Arling, Henry - Laborer, pe $50, w 15, p 308
Armstead, Joseph - Porter, pe $1,500, w 15, p 250
Armstrong, James - Porter, pe $200, w 15, p 54
Arthur, John - Waiter, pe $80, w 20, p 90
Ash, Thomas - Drayman, pe $300, w 14, p 58
Ashton, John - Drayman, pe $100, re $500, w 7, p 377
Askins, Henry - Waiter, pe $800, w 15, p 53
Aston, Theresa - Washerwoman, pe $20, w 8, p 294
Atwood, William - White Coaster, pe $100, w 20, p 227
Augustas, Henry - Waiter, pe $40, w 11, p 165
Augustas, Mary - Cake Woman, pe $15, w 11, p 239
Ayres, Henny - Washerwoman, pe $50, w 8, p 361

Black Real Estate and Personal Estate Holders, 1860

Black Estate Holders - 1860

Ayres, Henrietta - Cook, pe $30, w 11, p 173
Ayres, James - Sailor, pe $25, w 13, p 402
Ayres, James - Porter, pe $1,000, w 15, p 80
Ayres, Lewis - Drayman, pe $300, w 15, p 72
Ayres, William - Hack Driver, pe $50, w 11, p 164
Babtist, Jesse - Bricklayer, pe $25, w 11, p 44
Badden, Eliza - Washerwoman, pe $40, w 14, p 67
Baden, Mary - Washerwoman, pe $10, w 20, p 74
Badger, Eliza - Drayman, pe $50, re $1,000, w 17, p 7
Badgey, Frank - Blacksmith, pe $50, w 8, p 587
Badgill, Jarrett - Drayman, pe $300, re $1,000, w 16, p 200
Bafford?, Edward - Laborer, pe $100, w 18, p 376
Bahl, Asbury - Drayman, pe $100, w 12, p 199
Bailey, Ann - Servant, pe $10, w 16, p 70
Bailey, David - Barber, pe $200, w 2, p 60
Bailey, Francis - Sawyer, pe $10, w 17, p 10
Bailey, Robert - Laborer, pe $25, w 17, p 8
Bailey, Samuel - Caulker, pe $300, re $800, w 2, p 60
Bailey, William - Brickmaker, pe $10, w 17, p 10
Baily, Ellen - Washerwoman, pe $40, w 14, p 67
Baker, Charles - Brickmaker, pe $100, w 15, p 308
Baker, James - Laborer, pe $40, w 18, p 765
Baker, Nancy - Laundress, pe $10, w 20, p 95
Baldwin, Emma - Washerwoman, pe $50, w 14, p 128
Baldwin, Sarah - Washerwoman, pe $25, w 16, p 140
Baldwin, Singleton - Brickamker, pe $75, w 16, p 139
Ball, John - Hod Carrier, pe $50, w 16, p 33
Ball, William - Drayman, pe $300, w 15, p 265
Ballard, Caleb - Grain Measurer, pe $5, w 17, p 21
Ballard, James - Brickmaker, pe $75, w 16, p 101
Ballett, Church - Grain Measurer, pe $10, w 17, p 12
Balstel, Thomas - Hack Driver, pe $35, w 11, p 127
Banahan, Phebe - Washerwoman, pe $50, w 17, p 3
Banard, William - Waiter, pe $25, w 17, p 242
Baney, Solomon - Grain Measurer, pe $300, w 15, p 79
Banks, Elizabeth - pe $100, re $200, w 18, p 427
Banks, Ruth - Washerwoman, pe $10, w 20, p 124
Banks, William - Waiter, pe $100, w 16, p 138
Bantom, Indels - Sailmaker, pe $200, w 2, p 60
Banton, Sarah A. - Washerwoman, pe $40, w 20, p 216
Bantum, Harris - Porter, pe $400, w 15, p 76

Chapter 18

Black Estate Holders - 1860

Bantum, Henry - Whip Sawyer, pe $30, w 8, p 419
Barden, Perry - Whitewasher, pe $50, w 12, p 33
Barker, Nathan - Boot Black, pe $50, w 19, p 227
Barnes, Benjamin - Laborer, pe $50, w 16, p 70
Barnes, Emory - Barber, pe $100, w 14, p 11
Barnes, Franklin - Furnace, pe $270, w 20, p 204
Barnes, George - Wagoner, pe $200, w 7, p 308
Barnes, Joseph - Wagoner, pe $200, w 7, p 589z
Barnes, Samuel - Laborer, pe $25, w 16, p 68
Barnet, Elijah O. - Oyster Opener, pe $40, w 11, p 127
Barnet, Mary A. - Washerwoman, pe $50, w 7, p 359
Barney, Mary - Washerwoman, pe $25, w 13, p 412
Barney, William - Brickmaker, pe $50, w 17, p 95
Barrett, William - Drayman, pe $200, re $400, w 20, p 90
Barrwe, William? - Day Laborer, pe $100, w 2, p 72
Bass, John - Porter, pe $600, w 15, p 254
Bates, Caroline - Cook, pe $50, w 11, p 60
Bayley, Ellen - Washerwoman, pe $30, w 11, p 173
Bayley, Ennalls - Coachman, pe $40, w 11, p 65
Bayley, George - Waiter, pe $25, w 11, p 46
Baynard, Amanda - Washerwoman, pe $20, w 11, p 168
Bean, John H. - Day Laborer, pe $50, w 7, p 318
Beck, Francis J. - M. P. Clergyman, pe $75, w 11, p 240
Becker, Perry - Gardener, pe $15, w 20, p 60
Becket, William - Sailor, pe $20, w 17, p 24
Bee, William - Sailor, pe $25, w 17, p 8
Bell, George - Porter, pe $20, w 17, p 93
Bell, Hasen - Waiter, pe $300, w 12, p 29
Bell, John - Day Laborer, pe $50, w 7, p 505
Bell, Luoisa - Washerwoman, pe $50, w 7, p 308
Bell, Richard - School teacher, pe $200, w 17, p 175
Benjamin, John? - Day Laborer, pe $50, w 7, p 334
Bennet, Garrison - Drayman, pe $20, w 17, p 146
Bennett, Abraham - Laborer, pe $20, w 16, p 106
Bennett, Margaret - Washerwoman, pe $500, w 15, p 297
Benson, Catherine - Washerwoman, pe $10, w 11, p 239
Benson, John - Brickmaker, pe $20, w 17, p 287
Bentley, Grafton - Drayman, pe $75, w 8, p 547
Bentley, Obidiah - Coachman, pe $30, w 11, p 99
Benton, Aron - Brickmaker, pe $75, w 16, p 67
Bernard, William - Fisherman, pe $500, re $750, w 17, p 293

Black Real Estate and Personal Estate Holders, 1860

Black Estate Holders - 1860

Berry, Abram - Porter, pe $60, w 14, p 58
Berry, Andrea? - Nurse, pe $30, w 20, p 72
Berry, Celia - Cook, pe $200, w 12, p 202
Berry, Jacob? - Wood Sawyer, pe $25, w 16, p 23
Berry, James - Waiter, pe $50, w 8, p 583
Berry, Jeremiah - Drayman, pe $75, w 16, p 58
Berry, Mary - School Teacher, pe $100, w 12, p 215
Berryman, John C. - Caulker, pe $100, w 2, p 59
Betts?, Thomas - Laborer, pe $200, w 15, p 265
Bevans, Littleton - Varnisher, pe $500, w 15, p 91
Beyer, John - Brickmaker, pe $100, w 15, p 70
Bias, Alfred - Porter, pe $350, w 20, p 84
Bias, Perry - Drayman, pe $20, w 20, p 88
Binns, Sandy - Waiter, pe $100, w 11, p 54
Bires, William - Porter, pe $50, w 14, p 67
Bishop, Jacob - Waiter, pe $250, re $800, w 11, p 53
Bishop, John - Laborer, pe $75, w 16, p 50
Bishop, Peter - Tailor, pe $400, w 3, p 299
Bishop, Peter - Whitewasher, pe $100, w 3, p 180
Bishop, William H. - Barber, pe $300, re $3,000, w 11, p 108
Bitler, Eliza - Washerwoman, pe $200, w 15, p 74
Black, James - pe $50, w 16, p 163
Black, William - Seaman, pe $30, w 8, p 572
Blackston, Henry H. - Minister, pe $100, w 7, p 378
Blackston, Robert - Wood Sawyer, pe $50, w 13, p 468
Blake, Cato - pe $1,000, re $2,000, w 19, p 152
Blake, Julia - Washerwoman, pe $300, w 15, p 262
Blake, Julia A. - pe $100, w 7, p 377
Blake, Peter - Brickmaker, pe $500, w 15, p 248
Blake, Sarah - Huckster, pe $25, w 17, p 3
Blerew, Richard - Laborer, pe $300, w 15, p 71
Block, Robert - Steward, pe $500, w 15, p 245
Blunders, James - Porter, pe $300, w 15, p 247
Bodren, Nathaniel - Sailor, pe $100, re $300, w 2, p 48
Boghton, Louisa - Washerwoman, pe $50, w 16, p 104
Bohen, George - Laborer, pe $100, w 15, p 251
Bond, Andrew - Sailor, pe $100, w 7, p 252
Bond, Charles E. - Waiter, pe $50, w 8, p 356
Bond, Emory - Tavern Keeper, pe $500, re $1,700, w 11, p 109
Bond, Henny - pe $15, w 20, p 53
Bond, Isaac - Driver, pe $20, w 20, p 55

Chapter 18

Black Estate Holders - 1860

Bond, Maria - Laundress, pe $10, w 20, p 55
Bond, Nathan - Waiter, pe $30, w 11, p 175
Bond, Tower? - Laborer, pe $25, w 18, p 432
Bond, William - Laborer, pe $30, w 11, p 167
Bond, William - Hackman, pe $100, w 11, p 180
Book, Joseph - Seaman, pe $50, w 17, p 91
Boon, Alexander - Fireman, pe $300, w 15, p 247
Boon, Perry - Laborer, pe $50, w 17, p 2
Boon, Samson - Porter, pe $50, w 17, p 145
Boon, Samuel - Laborer, pe $50, w 15, p 289
Boon, Shoder - Laborer, pe $40, w 20, p 236
Boon, Sophia - Washerwoman, pe $100, w 15, p 1
Boone, Thomas - Sawyer, pe $10, w 17, p 46
Boos, Thomas - Drayman, pe $300, w 17, p 82
Booth, David - Whitewasher, pe $40, w 11, p 99
Booth, Edward - Whip Sawyer, pe $75, re $1,000, w 11, p 45
Booth, Nicholas - Drayman, pe $100, w 14, p 29
Booth, William - Carter, pe $100, w 12, p 192
Bordely, James - Brickmaker, pe $20, w 17, p 187
Bordley, Julia - Washerwoman, pe $60, w 14, p 57
Bordly, William - Brickamker, pe $100, w 16, p 104
Bordman, Hester - Waitress, pe $15, w 20, p 56
Borger, John - Drayman, pe $300, w 12, p 61
Boston, Ann - Washerwoman, pe $25, w 16, p 60
Boston, Harris - pe $10, w 20, p 54
Boston, Hester - Washerwoman, pe $5, w 17, p 50
Boston, James - Barber, pe $500, w 15, p 295
Boston, John - Day Laborer, pe $100, w 2, p 96
Boston, John - Drayman, pe $1,500, re $800, w 20, p 92
Boston, Richard - Laborer, pe $400, w 3, p 247
Boston, Robert - Brickmaker, pe $500, w 15, p 91
Boston, Robert - Brickmaker, pe $300, w 15, p 294
Boston, Sarah - Washerwoman, pe $30, w 20, p 232
Boston, Thomas - Laborer, pe $30, w 20, p 53
Boudley, Perry - Laborer, pe $130, w 20, p 91
Bouldin, Spencer - Laborer, pe $20, w 20, p 98
Bouldin, Spencer - Furnace, pe $80, w 20, p 229
Boury, Henry - Waiter, pe $60, w 14, p 119
Bovin, Charles - Porter, pe $600, w 12, p 28
Bowdin, Catharine - Servant, pe $600, w 20, p 52
Bowen, Charles - Sailor, pe $300, w 15, p 246

Black Real Estate and Personal Estate Holders, 1860

Black Estate Holders - 1860

Bower?, Frances - pe $25, w 16, p 58
Bowers, Francis - Porter, pe $10, w 17, p 9
Bowers, Mary - Washerwoman, pe $20, w 14, p 67
Bowers, Nathan - Carter, pe $600, w 12, p 184
Bowers, Rosetta - pe $25, w 17, p 86
Bowie, Margaret - Waiter, pe $20, w 17, p 94
Bowie, Phillip - Porter, pe $50, w 14, p 16
Bowie, Solomon - Porter, pe $20, w 17, p 288
Bowie, William - Laborer, pe $30, w 18, p 426
Bowley, Gabriel - Portter, pe $400, w 15, p 43
Bowser, Henrietta - Cook, pe $40, w 1, p 240
Bowser, James - Waiter, pe $500, w 12, p 21
Bowser, Lidia - Boarding House, pe $100, w 13, p 451
Bowser, Solomon - Waiter, pe 25, w 11, p 45
Bowser, William - Plasterer, pe $2, w 17, p 184
Boyd, Charles - Mariner, pe $400, w 15, p 71
Boyd, Thomas - Laborer, pe $5, w 7, p 58
Boyd, William - Whitewasher, pe $20, w 17, p 287
Boyer, Ellen - Washerwoman, pe $20, w 7, p 49
Boyles, Lewis - Waiter, pe $50, w 14, p 58
Bracken, Mary - Washerwoman, pe $50, w 8, p 547
Braddick, Henry - Hackman, pe $1,000, w 13, p 459
Bradford, Isaac - Porter, pe $150, w 12, p 22
Bradford, Jacob - Laborer, pe $100, w 15, p 1
Bradford, John - Porter, pe $60, w 14, p 54
Brant, Mrs. - Cap Maker, pe $10, w 17, p 14
Brashears, William - Barber, pe $50, w 13, p 458
Brashers, John - Brush Maker, pe $15, w 17, p 184
Braverwood, Daniel - Day Laborer, pe $100, w 7, p 382
Brewer, Joseph - Waiter, pe $50, w 13, p 412
Brice, John - Wagoner, pe $100, w 16, p 19
Brice, Samuel - Stevedore, pe $100, w 16, p 19
Bridge, John A. - Musician, pe $100, w 8, p 564
Briding, Abram - Porter, pe $40, w 20, p 62
Brien, Samuel - Waiter, pe $50, w 11, p 44
Bright, Isreal - Porter, pe $20, w 20, p 72
Bright, Mary A. - pe $50, w 7, p 387
Bright, Walter - Wagoner, pe $100, w 3, p 110
Brightman, Edward - Drayman, pe $300, w 14, p 68
Brightman, Stephen - Waiter, pe $100, w 14, p 91
Briscoe, Gabriel - Barber, pe $100, w 11, p 159

Chapter 18

Black Estate Holders - 1860

Briscoe, Henry - Barber, pe $300, w 11, p 158
Briscoe, Julia A. - Washerwoman, pe $20, w 8, p 293
Briscoe, Louis - Barber, pe $100, w 11, p 158
Brise, Alfred - Porter, pe $30, w 17, p 96
Britton, Catherine - Servant, pe $50, w 16, p 53
Brock, Perry - Waiter, pe $500, w 5, p 89
Brogel, Rialto - Shoemaker, pe $50, w 16, p 168
Brogton, Elizabeth - Washerwoman, pe $40, w 14, p 63
Brook, George - Waiter, pe $60, w 14, p 61
Brooks, Charles - Porter, pe $40, w 14, p 128
Brooks, David - Laborer, pe $40, w 18, p 432
Brooks, Eliza - Washerwoman, pe $50, w 16, p 23
Brooks, James - Butcher, pe $20, w 8, p 430
Brooks, John - Carpenter, pe $2,000, w 15, p 60
Brooks, John - Brickmaker, pe $50, w 16, p 139
Brooks, Rachael - Washerwoman, pe $100, w 12, p 27
Brooks, Samuel - Laborer, pe $40, w 20, p 84
Brooks, William - Laborer, pe $30, w 14, p 128
Broom, Major - pe $25, w 16, p 140
Brosy?, George - Drayman, pe $300, w 20, p 19
Brown, Alescander - Drayman, pe $200, w 17, p 94
Brown, Amelia - Seamstress, pe $100, w 6, p 111
Brown, Ann - Washerwoman, pe $100, w 19, p 226
Brown, Augustus - Laborer, pe $20, w 20, p 96
Brown, Benjamin - School teacher, pe $75, re $1,500, w 17, p 179
Brown, Benjamin - Laborer, pe $40, w 20, p 91
Brown, Charity - Washerwoman, pe $20, w 17, p 287
Brown, David - Teamster, pe $150, w 14, p 54
Brown, David - Laborer, pe $25, w 18, p 426
Brown, Edmund - Coachman, pe $50, w 11, p 63
Brown, Edward - Butcher, pe $100, w 8, p 306
Brown, Edward - Laborer, pe $60, w 18, p 767
Brown, Edwin - Carter, pe $20, w 17, p 188
Brown, Eliza - Washerwoman, pe $40, w 14, p 118
Brown, Eliza - Washerwoman, pe $300, w 15, p 80
Brown, Eliza - Washerwoman, pe $15, w 20, p 264
Brown, Emily - Washerwoman, pe $50, w 16, p 50
Brown, Ephraim - Barber, pe $75, w 11, p 108
Brown, Ephraim - Whitewasher, pe $200, w 20, p 247
Brown, George - Drayman, pe $40, w 11, p 173
Brown, Henry - Woodsawyer, pe $5, w 17, p 10

Black Real Estate and Personal Estate Holders, 1860

Black Estate Holders - 1860

Brown, Hezekiah - Brickmaker, pe $20, w 17, p 326
Brown, Hiram - Brickmaker, pe $50, w 15, p 290
Brown, Hiram - Mariner, pe $200, w 15, p 299
Brown, Isaac - Waiter, pe $50, w 11, p 108
Brown, Isaac - Laborer, pe $20, w 11, p 173
Brown, Jacob - Carter, pe $300, w 15, p 54
Brown, Jacob - Drayman, pe $200, w 17, p 297
Brown, James - Laborer, pe $350, w 3, p 7
Brown, James - Laborer, pe $100, w 15, p 1
Brown, James - Porter, pe $500, w 15, p 57
Brown, James - Wood Sawyer, pe $20, w 11, p 154
Brown, James M. - M. E. Clergyman, pe $300, w 11, p 132
Brown, John - Coachman, pe $500, w 15, p 249
Brown, John - Laborer, pe $300, w 15, p 250
Brown, John - Hackman, pe $10, w 16, p 58
Brown, John - Butcher, pe $75, w 16, p 165
Brown, John - Brickmaker, pe $10, w 17, p 14
Brown, John - Sailor, pe $5, w 17, p 45
Brown, John - Mariner, pe $40, w 20, p 58
Brown, John W. - Brickmaker, pe $100, w 16, p 145
Brown, Joseph - Carter, pe $100, w 17, p 12
Brown, Joseph - Laborer, pe $10, w 20, p 109
Brown, Joshua - Mariner, pe $40, w 14, p 119
Brown, Maria - Washerwoman, pe $25, w 17, p 326
Brown, Martha - Waiter, pe $10, w 8, p 269
Brown, Mary - pe $20, w 17, p 93
Brown, Mary - Laundress, pe $30, w 20, p 86
Brown, Moses - Tanner, pe $50, w 16, p 49
Brown, Mr. - Hod Carrier, pe $10, w 17, p 33
Brown, Mrs. - Servant, pe $25, w 17, p 9
Brown, Mutley - Laborer, pe $60, w 14, p 67
Brown, Nathan - Porter, pe $300, w 15, p 77
Brown, Nicholas - Whitewasher, pe $25, w 20, p 26
Brown, Perry - Drayman, pe $120, w 18, p 491
Brown, Philip - Cook, pe $100, re $600, w 8, p 369
Brown, Rachael - Barber, pe $5,000, w 9, p 68
Brown, Ruth - pe $50, w 16, p 67
Brown, Samuel - Driver, pe $50, w 20, p 91
Brown, Simon - Waiter, pe $150, re $400, w 11, p 146
Brown, Solomon - Laborer, pe $50, w 19, p 225
Brown, Stephen - Laborer, pe $50, w 16, p 100

Chapter 18

Black Estate Holders - 1860

Brown, Thomas - Carter, pe $150, w 16, p 72
Brown, Titus - Laborer, pe $20, w 20, p 57
Brown, William - Seaman, pe $40, w 8, p 587
Brown, William - Coachman, pe $50, w 11, p 62
Brown, William - Engineer, pe $75, w 16, p 81
Brown, William - Brickmaker, pe $20, w 17, p 203
Brown, William - pe $200, w 20, p 79
Browser, Joseph - Servant, pe $100, w 16, p 50
Bruce, John - Waiter, pe $10, w 20, p 62
Bryan, Lewis - Laborer, pe $500, w 3, p 247
Bryson, Hamilton - Barber, pe $60, w 14, p 58
Buchanan, George - Hod Carrier, pe $40, w 20, p 240
Buchanan, Nancy - Laundress, pe $10, w 20, p 57
Buchanan, Samuel - Laborer, pe $75, w 8, p 560
Buchanan, Thomas - Waiter, pe $50, w 11, p 85
Buck, Samuel - Wagoner, pe $100, w 3, p 113
Budd, Mary - Servant, pe $25, w 16, p 107
Bullen, Harriet - pe $600, w 20, p 81
Burges, Nelson - Stevedore, pe $5, w 17, p 13
Burgess, Asbury - Coachman, pe $70, w 20, p 236
Burgess, John - Whitewasher, pe $75, w 11, p 126
Burgess, Nathaniel - Drayman, pe $40, w 20, p 235
Burk, William - Caulker, pe $100, w 2, p 78
Burke, George S. - Porter, pe $500, w 12, p 197
Burke, Harriet - Washerwoman, pe $20, w 11, p 124
Burke, Henry - Gardener, pe $70, w 20, p 193
Burke, William - Baotman, pe $5, w 17, p 21
Burleigh, Hannah - Seamstress, pe $25, w 11, p 175
Burleigh, Osburn - Provisions, pe $1,500, re $5,000, w 11, p 106
Burns, John - Seaman, pe $30, w 17, p 91
Burns, Louis - Carter, pe $5, w 17, p 45
Burress, John - Laborer, pe $40, w 20, p 136
Burress, Lettiam - Washerwoman, pe $20, w 20, p 136
Burris, William - Waterman, pe $30, w 17, p 24
Bush, James - Mariner, pe $300, w 15, p 73
Butler, Abraham - Hooper, pe $15, w 14, p 12
Butler, Ann - pe $5,000, w 14, p 34
Butler, Aveline - Washerwoman, pe $50, w 16, p 145
Butler, Caroline - Washerwoman, pe $70, w 20, p 86
Butler, Cornelius - Waiter, pe $75, w 11, p 44
Butler, Edmond - Barber, pe $400, w 18, p 616

Black Real Estate and Personal Estate Holders, 1860

Black Estate Holders - 1860

Butler, George - Laborer, pe $300, w 15, p 80
Butler, Henry - wagoner, pe $30, w 13, p 471
Butler, Henry - Laborer, pe $15, w 18, p 429
Butler, Isabel - Washerwoman, pe $60, w 14, p 116
Butler, James - Waiter, pe $20, w 11, p 62
Butler, James - Caulker, pe $500, w 15, p 249
Butler, James - Servant, pe $25, w 17, p 8
Butler, John - Fireman, pe $50, w 11, p 45
Butler, John H. - Porter, pe $50, w 17, p 9
Butler, Margaret - Washerwoman, pe $40, w 14, p 61
Butler, Nancy - pe $100, re $800, w 8, p 511
Butler, Sydney A. - Washerwoman, pe $200, re $450, w 7, p 378
Butler, Thomas - Waiter, pe $100, w 12, p 28
Butler, William - Brickmaker, pe $100, w 15, p 90
Butler, William - Brickmaker, pe $5, w 17, p 22
Byran, Robert - Waiter, pe $100, w 13, p 470
Cagen, James - Speculator, pe $300, w 3, p 90
Cager?, James - Caulker, pe $3,000, w 3, p 144
Cain, William - Drayman, pe $200, w 17, p 33
Cakdwell, Nicholas - Physician, pe $100, re $300, w 11, p 21
Call, James - Waiter, pe $300, w 12, p 33
Calvert, Ann - Laundress, pe $10, w 20, p 122
Calvin, George - Sailor, pe $50, w 7, p 377
Calwell, Ann - Washerwoman, pe $300, w 15, p 259
Calwell, John - Hackman, pe $150, w 16, p 138
Cambell?, Peter - Brickmaker, pe $100, w 3, p 113
Camper, Levin - Whitewasher, pe $30, w 20, p 59
Camphor, John - Brickmaker, pe $50, w 17, p 177
Camphor, Moses - Laborer, pe $20, w 17, p 103
Cann, Isaac - Gardiner, pe $30, w 20, p 115
Capito, Ephraim - Laborer, pe $50, w 14, p 29
Capman?, James - Drayman, pe $100, w 3, p 77
Carda, Alexander - Drayman, pe $250, w 16, p 168
Carey, Peter - pe $10, w 17, p 13
Carmichael, Ann - Laundress, pe $15, w 20, p 113
Carpenter, Ann - Cook, pe $15, w 11, p 175
Carpenter, John - Porter, pe $150, w 12, p 184
Carpenter, John - Laborer, pe $300, w 15, p 59
Carr, Frederick - Grain Measurer, re $200, w 17, p 24
Carr, John - Brickmaker, pe 50, w 16, p 35
Carr, William - Brickmaker, pe $10, w 16, p 36

Chapter 18

Black Estate Holders - 1860

Carrish, George - Drayman, pe $500, w 12, p 35
Carroll, Charles - Porter, pe $50, w 13, p 459
Carroll, Henry - Laborer, pe $50, w 15, p 16
Carroll, John - Brickmaker, pe $20, w 15, p 15
Carroll, John - Brickmaker, pe $50, w 16, p 68
Carroll, Landry - Waiter, pe $20, w 11, p 240
Carroll, Phillip - Brickmaker, pe $50, w 16, p 68
Carroll, Samuel - Laborer, pe $300, w 15, p 55
Carroll, Samuel - Brickmaker, pe $25, w 16, p 68
Carson, Benjamin - Porter In Store, pe $75, w 8, p 520
Carter, Eliza - Preserver, pe $5, w 17, p 13
Carter, Henry - Whitewasher, pe $20, w 11, p 127
Carter, John - Porter, pe $250, w 12, p 13
Carter, Joseph - Drayman, pe $200, w 17, p 178
Carter, Joseph - Waiter, pe $400, w 17, p 869
Carter, Samuel - Hod Carrier, pe $25, w 16, p 142
Carter, Sophia - pe $10, w 16, p 66
Carter, William H. - Drayman, pe $25, w 11, p 44
Cassell, Christopher - Brickmaker, pe $20, w 17, p 202
Cassell, Evelina - Washerwoman, pe $30, w 14, p 68
Cassey?, Charles - Laborer, pe $75, w 16, p 101
Cassidy, Mrs. - pe $10, w 17, p 3
Cassidy, Nancy - Washerwoman, pe $10, w 16, p 101
Cassidy, Peter - Porter, pe $10, w 17, p 3
Casson, Alexander - Drayman, pe $100, w 16, p 166
Caster, James - Shoemaker, pe $50, w 16, p 141
Caster, Lucy - Boot Falter, pe $75, w 16, p 141
Castle, Virginia - Cake Woman, pe $40, w 11, p 189
Cater, Rebecca - Washerwoman, pe $100, w 14, p 11
Cater, Simon - Brickmaker, pe $500, w 15, p 266
Causey, Elizabeth - Washerwoman, pe $5, w 17, p 57
Cedars, Thomas - Brickmaker, pe $5, w 17, p 30
Chace?, Charles - Day Laborer, pe $50, w 7, p 319
Chair, Robert - Grain Measurer, pe $30, w 17, p 103
Chambers, Jane - Washerwoman, pe $20, w 11, p 165
Chambers, John - Brickmaker, pe $100, w 7, p 382
Chambers, John - Barber, pe $50, w 13, p 401
Chambers, Perry - Barber, pe $30, w 11, p 164
Chambers, Perry - Drayman, pe $75, w 16, p 164
Chaplain, Perry C. - Porter, pe $50, w 11, p 104
Chaplin, Sarah - pe $30, w 13, p 463

Black Real Estate and Personal Estate Holders, 1860

Black Estate Holders - 1860

Chaplins, Alice H. - pe $50, w 7, p 400
Chapman, N. - Servant, re $840, w 4, p 10
Chapman, Thomas - Seaman, pe $40, w 11, p 61
Chappell, David C. - Brickmaker, pe $40, w 11, p 238
Chappell, Jacob - Butcher, pe $50, re $300, w 8, p 518
Chappell, John - Stevedore, pe $50, w 8, p 518
Chappell, Richard - Shop Keeper, pe $100, re $3,000, w 8, p 518
Chase, Abscent - Laborer, pe $40, w 14, p 97
Chase, Elizabeth - Shop Keeper, pe $75, w 11, p 105
Chase, Henry - Laborer, pe $50, w 14, p 28
Chase, Henry - Wood Sawyer, pe $50, w 16, p 107
Chase, James - Stewart, pe $300, w 15, p 109
Chase, Samuel - Carter, pe $100, w 2, p 97
Chase, Samuel - Scool Teacher, pe $1,500, w 15, p 51
Chase, Samuel - Undertaker, pe $500, 15, p 51
Chase, Samuel - Drayman, pe $200, w 17, p 184
Chase, William - Lumber Piler, pe $300, w 15, p 261
Chester, Jeremiah - Caulker, pe $10, w 2, p 800
Chew, Elijah - Day Laborer, pe $5, w 7, p 3340
Chew, Henrietta - pe $20, w 17, p 146
Chew, Perry - Seaman, pe $20, w 17, p 188
Chew, Samuel - Sailor, pe $25, w 17, p 296
Chew, Stephen - Brickmaker, pe $500, w 15, p 263
Chim?, Addison - Brickmaker, pe $1,000, w 15, p 73
Chin, Henry - Laborer, pe $100, re $600, w 17, p 374
Chisler, Eliza - Washerwoman, pe $20, w 11, p 153
Chormas?, Jarrett - Waiter, pe $40, w 20, p 89
Church, Harriet - pe $75, re $2,000, w 7, p 498
Church, John - Seaman, pe $50, w 16, p 52
Clark, Charles - Laborer, pe $200, w 15, p 74
Clark, Charles - Laborer, pe $300, w 15, p 79
Clark, Charles - Laborer, pe $50, w 16, p 102
Clark, Edward - Drayman, pe $70, w 20, p 91
Clark, Eli - Gardener, pe $30, w 17, p 163
Clark, Henrietta - Servant, pe $25, w 17, p 296
Clark, Louis - Musician, pe $150, re $1,000, w 13, p 449
Clark, Robert - Waiter, pe $40, w 11, p 240
Clayton, John - Porter, pe $30, w 14, p 65
Clayton, Levi - Sailor, pe $500, w 15, p 246
Clayton, Moses - Baptist Minister, pe $600, w 6, p 2260
Clayton, Samuel - Waiter, pe $30, w 13, p 471

Chapter 18

Black Estate Holders - 1860

Clement, John - Drayman, pe $45, w 20, p 235
Clinton, David - Oysterman, pe $200, re $1,000, w 1, p 480
Coats, Clem - Drayman, pe $40, w 20, p 53
Coats, Leonard - Waiter, pe $50, w 11, p 41
Coats, Samuel - Porter, pe $20, w 11, p 154
Coats, Samuel - Porter, pe $25, w 20, p 92
Cobie, Milla - Quilting, pe $30, w 14, p 63
Cockey?, Jacob - Gardiner, pe $30, w 20, p 87
Coercy?, William - Hod Carrier, pe $25, w 16, p 140
Coffer, Jacob - Grain Measurer, pe $600, w 15, p 293
Coge?, Simon - Brickmaker, pe $50, w 15, p 291
Coje?, Walter - Brickmaker, pe $200, w 15, p 308
Colbert, William - Cooper, pe $700, w 20, p 78
Cole, Alexander - Laborer, pe $20, w 20, p 89
Cole, Caroline, - pe $10, w 20, p 62
Cole, Eliza - Huckster, pe $20, w 8, p 264
Cole, James - Porter, pe $40, w 11, p 167
Cole, James - Porter, pe $60, w 14, p 128
Cole, Joseph - Laborer, pe $40, w 20, p 236
Cole, Mary - Washerwoman, pe $25, w 16, p 33
Cole, Matilda - Washerwoman, pe $30, w 11, p 239
Coleman, John - Brickmaker, pe $300, w 15, p 71
Coleman, Thomas - Servant, pe $50, w 16, p 69
Colison, Henry - Waiter, pe $30, w 8, p 556
Collins, Charles - Boarding House, pe $300, w 2, p 166
Collins, Henry, - pe $20, w 17, p 91
Collins, James - Laborer, pe $100, w 3, p 316
Collins, John - Day Laborer, pe $100, w 7, p 370
Collins, Lende?, - pe $20, w 17, p 91
Collsin?, Hester - Servant, pe $16, w 10, p 6
Colman, Levin - Brickmaker, pe $20, w 17, p 58
Colson, William - Brickmaker, pe $25, w 17, p 87
Colwell, Charles - Stevedore, pe $30, re $2,000, w 1, p 460
Comeger, David - Porter, pe $20, w 17, p 93
Conaway, Eli - Fisherman, pe $50, w 17, p 337
Conaway, James - Caulker, pe $25, w 17, p 328
Conaway, John - Fisherman, pe $50, w 17, p 337
Conaway, Perry - Carpenter, pe $25, w 17, p 374
Conicks, Jane - Washerwoman, pe $75, w 11, p 62
Conkling, John - Sick Nurse, pe $40, w 8, p 352
Conner, Charlotte - Servant, pe $5, w 17, p 28

Black Real Estate and Personal Estate Holders, 1860

Black Estate Holders - 1860

Conner, Rebecca - School Teacher, pe $10, w 17, p 28
Conter?, William - Brickmaker, pe $50, w 16, p 138
Conway, Betsey - Washerwoman, pe $20, w 11, p 173
Conway, Jarret - Hair Picker, pe $20, w 11, p 173
Conway, Mina - General Worke, pe $25, w 11, p 63
Conway, Samuel - Boarding House, pe $200, re $800, w 2, p 750
Cook, Bar? - Laborer, pe $500, w 15, p 248
Cook, Charles - Caulker, pe $10, w 7, p 4130
Cook, Henrietta - Washerwoman, pe $50, w 17, p 5
Cook, Henry - Carpenter, pe $5, w 17, p 22
Cook, Henry - Mariner, pe $100, w 20, p 236
Cook, James - Barber, pe $30, w 11, p 155
Cook, John - Brickmaker, pe $100, w 16, p 163
Cook, John - Cooper, pe $500, w 18, p 352
Cook, Julia - Seamstress, pe $100, w 12, p 29
Cook, William - Whitewasher, pe $200, w 12, p 192
Cook, William - Cooper, pe $200, re $600, w 14, p 58
Cooper, Benjamin - Laborer, pe $25, w 16, p 145
Cooper, Edward - Drayman, pe $275, w 20, p 85
Cooper, Harriet - Washerwoman, pe $50, w 11, p 54
Cooper, Henry - Drayman, pe $1,000, w 15, p 42
Cooper, Henry - Stevedore, pe $25, w 16, p 165
Cooper, Iron - Caulker, pe $200, re $600, w 2, p 610
Cooper, James - Caulker, re $500, w 1, p 21
Cooper, James - Barber, pe $200, w 20, p 69
Cooper, Thomas - Caulker, pe $10, w 2, p 800
Cooper, William - Caulker, pe $300, re $500, w 1, p 480
Copper, Abraham - Porter, pe $25, w 17, p 183
Copper, James - Mariner, pe $200, w 15, p 295
Copper, John - Mariner, pe $200, w 15, p 292
Copper, Rachael - House Cleaner, pe $50, w 15, p 288
Corgs?, Annie - Washerwoman, re $500, w 16, p 140
Corgs?, Samuel - Brickamker, pe $50, w 16, p 140
Corm?, Elizabeth - Washerwoman, pe $70, w 20, p 222
Cornich, Henry - Brickmaker, pe $20, w 17, p 202
Cornish, Charles - Drayman, pe $500, w 15, p 246
Cornish, Charles - Wheelwright, pe $30, w 17, p 103
Cornish, Elijabeth - Washerwoman, pe $40, w 14, p 64
Cornish, George - Ropemaker, pe $300, w 15, p 90
Cornish, James - Hod Carrier, pe $20, w 17, p 178
Cornish, Samuel - Stevedore, pe $25, w 16, p 106

Chapter 18

Black Estate Holders - 1860

Cornish, Thomas - Laborer, pe $30, w 17, p 103
Corsair, Hamilton - Barber, pe $30, w 11, p 60
Corsey, Lucretia - Washerwoman, pe $20, w 11, p 99
Cosesy, Landel - Seaman, pe $20, w 17, p 146
Cotman, Samuel - Waiter, pe $25, w 13, p 402
Coultin, Samuel - Sailmaker, pe $50, w 6, p 580
Cox, John - Grain Measurer, pe $300, w 15, p 76
Cox, William - Waiter, pe $40, w 14, p 58
Crawford, Isaiah - Drayman, pe $20, w 20, p 59
Crawford, William C.   Sailor, pe $5, w 2, p 900
Creek, Ann - Servant, pe $200, w 15, p 72
Creek, John - W. - Druggist, pe $150, re $500, w 11, p 242
Creek, Samuel - Laborer, pe $20, w 8, p 269
Creis?, Edwrad - Brickmaker, pe $50, w 17, p 13
Cromwell, Garrison - Laborer, pe $25, re $1,000, w 17, p 309
Cromwell, Henrietta - Laundress, pe $10, w 20, p 109
Cromwell, Jihn - Carter, pe $150, w 17, p 330
Cromwell, Robert - Laborer, pe $40, w 20, p 109
Cross, Rachel - Washerwoman, pe $40, w 11, p 110
Crowley, Barbara - Nurse, pe $30, w 7, p 3100
Crume, Asbury - Whitewasher, pe $50, w 11, p 167
Crumper?, John - Laborer, pe $200, w 15, p 293
Cummings, John - Laborer, re $700, w 3, p 229
Curl, Wesley L. - Musician, pe $30, w 17, p 103
Curtis, Bedino? - Drayman, pe $150, w 8, p 380
Curtis, Hannah - Washerwoman, pe $25, w 16, p 42
Curtis, Jacob - Hack Driver, pe $30, w 11, p 60
Curtis, John H. - Porter, pe $50, w 20, p 57
Curtis, Joseph - Waiter, pe $20, w 17, p 203
Curtis, Mary - Cook, pe $15, w 11, p 187
Curtis, Robert - Huckster, pe $30, w 6, p 650
Curtis, William - Lumber Piler, pe $600, w 15, p 260
Curtis, William - Ostler, pe $75, w 16, p 105
Cyphus, Wesley - Waiter, pe $100, w 8, p 596
Darbey, John - Brickmaker, pe $10, w 17, p 296
Darey, David - Drayman, pe $150, w 17, p 184
Darey, Mathias - Grain Measurer, pe $150, w 17, p 188
Dary, William - Grain Measurer, pe $5, w 7, p 3770
Daugeter, Samuel - Caulker, pe $300, re $1,800, w 2, p 600
Davidge, Charles - Waiter, pe $40, w 11, p 63
Davidge, Frederick - Brickmaker, pe $20, w 17, p 50

Black Real Estate and Personal Estate Holders, 1860

Black Estate Holders - 1860

Davidge, Mary - Washerwoman, pe $100, w 11, p 86
Davies, Daniel - Steamboat Hand, pe $25, w 11, p 64
Davies, David - Brickmaker, pe $5, w 17, p 13
Davies, Henry - Laborer, pe $50, w 11, p 99
Davies, Henry - Laborer, pe $20, w 11, p 110
Davies, James H. - Cabinet Maker, pe $2,000, re $3,000, w 10, p 44
Davies, John - Barber, pe $40, w 20, p 124
Davies, Noah - Baptist Praecher, pe $30, w 13, p 471
Davies, William - Porter, pe $50, w 17, p 13
Davige, Eleanora - Washerwoman, pe $50, w 16, p 71
Davis, Ann - Servant, pe $30, w 17, p 176
Davis, Daniel - Cook, pe $50, w 17, p 58
Davis, Eliza - Washerwoman, pe $100, w 15, p 68
Davis, Elizabeth - Washerwoman, pe $100, w 15, p 70
Davis, Fanny - pe $100, w 15, p 69
Davis, George - Sailor, pe $400, w 15, p 76
Davis, George - Brickmaker, pe $300, w 15, p 249
Davis, Jefferson - Day Laborer, pe $50, w 7, p 361
Davis, John - Waiter, pe $30, w 20, p 84
Davis, Louisa - Washerwoman, pe $30, w 14, p 68
Davis, Perry - Brickmaker, pe $300, w 15, p 53
Davis, Rachel - Washerwoman, pe $100, w 16, p 110
Davis, Samuel - Laborer, pe $100, w 15, p 246
Davis, Samuel - Brickamker, pe $200, w 15, p 265
Davis, Sarah A. - Washerwoman, pe $30, w 11, p 173
Davison, Annie - pe $50, w 16, p 34
Dawsey, Lemeul - Drayman, pe $15, w 7, p 2820
Dawson, Perry - Grain Measurer, pe $50, re $500, w 17, p 329
Dawson, William - Drayman, pe $20, w 17, p 185
Day, Wilford - Brickmaker, pe $50, w 13, p 401
Deakins, John - Brickamker, pe $100, w 16, p 102
Deal, Henry - Brickmaker, pe $400, w 15, p 56
Deal, James - Laborer, pe $20, w 20, p 86
Dean, Alex - Porter, pe $60, w 18, p 408
DeBourney, Solomon - Waiter, pe $100, w 11, p 243
Dechilds, James - Drayman, pe $20, w 3, p 3230
Deefer, David - Laborer, pe $20, w 20, p 251
Deloshier, Mary - Washerwoman, pe $300, w 15, p 246
Denbee, Oston - Day Laborer, pe $50, w 7, p 253
Dennis, Litten - pe $50, w 12, p 29
Dennis, Robert - Waiter, pe $50, w 11, p 62

Chapter 18

Black Estate Holders - 1860

Densby, Wighton - Laborer, pe $307, w 7, p 590
Denton, Henry - Stevedore, pe $30, w 11, p 190
Dereny, John - Seaman, pe $40, w 17, p 96
Derick, Jonathan - Waiter, pe $20, w 20, p 85
Derrickson, Alford - Laborer, pe $50, w 16, p 59
Derry, Samuel - Grain Runner, pe $40, w 11, p 61
Deshall, Henry - Drayman, pe $200, w 3, p 3480
Deshields, John - Drayman, pe $6000, re $800, w 7, p 308
Deviteen?, Alexander - Cooper, pe $100, w 16, p 167
Devoter?, James - Brickmaker, pe $50, w 16, p 51
Dewey, Henry - Porter, pe $300, w 15, p 251
Dickenson, Henry - Waiter, pe $50, w 11, p 124
Dickerson, James - Waiter, pe $10, w 6, p 2190
Dickerson, Julia A. - pe $5, w 7, p 3820
Dickerson, William - Day Laborer, pe $1000, re $500, w 7, p 377
Dickison, James - Laborer, pe $50, w 17, p 176
Dicks, John - Waiter, pe $40, w 20, p 247
Difer?, Samuel - Waiter, pe $20, w 17, p 163
Diggs, Cyrus M. - Hay Dealer, pe $1500, re $500, w 8, p 569
Diggs, Lewis - Laborer, pe $30, w 11, p 154
Dilahey, James - Laborer, pe $25, w 17, p 254
Diller, John - Laborer, pe $25, w 17, p 187
Dirbois, Edward J. - Barber, pe $1,200, w 12, p 223
Distence, Charles - Day Laborer, pe $50, w 7, p 360
Dixon, Kaleb - Stevedore, pe $100, w 16, p 163
Dixon, Susan - Washerwoman, pe $75, w 16, p 141
Dixon, Thomas - Brickmaker, pe $20, w 17, p 378
Dobson, Henry - pe $20, w 20, p 54
Dobson, Peter - Laborer, pe $25, w 17, p 9
Dockins, Mrs. - Huckster, pe $25, w 17, p 30
Dody, Peter - Tailor, pe $1,400, re $400, w 9, p 320
Door, Henrietta - pe $50, re $5000, w 7, p 333
Dorman, Daniel - Grain Measurer, pe $10, re $300, w 17, p 24
Dorney, Mary - Washerwoman, pe $10, w 11, p 128
Dorsen, Malinda - Washerwoman, pe $60, w 14, p 116
Dorsey, Alexander - Ostler, pe $30, w 11, p 241
Dorsey, Allen - Waiter, pe $100, w 14, p 11
Dorsey, Benjamin - Sailor, pe $50, w 7, p 382
Dorsey, Charles - Grain Runner, pe $40, w 8, p 369
Dorsey, Cornelius - Barber, pe $400, w 12, p 41

Black Estate Holders - 1860

Dorsey, Ellen - Washerwoman, pe $20, w 11, p 109
Dorsey, Ellen - Washerwoman, pe $50, w 20, p 80
Dorsey, Ellen - Servant, pe $500, w 20, p 261
Dorsey, Henry - Laborer, pe $20, w 15, p 14
Dorsey, Henry - pe $50, w 16, p 163
Dorsey, James - Laborer, pe $200, w 15, p 297
Dorsey, James - Blacksmith, pe $100, w 20, p 79
Dorsey, Jerry - Potter, pe $25, w 16, p 51
Dorsey, John - Currier, pe $30, w 8, p 264
Dorsey, John - pe $100, w 12, p 118
Dorsey, John - Sailor, pe $10, w 17, p 26
Dorsey, John - Drayman, pe $175, w 20, p 73
Dorsey, Martha - Brickmaker, pe $200, w 15, p 109
Dorsey, Matilda - Washerwoman, pe $30, w 18, p 765
Dorsey, Philip - Ostler, pe $40, w 8, p 595
Dorsey, Richard - Brickmaker, pe $200, w 15, p 307
Dorsey, Richard - Stevedore, pe $25, w 16, p 16
Dorsey, Robert - pe $50, w 20, p 79
Dorsey, Samuel - Laborer, pe $20, w 20, p 109
Dorsey, Susan A. - Washerwoman, pe $25, w 16, p 33
Dosson?, Mary - Huckster, pe $50, re $1,000, w 13, p 468
Dotton, Nicholas - Carter, pe $300, w 11, p 108
Douglas, Benjamin - Sailor, pe $500, w 15, p 261
Douglas, Benjamin - Laborer, pe $45, w 18, p 431
Douglas, George - Waiter, pe $75, w 11, p 63
Douglas, Henry - Laborer, pe $60, w 18, p 428
Douglas, John H. - Waiter, pe $100, w 11, p 104
Douglas, Solomon - Waiter, pe $100, w 12, p 60
Dowder, Mary - Laundress, pe $20, w 20, p 125
Down, Violet - pe $50, w 16, p 32
Downs, Betsey - Washerwoman, pe $10, w 11, p 239
Downs, Charles - Laborer, pe $200, w 15, p 72
Downs, George - Laborer, pe $50, w 14, p 54
Downs, Harrison - Caulker, pe $200, re $400, w 2, p 720
Downs, Jefferson - Laborer, pe $25, w 20, p 62
Drake, William - Sailor, pe $50, w 7, p 370
Drigers, James - Coachman, pe $50, w 13, p 453
Driver, Charles - Brickmaker, pe $100, w 15, p 74
Driver, Edward - Carter, pe $1,000, w 15, p 90
Driver, Jerry - Brickmaker, pe $300, w 15, p 74

Chapter 18

Black Estate Holders - 1860

Druett, Mary - Washerwoman, pe $40, w 11, p 61
Drummer, Evan - Whip Maker, pe $100, w 14, p 136
Drury, Charles - Laborer, pe $50, w 15, p 301
Duff, Thomas - Waiter, pe $100, w 17, p 183
Duffen, Ann M. - Washerwoman, pe $40, w 11, p 175
Dugall, James - Steward, pe $100, w 3, p 230
Duglass, Lidia - Servant, pe $10, w 16, p 106
Dungan, Edward - Waiter, pe $75, w 11, p 62
Dunguns, Henny - Huckster, pe $100, w 19, p 263
Duniman, Hiram - Barber, pe $50, w 11, p 173
Dunkins, William - Laborer, pe $100, w 15, p 42
Dunn, John - Grain Measurer, pe $500, w 15, p 55
Durand, Ann - Dressmaker, pe $140, w 20, p 133
Durand, Nathaniel - Waiter, pe $30, w 11, p 244
Durham, Henry - Cooper, pe $50, w 16, p 61
Dutton, Charles - Grain Measurer, pe $40, w 8, p 369
Dutton, Henrietta - Washerwoman, pe $20, w 20, p 55
Duvall, John - Brickmaker, pe $100, w 14, p 12
Dyer, Joseph - Brickamker, pe $300, w 15, p 78
Dysett, Major - Driver, pe $400, w 15, p 247
Dyson, John - Drayman, pe $75, w 16, p 65
Eady, William - Laborer, pe $50, w 8, p 389
Earls, Harriet - Washerwoman, pe $30, w 11, p 241
Eastpet, Daniel - Brickmaker, pe $300, w 15, p 57
Eaton, Maria - Washerwoman, pe $20, w 11, p 128
Edward, Charles - Laborer, pe $25, w 16, p 138
Edwards, Abraham - Sailor, pe $10, w 17, p 46
Edwards, Edward - Laborer, pe $100, w 14, p 28
Edwards, Joseph - Waiter, pe $70, w 14, p 120
Edwards, Samuel - Market Man, pe $100, w 14, p 131
Effort, Thomas - Brickmaker, pe $50, w 16, p 136
Eilen, Isaac - Laborer, pe $20, w 11, p 168
Eisenback, Thomas - Storekeeper, pe $1,000, w 3, p 248
Elizabeth Brown - Washerwoman, pe $ 40, w 14, p 67
Ellicott, Ann M. - Dress Maker, pe $50, w 11, p 99
Ellicott, Isaac - Porter, pe $25, w 11, p 174
Elliott, John - Porter, pe $5, w 17, 23
Elliott, Robert - Waiter, pe $40, w 11, 174
Elliott, Samuel - Sawyer, pe $20, w 18, p 431
Ellis, George - Laborer, pe $200, w 15, p 76

Black Real Estate and Personal Estate Holders, 1860

Black Estate Holders - 1860

Ellis, John - Brickmaker, pe $5, w 17, p 44
Elows, Josiah - Laborer, pe $25, w 17, p 104
Elira, Elizabeth - Servant, pe $25, w 16, p 51
Emmerson, James - Porter, pe $50, w 13, p 458
Emory, Jacob - Porter, pe $50, w 11, p 86
Emory, Moses - Stevedore, pe $60, w 14, p 66
Ennig, Solomon - Laborer, pe $500, w 15, p 41
Evans, Maria - Washerwoman, pe $10, w 8, p 339
Evans, Thomas - Caulker, pe $1,000, w 15, p 1
Falston, Margaret - Washerwoman, pe $50, w 12, p 14
Farely, Hanson - Wagon Driver, pe $60, w 14, p 165
Farmton, Charles - Day Laborer, pe $50, w 7, p 334
Fater, Henry F. - Porter, pe $2,400, w 12, p 66
Fenwick, Mary - Washerwoman, pe $20, w 20, p 222
Ferguson, Clara - Servant, pe $50, w 15, p 287
Fernandes, Jonathan - Barber, pe $400, re $500, w 1, p 120
Findler, Joseph - Laborer, pe $50, w 20, p 247
Finley, Daniel - Moulder, pe $40, w 20, p 53
Finley, Lydia - Washerwoman, pe $25, w 16, p 110
Fisher, Caroline - Washerwoman, pe $50, w 13, p 402
Fisher, Charles - Caulker, pe $10, w 2, p 730
Fisher, George - Porter, pe $50, w 11, p 65
Fisher, George - Brickmaker, pe $30, w 17, p 96
Fisher, John - Lumber Yard, pe $1000, re $800, w 8, p 284
Fisher, John H. - Day Laborer, pe $10, w 2, p 960
Fisher, Samuel - Porter, pe $100, w 14, p 29
Fisher, Thomas - Blacksmith, pe $200, w 18, p 429
Fisher, William - Carter, pe $30, w 17, p 98
Flemer, Nicholas - Shoemaker, pe $25, w 20, p 54
Fleming, Catherine - Washerwoman, pe $30, w 11, p 124
Flemming, William - Engineer, pe $50, w 8, p 583
Flower, Robert - Drayman, pe $15, w 20, p 88
Floyd, Thomas - Musician, pe $50, w 16, p 105
Fopins?, Washington - Porter, pe $20, w 17, p 45
Ford, Arin - pe $50, w 11, p 156
Ford, George - Waiter, pe $40, w 11, p 105
Ford, Samuel - Laborer, pe $30, w 20, p 91
Foreman, Andrew - Coachman, pe $30, w 13, p 458
Foreman, David - Whitewasher, pe $75, w 8, p 511
Foreman, Elijah - Brickmaker, pe $25, w 16, p 144

Chapter 18

Black Estate Holders - 1860

Foreman, James - Drayman, pe $25, w 16, p 20
Foreman, John - Laborer, pe $25, w 11, p 174
Forman, Francis - Porter, pe $50, w 20, p 86
Forman, Maria - Washerwoman, pe $300, w 15, p 8
Forney, Jacob - Drayman, pe $100, w 14, p 63
Forrester, Perry - Tavern Keeper, pe $500, w 10, p 43
Fort, Elizabeth - Laundress, pe $10, w 20, p 57
Fortie, George - Shoemaker, pe $300, w 15, p 70
Fortito?, Lewis - School Teacher, pe $75, w 16, p 69
Fortune, John - Confectioner, pe $100, w 15, p 60
Forty, Charles - Barber, pe $30, w 11, p 165
Fossett, Levi - Church Sexton, pe $25, w 16, p 37
Foster, Mary - pe $10, w 11, p 154
Fountain, Margaret - Dressmaker, pe $3,000, w 20, p 73
Fowler, Israsel? - Barber, pe $10, w 7, p 4010
Fowler, Josiah - Brickmaker, pe $50, w 17, p 91
Fowler, Lenard - Brickmaker, pe $50, re $2,000, w 17, p 331
Fowler, William - Brickmaker, pe $20, w 17, p 328
Frances, William - Porter, pe $30, w 11, p 60
Francis, Ellen - Cook, pe $15, w 11, p 129
Francis, Francis - Drayman, pe $300, w 15, p 42
Francis, John - Boarding House, pe $20, w 2, p 770
Francis, John - Brickmaker, pe $10, w 17, p 11
Franklin, George - Whitewasher, pe $100, w 15, p 43
Franklin, George - Laborer, pe $50, w 15, p 43
Franklin, Perry - Whitewasher, pe $1,000, w 15, p 91
Franklin, Peter - Whitewasher, pe $1,200, w 15, p 43
Franklin, Thomas - Drayman, pe $650, w 16, p 168
Fredricks, Richard - Laborer, pe $50, w 14, p 55
Freeland, Frisby - Laborer, pe $10, w 15, p 15
Freeman, Cassia - Washerwoman, pe $10, w 16, p 58
Freeman, Isaac - Laborer, pe $50, w 11, p 61
Freeman, William - Huckster, pe $20, w 6, p 260
Fries, James - Huckster, pe $30, w 6, p 640
Frisby, Eliza - Washerwoman, pe $60, w 14, p 120
Frisby, Elizabeth - Washerwoman, pe $50, w 11, p 243
Frisby, John - Laborer, pe $200, w 15, p 9
Frisby, Joseph - Drayman, pe $125, w 20, p 229
Frisby, Matilda - Washerwoman, pe $15, w 20, p 236
Frisby, Thomas - Carter, pe $50, w 15, p 293

Black Real Estate and Personal Estate Holders, 1860

Black Estate Holders - 1860

Fruder, Leon - Laborer, pe $20, w 20, p 235
Fuller, Addison - Waiter, pe $75, w 16, p 57
Fumace?, Nancy - Huckster, pe $100, re $1,500, w 20, p 266
Furgeson, Charles - Carriage Driver, pe $40, w 20, p 87
Gabriel, Sister - Sister Of Charity, pe $600, re $8,000, w 11, p 66
Gailes, Susan - Washerwoman, pe $500, re $450, w 7, p 286
Gaines, Noah - Whitewasher, pe $10, w 17, p 50
Gains, Moses - Brickmaker, pe $500, w 15, p 108
Gaither, Washington - Store Keeper, pe $75, w 16, p 50
Gaitor, John - Laborer, pe $45, w 18, p 432
Gale, Auther - Brickmaker, pe $10, w 17, p 49
Gale, George - Laborer, pe $10, w 3, p 770
Gale, George C. - Carpenter, pe $15, w 7, p 4980
Gale, John - Day Laborer, pe $5, w 7, p 3170
Gale, Mary - Gardener, pe $1000, re $1,800, w 7, p 498
Gale, Robert - Whitewasher, pe $40, w 11, p 108
Galloway, John - Waiter, pe $3, w 8, p 4200
Galloway, Marinda - Washerwoman, pe $10, w 17, p 12
Galloway, William - Hod Carrier, pe $20, w 18, p 429
Gambert, Julius - Confectioner, pe $400, w 7, p 324
Gambill, Isaac - Carter, pe $25, w 16, p 34
Gamble, Serena - Washerwoman, pe $40, w 11, p 101
Ganes, Martin - Day Laborer, pe $5, w 2, p 780
Gant, Richard - Porter, pe $800, w 15, p 55
Gardener, James - Carter, pe $50, w 7, p 389
Gardner, John A. - Mariner, pe $300, w 15, p 91
Garner, Mary - Laundress, pe $40, w 20, p 50
Garnet, Richard - Porter, pe $40, w 14, p 60
Garnet, Solomon - Wood Sawyer, pe $20, w 11, p 99
Garrett, Daniel - Seaman, pe $75, w 16, p 57
Garrett, Edward - Whitewasher, pe $50, w 16, p 140
Garrett, Richard - Porter, pe $50, w 16, p 60
Garrett, Thomas - Stevedore, pe $50, w 14, p 97
Garrison, James - Laborer, pe $20, w 20, p 53
Garrison, Jeremia - Laborer, pe $25, w 16, p 204
Garrison, Jeremiah - Laborer, pe $300, w 15, p 264
Garrison, Jeremiah - Carter, pe $50, w 16, p 110
Garrison, John - Carter, pe $10, w 17, p 297
Garrison, Noble - Laborer, pe $20, w 17, p 99
Gasker, Hennie - Washerwoman, pe $10, w 20, p 111

Chapter 18

Black Estate Holders - 1860

Gasker, John - Drayman, pe $50, w 20, p 111
Gassaway, Francis - Carter, pe $15, w 20, p 58
Gassaway, Josiah - Laborer, pe $75, w 8, p 559
Gassaway, Nicholas - Porter, pe $30, w 20, p 84
Gebhart, Francis - Washerwoman, pe $50, w 16, p 57
Gennings?, Daniel - Farmer, pe $25, w 16, p 170
Gest, George - Caulker, pe $10, w 3, p 70
Gettings, Isaiah - Porter, pe $40, w 14, p 66
Gibbs, Mary - Seamstress, pe $100, w 16, p 51
Gibes?, James - Speculator, pe $500, w 3, p 323
Gibson, Benjamin - Drayman, pe $200, w 12, p 183
Gibson, Clara - Washerwoman, pe $20, w 18, p 433
Gibson, Lewis - Laborer, pe $100, w 19, p 178
Gibson, Malachia - Hackman, pe $3,000, w 15, p 41
Gibson, Mary - Washerwoman, pe $40, w 11, p 108
Giddings, Marshall - Porter, pe $25, w 16, p 59
Gidley, Daniel - Barber, pe $100, w 15, p 46
Gilbert, Jacob - Barber, pe $40, w 14, p 137
Gilbert, Jacob - Barber, pe $20, w 16, p 106
Gilbert, Martin - Brickmaker, pe $75, w 16, p 106
Gilbert, Paca T. - Whitewasher, pe $100, w 11, p 127
Gilbert, Sidney - pe $20, w 17, p 95
Giles, John - Wagoner, pe $40, w 11, p 60
Gilleot, Edward - Blacksmith, pe $3000, re $1,600, w 8, p 497
Gilleot, James - Blacksmith, pe $3000, re $1,600, w 8, p 497
Gilley, israel - Barber, pe $5, w 2, p 790
Gilliard, Charlotte - Washerwoman, pe $40, w 11, p 129
Gillman, Harriet - Washerwoman, pe $100, w 12, p 60
Gilmore, John - Laborer, pe $50, w 11, p 61
Gison, Charles - Brickmaker, pe $25, w 17, p 185
Gittings, Louisa - pe $10, w 17, p 185
Gittores, Sarah A. - Washerwoman, pe $50, w 11, p 123
Glasgow, James - Servant, pe $50, w 16, p 144
Glowber, Ariminta - Washerwoman, pe $40, w 14, p 128
Goehms, Catherine - Washerwoman, pe $75, w 11, p 63
Goings, Robert - Porter, pe $50, w 17, p 5
Goings, William - Mariner, pe $40, w 14, p 140
Golder, William - Shoemaker, pe $40, w 11, p 146
Goldsborough, Henry - Waiter, pe $25, w 11, p 45
Goldsborough, John - Cabinet Maker, pe $100, w 20, p 90

Black Real Estate and Personal Estate Holders, 1860

Black Estate Holders - 1860

Goldsborough, Sipes - Waiter, pe $200, re $1,000, w 19, p 236
Goldsborough, Washington - Brickmaker, pe $600, w 15, p 109
Gordon, John - Drayman, pe $200, w 20, p 236
Goring, James - Stewart, pe $1,000, w 6, p 223
Gould, David - Hackman, pe $30, w 13, p 484
Gould, John H. - Drayman, pe $250, w 17, p 81
Graham, Prissilla - Washerwoman, pe $40, w 11, p 126
Grandison, Charles - Porter, pe $5, w 8, p 2630
Grant, Charity - Washerwoman, pe $40, w 11, p 167
Grant, Nancy - pe $100, w 15, p 42
Grant, Ranson - Laborer, pe $100, w 15, p 42
Graso, Tobias - Brickmaker, pe $20, w 17, p 184
Grason, George - Brickmaker, pe $80, w 17, p 14
Grason, William - Brickmaker, pe $10, w 17, p 14
Grass, Frisby - Sailor, pe $500, w 15, p 261
Grasson, John - Brickmaker, pe $50, w 16, p 145
Gratefield, Eliza - Dress Maker, pe $100, w 13, p 459
Graves, Henry - Grain Runner, pe $40, w 11, p 167
Graves, Joseph - Grain Measurer, pe $25, w 17, p 184
Gray, Alford - Brickmaker, pe $75, w 16, p 47
Gray, Cumberland - Butcher, pe $75, w 8, p 587
Gray, Delia - Washerwoman, pe $100, w 15, p 72
Gray, George - Drayman, pe $25, w 16, p 60
Gray, James - Whitewasher, pe $75, w 20, p 230
Gray, Lucy - Washerwoman, pe $40, w 11, p 77
Gray, Perry - Laborer, pe $5, w 5, p 790
Gray, Rachel - Washerwoman, pe $200, w 15, p 91
Gray, Sarah - pe $100, w 15, p 43
Gray, Thomas - Brickmaker, pe $5, w 17, p 22
Gray, William - Steam Boat, pe $75, w 11, p 53
Gray, William J. - Cabinet Maker, pe $50, re $700, w 11, p 166
Green, Alfred - Cart Driver, pe $40, w 20, p 265
Green, Ann - Laundress, pe $50, w 19, p 86
Green, Caroline - pe $20, w 17, p 232
Green, Charles E. - Hod Carrier, pe $50, w 17, p 2
Green, David - Caulker, pe $200, w 2, p 46
Green, Edward - Hod Carrier, pe $40, w 18, p 495
Green, Eli - Coachman, pe $100, w 14, p 28
Green, Ephraim - Laborer, pe $50, w 19, p 87
Green, George - Caulker, pe $200, w 2, p 61

Chapter 18

Black Estate Holders - 1860

Green, George - Brickmaker, pe $100, w 15, p 43
Green, George - Whitewasher, pe $80, w 18, p 729
Green, Henry - Caulker, pe $100, w 2, p 81
Green, Henry - Waiter, pe $20, w 20, p 92
Green, Jacob - Seaman, pe $30, w 17, p 183
Green, Jane - Washerwoman, pe $20, w 18, p 431
Green, John - Brickmaker, pe $200, w 15, p 55
Green, Joseph - Porter, pe $400, w 12, p 190
Green, Joseph - Mariner, pe $60, w 20, p 56
Green, Rachael - Washerwoman, pe $200, w 15, p 42
Green, Rachel - Washerwoman, pe $20, w 20, p 80
Green, Samuel - Laborer, pe $200, w 15, p 55
Green, Samuel - Brickmaker, pe $50, w 16, p 145
Green, Thomas - Barber, pe $80, w 11, p 155
Green, William - Brickmaker, pe $25, re $1,000, w 17, p 349
Green, William - Hod Carrier, pe $40, w 18, p 428
Greene, Charles - Herb Doctor, pe $300, w 15, p 43
Greenn, Lucinda - Washerwoman, pe $800, w 6, p 233
Greenwich, Ely - Wood Sawyer, pe $750, w 16, p 68
Greenwich, John - Wood sawyer, pe $25, w 16, p 68
Greenwood, Jacob - Drayman, pe $50, w 11, p 44
Greenwood, John H. - Coach Printer, pe $100, w 7, p 413
Greenwood, Perry - Porter, pe $40, w 14, p 67
Greenwood, Samuel - Porter, pe $200, w 17, p 175
Gregg, America - Stevedore, pe $75, w 5, p 89
Gregg, Amos - Day Laborer, pe $50, w 7, p 401
Greves, Joseph - Drayman, pe $60, w 20, p 78
Griffen, Margaret - Washerwoman, pe $25, w 16, p 59
Griffen, Samuel - Brickmaker, pe $50, w 16, p 139
Griffin, Samuel - Brickmaker, pe $500, w 15, p 52
Griffin, Edward - Barber, pe $100, w 7, p 360
Griffin, George - Caulker, pe $100, w 3, p 230
Griffin, Henry - Day Laborer, pe $50, w 7, p 317
Griffin, James - Waiter, pe $300, w 15, p 245
Griffin, John - Brickmaker, pe $200, w 15, p 52
Griffin, Nelson - Laborer, pe $40, w 20, p 91
Griffin, Richard - Hackman, pe $600, w 15, p 298
Griffin, Samuel - Brickmaker, pe $100, w 15, p 52
Griffin, William - Brickmaker, pe $300, w 15, p 52
Griffin, William - pe $20, w 17, p 146
Griffith, John - Brickmaker, pe $300, w 15, p 51

Black Real Estate and Personal Estate Holders, 1860

Black Estate Holders - 1860

Griffith, Robert - Laborer, pe $25, w 16, p 23
Griffith, William - Hostler, pe $10, w 17, p 11
Griffith, William H. - Brickmaker, pe $100, w 15, p 2
Groer, Fransess - Washerwoman, pe $50, w 16, p 52
Groom, Elizabeth - Nurse, pe $30, w 11, p 241
Groom, Nat - Barber, pe $300, w 20, p 71
Grooms, John E. - Day Laborer, pe $50, w 7, p 389
Grooms, Nelson - Butcher, pe $50, w 8, p 592
Grooms, Otho - Drayman, pe $40, w 11, p 65
Gross, Benjamin - Laborer, pe $400, w 15, p 75
Gross, Benjamin - Drayman, pe $20, re $600, w 17, p 185
Gross, Diana - washerwoman, pe $200, w 15, p 71
Gross, Henry - Brickmaker, pe $10, w 17, p 30
Gross, James - Laborer, pe $100, w 15, p 320
Gross, James C. - Brickmaker, pe $500, w 15, p 61
Gross, John - Laborer, pe $200, w 15, p 75
Gross, Kinsey - Drayman, pe $25, w 17, p 2
Gross, Major - Laborer, pe $200, w 15, p 54
Gross, Phillip - Musician, pe $75, w 16, p 104
Gross, Samuel - Gardener, pe $25, w 16, p 103
Gross, Samuel - Brickmaker, pe $20, w 17, p 188
Gross, Sophia - Washerwoman, pe $100, w 15, p 68
Gross, Stephen - Laborer, pe $100, w 15, p 75
Gross, Stephen - Laborer, pe $100, w 15, p 75
Gross, Thomas - Laborer, pe $100, w 15, p 80
Gross, Wesley - Brickmaker, pe $30, w 17, p 92
Gross, William - Brickmaker, pe $30, w 17, p 186
Gun, Henrietta - pe $18,000, w 4, p ?
Gunson?, Richard - Grain Measurer, pe 500, w 15, p 294
Gusta, John - Sadler, pe $5, w 16, p 102
Guy, Charles - Coachman, pe $50, w 11, p 100
Guy, William - Brickmaker, pe $50, w 16, p 141
Howard, Betsie - Washerwoman, pe $30, w 14, p 63
Habram, Joseph - Waiter, pe $50, w 12, p 29
Hacket, Frederick - Day Laborer, pe $100, re $1,000, w 7, p 317
Hacket, William - Brickmaker, pe $50, w 7, p 376
Hackett, George - Coal Agebt, pe $600, w 6, p 222
Hackett, Martha - Servant, pe $10, w 16, p 70
Hackett, Mr. - Brickamker, pe $10, w 17, p 50
Hadeson, Wesley - Music Teacher, pe $70, w 20, p 91
Hagler, John - Drayman, pe $100, w 15, p 293

Chapter 18

Black Estate Holders - 1860

Hain, Robert - Brickmaker, pe $300, w 15, p 295
Hains, James - Brickmaker, pe $100, w 15, p 56
Hains, Philip - Drayman, pe $1,300, w 15, p 110
Haley, Alexander - Sailor, pe $200, re $700, w 2, p 95
Hall, Ann - Washerwoman, pe $25, w 16, p 186
Hall, Arthur - Furniture Cart, pe $200, w 6, p 229
Hall, Bazil - Tanner, pe $50, w 16, p 166
Hall, Edward - Waiter, pe $100, w 12, p 197
Hall, Elias - Drayman, pe $500, w 20, p 83
Hall, Freeborn - Brickmaker, pe $5, w 17, p 59
Hall, John - Porter, pe $300, w 15, p 68
Hall, John - Drayman, pe $250, w 20, p 72
Hall, John D. - Barber, pe $100, w 20, p 106
Hall, John W. - Seaman, pe $25, w 16, p 142
Hall, Kinsey - Butcher, pe $100, w 7, p 413
Hall, Louis - pe $10, w 17, p 10
Hall, Louisa - Washerwoman, pe $50, w 18, p 432
Hall, Nathan - Barber, pe $100, w 3, p 235
Hall, Sarah - Washerwoman, pe $40, w 14, p 131
Hall, Thomas - Laborer, pe $40, w 11, p 124
Hall, William - Brickmaker, pe $25, w 16, p 138
Hall, William - Sailor, pe $25, w 17, p 9
Halla, James - Drayman, pe $50, w 14, p 11
Hamilton, Agar - Laborer, pe $25, w 16, p 59
Hammond, John - Steamboat Hand, pe $75, w 8, p 464
Hammond, Lewis S. - Dr. Of Divinity, pe $1,000, w 12, p 144
Hammond, Sarah - Washerwoman, pe $50, w 5, p 88
Hancock, Ida - re $1,200, w 3, p 257
Handy, Anna - pe $600, re z$1,000, w 10, p 27
Handy, Isaac - Laborer, pe $500, w 20, p 111
Handy, James - Cabinetmaker, pe $500, w 3, p 18
Handy, Thomas - Coachman, pe $50, w 16, p 33
Hanson, Harriet - Washerwoman, pe $20, w 8, p 269
Hanson, Henrietta - Seamstress, pe $30, w 11, p 190
Hanson, James - Laborer, pe $100, w 3, p 230
Harden, James - Waiter, pe $100, re $1,000, w 8, p 586
Harden, Jeremiah - Waiter, pe $100, re $1,800, w 11, p 53
Harden, Rachel - Washerwoman, pe $40, w 20, p 96
Hardy, John - Waiter, pe $75, w 11, p 53
Hargroves, McKenzie - Drayman, pe $50, w 7, p 376
Harkins, James - Waiter, pe $100, w 12, p 28

Black Estate Holders - 1860

Harkner?, Walter - Drayman, pe $50, w 16, p 165
Harman, James - Day Laborer, pe $50, w 7, p 319
Harman, Terpit? - Laborer, pe $15, w 15, p 15
Harris, Alexander - Hod Carrier, pe $150, re $250, w 17, p 26
Harris, Angline - Huckster, pe $150, w 6, p 55
Harris, Bailey - Laborer, pe $10, w 20, p 56
Harris, Daniel - Store Keeper, pe $100, w 2, p 42
Harris, Harriett - Dressmaker, pe $50, w 16, p 105
Harris, Henry - Porter, pe $100, w 14, p 17
Harris, Henry - Brickmaker, pe $20, w 17, p 287
Harris, James - Sailor, pe $500, w 15, p 262
Harris, James - Brickmaker, pe $50, w 16, p 140
Harris, James - Brickmaker, pe $600, w 20, p 81
Harris, Letitia - Washerwoman, pe $20, w 11, p 173
Harris, Lewis - Wagon Driver, pe $50, w 7, p 388
Harris, Mary - Laundress, pe $500, w 19, p 86
Harris, Mintey - Servant, pe $75, w 16, p 16
Harris, Richard - Cook, pe $50, w 12, p 42
Harris, Richard - Laborer, pe $100, w 15, p 42
Harris, Robert - Waiter, pe $500, w 15, p 56
Harris, Thomas - Bricklayer, pe $100, w 3, p 227
Harris, Thomas - Carter, pe $25, w 17, p 7
Harris, William - Hod Carrier, pe $30, w 11, p 154
Harris, William - Brickmaker, pe $100, w 15, p 8
Harris, William - Butcher, pe $200, w 18, p 869
Harrison, Daniel - Laborer, pe $200, w 15, p 69
Harrison, Delia - Washerwoman, pe $40, w 11, p 187
Harrison, John F. - Carter, pe $50, w 7, p 364
Harry, Anthony - Laborer, pe $100, w 16, p 47
Harryman, Walter - Cabinet Maker, pe $800, w 3, p 248
Hart, Peonie - pe $40, w 18, p 368
Hart, Wilson - Brickmaker, pe $30, w 11, p 189
Hartman, Isaac - Waiter, pe $20, w 17, p 147
Harvey, Samuel - Whitewasher, pe $50, w 20, p 61
Harvey, Thomas - Barber, pe $25, w 17, p 1
Hasset, Harriet - pe $25, w 17, p 163
Hawkins, Ann - Washerwoman, pe $40, w 14, p 130
Hawkins, Daniel - Laborer, pe $15, w 20, p 56
Hawkins, Edward - Brickmaker, pe $2,000, w 15, p 78
Hawkins, Nathan - Waiter, pe $20, w 8, p 264
Hayes, Catharine - Washerwoman, pe $40, w 14, p 66

Chapter 18

Black Estate Holders - 1860

Hayes, Elizabeth - Washerwoman, pe $10, w 17, p 14
Hays, John W. - Brickmaker, pe $50, w 17, p 86
Hazleton, Henry - Laborer, pe $75, w 8, p 545
Heath, Mary - Seamstress, pe $10, w 17, p 49
Heath, Thomas - Brickmaker, pe $30, w 17, p 95
Heath, William - Wood sawyer, pe $10, w 17, p 50
Hedges, William H. - Seaman, pe $100, w 11, p 106
Heiner, Sarah J. - Seamstress, pe $100, re $800, w 8, p 284
Helbrew, John - Laborer, pe $35, w 20, p 49
Hemsley, Henry - Day Laborer, pe $50, w 7, p 360
Henry, Ann - Washerwoman, pe $30, w 11, p 61
Henry, Jonas - Sailor, pe $20, w 17, p 30
Henry, Mary - pe $20, w 17, p 93
Henry, Sarah - Washerwoman, pe $30, w 8, p 420
Hensler, Allen - Day Laborer, pe $50, w 7, p 360
Henson, Basil - Whitewasher, pe $30, w 13, p 472
Henson, James - Laborer, pe $30, w 13, p 469
Henson, John - Waiter, pe $100, w 19, p 177
Henson, John W. - Stevedore, pe $40, w 14, p 131
Hentson?, Levi - Pie Baker, re $400, w 7, p 588z
Herrod, Hester - pe $25, w 16, p 140
Herser, Samuel - Woodsawyer, pe $300, w 15, p 55
Hess, Charles - Carter, pe $25, w 16, p 115
Heynson, Peter - Laborer, pe $100, w 15, p 39
Hicks, Louis - Waiter, pe $50, w 8, p 356
Hicks, Thomas - Coachman, pe $40, w 20, p 83
High, James - Carter, pe $100, w 7, p 377
Hill, Ann - Cook, pe $30, w 11, p 241
Hill, David - Drayman, pe $50, w 19, p 122
Hill, Eliza - Washerwoman, pe $100, w 15, p 2
Hill, Joseph - Drayman, pe $100, w 14, p 28
Hill, Leonard - Servant, pe $75, w 15, p 2
Hill, Richard - Mariner, pe $60, w 14, p 59
Hill, Samuel - Ostler, pe $100, w 14, p 26
Hill, Sylvester - Porter, pe $100, w 14, p 28
Hill, Thomas - pe $200, re $350, w 17, p 81
Hillard, Hesekia - Porter, pe $100, re $1,100, w 6, p 36
Hinds, Isaac - Day Laborer, pe $50, w 7, p 361
Hiner, Jacob - Horseler, pe $600, w 6, p 58
Hinesman, James - Farmer, pe $4, w 17, p 44
Hinson, David - Brickmaker, pe $5, w 17, p 24

Black Real Estate and Personal Estate Holders, 1860

Black Estate Holders - 1860

Hinson, Mary - Nurse, pe $25, w 13, p 412
Hinson, William - Scowman, pe $100, w 6, p 73
Hinton?, Nathan - Fireman, pe $25, w 16, p 143
Hitchet, Henry W. - Caulker, pe $200, re $1,100, w 2, p 65
Hodge, Mary - Washerwoman, pe $5, w 17, p 11
Hodges, George - Drayman, pe $30, w 8, p 292
Hoe, Eliza - Housekeeper, re $100, w 20, p 267
Hoffman, Henry - Whitewasher, pe $100, w 15, p 8
Hoffman, Rebecca - Laundress, pe $20, w 20, p 122
Holden, Clelia - Servant, pe $25, w 16, p 47
Hollam, William - Laborer, pe $75, w 16, p 101
Hollands, Daniel - Drayman, pe $200, w 20, p 80
Holley, William - Laborer, pe $25, w 13, p 472
Holliday, Agnes - Washerwoman, pe $25, w 20, p 236
Holliday, Elizabeth - Washerwoman, pe $10, w 20, p 126
Holliday, John - Laborer, pe $300, w 15, p 77
Hollins, Edward - Drayman, pe $100, re $500, w 8, p 572
Holloway, William - Coal Yard, pe $50, w 8, p 306
Holmes, Henry - Carter, pe $200, w 15, p 79
Holmes, Solomon - Laborer, pe $200, w 15, p 70
Hooper, Charles - Laborer, pe $30, w 17, p 96
Hooper, George - Carter, pe $200, w 17, p 94
Hooper, Jacob - Laborer, pe $1,000, w 15, p 79
Hopkins, Henry - Porter, pe $50, w 7, p 256
Hopkins, James - Barber, pe $200, w 6, p 63
Hopkins, Robert - Brickmaker, pe $25, w 16, p 144
Horsey, John - Laborer, pe $10, w 17, p 55
Horsey, Nancy - Washerwoman, pe $20, w 11, p 154
Hoser?, Charles - Mariner, pe $50, w 15, p 296
Hough?, James - Carter, pe $100, re $400, w 7, p 587z
How, Robert - Scow Man, pe $100, w 7, p 371
Howard Samuel - Barber, pe $30, w 11, p 175
Howard, Amelia - Servant, pe $10, w 16, p 138
Howard, Andrew - Laborer, pe $20, w 18, p 426
Howard, Ann - Washerwoman, pe $40, w 18, p 768
Howard, Charles - Waiter, pe $100, w 6, p 60
Howard, Dennis - Brickmaker, pe $25, w 16, p 144
Howard, Dennis - Carter, pe $5, w 17, p 45
Howard, Eliza - Washerwoman, pe $15, w 11, p 187
Howard, Eliza - Washerwoman, pe $50, w 16, p 33
Howard, Elizabeth - Washerwoman, pe $75, w 8, p 601

Chapter 18

Black Estate Holders - 1860

Howard, Greenberg - Porter, pe $100, w 12, p 185
Howard, John - Laborer, pe $45, w 18, p 432
Howard, John - Waiter, pe $50, w 19, p 178
Howard, Lloyd - Barber, pe $50, w 14, p 13
Howard, Rebecca - Washerwoman, pe $20, w 8, p 294
Howard, Samuel - Brfickmaker, pe $200, w 15, p 56
Howard, Susan - pe $30, re $1,200, w 11, p 46
Howard, Wilson - Waiter, pe $25, w 13, p 463
Howell, Charles - Porter, pe $50, w 8, p 593
Howell, Joshua - Porter, pe $25, w 14, p 63
Hoy, Lucinda - Dressmaker, pe $100, w 210, p 26
Hubbard, james - Porter, pe $5, w 17, p 30
Hudson, Daniel - Waiter, pe $75, w 11, p 187
Hudson, James - Steward, pe $150, w 11, p 238
Hughes, Daniel - Farmer, pe $50, w 17, p 177
Hughes, Hester - Washerwoman, pe $10, w 17, p 56
Hughins, George - Brickmaker, pe $5, w 17, p 28
Hull, Joshua - Sailor, pe $5, w 17, p 57
Hult, Mary - School Teacher, pe $30, w 20, p 286
Hurt, John - Barber, pe $40, w 11, p 129
Husettan?, James - Scow Man, pe $50, w 7, p 382
Huston, John - Caulker, pe $50, w 7, p 361
Hutchins, Samuel - Drayman, pe $100, w 14, p 28
Hutta, John - Sailor, pe $100, w 2, p 77
Hyell?, Henry - Waiter, pe $500, w 15, p 261
Inloes, Nathaniel - Drayman, pe $200, w 12, p 64
Ireland, Perry - Confectioner, pe $100, w 10, p 41
Irens, Debrow - Washerwoman, pe $50, w 7, p 371
Irons, Stephen E. -Porter In Store, pe $100, w 11, p 126
Irvin, Catherine - Dress Maker, pe $50, w 11, p 76
Island, Jesse - Brickmaker, pe $30, w 17, p 103
Jacket, Jeremiah - Brickmaker, pe $50, w 16, p 186
Jackson, Alfred - Waiter, pe $50, w 11, p 63
Jackson, Arthur - Mariner, pe $500, w 15, p 56
Jackson, Benjamin F. - Caulker, pe $200, re $600, w 2, p 61
Jackson, Charles - Coachman, pe $30, w 11, p 100
Jackson, Eliza - Washerwoman, pe $25, w 11, p 129
Jackson, Elizabeth - Laundress, pe $40, w 20, p 86
Jackson, Emily - Washerwoman, pe $20, w 18, p 375
Jackson, George - Whitewasher, pe $25, w 17, p 378
Jackson, Henry - Huckster, pe $50, w 11, p 99

Black Real Estate and Personal Estate Holders, 1860

Black Estate Holders - 1860

Jackson, Henry - Porter, pe $25, w 13, p 402
Jackson, Henry - Farmer, pe $50, w 16, p 140
Jackson, Ignatius - Carter, re $300, w 7, p 584z
Jackson, James - Caulker, pe $400, re $2,000, w 1, p 26
Jackson, James - Porter, pe $100, w 14, p 65
Jackson, James - Porter, pe $700, w 15, p 72
Jackson, James - Brickmaker, pe $200, w 15, p 308
Jackson, James - Laborer, pe $30, w 20, p 96
Jackson, Joseph - Sailor, pe $100, w 2, p 98
Jackson, Julia - Washerwoman, pe $100, w 15, p 43
Jackson, Mary - Washerwoman, pe $100, w 15, p 70
Jackson, Mary - Washerwoman, pe $10, w 17, p 12
Jackson, Mary - Laundress, pe $35, w 20, p 86
Jackson, Milly - Servant, pe $100, w 15, p 41
Jackson, Peter - Ciachman, pe $50, w 11, p 164
Jackson, Rachael - Washerwoman, pe $50, w 11, p 65
Jackson, Randell - Wood Dealer, pe $800, w 3, p 258
Jackson, Samuel - Laborer, pe $25, w 16, p 68
Jackson, Thomas - Porter, pe $150, w 17, p 1
Jackson, Tilman - Driver, pe $200, re $600, w 20, p 202
Jackson, William - Caulker, pe $100, w 2, p 61
Jackson, William - Coachman, pe $50, w 11, p 76
Jackson, Willis - Shoemaker, pe $150, w 11, p 108
Jacobs, Nancy - Washerwoman, pe $25, w 11, p 174
Jakes, Henry - Caterer, pe $1,000, re $15,000, w 11, p 122
James, David - Painter, re $700, w 3, p 229
James, George - Drayman, pe $50, w 8, p 545
James, Henry - Waiter, pe $100, w 14, p 12
James, John H. - Drayman, pe $200, w 17, p 81
Jane La Fountain - Washerwoman, pe $800, w 20, p 89
Janey, Mary - Washerwoman, pe $30, re $800, w 17, p 327
Jarkins, Calvert - Barber, pe $200, w 12, p 41
Jefferson, Henry - Day Laborer, pe $50, w 7, p 320
Jefferson, Isabela - Washerwoman, pe $30, w 11, p 154
Jefferson, Richard - Brickmaker, pe $60, w 14, p 65
Jemison, Julia - Washerwoman, pe $100, w 15, p 92
Jemkins, William - Laborer, pe $30, w 13, p 468
Jenkins, Ann - Washerwoman, pe $100, re $500, w 2, p 98
Jenkins, Catharine - Washerwoman, pe $30, w 14, p 58
Jenkins, Clement - Coachman, pe $100, w 11, p 77
Jenkins, Eliza - Washerwoman, pe $50, w 16, p 165

Chapter 18

Black Estate Holders - 1860

Jenkins, John - Wood sawyer, pe $10, w 17, p 49
Jenkins, Maria - Washerwoman, pe $50, w 11, p 189
Jennings, Charles - Laborer, pe $50, w 20, p 50
Jennings, Henry - Porter, pe $15, w 20, p 60
Jennings, Maria - Washerwoman, pe $200, w 15, p 53
Jennings, Stephen - Laborer, pe $30, w 17, p 242
Jennings, Thomas - Oyster Shucker, pe $500, w 4, p 89
Johns, Alexander - Brickmaker, pe $15, w 17, p 56
Johns, Henry - Laborer, pe $50, w 11, p 252
Johns, Jefferson - Laundress, pe $15, w 20, p 58
Johns, John - Drayman, pe $300, w 20, p 85
Johns, William - Laborer, pe $100, w 17, p 56
Johnson, Adam - Wagoner, pe $300, w 13, p 463
Johnson, Alfred - Laborer, pe $100, w 15, p 74
Johnson, Amelia - Washerwoman, pe $200, w 15, p 265
Johnson, Ann M. - pe $40, w 20, p 125
Johnson, Anna - Washerwoman, pe $25, w 16, p 144
Johnson, Aquilla - Coal Dealer, pe $150, w 16, p 60
Johnson, Aron - Porter, pe $50, w 17, p 86
Johnson, Caroline - Washerwoman, pe $10, w 17, p 49
Johnson, Charles - Caulker, pe $100, re $500, w 2, p 96
Johnson, Charles - Porter, pe $50, w 14, p 55
Johnson, Charles - Laborer, pe $300, w 15, p 76
Johnson, Charles - Porter, pe $15, w 18, p 427
Johnson, Closter - Laundress, pe $15, w 20, p 95
Johnson, Dennis - Laborer, pe $50, w 19, p 224
Johnson, Edward - Hack Driver, pe $300, w 6, p 207
Johnson, Edward - Drayman, pe $150, w 20, p 54
Johnson, Eliza - Huckster, pe $200, w 6, p 60
Johnson, Eliza - Cook, pe $700, w 16, p 164
Johnson, Francis - Washerwoman, pe $200, w 15, p 108
Johnson, George - Laborer, pe $200, w 15, p 72
Johnson, George - Carter, pe $75, w 16, p 110
Johnson, George - Brickmaker, pe $10, w 17, p 10
Johnson, George - Carter, pe $100, w 17, p 45
Johnson, George - Brickmaker, pe $20, w 17, p 57
Johnson, George - Laborer, pe $40, w 18, p 431
Johnson, Hannah - Laundress, pe $10, w 20, p 88
Johnson, Hardester - Boarding House, pe $300, re $3,000, w 2, p 159
Johnson, Harriett - Washerwoman, pe $25, w 16, p 52
Johnson, Henry - Porter, pe $25, w 20, p 109

Black Real Estate and Personal Estate Holders, 1860

Black Estate Holders - 1860

Johnson, Horace - Whitewasher, pe $25, w 16, p 68
Johnson, Horace - Coachman, pe $40, w 18, p 408
Johnson, James - Barber, pe $200, w 13, p 441
Johnson, James - Carter, pe $1,000, w 15, p 108
Johnson, James - Carter, pe $5, w 17, p 45
Johnson, James - Laborer, pe $25, w 17, p 178
Johnson, James - Waiter, pe $20, w 17, p 203
Johnson, James - Coachman, pe $60, w 18, p 429
Johnson, Jarret - Hay Dealer, pe $1,000, w 20, p 56
Johnson, John - Brickmaker, pe $50, w 7, p 370
Johnson, John - Laborer, pe $200, w 18, p 376
Johnson, Joseph - Drayman, pe $500, w 15, p 51
Johnson, Julia - Washerwoman, pe $200, w 15, p 59
Johnson, Maria - Cook Shop, pe $500, w 15, p 259
Johnson, Maria - Washerwoman, pe $300, w 15, p 263
Johnson, Maria - Huckster, pe $50, w 17, p 30
Johnson, Marris? - Brickmaker, pe $50, w 16, p 106
Johnson, Mary - Washerwoman, pe $60, w 14, p 63
Johnson, Perry - Grain Measurer, pe $50, w 17, p 104
Johnson, Philip - Carter, pe $500, w 15, p 109
Johnson, Pleasant - Drayman, pe $100, w 6, p 121
Johnson, Rachel - Servant, pe $50, w 16, p 59
Johnson, Rebeca - Washerwoman, pe $60, w 14, p 62
Johnson, Rebecca - Washerwoman, pe $100, w 16, p 106
Johnson, Richard - Waiter, pe $100, w 16, p 69
Johnson, Samuel - Drayman, pe $400, w 15, p 78
Johnson, Samuel - Drayman, pe $25, w 17, p 2
Johnson, Samuel - Porter, pe $40, w 18, p 408
Johnson, Sarah - pe $100, w 15, p 77
Johnson, Sarah - Washerwoman, pe $25, w 18, p 427
Johnson, Solomon - Grain Measurer, pe $600, w 12, p 59
Johnson, Stanley - Waiter, pe $30, w 13, p 468
Johnson, Stephen - Waiter, pe $100, w 15, p 30
Johnson, Thomas - Day Laborer, pe $50, w 2, p 78
Johnson, Thomas - Brickmaker, pe $30, w 13, p 472
Johnson, Thomas - pe $70, w 14, p 60
Johnson, Thomas P. - Market Man, pe $200, w 14, p 57
Johnson, Walter - Barber, pe $800, w 6, p 147
Johnson, William - Sailor, pe $100, w 2, p 77
Johnson, William - Carter, pe $200, w 16, p 106
Johnson, William - Brickmaker, pe $25, w 17, p 104

Chapter 18

Black Estate Holders - 1860

Johnson, William - Waiter, pe $30, w 20, p 125
Johnson, Samuel - Porter, pe $100, w 16, p 70
Johnston, Anna - Washerwoman, pe $25, w 16, p 70
Johnston, Appolona - Washerwoman, pe $30, w 11, p 173
Johnston, Catherine - Washerwoman, pe $20, w 8, p 350
Johnston, Darius - Teamster, pe $50, w 8, p 572
Johnston, Elizabeth - Cook, pe $40, w 11, p 101
Johnston, George - Waiter, pe $100, re $400, w 11, p 106
Johnston, George H. - Wood Sawyer, pe $20, w 11, p 154
Johnston, Henry - Coachman, pe $500, w 15, p 254
Johnston, Hester - pe $100, w 16, p 101
Johnston, James - Shoemaker, pe $100, w 5, p 88
Johnston, John - Cooper, pe $200, re $500, w 11, p 45
Johnston, John - Waiter, pe $25, w 16, p 60
Johnston, John T. - Laborer, pe $30, w 11, p 168
Johnston, Julia - Washerwoman, pe $50, w 15, p 290
Johnston, Mary - Washerwoman, pe $50, w 8, p 284
Johnston, Nicholas - Cooper, pe $100, w 14, p 16
Johnston, Richard - Laborer, pe $40, w 11, p 126
Johnston, Sarah - Cook, pe $20, w 11, p 244
Johnston, Susan - Washerwoman, pe $20, w 11, p 156
Johnston, William - Porter In Store, pe $30, w 11, p 128
Johnston, William - Ostler, pe $25, w 11, p 174
Joice, Sophia - Washerwoman, pe $20, w 11, p 127
Jones, Aaron - Pedler, pe $300, w 15, p 290
Jones, Alfred - Brickmaker, pe $300, w 15, p 53
Jones, Amos - Woodsawyer, pe $600, w 15, p 297
Jones, Andrew - Wine Bottler, pe $600, w 6, p 224
Jones, Aron - Laborer, pe $10, w 16, p 59
Jones, Arther - Cook Shop, pe $200, w 7, p 334
Jones, Arthur - Waiter, pe $5, w 17, p 13
Jones, Asbury - Waiter, pe $50, w 5, p 78
Jones, Asbury - Waiter, pe $40, w 11, p 60
Jones, Caroline - Washerwoman, pe $50, w 15, p 42
Jones, Charles - Caulker, pe $1,000, w 6, p 223
Jones, Charles - Waiter, pe $25, w 8, p 294
Jones, Charlotte - pe $10, w 20, p 61
Jones, David - Porter, pe $100, w 14, p 120
Jones, Doria - Washerwoman, pe $30, w 13, p 469
Jones, Drucilla - Seamstress, pe $5, w 17, p 58
Jones, Edward - Sailor, pe $500, w 15, p 43

Black Real Estate and Personal Estate Holders, 1860

Black Estate Holders - 1860

Jones, Eliza - Washerwoman, pe $50, w 11, p 124
Jones, Elizabeth - Huckster, pe $300, w 15, p 80
Jones, Hamilton - Brickmaker, pe $200, w 15, p 69
Jones, Henry - Barber, pe $100, w 7, p 505
Jones, Henry - Coachman, pe $50, w 11, p 110
Jones, Henry - Woodsawyer, pe $25, w 16, p 60
Jones, Henry - Laborer, pe $5, w 17, p 57
Jones, Henry - pe $20, w 17, p 145
Jones, Henry - Sawyer, pe $10, w 17, p 177
Jones, Horace - Waiter, pe $60, w 14, p 140
Jones, Horice? - Waiter, pe $75, w 16, p 51
Jones, Hugh - Porter, pe $25, w 17, p 203
Jones, Isaac - Laborer, pe $60, w 18, p 431
Jones, James - Waiter, pe $50, w 20, p 87
Jones, James A. - pe $100, w 17, p 82
Jones, Jenkins - Drayman, pe $200, w 17, p 8
Jones, John - Master Barber, pe $500, re $4,200, w 4, p 122
Jones, John - Laborer, pe $500, w 15, p 53
Jones, John P. - Provision Dealer, pe $500, re $800, w 11, p 52
Jones, John W. - Sawyer, pe $25, w 13, p 402
Jones, Joshua - Caulker, pe $200, w 15, p 79
Jones, Littleton - Brickmaker, pe $5,000, w 15, p 60
Jones, Mary - Washerwoman, pe $25, w 8, p 369
Jones, Mary - Washerwoman, pe $50, w 14, p 66
Jones, Mary - Washerwoman, pe $25, w 18, p 383
Jones, Nancy - pe $10, w 15, p 15
Jones, Nathan - Waiter, pe $50, w 11, p 46
Jones, Noah - Waiter, pe $50, w 11, p 99
Jones, Prince - Waiter, pe $50, w 11, p 86
Jones, Reuben - Laborer, pe $100, w 15, p 55
Jones, Sarah - pe $50, w 16, p 52
Jones, Susan - Whitewasher, pe $50, w 16, p 139
Jones, Thomas - Laborer, re $700, w 3, p 230
Jones, Thomas - Grain Measurer, pe $5, w 17, p 12
Jones, Thomas - Shoemaker, pe $25, w 17, p 179
Jones, William - Coachman, pe $40, w 14, p 65
Jones, William - Porter, pe $100, w 16, p 144
Jones, William - Sailor, pe $25, w 17, p 296
Jones, William W. Waiter, pe $20, w 11, p 175
Jourdon, Julia - Cook, pe $30, w 11, p 190
Justus, Rebecca - Washerwoman, pe $25, w 16, p 69

Chapter 18

Black Estate Holders - 1860

Kain, Richard - Whitewasher, pe $100, w 15, p 46
Kain, Samuel - Hod Carrier, pe $100, w 15, p 288
Kane, Elisha - Laborer, pe $5, w 17, p 29
Kane, George - Brickmaker, pe $10, w 17, p 29
Kane, Henry - Ship Carpenter, pe $30, w 17, p 104
Kane, Peter - pe $20, w 17, p 90
Karmoh?, John - Drayman, pe $200, re $500, w 7, p 377
Kee, James - Day Laborer, pe $100, w 2, p 72
Keeth, Charles - Caulker, pe $100, w 2, p 77
Kell, James - Brickmaker, pe $50, w 16, p 57
Keller, George - Barber, pe $50, w 14, p 59
Kelley, Joseph - pe $50, w 13, p 402
Kelly, John - Waiter, pe $200, w 15, p 261
Kemp, John - Waiter, pe $40, w 11, p 241
Kemp, Henry - Sailor, pe $25, w 17, p 4
Kennard, Isaac - Laborer, pe $50, w 13, p 401
Kennard, James - Waiter, pe $200, w 12, p 21
Kennis, Ellen E. - Washerwoman, pe $40, w 8, p 363
Kent, Catherine - Washerwoman, pe $25, w 17, p 296
Kent, Joseph - Brickmaker, pe $25, w 17, p 263
Kent, William - Whitewasher, pe $100, w 5, p 87
Kerr, Maria - Washerwoman, pe $50, w 16, p 51
Keyes, Edward - Carter, pe $150, w 17, p 310
Keys, James - Day Laborer, pe $100, w 7, p 317
Keys, William - Laborer, pe $20, w 20, p 98
Keyser, John - Laborer, pe $10, w 17, p 8
King, William - Seaman, pe $20, w 17, p 310
Kirkley, Louis - Carter, pe $40, w 16, p 59
Kitney, Eliza - Washerwoman, pe $100, w 15, p 90
Lamman, William - Brickmaker, pe $30, w 17, p 103
Landis, Henry - Drayman, pe $5, w 17, p 58
Landsey, William - Waiter, pe $50, w 11, p 164
Lane, Abraham - Coachman, pe $40, w 11, p 165
Lanzer, Amos - Laborer, pe $25, w 20, p 98
Larkins, Emele - Barber, pe $25, w 11, p 174
Lasker, John T. - Sailor, pe $50, w 2, p 75
Lattemore, Robert - Sailor, pe $100, w 2, p 80
Latti, John H. - Seaman, pe $75, w 16, p 51
Launy?, John - Laborer, pe $60, w 18, p 408
Laurence, Cornelius - Cook, pe $1,000, w 15, p 109
Laurence, Henry - Market Man, pe $100, w 14, p 118

Black Estate Holders - 1860

Laurence, Jesse - Wood Sawyer, pe $20, w 18, p 427
Laurence, John - Brickmaker, pe $200, w 15, p 301
Laurence, John - Laborer, pe $50, w 19, p 225
Lawes, Robert - Day Laborer, pe $50, w 7, p 376
Lawrence, Henry - Laborer, pe $25, w 20, p 97
Leary, Charles - Drayman, pe $250, w 15, p 320
Leatherberry, Windis? - Brickamker, pe $25, w 17, p 29
Leatherby, Charity - Washerwoman, pe $25, w 17, p 28
LeCoursey, David - Coachman, pe $70, w 20, p 85
Lee, Bessy - Washerwoman, pe $25, w 11, p 41
Lee, Charles - Porter, pe $50, w 13, p 402
Lee, Deboarh - pe $25, w 11, p 54
Lee, Ella - Washerwoman, pe $70, w 18, p 495
Lee, Harriet - Seamstress, pe $40, w 11, p 187
Lee, James - Drayman, pe $500, w 15, p 54
Lee, James - Drayman, pe $25, w 16, p 35
Lee, Jesse - Porter, pe $100, w 16, p 164
Lee, Levi - Porter, pe $35, w 20, p 240
Lee, Martin - Day Laborer, pe $100, w 7, p 396
Lee, Rebecca - Washerwoman, pe $100, w 7, p 378
Lee, Sarah - Servant, pe $50, w 16, p 55
Lemon, William - Drayman, pe $200, w 7, p 583z
Lenard, Robert - Whitewasher, pe $50, w 17, p 43
Lenenberger, Ann - Washerwoman, pe $50, w 16, p 139
Leonard, Robert - Whitewasher, pe $200, w 15, p 296
Lesley, John - Brickmaker, pe $200, w 17, p 94
Lester, George W. - Huckster, pe $1,200, w 15, p 55
Lester, James - pe $50, p 139
Lever, Charles - Butcher, pe $800, w 6, p 58
wLevin, William - Brickmaker, pe $25, w 17, p 6
Lewis, Andrew - Locksmith, pe $1,000, w 12, p 198
Lewis, Ann - Washerwoman, pe $30, w 13, p 468
Lewis, Edward - Ferryman, pe $50, w 12, p 58
Lewis, Frances - Grain Measurer, pe $100, w 19, p 178
Lewis, George - Laborer, pe $75, w 11, p 61
Lewis, John - Coachman, pe $100, w 6, p 67
Lewis, John - Butcher, pe $50, w 8, p 601
Lilly, Coleman - Huckster, pe $40, w 8, p 440
Lilly, Peter - Blacksmith, pe $20, w 16, p 66
Linberry, Washington - Porter, pe $75, w 11, p 77
Linn, Caleb - Brickmaker, pe $15, w 17, p 203

Chapter 18

Black Estate Holders - 1860

Little, Rufus - Laborer, pe $50, w 15, p 292
Lloyd, William - Locksmith, pe $125, w 18, p 704
Lockerman, Daniel - Wood Sawyer, pe $20, w 8, p 264
Lockerman, Daniel - Whitewasher, pe $15, w 20, p 54
Lockling, Henrietta - Washerwoman, pe $30, w 13, p 471
Locks, John - Hackman - pe $200, re $1,500, w 7, p 596z
Logan, Hanson - Laborer, pe $70, w 18, p 368
Lojings?, Peter - Porter, pe $20, w 20, p 73
Lomack, Thomas - Market Man, pe $100, w 14, p 54
Loney, John - Caulker, pe $100, re $400, w 2, p 78
Long, Luoisa - Washerwoman, pe $30, w 11, p 241
Lossom?, William - Brickmaker, pe $15, w 17, p 11
Louday?, Perry - Drayman, pe $500, w 15, p 248
Loundon, Prisilla - Washerwoman, pe $50, w 8, p 567
Lowman, Ann - Washerwoman, pe $25, w 13, p 484
Loyd, Robert - Woodsawyer, pe $200, w 15, p 296
Loyd, William - Caulker, pe $200, re $600, w 2, p 46
LU?, John - Stevedore, re $1,500, w 4, p 10
Lucas, Joshua - Brickmaker, pe $50, w 16, p 143
Lucas, Peter - Grain Measurer, pe $1,000, w 15, p 308
Luerry?, James - Laborer, pe $50, w 14, p 128
Lyles, Daniel - Tanner, pe $35, w 20, p 58
Lyles, Richard - Stevedore, pe $100, w 16, p 70
Lyman, Charles - Waiter, pe $200, re $800, w 11, p 52
Lymas, Maria - Whitewasher, pe $30, w 11, p 164
Lynch, Abram - Whitewasher, pe $80, w 18, p 495
Lynch, Nicklaus - Sailmaker, pe $200, w 3, p 248
Lynn, Marshall - Brickmaker, pe $50, w 14, p 12
Lyons, Charles - Drayman, pe $200, w 15, p 246
Lyons, Charles - Brickmaker, pe $50, w 15, p 289
Maberry, Mark - Brickamker, pe $100, w 16, p 104
Madden, French - Porter, pe $100, w 19, p 177
Madden, Henry - Seaman, pe $50, w 8, p 545
Madden, Peter - Porter, pe $70, w 14, p 68
Madden, Samuel - Minister, pe $125, w 19, p 177
Maddox, Charles - Laborer, pe $50, re $500, w 17, p 14
Maddox, George - Brickamker, pe $400, w 15, p 70
Maddox, Lewis - Brickmaker, pe $800, w 15, p 265
Maddox, Robert - Brickmaker, pe $100, w 15, p 2
Maddox, William - Laborer, pe $300, w 15, p 251
Madonney, Henry - Day Laborer, pe $100, re $500, w 2, p 97

Black Real Estate and Personal Estate Holders, 1860

Black Estate Holders - 1860

Magill, Isiah - Carter, pe $75, w 16, p 36
Mahoney, John - Brickmaker, pe $25, w 17, p 185
Mahoney, Sophia - Washerwoman, pe $100, w 16, p 36
Major, Joseph - Coachman, pe $100, w 16, p 142
Mallory, Fenton - Waiter, pe $75, w 11, p 53
Maloney, Nathan - Carter, pe $1,600, w 20, p 116
Maner, Samson - Express Wagon, pe $125, w 14, p 64
Mannocks, Emily - Washerwoman, pe $40, w 8, p 444
Mara, Richard - Drayman, pe $500, w 12, p 59
Marbery, Luke - Waiter, pe $30, w 13, p 471
Margay?, Elizabeth - Servant, pe $100, w 15, p 248
Marshal, Edward - Porter, pe $60, w 14, p 137
Martin, Jane - Washerwoman, pe $30, w 13, p 458
Martin, William - Drayman, pe $100, w 16, p 165
Martin, William H. - Porter, pe $60, w 14, p 65
Mase, Joseph? - Waiter, pe $100, w 18, p 432
Mason, George - Confectioner, pe $400, w 13, p 421
Mason, Harrison - Waiter, pe $50, w 10, p 68
Mason, James - Sailor, pe $40, w 17, p 25
Mason, John - Cook, pe $100, w 17, p 25
Mason, Joseph - Waiter, pe $40, w 11, p 240
Mason, Noah - Drayman, pe $400, w 20, p 222
Mason, Richard - Master Shoemaker, pe $400, w 4, p 108
Mason, Susan - re $800, w 4, p 10
Mathe?, Thomas - Sailor, pe $50, w 2, p 90
Mathews, Henry - Whitewasher, pe $10, w 14, p 28
Mathews, Maria - Washerwoman, pe $500, w 12, p 198
Mathews, Samuel - Waiter, pe $1,000, w 12, p 198
Mathews, Henry - Waiter, pe $100, w 17, p 82
Matthews, Ellen - Washerwoman, pe $40, w 14, p 63
Matthews, George - Porter, pe $100, w 14, p 11
Matthews, Harriet - Laundress, pe $20, w 20, p 61
Matthews, James H. - Porter, pe $40, w 20, p 111
Matthews, Jane - Brickmaker, pe $75, w 16, p 106
Matthews, John - Drayman, pe $100, w 14, p 11
Matthews, Mary - Washerwoman, pe $50, w 16, p 15
Matthews, Reazin - Laborer, pe $45, w 18, p 412
Matthews, Richard - Whitewasher, pe $60, w 18, p 729
Matthews, Thomas - Drayman, pe $100, w 14, p 29
Matthews, William - Drayman, pe $30, w 11, p 164
Mayberry, John - Brickmaker, pe $300, w 15, p 70

Chapter 18

Black Estate Holders - 1860

Mays, Henry - Caulker, pe $200, re $600, w 2, p 46
McCabe, Jefferson - Steamboat Hand, pe $150, w 8, p 463
McCabe, Solomon - Master Barber, pe $500, re $6,000, w 11, p 122
McCleary, Matilda - Washerwoman, pe $10, w 11, p 239
McCubbins, Jerry - Laborer, pe $50, w 14, p 28
McDanlit, Mary A. - Washerwoman, pe $150, w 12, p 14
McJumper, Henry - Preacher, pe $100, w 3, p 348
McKonkey, Joseph - Brickmaker, pe $75, w 16, p 61
McLean, Alfred - Laborer, pe $25, w 20, p 60
McLean, Margaret - Washerwoman, pe $15, w 60, p 60
McPherson, Alesconder - Cabonet Maker, pe $30, w 13, p 451
McPherson, Caroline - pe $25, w 17, p 177
Meads, George W. - Stevedore, pe $150, w 9, p 12
Meads, Samuel - Driver, pe $1,000, w 15, p 251
Melin, Reuben - Sailor, pe $10, w 17, p 45
Melter, John - Waiter, pe $20, w 16, p 60
Meridith, Richard - Grain Measurer, pe $25, re $800, w 17, p 179
Merine, Richard - Brickmaker, pe $10, w 17, p 11
Merrein, Jeremiah - Laborer, pe $25, w 17, p 243
Merridie, John - Grain Measurer, pe $5, w 17, p 25
Meyers, Henry - Brickmaker, pe $50, w 16, p 165
Meyers, Jacob - Brickmaker, pe $50, w 16, p 186
Meyers, Sarah A. - pe $50, w 7, p 387
Milburn, George - Drayman, pe $150, w 17, p 176
Milburn, Levering - Waiter, pe $30, w 11, p 154
Miles, Daniel - Whitewasher, pe $100, w 14, p 29
Miles, Mary - Servant, pe $10, w 17, p 10
Milikin, Charles - Laborer, pe $5, w 17, p 180
Miller, Amelia - Washerwoman, pe $20, w 8, p 269
Miller, Catharine - Hair Picker, pe $50, w 15, p 2
Miller, Emory - Carter, pe $200, w 15, p 90
Miller, Hannah - Washerwoman, pe $50, w 2, p 91
Miller, Henry - Laborer, pe $100, w 16, p 50
Miller, Horace - Brickmaker, pe $300, w 15, p 298
Miller, James - Coachman, pe $20, w 11, p 156
Miller, James - Oyster Shucker, pe $40, w 20, p 89
Miller, Louise - Washerwoman, pe $10, w 20, p 98
Miller, William - Drayman, pe $300, w 15, p 59
Milligan, Moses - Brickmaker, pe $50, w 7, p 361
Mills, Catharine - pe $30, w 10, p 17
Ming?, James - Blacksmith, pe $50, w 7, p 388

Black Estate Holders - 1860

Mitchel, Emanuel - Shoemaker, pe $1,000, w 15, p 250
Mitchel, Francis - Washerwoman, pe $10, w 17, p 11
Mitchel, William - Drayman, pe $150, w 14, p 16
Mitchell, Cyrus - Drayman, pe $500, w 15, p 109
Mitchell, Elisha - Sawyer, pe $200, re $600, w 1, p 134
Mitchell, James - Caulker, pe $400, re $2,000, w 1, p 59
Mitchell, James - Hod Carrier, pe $40, w 18, p 427
Mitchell, Josiah - Brickmaker, pe $10, w 17, p 12
Mitchell, Ralph - Sawyer, pe $5, w 17, p 46
Mitchell, Samuel - Coffee Roaster, pe $75, w 16, p 141
Mohaney, Benjamin - Whitewasher, pe $50, w 7, p 347
Molison, Henry - Doctor, pe $200, w 16, p 117
Monroe, James - Laborer, pe $25, re $800, w 17, p 178
Montgomery, Charles - Waiter, pe $50, w 11, p 99
Moody, John - Confectioner, pe $50, w 16, p 69
Moody, Joseph - Whitewasher, pe $50, w 13, p 402
Moore, Charles H.   Porter, pe $60, w 14, p 118
Moore, Daniel - Porter, pe $50, w 17, p 4
Moore, Daniel - Preacher, pe $30, w 17, p 185
Moore, Edward - Mariner, pe $50, w 18, p 346
Moore, John - Brickmaker, pe $300, w 15, p 56
Moore, John - Grain Measurer, pe $1,000, w 15, p 296
Moore, John - Drayman, pe $30, w 20, p 102
Moore, Leonard - Laborer, pe $40, w 14, p 64
Moore, Loyd - Coachman, pe $25, w 13, p 402
Moore, Mathew - Caulker, re $400, w 7, p 582z
Moore, Richard - Laborer, pe $25, w 14, p 63
Moore, Sarah - Washerwoman, pe $2, w 16, p 138
Moore, Simon - Laborer, pe $50, w 15, p 294
Morgan, Benjamin - Waiter, pe $50, w 20, p 88
Morgan, Daniel - Laborer, pe $40, w 14, p 64
Morgan, George - Drayman, pe $150, w 8, p 560
Morgan, John - Waiter, pe $20, w 20, p 81
Morgan, Mary - Washerwoman, pe $10, w 11, p 239
Morgan, Mary - Washerwoman, pe $50, w 14, p 128
Morgan, Thomas - Laborer, pe $100, w 11, p 86
Morgan, William H. - Driver, pe $40, w 20, p 111
Morris, George - Waiter, pe $100, w 12, p 22
Morris, Joseph - Brick Maker, pe $100, w 3, p 11
Morris, Richard - re $400, w 7, p 588z
Morsel, Catharine - Washerwoman, pe $10, w 17, p 13

Chapter 18

Black Estate Holders - 1860

Moses, John - Brickmaker, pe $10, w 15, p 2
Mowton?, Charles - Coachman, pe $30, w 11, p 167
Mueney?, William - Huckster, pe $100, w 8, p 503
Muney, Samuel - Porter, pe $200, re $1,000, w 19, p 236
Murphy, Benjamin - Whitewasher, pe $100, w 14, p 63
Murphy, Dennis - Whitewasher, pe $60, w 14, p 62
Murphy, Elizabeth - Washerwoman, pe $100, w 14, p 64
Murray, Jacob - Barber, pe $150, w 11, p 105
Murray, Levin - Drayman, pe $50, re $500, w 17, p 82
Murray, Robert - Professor, pe $600, w 5, p 88
Murray, William H. - Barber, pe $200, re $600, w 13, p 470
Murrey, Rebecca, pe $50, p 462
Murrey, Spencer - Waiter, pe $30, w 13, p 472
Murry, Mary - Washerwoman, pe $300, w 15, p 75
Murry, Susan - Washerwoman, pe $20, w 20, p 53
Mussey, William - Laborer, pe $300, w 15, p 69
Myers, Daniel - Mariner, re $4,000, w 3, p 19
Myers, David - Whitewasher, pe $30, w 11, p 187
Myers, Eliza - Dress Maker, pe $40, w 11, p 128
Myers, George - Drayman, pe $200, w 11, p 187
Myers, Harriet - Washerwoman, pe $40, w 14, p 65
Myers, Henry - Storekeeper, pe $400, w 17, p 9
Myers, Isiah - Whitewasher, pe $60, w 14, p 60
Myers, Jacob - Caulker, pe $100, w 2, p 62
Myers, Jeremiah - Porter, pe $90, w 14, p 67
Myers, Oliver - Waiter, pe $40, w 14, p 137
Myers, Philip - Waiter, pe $25, w 13, p 402
Myers, Stephen - Carriage Driver, pe $35, w 20, p 201
Nash, William - Waiter, pe $50, w 11, p 44
Neal, Lewis - Laborer, pe $40, w 18, p 433
Neals, Thomas - Gardener, pe $50, w 20, p 230
Neile, Albert W. - Farmer, pe $6,000, w 15, p 51
Neile, Robert - Brickmaker, pe $20, w 17, p 186
Nelson, Ara N. ? - Chambermaid, pe $300, w 15, p 71
Nelson, Catharine - pe $1,000, w 6, p 223
Nelson, Emanuel - Laborer, pe $100, w 19, p 263
Nelson, Henry H. - Waiter, pe $40, w 11, p 189
Nelson, Robert - Wagoner, pe $200, w 15, p 295
Nelson, Susan - Washerwoman, pe $100, w 15, p 71
Netter, Simon - Laborer, pe $500, w 15, p 248
Netter?, Henry - Brickmaker, pe $100, w 16, p 102

Black Real Estate and Personal Estate Holders, 1860

Black Estate Holders - 1860

Nettles, John - Brickmaker, pe $50, w 17, p 254
Newman, Charles - Brickyard, pe $20, w 11, p 168
Newman, Jacob - Drayman, pe $25, w 20, p 122
Newman, John - Brickmaker, pe $25, w 17, p 258
Nicholas, Abby - pe $100, re $3,000, w 10, p 46
Nicholas, Wesley - Master Barber, pe $300, w 4, p 125
Nichols, Angeline - Washerwoman, pe $3, w 17, p 45
Nichols, Letitia - Washerwoman, pe $25, w 13, p 463
Nicholson, James - Porter, pe $100, w 14, p 72
Nicholson, James - Laborer, pe $48, w 18, p 426
Nicholson, Joseph - Butcher, pe $100, w 8, p 546
Nicholson, Joseph - Waiter, pe $300, w 15, p 72
Nicholson, Susan - Washerwoman, pe $40, w 11, p 54
Nickleson, Charles - Brickmaker, pe $50, w 12, p 28
Nickols, Hemsley - Laborer, pe $20, w 17, p 179
Nickolson, Jacob - Brickmaker, pe $30, re $1,000, w 17, p 170
Nisen, Charles - Seaman, pe $50, w 17, p 93
Noel, John - Barber, pe $50, re $1,500, w 13, p 468
Norris, Adam - Grain Measurer, pe $25, w 17, p 263
Norris, Eliza - Washerwoman, pe $50, w 19, p 222
Norris, John - Grain Measurer, pe $25, w 17, p 264
Norris, Mary - Washerwoman, pe $25, w 13, p 471
Norris, Nimrod? - Huckster, pe $100, w 7, p 352
Norris, William - Brickmaker, pe $20, w 17, p 30
Norris, William - Grain Measurer, pe $25, w 17, p 264
Nucklis, Henry - Waiter, pe $500, w 12, p 31
Ockemie, Aaron - Whitewasher, pe $60, w 14, p 66
Ockmay, James - Drayman, pe $300, w 17, p 176
Oerch?, William - Brickmaker, pe $50, w 16, p 164
Oldham, William - Master Barber, pe $1,500, w 5, p 119
Oliver, Allen - Wood Sawyer, pe $70, re $200, w 18, p 498
Oliver, Elizabeth - Washerwoman, pe $20, w 11, p 127
Osborn, Edward - Hod Carrier, pe $25, w 16, p 15
Osedet?, Bushrod - Drayman, pe $400, w 18, p 570
Ossett, Thomas - Brickmaker, pe $300, w 15, p 79
Othor, Samuel - Laborer, pe $40, w 20, p 204
Owens, Basil - Cooper, pe $25, w 17, p 95
Owens, Ellen - Washerwoman, pe $30, w 11, p 99
Owens, Jacob - Drayman, pe $100, w 14, p 65
Owens, James T. - Drayman, pe $150, w 17, p 176
Owens, John - Day Laborer, pe $50, w 7, p 377

Chapter 18

Black Estate Holders - 1860

Owens, John - Brickmaker, pe $300, w 15, p 248
Owens, Otho - Waiter, pe $50, w 16, p 36
Owens, Richard - Porter, pe $50, w 17, p 1
Page, Moses - Whitewasher, pe $200, w 15, p 295
Page, Thomas - Cabinet Maker, pe $40, w 11, p 62
Paine, Theodore - Coachman, pe $50, w 19, p 222
Paine, William - Barber, pe $40, w 11, p 174
Palmer, George - Porter, pe $25, w 17, p 263
Palmer, James - Coachman, pe $75, re $600, w 11, p 63
Paraway, Amelia - Washerwoman, pe $40, w 14, p 120
Paraway, Oliver - Drayman, pe $40, w 11, p 164
Parker, Daniel - Waiter, pe $50, w 16, p 41
Parker, George - pe $50, w 11, p 126
Parker, Peter - Laborer, pe $40, w 18, p 431
Parker, Simon - Waiter, pe $100, w 12, p 42
Parker, Susan - Washerwoman, pe $100, w 15, p 68
Parker, Thomas - Stevedore, pe $10, w 17, p 22
Parker, William - Laborer, pe $50, w 16, p 67
Parker, William - Laborer, pe $40, w 18, p 408
Parks, Manuel - Laborer, pe $25, w 20, p 113
Parks, Nicholas - Waiter, pe $50, w 11, p 109
Parren, Caroline - Washerwoman, pe $50, w 15, p 2
Pasaway, Owen - Laborer, pe $30, w 18, p 432
Paschal, Cornelius - Day Laborer, pe $50, w 7, p 383
Patterson, Adeline - Washerwoman, pe $30, w 8, p 596
Patterson, Henry - Laborer, pe $50, w 13, p 470
Patterson, Rachel - Washerwoman, pe $200, w 15, p 185
Patterson, William - Caulker, pe $100, w 2, p 96
Payne, Ameila - pe $50, re $400, w 17, p 330
Payne, Washington - Carpenter, pe $20, w 17, p 174
Peach, Dorgus - pe $20, w 17, p 147
Peacock, John - Waiter, pe $50, w 19, p 178
Peaker, John - Porter, pe $60, w 14, p 97
Pearce, John - Barber, pe $100, w 2, p 92
Pearce, Weston - Waiter, pe $15, w 20, p 80
Peck, Nathaniel - Whitewasher, pe $200, re $800, w 11, p 125
Peck, Nathaniel - Whitewasher, pe $100, w 11, p 129
Peck, Susan - pe $40, w 8, p 587
Peirce, Simon - Laborer, pe $20, w 17, p 288
Peire, Pery - Laborer, pe $25, w 17, p 243
Pembrook, Samuel - Drayman, pe $5, w 17, p 11

Black Real Estate and Personal Estate Holders, 1860

Black Estate Holders - 1860

Pempleton, John - Waiter, pe $20, w 17, p 146
Penelton, Reason - Brickamker, pe $50, w 16, p 105
Penn, Edward - Waiter, pe $100, w 18, p 413
Penn, Isabella - Washerwoman, pe $60, w 14, p 131
Pennington, Nancy - Washerwoman, pe $40, w 8, p 587
Penwines, Joseph J. - Drayman, pe $100, re $300, w 7, p 283
Perines?, Josiah - Sailor, pe $100, w 12, p 30
Perkins, Catharine - Servant, pe $100, w 15, p 3
Perkins, James - Grain Measurer, pe $1,500, w 15, p 3
Perkins, Rachel - Washerwoman, pe $10, w 17, p 9
Perkins, Washington - Grain Measurer, pe $50, w 17, p 145
Perkins, William - Porter, pe $300, w 15, p 3
Perry, Charles - Boot Black, pe $100, w 16, p 164
Perting, Lois - Washerwoman, pe $20, w 20, p 136
Peters, Letitia - Washerwoman, pe $25, w 13, p 402
Peters, Rose - Washerwoman, pe $50, w 7, p 359
Peterson, Daniel - Caulker, pe $100, w 3, p 227
Philips, James - Laborer, pe $100, w 3, p 135
Phillips, Catharine - Washerwoman, pe $120, w 20, p 72
Phillips, Eliza - Ostler, pe $20, w 15, p 15
Phillips, Luois - Ostler, pe $20, w 15, p 15
Phillips, Tagard - Day Laborer, pe $50, w 2, p 115
Phillips, Thomas - Drayman, pe $50, w 14, p 11
Phineba?, William - Shoemaker, pe $25, w 17, p 14
Pierce, Ann - Laundress, pe $20, w 20, p 58
Pierce, Butler - Laborer, pe $60, w 14, p 68
Pierce, Harriett - Washerwoman, pe $50, w 16, p 52
Pierce, Jacob - Grain Measurer, pe $500, w 15, p 264
Pierce, John - Drayman, pe $150, w 20, p 83
Pierce, Perry - Laborer, pe $25, w 16, p 33
Pimbrook, Basil - Laborer, pe $300, w 15, p 77
Pinckney, Maria - Washerwoman, pe $40, w 11, p 168
Pindall, Ashman - Barber, pe $40, w 11, p 110
Pindle, Durham - Sailor, pe $50, w 7, p 376
Pindle, James - Carter, pe $50, w 16, p 50
Pindle, Prisey - Washerwoman, pe $50, w 19, p 264
Pinkey, Charles - pe $20, w 17, p 96
Pinkney, Abraham - Brickmaker, pe $10, w 17, p 297
Pinkney, Ellen - pe $300, w 19, p 64
Pinkney, James - Waiter, pe $100, w 3, p 110
Pinkney, Sarah - Washerwoman, pe $75, w 8, p 511

Chapter 18

Black Estate Holders - 1860

Pinkstan, John - Day Laborer, pe $50, w 2, p 27
Pipes, Frederick - Waiter, pe $50, w 18, p 431
Pitt, Frederick - Laborer, pe $60, w 14, p 67
Plater, Charles - Mariner, pe $100, w 15, p 3
Plater, Jane - Servant, pe $50, w 15, p 289
Plater, John - Brickmaker, pe $20, w 17, p 92
Plater, Joseph - Whitewasher, pe $75, w 16, p 138
Plater, Mary - Servant, pe $50, w 15, p 294
Pokdy, John - Brickmaker, pe $10, w 17, p 11
Polk, Mary - Washerwoman, pe $100, w 15, p 71
Pool, Zecariah - Brickmaker, pe $50, w 16, p 101
Porter, Emaline - pe $700, w 16, p 143
Porter, Jane - Washerwoman, pe $100, w 15, p 133
Porter, Robert - Porter, pe $300, w 15, p 262
Posey, George - Wood Sawyer, pe $300, w 15, p 300
Powell, Charles - Laborer, pe $40, w 14, p 60
Powell, John - Wagoner, pe $200, w 3, p 348
Powell, John W. - Musician, pe $40, w 11, p 133
Powell, Joshua - Ostler, pe $200, w 15, p 1
Pratt, John - Waiter, pe $300, w 15, p 70
Pratt, Martha - Washerwoman, re $30, w 20, p 95
Pratt, Truman - Carter, pe $150, w 20, p 82
Price, Eliza - Washerwoman, pe $50, w 15, p 30
Price, Lucy - Seamstress, pe $10, w 16, p 58
Price, Richard - Porter, pe $20, w 11, p 189
Price, Romeo - Waiter, pe $150, re $800, w 11, p 108
Price, William - Laborer, pe $20, w 11, p 127
Prichet, Thomas - Day Laborer, pe $50, w 7, p 360
Procter, Mary V. - Washerwoman, pe $25, w 16, p 34
Proctor, Charles - Porter, pe $40, w 14, p 55
Prout, Israel - Hod Carrier, pe $25, w 17, p 7
Pulaski, Alexander - Barber, pe $20, w 11, p 165
Pumphry, Joshua - Blacksmith, pe $50, re $500, w 17, p 82
Purnell, Daniel - Drayman, pe $1,000, w 12, p 197
Purnell, Isaac - Sailor, pe $20, w 17, p 24
Purnell, Susan - Washerwoman, pe $5, w 17, p 10
Purnell, William - Waiter, pe $80, w 20, p 85
Purviance, Mary - pe $10, w 20, p 204
Pwerkins, Emily - Washerwoman, pe $50, w 15, p 3
Quebec, Caroline - Washerwoman, pe $25, w 11, p 153
Queen, Ann - Washerwoman, pe $20, w 17, p 3

Black Estate Holders - 1860

Queen, Daniel - Carter, pe $125, w 17, p 28
Queen, Edward - Laborer, pe $50, w 14, p 13
Queen, Edward - Brickmaker, pe $100, w 15, p 68
Queen, Isaac - Seaman, pe $25, w 16, p 170
Queen, James - Laborer, pe $75, w 8, p 564
Queen, James - Waiter, pe $25, w 17, p 178
Queen, James - Rope Maker, pe $10, w 17, p 263
Queen, John - Seaman, pe $50, w 16, p 171
Queen, Matilda - Washerwoman, pe $40, w 14, p 136
Queen, Noah - Drayman, pe $300, w 15, p 74
Queen, Robert - Brickmaker, pe $50, w 16, p 139
Queen, Sophia - Washerwoman, pe $50, w 16, p 186
Queen, William - Brickmaker, pe $20, w 17, p 178
Quigley, Henry C. - Carpenter, pe $30, w 11, p 243
Rainer, Mary - Chambermaid, pe $100, w 15, p 297
Ralph, George - Sailor, pe $100, w 2, p 74
Ramsey, Ellen - Washerwoman, pe $25, w 16, p 107
Rassie?, Clemm - Coachman, pe $100, w 12, p 14
Ray, Charles - pe $15, w 20, p 54
Reasin, James - Carter, pe $50, w 15, p 15
Reasin, Noah - Sailor, pe $200, w 15, p 205
Reden, Harriet - Huckster, pe $50, w 9, p 12
Redman, Henry - Carriage Driver, pe $10, w 13, p 401
Reed, Abraham - Waiter, pe $500, w 15, p 261
Reed, Ami? - Cake Shop, pe $300, w 15, p 52
Reed, Essex - Brickmaker, pe $300, w 15, p 52
Reed, George - Sailor, pe $200, re $400, w 7, p 371
Reed, Hester - Washerwoman, pe $25, w 11, p 105
Reed, Josiah - Drayman, pe $100, w 15, p 2
Reed, Mary - Dress Maker, pe $300, w 15, p 90
Reed, Perry - Driver, pe $1,000, w 15, p 259
Reese, Mary - Washerwoman, pe $25, w 13, p 472
Reeves, John - Brickmaker, pe $300, w 15, p 40
Reid, Perry - Drayman, pe $25, w 17, p 2
Reubens, Stephen - Cooking, pe $300, w 12, p 122
Reynolds, James - Sailor, pe $300, w 15, p 246
Rhodes, Abraham - Drayman, pe $200, w 8, p 389
Rice, Cayo - Drayman, pe $50, w 11, p 62
Rice, Wiliam - Seaman, pe $40, w 8, p 430
Rich, Bass? - Brickmaker, pe $30, w 8, p 390
Rich, Eliza - Washerwoman, pe $5, w 17, p 24

Chapter 18

Black Estate Holders - 1860

Richards, Frisby - Coachman, pe $60, w 20, p 78
Richards, John - Day Laborer, pe $50, w 2, p 81
Richards, Sarah - Servant, pe $50, w 16, p 53
Richards, Solomon - Lumber Piler, pe $50, w 8, p 361
Richardson, Alfred - Coachman, pe $100, w 20, p 230
Richardson, Eliza - Washerwoman, pe $500, w 15, p 263
Richardson, Henry - Hack Driver, pe $40, w 11, p 64
Richardson, Henry - Barber, pe $100, w 12, p 122
Richardson, James - Laborer, pe $20, w 20, p 54
Richardson, Jane - Washerwoman, pe $10, w 20, p 117
Richardson, Samuel - Whitewasher, pe $70, w 11, p 156
Richardson, Thomas - Carter, pe $25, w 20, p 240
Richardson, William - Porter, pe $50, w 15, p 76
Richardson, William - Stevedore, pe $50, w 16, p 140
Richardson, William - Seaman, pe $30, w 17, p 91
Richfield, Amanda - pe $30, w 13, p 472
Ridgaway, Daniel - Coachman, pe $70, w 14, p 61
Ridgaway, James - Laborer, pe $5, w 17, p 22
Ridgeaway, Henry - Laborer, pe $3,000, re $500, w 15, p 185
Ridgeley, Robert - Waiter, pe $40, w 11, p 77
Ridgely, John - Laborer, pe $10, w 20, p 59
Ridgely, Lucy - Washerwoman, pe $100, w 11, p 62
Ridgeway, William H. - Day Laborer, pe $100, w 2, p 97
Riely, William - pe $25, w 17, p 186
Riggs, John - Boot Black, pe $100, w 13, p 442
Rigley, Anna - pe $25, w 13, p 463
Riley, George - Wheelwright, pe $50, w 16, p 52
Riley, Thomas - Laborer, pe $25, w 17, p 185
Ringgold, Catherine - Washerwoman, pe $30, w 11, p 173
Ringgold, Henry - Drayman, pe $350, w 20, p 125
Ringgold, Hezekiah - Drayman, pe $100, w 6, p 134
Ringgold, Maria - Washerwoman, pe $40, w 11, p 129
Ringgold, Richard - Wood Sawyer, pe $30, w 11, p 187
Ringold, Abraham - Laborer, pe $25, w 16, p 78
Ringold, Perry - Grain Measurer, pe $20, w 17, p 59
Ringold, Sarah - Washerwoman, pe $50, w 16, p 105
Roache, Charles - Huckster, pe $500, w 15, p 205
Robbins, Edward - Waiter, pe $300, w 15, p 260
Roberts, August - Barber, pe $20,000, w 9, p 68
Roberts, Charles - Brickmaker, pe $75, w 16, p 60
Roberts, Cheeseman - Whitewasher, pe $40, w 8, p 445

Black Real Estate and Personal Estate Holders, 1860

Black Estate Holders - 1860

Roberts, George R. - Laborer, pe $100, re $400, w 1, p 340
Roberts, John - Brickmaker, pe $100, w 15, p 205
Roberts, William - Porter, pe $30, w 17, p 93
Robertson, Lewis - Laborer, pe $100, w 12, p 58
Robins, Levin - Drayman, pe $300, w 15, p 76
Robinson, Charles - Huckster, pe $100, w 8, p 593
Robinson, George - Ostler, pe $25, w 8, p 587
Robinson, Henry - Drayman, pe $600, re $2,500, w 18, p 786
Robinson, Henry - Laborer, pe $20, w 20, p 247
Robinson, James - Grain Measurer, pe $50, w 17, p 104
Robinson, John - Waiter, pe $100, w 14, p 11
Robinson, Lewis - Livery Stable, pe $7,000, w 20, p 232
Robinson, Peter - Porter, pe $30, w 18, p 765
Robinson, Robert - Porter, pe $40, w 20, p 61
Robinson, Zachariah - Caulker, pe $100, w 2, p 78
Robison, Francess - Washerwoman, pe $50, w 16, p 59
Roche, George - Whitewasher, pe $200, w 15, p 39
Rodes, John - Fireman, pe $20, w 17, p 203
Rogers, Grace A. - Washerwoman, pe $50, w 20, p 82
Rollins, George - Drayman, pe $25, w 20, p 102
Rollins, Henry - Brickmaker, pe $5, w 17, p 10
Rollins, James - Mariner, pe $300, w 15, p 71
Rollins, William - Mariner, pe $100, w 15, p 71
Rosburn, Ellen - pe $300, re $1,000, w 2, p 41
Ross, Daniel - Grain Measurer, pe $25, w 17, p 30
Ross, James - Minister, pe $300, w 6, p 55
Ross, John R. - Laborer, pe $50, w 20, p 239
Ross, Lloyd - Drayman, pe $100, w 16, p 51
Ross, Margaret - Servant, pe $25, w 16, p 51
Ross, Thomas - Laborer, pe $35, w 20, p 62
Ross, William - Porter, pe Porter, w 14, p 119
Roughs, Benjamon W. - Drayman, pe $300, w 11, p 63
Rowles, Jesila? - pe $150, w 13, p 475
Ruben, Henry - Brickmaker, pe $50, w 16, p 100
Ruff, John W. - Porter, pe $50, w 14, p 29
Russell, George - Hay Huckster, pe $300, re $1,500, w 18, p 786
Russell, John - Ostler, pe $50, w 12, p 28
Ryder, Moris - Sailor, pe $20, w 17, p 174
Saddler, James - Porter, pe $60, w 14, p 137
Saford, David - Carpenter, pe $25, w 17, p 287
Saison, Charles - Drayman, pe $25, w 16, p 65

Chapter 18

Black Estate Holders - 1860

Sales, Harriet - Washerwoman, pe $20, w 11, p 155
Sammond, Salley - pe $30, w 8, p 337
Sampson, Jospeh - Day Laborer, pe $50, w 7, p 400
Sampson, Richard - Carter, pe $50, w 17, p 2
Sanders, Alfred - Porter, pe $100, w 7, p 359
Sanders, Henry - Waiter, pe $75, w 11, p 54
Sanders, John - Barber, pe $75, w 20, p 78
Sanders, William - Musician, pe $200, w 6, p 26
Sanders, William - Barber, pe $60, w 20, p 78
Sanders, William H. T. - pe $100, w 7, p 388
Sandey, Thomas - Trader, pe $3,500, re $500, w 6, p 221
Sands, Edward - Porter, pe $50, w 16, p 145
Sanford, Joseph - Porter, pe $50, w 5, p 89
Sank, Wonda? - Porter, pe $100, w 16, p 51
Sanks, Charles - Drayman, pe $200, w 17, p 183
Sanks, Eliza - Washerwoman, pe $200, w 15, p 54
Sanks, James - Drayman, pe $20, w 17, p 92
Sanks, John - Stevedore, pe $100, w 16, p 199
Sanks, John - Brickmaker, pe $30, w 17, p 94
Sanks, John - Brickmaker, pe $25, w 17, p 202
Sanks, Mary - Washerwoman, pe $5, w 17, p 28
Sanks, Spencer - Drayman, pe $400, w 15, p 73
Sappinglaw?, Margaret - pe $50, w 2, p 89
Sarrell, Richard - Laborer, pe $20, w 17, p 49
Saseton?, John - Laborer, pe $25, w 13, p 458
Saul, McCarthy - Stevedore, pe $700, w 16, p 164
Saul, Stephen - Porter, pe $100, w 16, p 164
Saulsby, William - Laborer, pe $50, w 8, p 584
Savage, Isaac - Sailor, pe $5, w 17, p 34
Savoy, Basil - Brickmaker, pe $20, w 17, p 187
Savoy, Francis - Whitewasher, pe $50, w 11, p 130
Scott, Benjamin - Grain Measurer, pe $60, w 18, p 495
Scott, Benjamon - M. P. Clergyman, pe $100, w 8, p 462
Scott, Candy - pe $30, w 17, p 145
Scott, Charles - Brickmaker, pe $25, w 17, p 5
Scott, Isaac - Barber, pe $100, w 16, p 72
Scott, James - Grain Measurer, pe $100, w 6, p 60
Scott, James - Brickmaker, pe $25, w 16, p 16
Scott, James - Waterman, pe $50, w 19, p 86
Scott, John - Stevedore, pe $10, w 17, p 10
Scott, John G. - Brickmaker, pe $100, w 15, p 60

Black Real Estate and Personal Estate Holders, 1860

Black Estate Holders - 1860

Scott, Joseph - Waiter, pe $75, w 16, p 67
Scott, Louis - Whitewasher, pe $20, w 20, p 113
Scott, Mary - Washerwoman, pe $40, w 14, p 61
Scott, Mary - Hireling, pe $25, w 17, p 3
Scott, Perry - Sailor, pe $300, w 15, p 250
Scott, Resin - Day Laborer, pe $100, re $500, w 7, p 333
Scott, Richard - Brickmaker, pe $100, w 16, p 103
Scott, Robert - Laborer, pe $275, w 7, p 590z
Scott, Samuel - Caulker, pe $100, w 2, p 81
Scott, Sarah - Washerwoman, pe $10, w 17, p 25
Scott, Thomas - Laborer, pe $35, w 11, p 109
Scroggins, George - Wagoner, pe $40, w 11, p 129
Scroggins, William - Whitewasher, pe $75, w 16, p 47
Scythe, Edward - Cook, pe $100, re $900, w 11, p 106
Sedgewick, Keziah - Washerwoman, pe $20, w 20, p 88
Seevers, Henry - Carriage Driver, pe $100, w 14, p 54
Sefus, Emory - Laborer, pe $50, w 19, p 229
Senna, Hester - Washerwoman, pe $10, w 17, p 30
Serrell?, Walter - Barber, pe $2,000, w 15, p 60
Severs, Thomas - Brickmaker, pe $30, w 17, p 104
Sevoy, Albert - Waiter, pe $40, w 14, p 137
Sevoy, Daniel - Laborer, pe $100, w 14, p 54
Sewell, J. - Brickmaker, pe $25, w 17, p 104
Sewell, Polly - pe $10, w 17, p 146
Sharp, Joshua - Caulker, pe $10, w 17, p 174
Shaw, Henry - Caulker, pe $150, w 2, p 96
Sheckles, John - Laborer, pe $100, w 15, p 287
Sheppard, Maria - Washerwoman, pe $15, w 11, p 155
Sheppard, Peter - Hostler, pe $100, w 18, p 729
Shepphard, Benjamin - Porter, pe $75, w 20, p 240
Sherwood, Jacob - Saeman, pe $50, w 16, p 103
Shickman, Samuel - Brickamker, pe $400, w 15, p 80
Shields, Ann - Washerwoman, pe $20, w 8, p 337
Shields, Jacob - Porter, pe $40, w 11, p 242
Shomter, Isabella - pe $50, w 2, p 79
Shorden, Thomas - pe $15, w 20, p 62
Shorter, John - Porter, pe $25, w 20, p 57
Silbey, Joshua - Laborer, pe $25, w 16, p 33
Simmons, Ellen - Laundress, pe $40, w 20, p 126
Simms, Benjamin - Drayman, pe $200, w 14, p 66
Simms, Benjamon - Waiter, pe $30, w 11, p 60

Chapter 18

Black Estate Holders - 1860

Simms, Henry - Porter, pe $60, w 14, p 60
Simms, James - Drayman, pe $150, w 11, p 65
Simms, John - Drayman, pe $100, w 14, p 16
Simms, Peter - Drayman, pe $15, w 20, p 62
Simms, Thomas - Day Laborer, pe $50, w 7, p 320
Simms, William - Laborer, pe $70, w 14, p 61
Simon, Jane - Washerwoman, pe $100, w 15, p 70
Simons, George - Waterman, pe $100, w 15, p 288
Simpson, James - Brickmaker, pe $25, w 17, p 8
Simpson, William - Day Laborer, pe $100, w 7, p 378
Sims, John - Stevedore, pe $20, w 16, p 115
Simson, Rosa - pe $100, w 16, p 57
Singer, Daniel - Drayman, pe $10, w 20, p 61
Skinner, Edward - Waiter, pe $40, w 8, p 587
Skinner, Ellen - Servant, pe $50, w 15, p 2
Skinner, Ellen - Washerwoman, pe $100, w 15, p 54
Skinner, Ellen - pe $5, w 17, p 45
Skinner, Robert - Caulker, pe $100, w 15, p 79
Slater, Robert - Caulker, pe $500, w 15, p 43
Slater, William - Servant, pe $300, w 15, p 308
Slaughter, Mary - Servant, pe $5, w 17, p 178
Slaughter, Rosanna - Washerwoman, pe $5, w 17, p 179
Sletters, Phillip - Cooper, pe $50, w 16, p 104
Sloan, Samuel - Carter, pe $25, w 16, p 101
Slodner, Joseph - Ship Carpenter, pe $1,100, w 15, p 43
Small, Ellen - Washerwoman, pe $25, w 17, p 177
Small, George - Coachman, pe $150, w 6, p 36
Small, Moses - Waiter, pe $30, w 13, p 472
Small, Susan - Huckster, pe $200, w 6, p 36
Small, Virginia - Washerwoman, pe $40, w 11, p 130
Smallwood, John - Drayman, pe $200, w 20, p 72
Smallwood, Mary - Washerwoman, pe $300, w 15, p 43
Smallwood, Nicholas - Whitewasher, pe $500, w 15, p 43
Smith, Arthur - Brickmaker, pe $30, w 17, p 187
Smith, Augustus - Coachmen, pe $75, w 11, p 62
Smith, Benjamin - Laborer, pe $200, w 15, p 247
Smith, Charles - Whitewasher, pe $50, re $600, w 7, p 401
Smith, Charles - Seaman, pe $40, w 11, p 126
Smith, Charles - Porter, pe $25, w 17, p 13
Smith, Charles - Laborer, pe $20, w 20, p 56
Smith, Daniel - Drayman, pe $40, w 20, p 235

Black Estate Holders - 1860

Smith, Edward - Whitewasher, pe $25, w 11, p 43
Smith, Elizabeth - Washerwoman, pe $20, w 17, p 327
Smith, Ellen - Washerwoman, pe $50, w 17, p 4
Smith, Emily - Dressmaker, pe $100, w 5, p 88
Smith, Harriet - Washerwoman, pe $50, w 14, p 137
Smith, Henry - Waiter, pe $500, w 12, p 23
Smith, Israel - House Cleaner, pe $30, w 11, p 62
Smith, James - Day Laborer, pe $100, w 2, p 78
Smith, James - Porter, pe $75, w 5, p 78
Smith, James - Sailor, pe $5, w 17, p 34
Smith, John - Day Laborer, pe $100, w 2, p 82
Smith, John - Waiter, pe $100, w 14, p 59
Smith, John - Drayman, pe $100, w 14, p 137
Smith, John - Cooper, pe $200, w 15, p 53
Smith, John - Laborer, pe $50, w 16, p 42
Smith, John - Whitewasher, pe $180, w 17, p 1
Smith, John H. - Hackman, pe $700, re $6,000, w 11, p 122
Smith, John H. - Drayman, pe $350, w 20, p 72
Smith, Joseph - Porter, pe $25, w 16, p 58
Smith, Joseph - Laborer, pe $20, w 20, p 114
Smith, Joseph - Drayman, pe $30, w 20, p 118
Smith, Julia - Servant, pe $25, w 16, p 53
Smith, Louisa - Washerwoman, pe $30, w 14, p 63
Smith, Lydia - Huckster, pe $20, w 17, p 59
Smith, Maria - Washerwoman, pe $200, re $2,000, w 11, p 14
Smith, Mary - Washerwoman, pe $300, w 15, p 43
Smith, Matilda - pe $100, w 15, p 43
Smith, Nait - Laborer, pe $10, w 20, p 113
Smith, Nathan - Hod Carrier, pe $50, w 16, p 23
Smith, Olivia - pe $10, w 20, p 61
Smith, Owen - Waiter, pe $40, w 11, p 65
Smith, Peter - Waiter, pe $3,000, re $1,000, w 15, p 191
Smith, Rachel - Washerwoman, pe $75, w 16, p 105
Smith, Rachel - pe $30, w 20, p 78
Smith, Robert - Waiter, pe $75, w 11, p 44
Smith, Samuel - Cooper, pe $500, w 15, p 53
Smith, Samuel - Driver, pe $500, w 15, p 250
Smith, Samuel - Brickmaker, pe $500, w 15, p 262
Smith, Samuel - Laborer, pe $100, w 16, p 166
Smith, Samuel - Sailor, pe $20, w 17, p 50
Smith, Samuel - Drayman, pe $250, w 20, p 236

Chapter 18

Black Estate Holders - 1860

Smith, Sarah - Washerwoman, pe $200, w 15, p 77
Smith, Simon - Carter, pe $400, w 20, p 55
Smith, Susan - pe $15, w 17, p 147
Smith, Thomas - Laborer, pe $5, w 17, p 49
Smith, Thomas - Drayman, pe $100, w 18, p 729
Smith, William - Sailor, pe $50, w 17, p 59
Smith, Wilson - Sailor, pe $50, w 17, p 6
Smithers, Henrietta - Washerwoman, pe $300, w 15, p 262
Smuthers, Jesse - Porter, pe $500, w 15, p 240
Snead, Dianna - pe $75, w 16, p 138
Snell, Charles - Laborer, pe $70, w 14, p 62
Snell, William - Laborer, pe $20, w 18, p 768
Snowden, Arianna - Washerwoman, pe $15, w 11, p 155
Snowden, John - Dressmaker, pe $300, w 20, p 125
Snyder, Caroline - Washerwoman, pe $10, w 20, p 72
Sollers, John - Drayman, pe $10, w 11, p 156
Sommerfield, Robert - Waiter, pe $50, w 16, p 49
Sorrell, Darius - Stevedore, pe $50, w 11, p 45
Sorrell, Edward - Drayman, pe $150, w 17, p 175
Sorrell, Henry - Porter, pe $50, w 17, p 2
Sorrell, John - Drayman, pe $150, w 11, p 53
Sorrell, William - Porter, pe $50, w 17, p 4
Southwood, John - Porter, pe $30, w 14, p 128
Sowden, Charles - Brickmaker, pe $25, w 17, p 186
Sparrow, Richard - Laborer, pe $75, w 16, p 34
Spence, Frisby - Brickmaker, pe $30, w 17, p 104
Spence, Isaac - Brickmaker, pe $25, w 17, p 187
Spencer, William H. - Farm Hand, pe $25, w 16, p 23
Spindle, Elizabeth - pe $30, w 20, p 229
Spindle, Thomas - pe $40, w 20, p 229
Spridle, Fempy - Seamstress, pe $8, w 17, p 50
Spridle, Jelsu? - Drayman, pe $300, w 17, p 4
Spridle?, Addison - Drayman, pe $150, w 17, p 4
Sprigg, Francis - Washerwoman, pe $25, w 13, p 472
Sprigs, James - Drayman, pe $100, w 17, p 1
Squirrel, Isaac - Whitewasher, pe $40, w 20, p 251
Stanley, Smart - Day Laborer, pe $50, w 7, p 320
Stansbury, George - Brickmaker, pe $50, w 16, p 69
Stansbury, James - Brickmaker, pe $300, w 15, p 78
Stansbury, Sarah - Washerwoman, pe $25, w 16, p 145
Stansbury, Susan - pe $200, w 16, p 47

Black Real Estate and Personal Estate Holders, 1860

Black Estate Holders - 1860

Staten, William - Cook, pe $50, w 17, p 25
Staunton, James - Waiter, pe $30, w 20, p 53
Stephens, John - Porter, pe $200, w 15, p 263
Stephenson, Arena - Washerwoman, pe $10, w 17, p 50
Stephenson, Sarah - Washerwoman, pe $70, w 14, p 66
Steuart, George - Farmer, pe $5, w 17, p 58
Steuart, George - Porter, pe $20, w 17, p 184
Steuart, John E. - Drayman, pe $150, w 17, p 11
Steuart, William - Carter, pe $150, w 17, p 288
Stevens, Benjamon - Hackman, pe $25, w 11, p 64
Stevens, Charles - Waiter, pe $10, w 20, p 54
Stevens, Jane - Washerwoman, pe $40, w 20, p 222
Stevens, John - Laborer, pe $45, w 18, p 368
Stevenson, Elizabeth - Washerwoman, pe $20, w 13, p 484
Stevenson, Mary - Huckster, pe $600, w 15, p 43
Stevenson, Solomon - Day Laborer, pe $50, re $400, w 7, p 352
Stewart, Ann - Washerwoman, pe $75, w 8, p 547
Stewart, Charles - Drayman, pe $30, w 20, p 240
Stewart, Christiana - Washerwoman, pe $100, w 15, p 41
Stewart, Daniel - Brickmaker, pe $300, w 15, p 90
Stewart, Edward - Currier, pe $30, w 11, p 155
Stewart, Enoch - Waiter, pe $800, w 15, p 263
Stewart, Isaac - Seaman, pe $40, w 11, p 187
Stewart, James - Drayman, pe $100, w 15, p 300
Stewart, Lewis - Hay Dealer, pe $100, w 20, p 113
Stewart, Margeret - Washerwoman, pe $50, w 8, p 363
Stewart, Maria - Washerwoman, pe $30, w 8, p 264
Stewart, Maria - Teacher, pe $15, w 11, p 61
Stewart, Mary - Laundress, pe $40, w 20, p 125
Stewart, Mary - Washerwoman, pe $20, w 20, p 126
Stewart, Sarah - Washerwoman, pe $300, w 15, p 90
Stewart, Thomas - Porter, pe $50, w 8, p 263
Stewrat, John - Brickmaker, pe $20, w 16, p 66
Stuart, Ephraim - Whitewasher, pe $500, w 15, p 260
Sunger?, George - Laborer, pe $100, w 15, p 288
Suter, Eliza - Washerwoman, pe $5, w 17, p 22
Sutton, Richard - Whitewasher, pe $60, w 20, p 60
Sutton, Susan - Laundress, pe $20, w 20, p 58
Sylvester, James - Coachman, pe $50, w 14, p 12
Syneris, Robert - Carter, pe $100, w 12, p 22
Tabb, Mary - Washerwoman, pe $30, w 13, p 462

Chapter 18

Black Estate Holders - 1860

Talbert, Julia A. - Washerwoman, pe $50, w 7, p 389
Talbot, Mary - Washerwoman, pe $50, w 11, p 101
Talbot, Robert - Laborer, pe $50, w 16, p 68
Talbot, Samuel - Laborer, pe $800, w 15, p 72
Tally, James - Drayman, pe $25, w 11, p 155
Tally, Sarah - Cake Woman, pe $20, w 11, p 173
Tates, Hiram - Drayman, pe $100, w 19, p 86
Tates, Simon - Drayman, pe $100, w 6, p 34
Taylor, Abraham - Caulker, pe $100, w 3, p 258
Taylor, Allard - Coachsmith, pe $50, w 7, p 334
Taylor, Charlotte - Washerwoman, pe $20, w 8, p 339
Taylor, Eliza - Servant, pe $50, w 16, p 104
Taylor, George - Whitewasher, pe $30, w 13, p 463
Taylor, H. William - Brickmaker, pe $300, w 15, p 301
Taylor, Isaac - Plasterer, pe $30, w 18, p 428
Taylor, Isaac - Laborer, pe $40, w 18, p 432
Taylor, Isaac - Restaurant, pe $900, w 10, p 77
Taylor, James - Grain Measurer, pe $30, re $800, w 17, p 188
Taylor, James - Whitewasher, pe $10, w 20, p 95
Taylor, Joseph - Waiter, pe $100, w 11, p 242
Taylor, Maria - Washerwoman, pe $10, w 11, p 242
Taylor, Mary - Washerwoman, pe $25, w 13, p 411
Taylor, Mary - Washerwoman, pe $50, w 16, p 105
Taylor, Rachel - Washerwoman, pe $200, re $2,000, w 2, p 60
Taylor, Richard - Porter, pe $200, w 16, p 16
Taylor, William - Brickmaker, pe $20, w 17, p 99
Taylor, William F. - Caulker, pe $50, w 7, p 243
Teacle, Henry - Waiter, pe $30, w 11, p 61
Teirnan, Patrick - Porter, pe $300, re $1,000, w 19, p 236
Thomas, Amal - Sailor, pe $100, w 2, p 78
Thomas, Caroline - Washerwoman, pe $75, w 16, p 103
Thomas, Catharine - pe $100, w 14, p 85
Thomas, Charles - Waiter, pe $30, w 11, p 167
Thomas, Deborah - Washerwoamn, pe $40, w 11, p 155
Thomas, Elizabeth - Washerwoman, pe $40, w 14, p 55
Thomas, Garrison - Grain Measurer, pe $8,000, w 15, p 43
Thomas, Gear? - Brickmaker, pe $300, w 15, p 51
Thomas, George - Waiter, re $300, w 7, p 596z
Thomas, George - Waiter, pe $30, w 11, p 62
Thomas, George - Carpenter, pe $100, w 12, p 194
Thomas, George - Laborer, pe $5, w 17, p 179

Black Real Estate and Personal Estate Holders, 1860

Black Estate Holders - 1860

Thomas, Harriet - Washerwoman, pe $25, w 13, p 472
Thomas, Hazel - Drayman, pe $350, w 14, p 59
Thomas, Hiram - pe $30, w 17, p 94
Thomas, James - Day Laborer, pe $50, w 7, p 361
Thomas, James - Laborer, pe $40, w 18, p 375
Thomas, Jane - Washerwoman, pe $5, w 17, p 50
Thomas, John - Whitewasher, pe $50, w 8, p 556
Thomas, John - Wood Sawyer, pe $100, w 12, p 41
Thomas, John - Drayman, pe $75, w 16, p 166
Thomas, John - Fireman, pe $20, w 17, p 87
Thomas, John - Drayman, pe $200, w 17, p 99
Thomas, Joseph - Laborer, pe $70, w 14, p 137
Thomas, Juila - Servant, pe $10, w 17, p 34
Thomas, Mary - Laundress, pe $10, w 20, p 122
Thomas, Perry - Cook, pe $200, w 12, p 28
Thomas, Rachel - Washerwoman, pe $50, w 13, p 475
Thomas, Sarah - Washerwoman, pe $40, w 11, p 63
Thomas, Shadricse? - Mariner, pe $200, w 15, p 69
Thomas, Walter - Fireman, pe $50, w 16, p 141
Thomas, Wesley - Brickamker, pe $75, w 16, p 105
Thomas, William - Wood Sawyer, pe $40, w 11, p 62
Thomas, William - Brickmaker, pe $75, w 15, p 2
Thomas, William - Mariner, pe $40, w 18, p 368
Thomas, William - Drayman, pe $350, w 20, p 73
Thomas, William - Drayman, pe $200, w 20, p 73
Thomas, William - Drayman, pe $50, w 13, p 411
Thomes, Mary A. - Washerwoman, pe $40, w 11, p 129
Thompson, Ann - Washerwoman, pe $50, w 14, p 119
Thompson, Ann - Huckster, pe $200, w 15, p 75
Thompson, Catharine - pe $50, w 13, p 451
Thompson, Dianah - pe $10, w 17, p 297
Thompson, Emily L. - pe $50, w 7, p 364
Thompson, George - Seaman, pe $25, w 13, p 472
Thompson, Harrison - Drayman, pe $60, w 14, p 12
Thompson, James - Waiter, pe $50, w 17, p 1
Thompson, Jarrett - Brickmaker, pe $50, w 16, p 58
Thompson, John - Waiter, pe $500, w 15, p 265
Thompson, William - Drayman, pe $100, w 14, p 12
Thompson, William - Porter, pe $100, w 14, p 16
Thompson, William - Farm Hand, pe $30, w 18, p 427
Tidings, Elizabeth - Seamstress, pe $5, w 17, p 11

Chapter 18

Black Estate Holders - 1860

Tiler, Thomas - Brickamker, pe $5, w 17, p 33
Tilghman, David - Grain Measurer, pe $25, w 17, p 183
Tilghman, James - Sailor, pe $25, w 17, p 2
Tilghman, William - Grain Measurer, pe $30, w 17, p 104
Tilison, Theodore - Brickmaker, pe $30, w 17, p 92
Tillman, William - Laborer, pe $300, w 15, p 91
Tilman, Francis - Drayman, pe $50, w 7, p 388
Times, William - Laborer, pe $30, w 20, p 109
Togood, James H. - Carter, pe $25, w 16, p 16
Tolers, Mary - Washerwoman, pe $50, w 15, p 205
Toleson, Daniel - Porter, pe $500, w 15, p 250
Tolson, Daniel - pe $30, w 17, p 99
Tolson, James - Laborer, pe $50, w 17, p 178
Tomie, William - Laborer, pe $50, w 16, p 60
Toogood, Tate - Brickmaker, pe $20, w 16, p 66
Toomey, James - Carter, pe $100, w 15, p 293
Tophan, Charles - Drayman, pe $40, w 20, p 118
Toupt?, John - Wood Sawyer, pe $20, w 11, p 240
Travers, Ephraim - Seaman, pe $20, w 17, p 203
Travers, James - pe $100, w 15, p 73
Travers, William - Brickmaker, pe $600, w 15, p 55
Travis, Edward - Church Sexton, pe $100, re $1,000, w 17, p 7
Travis, Mrs. - Washerwoman, pe $3, w 17, p 23
Travis, Robert - Sailor, pe $100, w 2, p 97
Tripp, Fanney - Servant, pe $25, w 16, p 57
Tripp, Richard - Carter, pe $100, w 16, p 102
Trippe, Harrison - Brickmaker, pe $50, w 15, p 291
Trusty, George - Woodsawyer, pe $15, w 20, p 54
Trusty, John - Day Laborer, pe $200, w 2, p 61
Trusty, Samuel - Whitewasher, pe $100, re $500, w 8, p 369
Tugman, Jerry - Laborer, pe $15, w 15, p 10
Tuken, James H. - Porter, pe $300, w 12, p 59
Turner, Frances - Barber, pe $1,200, re $4,500, w 11, p 41
Turner, John - Laborer, pe $100, w 15, p 41
Turner, John - Clerk, pe $300, w 20, p 73
Turner, Thomas - Brickmaker, pe $200, w 15, p 68
Turner, William - Mariner, pe $300, w 15, p 41
Tyler, Charles - Brickmaker, pe $25, w 16, p 33
Tyler, Eliza - Washerwoman, pe $25, w 13, p 458
Tyson, William - Mariner, pe $700, w 15, p 1
Uncle, Lorenzo - Blacksmith, pe $100, w 14, p 12

Black Real Estate and Personal Estate Holders, 1860

Black Estate Holders - 1860

Unkle, Philip - Drayman, pe $300, w 15, p 245
Uwell, Piney - Washerwoman, pe $100, w 16, p 165
Valentine, John - Seaman, pe $50, w 9, p 12
Vanbiber, Hezekiah - Laborer, pe $25, w 20, p 126
Vandel Sulle, Perry - Porter, pe $500, w 12, p 59
Verry, Charles - Laborer, pe $100, w 8, p 564
Vincent, Isaac - Grain Measurer, pe $200, re $3,000, w 17, p 330
Vinson, Perry - Porter, pe $100, w 14, p 58
Whitson, James - Hay Packer, pe $50, w 8, p 503
Wadaling, John - Stevedore, pe $50, w 16, p 186
Wade, Alexander - Waiter, pe $100, w 12, p 28
Wadkie, Daniel - Hod Carrier, pe $25, w 17, p 2
Walker, Eliza - Washerwoman, pe $45, w 18, p 346
Walker, Henry - Grain Measurer, pe $20, w 17, p 29
Walker, Joseph - Laborer, pe $25, w 16, p 23
Walker, Joseph - Brickmaker, pe $10, w 17, p 57
Walker, Terresa - Washerwoman, pe $30, w 13, p 472
Walker, Truman - Laborer, pe $50, w 20, p 74
Wallace, Caleb - Brickamker, pe $100, w 14, p 28
Wallace, Charles - Brickmaker, pe $75, w 16, p 104
Wallace, David - Carter, pe $100, re $1,000, w 20, p 188
Wallace, Garrison - Brickamker, pe $75, w 16, p 105
Wallace, Jacob - Porter, pe $50, w 14, p 11
Wallace, James - Laborer, pe $90, w 14, p 66
Wallace, Sarah J. - Tavern Keeper, pe $300, w 11, p 238
Wallace, William - Sailor, pe $20, w 17, p 177
Wallacve, John W. - Brickmaker, pe $25, w 17, p 96
Wallis, Elemuel - Day Laborer, pe $50, w 2, p 81
Wallis, Jarrett - Drayman, pe $120, w 20, p 79
Wallis, Richard - Porter, pe $50, w 17, p 3
Walters, Isaac - Porter, pe $50, w 12, p 23
Wangers, Jenkins - Porter, pe $100, re $600, w 17, p 81
Ward, James - Musician, pe $30, w 11, p 187
Warfield, Adam - Day Laborer, pe $100, w 2, p 97
Warfield, George - Laborer, pe $300, w 15, p 205
Warfield, John H. - Porter, pe $100, w 14, p 132
Warner, Joseph - Laborer, pe $100, w 12, p 184
Warner, Robert - Whitewasher, pe $25, re $500, w 17, p 184
Warner, Ruth - Washerwoman, pe $100, w 15, p 71
Warren, Adam - Whitewasher, pe $75, w 16, p 67
Warwick, Harriet - Cook, pe $50, w 11, p 167

Chapter 18

Black Estate Holders - 1860

Wary, Alice - Washerwoman, pe $5, w 17, p 23
Washington, Felix - Brickmaker, pe $25, w 16, p 170
Washington, Fredrich - Drayman, pe $250, w 7, p 413
Washington, George - Servant, pe $75, w 16, p 20
Washington, Mary - Washerwoman, pe $40, w 18, p 432
Watby, Addison - Drayman, pe $50, w 16, p 171
Waters, Charles - Brickamker, pe $300, w 15, p 245
Waters, George - Laborer, pe $20, w 17, p 184
Waters, Gilbert - Laborer, pe $100, w 17, p 81
Waters, Harriett - Servant, pe $600, w 18, p 718
Waters, Henny - Washerwoman, pe $40, w 18, p 736
Waters, John - Laborer, pe $200, w 3, p 212
Waters, Levin - Stevedore, pe $5, w 17, p 22
Waters, Major - Laborer, pe $75, w 16, p 102
Waters, Wiliam H. - M. E. Clergyman, pe $100, re $400, w 8, p 583
Waters, William - Drayman, pe $100, w 3, p 323
Waters, William - Drayman, pe $100, re $400, w 8, p 527
Watkins, George - Laborer, pe $50, w 5, p 78
Watkins, George H. - Porter, pe $400, w 15, p 40
Watkins, George T. - Teacher, pe $120, w 20, p 83
Watkins, Isaac - Laborer, pe $75, w 11, p 53
Watkins, Joseph - Drayman, pe $200, w 20, p 84
Watkins, Maria - Washerwoman, pe $10, w 11, p 239
Watkins, Thomas - Porter, pe $1,000, w 4, p 7
Watson, Hampton - Bootblack, pe $50, re $400, w 13, p 472
Watson, John - Brickmaker, pe $25, w 20, p 130
Watts, Anna - pe $30, w 17, p 96
Watts, Charles - Seaman, pe $30, w 17, p 96
Watts, Daniel - Laborer, pe $200, w 15, p 71
Watts, Georgiana - Servant, pe $10, w 17, p 59
Watts, Harriet - Washerwoman, pe $25, w 16, p 23
Watts, Henry - Laborer, pe $30, w 13, p 468
Watts, Jeremiah - Brickmaker, pe $100, w 15, p 72
Watts, John - Day Laborer, pe $50, w 2, p 61
Watts, Martha - Huckster, pe $300, w 15, p 60
Watts, Nancy - pe $50, w 17, p 95
Watts, Nelson - Wood Sawyer, pe $100, w 17, p 49
Watts, Susan - Washerwoman, pe $75, w 11, p 86
Weaver, Benjamin - Drayman, pe $25, w 16, p 69
Weaver, James - Brickmaker, pe $30, w 17, p 103
Weaver, Thomas - Porter, pe $100, w 17, p 81

Black Real Estate and Personal Estate Holders, 1860

Black Estate Holders - 1860

Webb, Harrison - Musician, pe $100, w 7, p 401
Webb, Harrison H. - P. E. Clergyman, pe $100, re $500, w 8, p 568
Webb, Peter - Drayman, pe $30, w 17, p 92
Webster, Isaac - Porter, pe $50, re $1,000, w 17, p 7
Webster, Joseph - Wagoner, pe $25, re $500, w 17, p 185
Webster, Robert - Barber, pe $20, w 20, p 80
Weeks, Caleb - Sailor, pe $50, w 7, p 364
Weeks, Cornelius - Waiter, pe $20, w 17, p 91
Weeks, Jeremiah - Whitewasher, pe $50, w 14, p 97
Weeks, Peter - Drayman, pe $40, w 20, p 99
Weems, Matilda - Washerwoman, pe $10, w 20, p 247
Weems, Stephen - Baker, pe $500, w 15, p 292
Weer, Charles - Driver, pe $20, w 20, p 240
Weigh, Thomas - Day Laborer, pe $100, re $350, w 2, p 59
Weimes, James - Waiter, pe $150, w 12, p 22
Wells, Anna - re $550, w 7, p 317
Wells, David - Day Laborer, pe $50, w 7, p 359
Wells, Elizabeth - Washerwoman, pe $50, w 14, p 28
Wells, George - Carter, pe $500, w 7, p 317
Wells, George - Drayman, pe $300, w 17, p 176
Wells, Henry - Drayman, pe $50, w 16, p 103
Wells, Philip - Laborer, pe $100, w 15, p 78
Wesley, John - Brickmaker, pe $25, w 17, p 203
West, James T. - Laborer, pe $500, w 15, p 260
Wey, Philip - Day Laborer, pe $100, w 2, p 46
Wheatley, Daniel - Caulker, re $400, w 7, p 591z
Wheatly, Henry - Laborer, pe $50, w 14, p 119
Wheeler, David - Laborer, pe $400, w 15, p 68
Wheeler, Rose - Washerwoman, pe $40, w 20, p 222
Whipper, George - Drayman, pe $100, w 15, p 254
White, Charles - Porter, pe $100, w 12, p 192
White, Charles - Drayman, pe $150, w 17, p 175
White, Henry - Porter, pe $100, w 2, p 81
White, James - Porter, pe $60, w 14, p 65
White, James - Barber, pe $10, w 17, p 50
White, John - Mariner, pe $50, w 15, p 289
White, John - Caulker, pe $10, w 17, p 179
White, Ruth - Cook, pe $15, w 11, p 129
White, Samuel - Waiter, pe $50, w 14, p 16
Whittington, Elizabeth - Washerwoman, pe $50, w 11, p 99
Wickly, Henry - Laborer, pe $25, w 16, p 65

Chapter 18

Black Estate Holders - 1860

Wicks, Abraham - Porter, pe $100, w 11, p 60
Wicks, John H. - Washerwoman, pe $700, w 14, p 66
Wicks, Mary - Washerwoman, pe $100, w 8, p 464
Wiliams, George H. - Laborer, pe $500, w 15, p 260
Wiliams, Mary - Washerwoman, pe $20, w 8, p 269
Wilkins, George - Drayman, pe $150, w 17, p 10
Willet, William - Porter, pe $500, w 15, p 265
Williams, Alexander - Sailor, pe $50, w 7, p 388
Williams, Alexander - Tinner, pe $120, w 16, p 103
Williams, Amelia - Huckster, pe $1,000, w 6, p 223
Williams, Andrew - Carter, pe $50, w 16, p 138
Williams, Anna - Washerwoman, pe $50, w 7, p 359
Williams, Anthoney - Wood Sawyer, pe $10, w 17, p 29
Williams, Archibald - Drayman, pe $150, w 20, p 80
Williams, Benjamin - Waiter, pe $100, w 14, p 26
Williams, Benjamin - Porter, pe $20, w 20, p 111
Williams, Charity - Washerwoman, pe $50, w 16, p 144
Williams, David - Waiter, pe $25, w 20, p 111
Williams, Delia - Laundress, pe $50, w 20, p 87
Williams, George - Drayman, pe $75, w 16, p 50
Williams, Harriet - Washerwoman, pe $100, re $1,000, w 17, p 7
Williams, Henrietta - pe $50, w 11, p 65
Williams, Henry - Stewart, pe $500, w 15, p 75
Williams, Henry C. - Steward, pe $100, w 6, p 56
Williams, Horace - Stevedore, pe $30, w 11, p 126
Williams, James - Carter, pe $150, w 8, p 486
Williams, james - Brickmaker, pe $100, w 16, p 35
Williams, James - Brickmaker, pe $20, w 18, p 422
Williams, James H. - Carpenter, pe $100, w 20, p 59
Williams, Jerry - Hod Carrier, pe $10, w 20, p 117
Williams, John - Brickmaker, pe $100, w 15, p 1
Williams, John - Laborer, pe $300, w 15, p 69
Williams, John - Laborer, pe $100, w 15, p 287
Williams, John - Grain Measurer, pe $4, w 17, p 45
Williams, John - Barber, pe $100, w 17, p 64
Williams, Joseph - Laborer, pe $50, w 8, p 595
Williams, Joseph - Mariner, pe $300, w 15, p 78
Williams, Joseph - Drayman, pe $120, w 20, p 87
Williams, Lewis - Laborer, pe $200, w 15, p 296
Williams, Louisa - Washerwoman, pe $20, w 16, p 103
Williams, Mary - Washerwoman, pe $50, w 8, p 596

Black Real Estate and Personal Estate Holders, 1860

Black Estate Holders - 1860

Williams, Nathan - Drayman, pe $250, re $600, w 20, p 90
Williams, Nelson - Coachman, pe $50, w 11, p 124
Williams, Noah - Blacksmith, pe $1,000, w 15, p 249
Williams, Rachel - pe $15, w 17, p 184
Williams, Richard - Bar Keeper, pe $50, w 11, p 189
Williams, Richard - Carter, pe $500, w 15, p 108
Williams, Robert - Bricklayer, pe $400, w 12, p 13
Williams, Robert - Hod Carrier, pe $50, w 16, p 142
Williams, Rodney - Drayman, pe $150, w 20, p 74
Williams, Samuel - Sailor, pe $50, re $650, w 7, p 333
Williams, Sarah - Washerwoman, pe $500, w 15, p 249
Williams, Thomas - Laborer, pe $40, w 14, p 118
Williams, Thomas - Laborer, pe $25, w 16, p 34
Williams, Thomas - Coachman, pe $40, w 20, p 61
Williams, Thomas - Hostler, pe $20, w 20, p 232
Williams, William - Minister, pe $300, w 5, p 114
Williams, William - pe $500, w 15, p 43
Williams, William D. - Pickler, pe $50, w 16, p 103
Williams, William - Carter, pe $50, w 16, p 103
Willie, Dumb - Brickmaker, pe $10, w 17, p 25
Wilmer, John - Laborer, pe $40, w 20, p 235
Wilmina, Chester - pe $600, w 3, p 19
Wilos, Joseph? - Caulker, pe $100, w 3, p 68
Wilson, Ada - Washerwoman, pe $100, w 15, p 76
Wilson, Adam - Day Laborer, pe $50, w 7, p 370
Wilson, Benjamin - Laborer, pe $50, w 14, p 137
Wilson, Charles - Sailor, pe $100, w 2, p 97
Wilson, Charles - Day Laborer, pe $400, w 7, p 505
Wilson, Charles - Laborer, pe $200, w 12, p 33
Wilson, Durham - Waiter, pe $50, w 11, p 146
Wilson, Eliza - Washerwoman, pe $30, w 11, p 173
Wilson, Elizabeth - pe $300, w 12, p 66
Wilson, Frederick - Patent Med., pe $800, re $300, w 6, p 225
Wilson, George - Drayman, pe $40, w 8, p 587
Wilson, Greenbay - Waiter, pe $200, w 20, p 69
Wilson, Henry - Day Laborer, pe $100, w 7, p 334
Wilson, Henry - Herb Doctor, pe $90, w 20, p 61
Wilson, Jacob - Laborer, pe $300, w 15, p 54
Wilson, James - Wood Sawyer, pe $50, w 11, p 65
Wilson, James - Carter, pe $75, w 16, p 50
Wilson, James - Waiter, pe $200, re $800, w 20, p 68

Chapter 18

Black Estate Holders - 1860

Wilson, Jane - Washerwoman, pe $5, w 17, p 22
Wilson, Jefferson - Laborer, pe $10, w 17, p 145
Wilson, Jeremiah - Grain Measurer, pe $200, w 15, p 76
Wilson, John - Day Laborer, pe $50, w 2, p 80
Wilson, Lucy - pe $400, w 6, p 223
Wilson, Margaret - Washerwoman, pe $75, w 16, p 140
Wilson, Maria - Washerwoman, pe $30, w 11, p 154
Wilson, Mary J. - Washerwoman, pe $40, w 11, p 239
Wilson, Matilda - Laundress, pe $25, w 20, p 57
Wilson, Rachael - Washerwoman, pe $50, w 11, p 85
Wilson, Samuel - Drayman, pe $60, w 14, p 68
Wilson, Samuel - Laborer, pe $100, w 15, p 52
Wilson, Samuel - Sailor, pe $10, w 17, p 56
Wilson, Thomas - Laborer, pe $25, w 17, p 176
Wilson, William - Laborer, pe $100, w 3, p 180
Wilson, William - Scow Man, pe $50, w 7, p 388
Wilson, William - Carter, pe $500, w 14, p 68
Wilson, William - Fireman, pe $50, w 16, p 70
Wilson, William - Seaman, pe $25, w 17, p 188
Wilson, William H. - Hod Carrier, pe $300, w 15, p 299
Wimps, Henry - Waiter, pe $100, w 12, p 29
Windmore, Rebecca - Washerwoman, pe $10, w 11, p 155
Wing, David - Brickmaker, pe $25, w 17, p 7
Wing, John - Pinting, pe $20, w 17, p 11
Winks, Mary - Washerwoman, pe $50, w 16, p 141
Winn, Thomas - Waiter, pe $100, w 11, p 85
Winor, Joseph - Drayman, pe $150, w 17, p 188
Winson, James - pe $30, w 17, p 104
Wise, Joseph - Waiter, pe $500, w 15, p 109
Wisher, Andrew - Shoemaker, pe $10, w 20, p 54
Wisher, Isaac - Brickmaker, pe $10, w 17, p 297
With, James - Waiter, pe $200, w 12, p 21
Wolson, Benjamin - Laborer, pe $40, w 8, p 362
Wood, Hiram - Carter, pe $250, w 16, p 168
Wooden, Edward - Sailor, pe $5, w 17, p 45
Woods, Augustus - Drayman, pe $500, w 15, p 245
Woods, Bradly - Brickmaker, pe $500, w 15, p 245
Woods, Jeremiah - Drayman, pe $100, w 8, p 486
Woods, Walter - Porter, pe $5, w 17, p 13
Woodyard, Ellen - House Cleaner, pe $50, w 11, p 241
Woodyard, Jerrey - Drayman, pe $200, w 20, p 91

Black Estate Holders - 1860

Woolford, Barth - Carter, pe $250, w 17, p 243
Woolford, Emory - Brickmaker, pe $10, w 17, p 13
Woolford, Willis - Hod Carrier, pe $10, w 17, p 296
Wormsley, Isaac - Sailor, pe $50, w 7, p 376
Worrell, John - Laborer, pe $50, w 16, p 61
Worthington, Sarah - Laundress, pe $10, w 20, p 59
Wright, James - Brickmaker, pe $100, w 3, p 68
Wright, Maria - Cook, pe $25, w 16, p 70
Wright, Robert - Day Laborer, pe $100, w 2, p 72
Wright, Thomas - Barber, pe $30, w 11, p 153
Wright, William - Brickmaker, pe $100, w 16, p 72
Yearby, Mary - pe $20, re $1,500, w 17, p 95
Yoney?, Stephen - Brickmaker, pe $100, w 15, p 76
Young, Ellen - Washerwoman, pe $30, w 11, p 243
Young, Hamison? - Brickmaker, pe $50, w 16, p 60
Young, Isaac H. - Weaver, pe $100, w 7, p 361
Young, John - Brickmaker, pe $20, w 17, p 203
Young, Joseph - pe $1,000, w 15, p 251
Young, Michael - Waiter, pe $100, w 11, p 106
Young, Mr. - Sailor, pe $10, w 17, p 177
Zeppories?, Benjamin - Coachman, pe $80, w 18, p 432

19
Mortality in the Free Black and Slave Population of Baltimore, 1850

By 1850 enumerators collecting population census figures in Baltimore were also expected to gather slave schedules and mortality schedules. Mortality schedules covered households where a death had occured within a twelve month period prior to the collection of the census.

These schedules provide the name, race, age, month and year of death, occupation, cause of death, and area (Ward) in which the deceased had lived. The schedules also recorded the status (slave or free) of those living in the Black community.

Baltimore city's Mortality records for 1850 provide information on the deaths of more than 700 members of the Black community. In a time period when other sources of information on mortality in the Black family are difficult to locate, the schedules provide insight into the causes as well as the numbers of deaths.

Baltimore's schedules do not provide an official record of all deaths as is clearly evidenced by official weekly death counts and the identification of deaths of an unusual nature that are revealed in local papers. By cross referencing unusual deaths listed in local newspapers with Mortality Records, unique insight is provided into the types of deaths occuring in the Black community.

The following is representative of one such article that appeared in the *Baltimore Sun* on March 25, 1850.

> *Inquest - A man burned to death. Coroner Reilly was called early yesterday morning to hold an inquest on the body of a colored man, named Perry Talbot, aged abput forty - five years, who was found dead in his dwelling in a little court between Caroline and Spring Streets, south of Pratt. He lived by himself and had not been seen since friday last. When found, he was on his hands and knees with his head in the fireplace directly over the spot where the fire had been. He was literally roasted, all his face and nearly all of his head being burnt off. His bed was immediately alongside the fire, and the wonder is that it was not burnt. The deceased is represented to have been a man of sober habits. The jury rendered a verdict of accidental death, caused while falling into the fire while in a fit, sometime during the night of friday last.*

(See index under Talbot, Perry.)

Chapter 19

in a fit, sometime during the night of friday last.
(See index under Talbot, Perry.)

Interestingly, there are a number of names in such notices that do not appear in the mortality schedules. A combination of deaths reported in the local papers and mortality schedules for Baltimore in 1850 and 1860 would provide the cause of death for close to 2, 000 Black Baltimoreans.

Although consumption traditionally led as the prevailing cause of death in the Black community in mid nineteenth century Baltimore, it is unusual to see as many typhoid deaths as reflected in the records of 1850. Of 702 reported deaths, 51 were from typhoid, an extremely high number. There are also an unusual number of deaths by cholera: 14.

A search of the Baltimore Sun of the spring and summer of 1849 provided an answer to the mystery. A large number of families in the Black community of Baltimore lived in alleys scattered throughout the city. The conditions in a number of the alleys were unsanitary, placing the Black families residing there at greater risk than the general populace when a typhoid epidemic struck Baltimore in late May and June of 1849.

An article in the Baltimore Sun of May 24th of that year noted *"This fell disease appears to be doing a fatal business among the colored people in some sections of the city."* The deaths were attributed to the *"loathsome and filthy conditions"* under which the Black victims lived. Furthermention is made of the Health departments visits to the various *"filthy alleys and dwellings"* in order to attempt to disinfect the area.

Although some whites also died of the disease a disproportionate number of the total deaths occurred in the Black community. By the end of the third week in June the almshouse was filled to capacity with the sick and dying. The members of the Board of Health opened an old Hospital near Fairmont in the city to care for the overflow of patients.

By the end of June the disease was on the wane. Most of the deaths were spread throughout the city which seems to suggest that the deplorable conditions mentioned in the series of Sun articles were prevalent in a large number of alleys occupied by Black Families. Wards hardest hit were the 5th, 15th, and 17th wards.

No sooner had the typhoid epidemic waned when an equally unusual epidemic of cholera struck the city. Victims were to be found in all sectors of the city, regardless of race or residence. Poor living conditions and health care available to the members of the Black community was once again reflected in the Health departments statistics which covered the disease through the month of July. Of 14 cases reported in a three week period in the Black community 11 died. This represented a death rate of

Mortality in the Free Black and Slave Population, 1860

78%. During the same period only 12 of 34 cases in the white community ended in death. This represented a death rate in the white communmity of 35%.

Below listed are statistics obtained from a study of the mortality schedules for the Black community of Baltimore between the summer of 1849 and the summer of 1850.

Age Groupings Of Deceased (when indicated)

Age Group	Number of Deaths
0- 5	289
6- 10	45
11- 15	21
16- 20	35
21- 30	91
31- 45	91
46- 60	80
61-over	46

Children five years of age and under represented 49% of all deaths while less than 7% of those listed lived past the age of 60.

Slave Deaths - 45 (22male and 23 female)

The following is an index to the deaths of free blacks and slaves in the 1850 mortality schedules of Baltimore. The index is organized as follows:

Surname and first name of deceased, age at time of death, ward where deceased resided, cause of death.

A sample entry would read as follows:

Aldridge, James E. - 2, wd 15, inflammation of bowels

The translation would be: James E. Aldridge died at the age of two in the 15the ward of Baltimore city.

For children under a year the following abbreviations have been used: m - month(s), w - week(s), d - day(s). For example: *Ackwood, Maria L. - 3m* indicates that Maria died at the age of three months.

Chapter 19

Mortality in Free Blacks & Slaves - 1860

?, Charles - 60
?, Elizabeth - 48, w 12, Consumption
Ackwood, Maria L. - 3m, w 11, Typhoid
Adams, Randolph - 7m, w 16, Teething
Adgeby, Mary A. - 3m, w 11, Water On Brain
Aldridge, James E. - 2, w 15, Inflammation Of Bowels
Anderson, Eliza - 3m, w 7
Anderson, Joseph - 3, w 7, Bilious Fever
Anderson, Laura - 2m, w 12
Anderson, Rachel - 2m, w 12
Anderson, Susan - 24, w 12
Anthony, Charles - 1, w 12
Anthony, Jacob - 1, w 6, Brain Fever
Anthony, Rachel - 69, w 6, Old Age
Anthony, Samuel - 1, w 12
Askins, Carlos - 19, w 15
Augustus, Charles - 46, w 16, Consumption
Aurmann, Caroline - 1 , w 12, Brain Fever
Aurmann, Jessica P. - 1, w 14
Bailey, Ann - 30, w 16, Typhoid
Bailey, James - 30, w 16, Smallpox
Bailey, William - 40, w 3, Dropsy
Banhorn, Henry - 52, w 11, Burned
Banks, Robert - 5m, w 6, Summer Complaint
Barnet, Susan - 60, w 3, Diarrhea
Barnett, Mary E. - 9, w 18, Burned
Beckett, Elizabeth - 54, w 17, Consumption
Bell, Eliza - 2, w 20, Water On Brain
Benson, John - 50, w 6, Consumption
Benson, Sarah J. - 38, w 2, Consumption
Bent, Richard - 20, w 14, Consumption
Benton, Mary L. - 2, w 17
Berry, Mary S. - 11, w 3, Consumption
Biddle, Marcellana - 8m, w 16, Brain
Birch, Jane - 28, w 12, Consumption
Birch, Lewis - 9, w 12, Diarrhea
Biscoe, Louisa - 2, w 18, Croup
Black, Josephine - 11, w 16, Consumption
Black, Mary - 20, w 8, Congestion Of Brain
Blackstone, Mary - 5, w 6, Consumption
Blake, Henry - 4, w 12, Inflammation Of Lungs
Blake, Isaac - 80, w 1, Consumption
Blake, Margaret - 19, w 18, Kidney
Bond, James - 3, 6, Scarlet Fever
Bond, William - 1m, w 10, Catarrh
Bond, William - 1, w 12, Scalded
Boon, John W. - 1, w 17
Booth, Jeremiah - 2m, w 11, Dysentery
Bordley, Adam - 75, w 13, Consumption
Bordley, John - 22, w 1, Brain Fever
Boston, Miss - 18, w 14, Consumption
Bowden, Polly - 60, w 6, Dropsy

Mortality in Free Blacks & Slaves - 1860

Bowen, Benjamin - 39, w 6, Fell From House
Bowen, Edward - 25, w 15, Cholera
Bowen, Elihu - 32, w 5, Dyspepsia
Bowen, Maria - 42, w 17, Typhoid
Bowen, Mary P. - 10m, w 15, Teetning
Bowen, Sarah - 1m, w 6, Spasms
Bowie, Jacob - 1, w 15, Scropula
Bowley, Joseph - 1, w 3, Water On Brain
Bowman, Georgiana - 14, w 3, Typhoid
Boyd, Ann E. - 5, w 15, Whooping Cough
Boyer, Henry - 50, w 20
Brack, Henrietta - 70, w 12, Dropsy
Bradford, Annie - 26, w 3, Consumption
Brady, Ann - 54, w 16, Consumption
Brice, Tom - 19, w 12
Bright, Ann - 60, w 5
Bright, Josephine - 9m, w 4, Consumption
Bright, Major - 51, w 6, Inflammation Of Lungs
Bright, Major W. - 20, w 6, Typhoid
Brightman, John W. - 50, w 11, Typhoid
Briscoe, Margaret - 7m, w 11, Whooping Cough
Brooks, Charlette - 3, w 18, Water On Brain
Brooks, John H. - 8m, w 18, Water On Brain
Brooks, Minty - 4m, w 11, Water On Brain
Brooks, Rachel G. - 2, w 6, Whooping Cough
Brooks, Samuel - 8m, w 6, Whooping Cough
Brown, Alfred - 17, w 5, Cold
Brown, Arthur - 17, w 5, Pleurisy
Brown, Charity - 4m, w 6, Summer, Complaint
Brown, Eliza - 17, w 14, Consumption
Brown, Eliza - 30, w 12, Consumption
Brown, Elizabeth - 80, w 14, Consumption
Brown, Elizabrth - 8, w 5, Worms
Brown, Ellen - 40, w 6, Consumption
Brown, Hwenry - 30, w 5, Fits
Brown, James - 55, w 2, Cold
Brown, Josephine - 6m, w 16, Teething
Brown, Lucinda - 2, w 13
Brown, Mary - 12, w 4, Consumption
Brown, Matilda - 45, w 15, Heart Disease
Brown, Sarah - 2, w 14, Fits
Bryer, William - 6m, w 20, Fall
Buchanan, Thomas - 25, w 6, Inflammation Of Lungs
Buckey, Mary - 60
Burgess, Margaret - 100, w 15, Old Age
Burk, Susana - 1, w 3, Gastric Fever
Burkley, James - 7m, w 11
Burns, Harriet - 22, w 18, Typhoid
Butler, Elizabeth - 1, w 11, Whooping Cough
Butler, Felis - 78, w 18, Old Age
Butler, Moses - 55, w 13, Typhoid

Chapter 19

Mortality in Free Blacks & Slaves - 1860

Butler, Sally - 1h, w 11, Injuries
Butler, William H. - 3m, w 16, Smallpox
Campbell, Fanny - 80, w 2, Consumption
Campbell, George - 20, w 13
Camphor, Rhoda - 90, w 15, Old Age
Carey, George - 40, w 7, Bleeding Nose
Carmack, Joel P. - 42, w 6, Typhoid
Carr, James H. - 5, w 15, Hip Disease
Carroll, David - 1, w 15, Cold
Carter, Martha - 42, w 18, Consumption
Cassel, Sarah - 71, w 14
Castor, Jane - 3w, w 15
Castor, Thomas J. - 8, w 15, Inflamation of Bowels
Chamber, George - 2, w 17, Head Disease
Chamber, Harriet - 52, w 17, Typhoid
Chambers, Mary E. - 2, w 14
Chaney, Robert - 5m, w 4, Cholera Infantile
Chapman, Henry - 22, w 11, Heart
Chappell, Edna S. - 1m, w 7
Chappell, Mary E. - 2, w 7
Chase, John - 80, w 6
Chase, Joseph - 3m, w 16, Croup
Chesley, Thomas - 5, w 6, Consumption
Chew, Abraham - 50, w 3, Typhoid
Chew, John H. - 4m, w 15
Chin, Robert H. - 2, w 17, Teething
Chrim, William - 11m, w 5, Consumption

Christmas, Sarah - 75, w 5
Clark, Ann M. - 4m, w 15
Coiles, Harris - 27, w 1, Broken Heart
Coker, Daniel - 45, w 15, Heart Disease
Cole, Betsy - 30, w 14, Consumption
Cole, John - 1, w 6, Scarlet Fever
Cole, Julia Ann - 1, w 6, Scarlet Fever
Cole, Sarah A. - 7, w 6, Scarlet Fever
Cole, Thomas - 4, w 6, Scarlet Fever
Cole, Thomas - 15, w 14, Consumption
Coleman, Isaac - 30, w 3, Consumption
Comeger, Betsey - 30, w 15, Pleurisy
Coney, Henrietta - 18, w 16, Typhoid
Derry, Richard J. - 1, w 16, Catarrh Fever
Desson, Lewis T. - 1, w 4, Croup
Devetier, Benjamin - 1, w 16, Summer Complaint
Dewine, John - 2, w 17, Fits
Dickerson, Maria - 40, w 11, Inflammation Of The Lungs
Dickinson, Eliza - 50, w 3, Cancer
Dickson, James - 1, w 6, Dropsy
Dickson, John - 18, w 6, Sun Stroke
Dickson, Kaziah - 24, w 6, Typhoid
Diggs, Carroll S. - 3m, w 6, Inflammation Of Brain
Diggs, Clara - 54, w 13, Dropsy
Diggs, William W. - 1, w 19, Decline

Mortality in Free Blacks & Slaves - 1860

Dixon, Adeline A. - 18, w 16, Dropsy In Chest
Dixon, Eliza - 45, w 3, Paralytic
Dixon, James - 70, w 1, Fits
Dobson, Thomas H. - 23, w 5, Smallpox
Dodson, Josephine - 5m, w 5, Summer Complaint
Dorsey, Elisa - 46, w 15, Bilious Fever
Dorsey, Isaac - 45, w 7
Dorsey, John H. - 2, w 15, Teething
Dorsey, - Lucinda, w 16
Downs, Horace - 35, w 8, Dysentery
Downs, Jeff - 4m, w 19, Lungs
Downs, Virginia - 4m, w 19, Lungs
Dudley, Eliza - 115, w 14, Consumption
Dunn, John Jr. - 4m, w 15, Croup
Dutton, Overton - 55, w 6, Typhoid
Edgely, John - 2, w 19, Dropsy
Effort, Mary J. - 26, w 18, Diarrhea
Elborn, Henry - 40, w 14
Emmens, John - 10, w 3, Convulsions
Estep, ? - 1d, w 15, Premature Birth
Farnandis, John - 63, w 1, Consumption
Farrow, James - 3, w 3, Cholera
Ferguson, Elizabeth - 50, w 12, Paralytic
Fields, Ann C. - 11, w 7
Finley, Rachel - 59, w 15, Tumor
Firr, George - 50, w 19, Fall
Fisher, Edwrad - 1, w 13
Flemming, Rachel A. - 4m, w 6, Summer Croup
Flemming, William H. - 1, w 6, Summer Croup
Foose, Sarah - 1, w 4, Typhoid
Ford, Eliza - 37, w 1, Consumption
Ford, Frank - 1, w 11, Whooping Cough
Ford, Rachel - 8m, w 1, Scarlet Fever
Ford, Theopilus - 1, w 11, Whooping Cough
Foreman, George - 1, w 5, Head Complaint
Foreman, Sandy - 60, w 10, Pleurisy
Fowler, Lydia F. - 2, w 5, Consumption
Francis, Mary - 1, w 13, Catarrh Fever
Franklin, Mary E. - 6, w 3, Dysentery
Frisby, William - 1m, w 6, Sudden
Furr, Sarah - 20, w 11, Cold
Gaines, Chaney - 60, w 15, OLd Age
Gaines, Mary E. - 10m, w 4, Lungs
Gaines, William - 2, w 15, Teething
Gallagher, Rose - 15, w 14
Gant, H. - 5, w 20, Consumption
Gantt, A. - 10, w 10, Scarlet Fever
Garrison, Cornelia - 30, w 16, Consumption
Garrison, John F. - 1, w 16, Teething
Garrison, Mary V. - 24, w 16, Spasms
Garrison, Richard - 11, w 1, Cholera
Gibbs, William - 39, w 17, Hard Drink
Gibson, Affra - 70, w 4, Old Age

Chapter 19

Mortality in Free Blacks & Slaves - 1860

Gibson, Josephine - 14, w 15, Typhoid
Gibson, Maria - 30, w 14, Consumption
Giddings, James H. - 1m, w 15, Fits
Giles, Isaiah - 24, w 13, Consumption
Glascoe, Rebecca - 40, w 5, Cancer Of Breast
Goaeus, George W. - 1, w 5, Consumption
Goaeus, Margaret Ann - 10, w 5, Cold
Gold, Catherine - 25, w 8, Child Bearing
Goldsborough, Daniel - 11m, w 3, Cholera Infantile
Goodham, John - 16, w 14
Gould, Rosette - 2m, w 15, Spasms
Goulden, Sarah - 30, w 6, Consumption
Grain, William - 4m, w 5, Head Complaint
Grant, Jesse - 29, w 14
Graves, Charles - 55, 5, Heart Disease
Gray, Mary A. - 6, w 4, Typhoid
Green, David - 40, w 15
Green, Lemuel - 21, w 15, Fall
Green, Mary E. - 14, w 15
Greenwood, Fanny - 2, w 5, Consumption
Greenwood, Fanny - 21, w 5, Consumption
Grey, John - 35, w 17, Dysentery
Griffin, Henry - 53, w 15, Consumption
Griffin, Maria - 30, w 7, Consumption
Griffin, Nathan - 5m, w 6, Consumption
Grimes, Anna - 4, w 4, Cholera Infantile
Grooms, M. - 23, w 5, Typhoid
Gross, Georgianna - 7, w 13, Dysentery
Gross, Gideon - 50, w 8, Dropsy
Gross, John - 70, w 15, Consumption Of Bowels
Gross, Jonathan - 50, w 15, Dropsy
Gross, Levi - 21, w 15, TYphoid
Grover, Tracey - 36, w 20, Spine Disease
Guyton, Matilda - 35, w 5, Consumption
Habun, Frederick - 5m, w 11, Head Disease
Hacket, John - 80, w 5, Old Age
Hall, Elizabeth - 9, w 1, Consumption
Hall, Randall - 50, w 15, Love Leg
Hamer, Hezekiah - 25, w 7, fever
Hammond, John - 1, w 6, Summer Complaint
Handy, Emael - 26, w 3
Hanson, Elisa - 35, w 5, Consumption
Hardey, Isaac - 33, w 8, Consumption
Hardy, Mary E. - 1, w 5
Harman, William - 5m, w 3, Water On The Brain
Harman, William H. - 5m, w 6, Water On The Brain
Harris, George - 2, w 6, Scarlet Fever
Harris, Hannah - 35, w 20, Cold
Harris, John W. - w 6, Scarlet Fever
Harris, Luds - 5, w 6, Scarlet Fever

334

Mortality in the Free Black and Slave Population, 1860

Mortality in Free Blacks & Slaves - 1860

Harris, Rosetta - 56, w 7, Consumption
Harris, Samuel - 7m, w 19, Catarrh Fever
Harris, William - 11, w 6, Scarlet Fever
Harris, William - 26, w 16, Cold
Harvey, Isaiah - 8, w 17, Spine Disease
Haskins, Thomas - 21, w 18
Hawkins, Mary - 2, w 16
Hays, Peter - 30, w 11, Consumption
Henderson, H. - 24, w 20, Consumption
Henrick, Lewis - 50, w 20
Henson, Edney - 60, w 6, Jaundice
Henson, Georgeanna - 1, w 15, Cold
Henson, James - 44, w 9, Liver Compalint
Henson, Margaret - 1m, w 15
Henson, Mary - 1m, w 15
Henson, Mary A. - 8m, w 10, Neuralgia
Hewston, Ida J. - 2m, w 3, Liver Complaint
Hicks, Dolly - 60, w 3, Asthma
Hill, Caroline - 21, w 6, Dyspepsia
Hill, William T. - 7m, w 5, Intermittent Fever
Hinson, George - 5m, w 17, Teething
Hinson, Joseph - 3m, w 3, Cholera Infantile
Hinson, Sarah - 2, w 17
Honan, John W. - 2m, w 14, Summer Complaint
Honey, Thomas - 4m, w 7
Hooper, Elenora - 7, w 1, Cold
Hooper, James H. - 3, w 1, Cold
Hooper, John W. - 3, w 1, Cold
Hooper, Miles - 35, w 1, Dropsy
Houston, Araminta - 50, w 5, Visitation Of God
Houston, Henry - 27, w 17, Drowned
Howard, Albert - 9, w 3, Worms
Howard, James - 82, w 13, Old Age
Howard, - Samuel - w 16, Teething
Howard, Sarah - 58, w 14
Hubbard, Rebecca B. - 2, w 6, Smallpox
Hughes, Charles - 1, w 3, Consumption
Hughes, James - 36, w 4, Typhoid Fever
Hutchins, Catherine A. - 16, w 6, Consumption
Hutton, Henry H. - 10m, w 6, Croup
Hutton, Laura J. - 2, w 3, Teething
Hynes, Margaret A. - 1, w 6, Teething
Isaacs, Joseph - 29, w 14, Dropsy
Isaacs, Joseph - 30, w 6, Dropsy
Jack, William - 1, w 12, Diarrhea
Jackson, Ann L. - 7m, w 15, Spasms
Jackson, Ann R. - 3m , w 6, Croup
Jackson, Celia - 40, w 14, Consumption
Jackson, John - 30, w 11, Consumption
Jackson, Mary C. - 4, w 15, Smallpox
Jackson, Sarah - 1, w 20
Jackson, Sophia - 104, w 13, Old Age
James, Caleb - 40, w 12, Smallpox

Chapter 19

Mortality in Free Blacks & Slaves - 1860

James, Flora - 80, w 15, Dropsy
James, Stephen - 62, w 11, Typhoid
Janey, Hugh J. - 5m, w 15, Cold
Jenkins, Daniel - 1, w 3, Cholera Infantile
Jenkins, George - 5m, w 16, Brain Fever
Jennings, Ann - 21, w 20, Decline
Jensen, Rye - 19, w 12, Consumption
Jinks, Columbus - 28, w 11, Inflammation Of The Lungs
Johns, Mary - 30, w 20, Childbearing
Johnson, Ambrosia - 1, w 13, Scalded
Johnson, Ann - 100, w 19, Old Age
Johnson, Clement - 75, w 14
Johnson, George W. - 8m, w 16, Brain Fever
Johnson, Hamilton - 2, w 3, Cramp Cholera
Johnson, Jane - 14, w 20, Consumption
Johnson, John F. - 1, w 6, Smallpox
Johnson, Malvina - 8m, w 16, Consumption
Johnson, Richard - 38, w 14, Smallpox
Johnson, Richard - 39, w 14, Rheumatism
Johnson, Robinson - 31, w 2, Smallpox
Johnson, Sarah - 32, w 2, Diarrhea
Johnson, W. H. - 1, w 19, Dysentery
Johnston, Addella - 2, w 7, Whooping Cough
Johnston, Gold - 6, w 7

Johnston, Kitty - 48, w 8, Consumption
Jones, Ann - 9m, w 6, Consumption
Jones, Deborah - 20, w 15, Consumption
Jones, Fanny - 33, w 5
Jones, George - 9m, w 15, Inflammation Of Stomach
Jones, John - 10, w 15, Fall
Jones, John W. - 11m, w 11
Jones, Josiah - 10, w 15, Inflammation Of Stomach
Jones, Mary - 1, w 12, Sun Complication
Jones, Matthew - 46, w 3, Hepatitis
Jones, Nathan - 2, w 16, Consumption
Jones, Pochantas C. - 1, w 1, Consumption
Jones, Racheal - 5m, w 11, Fits
Jones, Samuel - 40, w 15
Jones, Stephen - 19, w 8, Dysentery
Jones, Sylvia - 90, w 6, Typhoid
Jordan, James - 39, w 16, Throat
Kelly, Mary L. - 2, w 6, Croup
Kemp, Emma S. - 8m, w 16, Teething
Kemp, Isaiah - 19, w 15, Rheumatism
Kemp, John - 18, w 5, Typhoid
Kid, Ann M. - 8, w 3, Bilious Fever
Kid, Sarah - 26, w 3, Heart
King, Alice - 3m, w 18
Lansdale, E. L. - 40, w 11, Cold
LeCompt, Eliza - 59, w 3, Brain Fever
Lee, Catherine - 22, w 6, Breast

Mortality in Free Blacks & Slaves - 1860

Cancer
Lee, Charles - 54, w 6, Dropsy
Lee, Elizabeth A. - 30, w 7, Neuralgia
Lee, Henrietta - 19, w 4, Consumption
Lee, Henry - 60, w 5
Levi, Elizabeth - 2, w 20, Sun Complaint
Lewis, Neomi - 48, w 14, Dropsy
Lewis, Susan - 2, w 19, Consumption
Lewis, William - 47, w 11, Consumption
Lily, Elisa - 18, w 16, Cold
Limberry, George W. - 2, w 13, Cholera Morbus
Limberry, Martha Ann - 4, w 13, Catarrah Fever
Locks, Stephen - 50, w 3, Dropsy
Lodge, Isaac - 24, w 1, Heart Disease
Logan, John H. - 5m, w 15, Whooping Cough
Logie, John - 33, w 15, Typhoid
Love, Liney - 60, w 11, Cold
Lowdin, Mary V. - 3, w 1, Consumption
Lowdin, Simon - 60, w 1, Apoplexy
Lowe, Charles - 30, w 15, Consumption
Luther, James S. - 50, w 1, Consumptiom
Madden, Jonas - 43, w 17, Inflammation Of Lungs
Marsell, Peter - 56, w 17, Cold
Marshall, Elizabeth - 9m, w 12, Sun
Martin, Leeds - 1, w 3, Cholera Infantile
Martin, Mary - 3m, w 3, Fits
Mason, Sarah - 39, w 11, Typhoid
Mathews, Mary E. - 16, w 18, Heart Disease
Matthews, William - 6, w 19, Poison
McCabe, Nancy - 25, w 5
McKim, John H. - 2, w 6, Water On The Brain
McLaughlin, William H. - 3, w 15, Lung Disease
Meekins, Hannah J. - 10, w 6, Consumption
Milbourne, George W. - 5m, w 16, Catarrh Fever
Miles, Cornelius - 39, w 15, Cramp Colic
Miller, Asbury - 50, w 1, Herat Disease
Miller, Cata - 30, w 3, Consumption
Mills, F. - 8m, w 5, Brain Disease
Mills, John A. - 3m, w 8, Smallpox
Mills, John J. - 20, w 8, Consumption
Moan, Larry - 4, w 4, Fever
Moor, Levin - 39, Typhoid
Moore, John - 21, w 6, Sun Struck
Moorison, Mary E. - 7m, w 2, Water On the Brain
Mould, Charles - 50, w 5, Dropsy
Murray, Georgeanna - 3, w 5, Diarrhea
Murray, Jane - 18, w 15, Cold
Murray, John - 40, w 16, Smallpox
Murray, Maria - 1m, w 5
Myers, Andrew - 35, w 16, Consumption
Myers, George - 1, w 3
Myers, Jerry - 2, w 11, Dysentery
Nash, Mary - 34, w 12, Consumption

Chapter 19

Mortality in Free Blacks & Slaves - 1860

Naylor, Julia A. - 5, w 16, Brain
Netter, Harriet - 1, w 15, Cold
Newman, George H. - 10m, w 4, Teething
Nichelson, Sophia - 30, w 8, Paralytic
Nicholas, Elizah - 40, w 2, Cold
Nichols, John - 42, w 3, Consumption
Nicholas, Edwrad H. - 1, Dysentery
Nicholson, James - 2, w 12, Catarrh Fever
Nicholson, Susan J. - 3, w 15, Consumption
Noon, Benjamin - 1, w 4, Water On The Brain
Oakcliffe, Ann R. - 2, w 19, Brain Fever
Offitt, Caroline - 21, w 14, Typhoid
Ogle, Catherine - 5, w 18, Dropsy
Oliver, Isaac - 20, Lung Disease
Osbourne, George - 6m, w 19, Spasms
Osbourne, Mary - 40, w 19, Decline
Osbourne, Nat - 13, w 19, Consumption
Otho, Elizabeth - 23, w 12, Dropsy
Palmer, Francis - 9, w 12, Consumption
Palmer, James - 74, w 12
Paraway, Charles - 50, w 18, Cholera
Paraway, James - 1, w 5
Paraway, James - 54, w 12, Debility
Parker, James R. - 2, w 15, Croup
Patterson, Ann - 37, w 13, Childbearing
Patterson, Joshua - 54, w 3, Consumption
Patterson, Thomas - 30, w 3, Consumption
Paul, Lewis - 3, w 3, Typhoid
Perry, Henry - 15, w 15, Bilious Fever
Perry, Mary J. - 18, w 15, Consumption
Peterkin, Elizabeth - 22, w 17, Consumption
Philips, Nicholas S. - 17, w 8, Dropsy
Pier, Samuel - 6, w 3, Consumption
Pikes, Risden - 35, w 3, Typhoid
Pinkert, Abraham - 11m, w 15
Pinkett, John - 1, w 17
Polk, James - 35, w 12, Typhoid
Polk, Marie - 43, w 12, Typhoid
Porter, Susan - 33, w 17, Typhoid
Powell, Ann M. - 3m, w 6, Consumption
Powell, George - 1, w 12, Brain Fever
Powell, Lydia - 80, w 12, Old Age
Pullet, George - 50, w 15, Pleurisy
Purnell, Daniel - 3, w 12, Sun Complication
Purviance, George A. - 15, w 8, Mania
Purviance, Hannah - 36, w 8, Heart Broke
Purviance, Samuel - 8, w 8
Purviance, Wesley - 25, w 8, Mania
Queen, Mary E. - 4, w 3, Dropsy
Quill, Fanny - 84, w 12, Diarrhea
Rainbow, Charles - 8, w 4, Diarrhea
Randall, Alice - 5m, w 19, Spasms
Randall, James - 10, w 19, Decline

Mortality in Free Blacks & Slaves - 1860

Ray, Susan - 19, w 5
Reister, R. - 40, w 5, Typhoid
Richards, Jefferson - 40, w 5, Typhoid
Richardson, Benjamin B. - 10, w 15, By A Kick
Richardson, Harriet - 22, w 6, Diarrhea
Richardson, Mary - 26, w 5, Typhoid
Richardson, Paluna - 59, w 12, Consumptiion
Rideout, Isabella - 1, w 7, Cold
Ridgeway, Rosella - 50, w 6, Consumption
Ringgold, Jacob - 6m, w 6, Inflammation Of Head
Ringgold, Ruth - 70, w 15, Old Age
Ringold, Eliza - 50, w 17, Typhoid
Ringold, Mary - 60, w 16, Dropsy
Roberts, Harriet - 20, w 11, Diarrhea
Robinson, Levi - 2, w 7, Smallpox
Robinson, Martha - 1, w 12, Deleria
Rogers, James - 8, w 20, Consumption
Rogers, Sarah - 10m, w 20, Brain Fever
Rogers, William - 9, w 13, Consumption
Ross, Augustus - 4m, w 4, Fits
Ross, Maria - 30, w 5, Typhoid
Rowles, Lewis - 1, w 1, Cholera
Sales, Louisa - 50, w 6, Consumption
Salter, Charles - 25, w 3, Consumption
Sanders, George - 60, w 1, Diarrhea
Sanders, Rosetta - 14, w 1, Fits
Savoy, Elisabeth - 1d, w 15, Fits
Scott, Eleanor - 25, w 15, Childbirth
Scott, J. - 8d, w 15, Colic
Scribner, George - 14, w 15, Cold
Seister, Solomon - 2m, w 17
Selwell, Hester - 75, w 6, Old Age
Sevatt, Lydia - 10m, w 6, Croup
Sewell, Thomas E. - 1, w 5, Intermittent Fever
Shank, Maria - 36, w 18
Sharp, Jacob O. - 7m, w 1, Teething
Sharp, James - 98, w 1, Old Age
Sharper, Maria - 25, w, 14, Consumption
Sheaf, Ann M. - 1m, w 6, Scarlet Fever
Sherwood, Emily - 25, w 6, Inflammation Of Bowels
Sholes, Rhoda - 3, w 12, Brain Fever
Shorter, William - 12, w 13, Consumption
Siddons, David - 27, w 20, Heart Disease
Siddons, Dorothea - 89, w 10, Old Age
Simms, Catherine - 1, w 19, Typhoid
Simms, Jolin - 5, w 12
Simpson, John J. - 1, w 18, Croup
Sloan, James - 9, w 12
Smith, Alexander - 50, w 11, Mania
Smith, Anna - 23, w 6, Consumption
Smith, Benjamin - 2, w 15, Catarrh Fever
Smith, Catherine - 53, w 5, Bilious Fever

Chapter 19

Mortality in Free Blacks & Slaves - 1860

Smith, Ellen - 24, w 14
Smith, George - 3, w 9, Consumption
Smith, James - 21, w 3, Stroke
Smith, Joseph - 6, w 6, Inflammation Of Lungs
Smith, Julieyya - 2, w 9, Lung Disease
Smith, Martha J. - w 14, Teething
Smith, Peter - 8m, w 1, Summer Complications
Smith, Richard - 23, w 14, Consumption
Smith, Richard - 24, w 14, Consumption
Smith, Sarah - 47, w 17, Typhoid
Smith, Sarah - 56, w 6, Inflammation Of Lungs
Smith, Susan - 7, w 10, Whooping Cough
Smithers, Henry - 29, w 14, Rheumatism
Snell, ? - 3m, w 16
Snoden, Edward - 79, w 18, Consumption
Snowden, James - 40, w 19, Insane
Somerville, Susan - 34, w 3, Drowned
Sommerwell, Samuel - 45, w 3, Pleurisy
Sparrow, Paddy - 35, w 3, Childbirth
Sprigg, Alser R. - 2, w 18, Head Disease
Stanley, Charles - 40, w 15, Typhoid
Stanley, George W. - 4m, w 12, Croup
Stanley, Lucinda - 7, w 3, Catarrh Fever
Stansbury, Elizah - 39, w 14, Typhoid
Starett, Celia - 2m, w 11
Stephens, John - 40, w 20, Inflammation Of Lungs
Sterrett, Margaret A. - 33, w 6, Lung Disease
Stevens, Rachel - 12, w 6, Consumption
Stevenson, Francis F. - 12h, w 16
Stewart, George - 6, w 6, Dysentery
Stewart, Hester - 40, w 15
Stewart, William - 6m w 4, Brain Fever
Stewart, William - 80, w 5, Old Age
Stewrat, John - 8m, w 10, Spasms
Stuart, Sarah J. - 1, w 11, Whooping Cough
Stump, George - 27, w 3, Inflammation Of Lungs
Sutton, Rezin - 1, w 6, Inflammation Of Lungs
Tachsum, Sally - 1, w 1
Talbot, Ann M. - 32, w 6, Consumption
Talbot, Perry - 40, w 3, Burnt
Talbott, ? - 2, w 15
Talbott, Martha A. - 2d, w 15
Talbott, Mary E. - 3w, w 15
Tate, ? - 2d, w 15, Premature Birth
Taylor, Charlotte - 57, w 17
Taylor, John - 32, w 16, Smallpox
Taylor, Thomas - 5m, w 4, Spasms
Thomas, Amelia - 26, w 6, Consumption
Thomas, Andrew - 29, w 10, Smallpox
Thomas, Charles - 1, w 12, Spasms
Thomas, Edward - 32, w 10, Smallpox

Mortality in Free Blacks & Slaves - 1860

Thomas, Eliza A. - 1, w 3, Consumption
Thomas, James - 41, w 12, Cold
Thomas, John - 1m, w 15
Thomas, John - 4m, w 16, Summer Complaint
Thomas, John William - 6, w 5
Thomas, Joseph S. - 2m, w 17
Thomas, Maria - 30, w 17, Dropsy
Thomas, Mary - 2m, w 6, Croup
Thomas, Mary J. - 1, w 11, Teething
Thomas, Mary J. - 8, w 16, Dropsy
Thomas, W. H. - 2m, w 19, Hip Disease
Thomas, William - 10m, w 19, Fall
Thomas, William - 35, w 5, Typhoid
Thompson, Charlotte - 53, w 16, Typhoid
Thompson, George - 7m, w 6, Measles
Tilman, Lucy - 70, w 20, Inflammation - Rheumatism
Tilman, Morris - 27, w 12, Cholera
Toogood, George - 25, w 14, Typhoid
Topping, Julia - 1, w 20, Brain Fever
Travers, Spencer - 21, w 15, Typhoid
Tripp, Henry - 31, w 11, Dropsy
Tripp, Henry - 40, w 13, Consumption
Tripp, Mary L. - 6m, w 4, Consumption
Truxsen, John - 21, w 3, Brain Fever
Turner, Ann - 5m, w 12, Scarlet Fever
Turner, Rebecca - 27, w 15, Childbearing
Turner, Rebecca - 72, w 17, Mortification Of Toe
Tyler, Isaac - 50, w 18, Typhoid
Tyler, Ruth A. - 45, w 18, Typhoid
Walker, Elizabeth - 1m, w 12, Fits
Wallace, H. - 6, w 14, Dropsy
Wallace, L. - 8, w 5
Walters, James - 40, w 3, Cholera
Wares, Sarah - 20, w 3, Consumption
Washington, Alphonsa - 48, w 13, Consumption
Washington, S. J. - 18, w 10
Washington, Sarah - 7m, w 20, Typhoid
Waters, Charles - 34, w 8, Consumption
Waters, James - 19, w 5
Waters, Joseph - 9m, w 16, Summer Complaint
Waters, Luke - 40, w 3, Ship Fever
Waters, Priscilla - 13, w 16, Typhoid
Waters, Rebecca - 2, w 3
Waters, William J. - 28, w 16, Consumption
Watkins, John - 5, w 18, Consumption
Watkins, Maria - 1, w 11, Spasms
Webster, Polly - 38, w 5, Paralytis
Weeks, Isaac - 32, w 12, Cold
Wells, George - 3, w 6, Lung Disease
Wells, Mary - 64, w 17, Dropsy
West, James H. - 1m, w 2
Wheeler, Andrew - 6m, w 7, Fits
White, Andrew - 6m, w 20, Decline
White, George - 4, w 12, Smallpox
White, Henry - 780, w 11, Old Age
White, Jane - 21, w 12, Dysentery

Chapter 19

Mortality in Free Blacks & Slaves - 1860

White, Sarah - 6, w 16, Consumption
White, Virginia - 1, w 20, Consumption
White, W. H. - 10, w 20
Whittington, John - 2, w 3, Brain
Wilkinson, John H. - 1d, w 11, Stillborn
Wilkinson, John H. - 2, w 11
Willett, Thomas - 1, w 15, Typhoid
Williams, Benjamin - 1m, Spasms
Williams, Catherine - 57, w 15, Heart Disease
Williams, Charlotte - 73, w 12, Heart Disease
Williams, Eleanora - 1, w 16, Teething
Williams, Eliza A. - 8, w 3, Consumption
Williams, Francis - 34, w 12, Consumption
Williams, George H. - 22, w 7, Consumption
Williams, Henry - 46, w 6, Ship Fever
Williams, James - 26, w 12, Consumption
Williams, James E. - 11m, w 16, Teething
Williams, John - 60, w 11, Pleurisy
Williams, Lloyd - 2, w 12, Water On Brain
Willis, John - 2m, w 18, Dysentery
Wilson, Daniel - 5m, w 1, Consumption
Wilson, Ellen - 30, w 4, Childbirth
Wilson, James A. - 1, w 11, Catarrh
Wilson, Joseph - 18, w 4, Cramp
Wilson, Robert - 1d, w 11
Wilson, Susan - 80, w 11, Consumption
Winchester, Frank - 3, w 18, Inflammation Of Lungs
Winder, William - 54, w 10, Consumption
Woodland, John - 2, w 15, Summer Complaint
Woolford, Daniel - 8m, w 5, Bilious Pleurisy
Wright, Sarah - 35, w 12, Herat Disease
Wye, Renny - 1, w 12, Decline
Wynn, Georgeanna - 6m, w 3, Catarrah Fever
Young, Emily J. - 9m, w 6, Inflammation
Young, Jacob - 60, w 4, Inflammation Of lungs
Young, Martial - 31, w 7, Mashed To Death
Young, Simpson, 1m

Reprinted with the kind permission of the *Flower of the Forest - Black Genealogical Journal*: Mortality Schedules For the Free Black and Slave Population of Baltimore v. 1, no. 6, 1987.

Notes to Chapters 1 - 9

Chapter 1
The Slaveholder

1.) The New Webster Encyclopedic Dictionary of the English Language (Chicago 1971)
2.) Laws of Maryland, February 25, 1842, chp. 232
3.) Ibid, February 25, 1847, chp. 144
4.) Ibid, May 30, 1853, chp. 413
5.) Ibid, March 6, 1856, chp. 207
6.) Ibid, May 8, 1852, chp. 207

Chapter 2
The Hiring Out of Slaves

7.) *Port Tobacco Times*, January 3, 1856, p. 3
8.) Ralph Clayton, *Black Baltimore 1820 - 1870*, (Bowie, Maryland 1987) pp. 13 - 14
9.) U. S. Bureau of the Census, Fifth Census of the United States, 1830, Baltimore, Maryland, ward 3, p. 110
10.) Ibid, ward 3, p. 138
11.) Ibid, ward 3, p. 124
12.) Ibid, ward 5, p. 224
13.) Carter Woodson, Free Negro Owners of Slaves in the United States in 1830 (Washington, 1924) pp. 16 - 22
14.) Ibid
15.) The Baltimore Sun, September 20, 1850, p. 3
16.) Ibid, March 11, 1850, p. 3
17.) Ibid, December 1, 1852, p. 2
18.) Ibid, April 14, 1852, p. 3
19.) Ibid, October 4, 1852, p. 2
20.) Ibid, January 30, 1855, p. 3
21.) Ibid, February 1, 1850, p. 3
22.) Ibid, January 1, 1855, p. 4
23.) Ibid, June 8, 1858, p. 3
24.) Ibid, May 5, 1852, p. 4
25.) Ibid, January 25, 1853, p. 2
26.) Ibid, June 2, 1852, p. 4
27.) The Liberator, January 18, 1850, p. 1
28.) Sun, April 17, 1852, p. 2
29.) Field assessor work book, Baltimore City, ward 11, 1858, Balti-

Notes to Pages -

    more City Archives
30.) Ibid
31.) Ibid
32.) Ibid
33.) Ibid

Chapter 3
The Sale of Slaves

34.) Sun, May 14, 1850, p. 4
35.) Ibid, February 29, 1860, p. 4
36.) Ibid, April 1, 1852, p. 4
37.) Ibid, January 7, 1850, p. 3
38.) Ibid, June 21, 1850, p. 3
39.) Ibid, January 17, 1848, p. 1
40.) Ibid, June 21, 1850, p. 3
41.) Ibid, October 18, 1853, p. 3
42.) Ibid, March 1, 1856, p. 3
43.) The Baltimore American, July 3, 1860, p. 3
44.) Sun, July 11, 1848, p. 2
45.) Sun, May 13, 1850, p. 2
46.) Sun, April 15, 1858, p. 2
47.) Sun, February 20, 1850, p. 3
48.) Sun, March 15, 1850, p. 2
49.) Sun, November 23, 1852, p. 2
50.) Sun, December 12, 1854, p. 2

Chapter 4
The Slave Trade Hierarchy

51.) Frederic Bancroft, Slave Trading in the Old South, (Baltimore, 1931), pp. 122 - 123
52.) The Liberator, September 6, 1850, p. 4
53.) Sun, December 21, 1854, p. 2
54.) Ibid, January 1, 1850, p. 4
55.) Ibid, September 17, 1853, p. 2
56.) Ibid, October 12, 1848, p. 2
57.) Ibid, November 26, 1850, p. 4
58.) Ibid, April 15, 1851, p. 4
59.) Ibid, December 16, 1852, p. 4
60.) Ibid, May 22, 1854, p. 4
61.) Ibid, November 28, 1857, p. 3

62.) Ibid, January 6, 1845, p. 4
63.) Stanton Tiernan, "Baltimore's Old Slave Markets," Sun, September 13, 1936
64.) Sun, July 14, 1848, p. 4 and The Liberator, January 18, 1850, p. 1
65.) Petition #129, Baltimore City Archives
66.) Henry Stockbridge Sr., "Baltimore in 1846," Maryland Historical Magazine, v. 6, 1911, p. 26
67.) Ibid, p. 27
68.) Ibid, p. 27
69.) Ibid, p. 27
70.) Frederick Douglass, The Frederick Douglass Papers, (New York, 1982), pp. 373 - 374
71.) Leeds Anti-Slavery Series, #9, 1847 (located in the Schomburg Collection)
72.) Charles H. Wesley, "Manifests of Slave Shipments Along the Waterways," Journal of Negro History p. 171
73.) Ibid
74.) Tiernan, "Baltimore's Old Slave Markets," Sun, September 13, 1936
75.) Frederic Bancroft, Slave Trading in the Old South, (Baltimore, MD 1931) p. 373
76.) Daniel Drayton, Personal Memoir (recounted in Bancroft's Slave Trading in the Old South), pp. 59 - 60
77.) Sun, July 14, 1848, p. 4
78.) Sun, December 16, 1852, p. 4
79.) U. S. Bureau of the Census, Eighth Census of the United States; slave schedules, 1860
80.) Fred Fowler, "Some Undistinguished Negroes," Journal of Negro History, v. 5, October 1920, p. 477
81.) Edward Ingle, The Negro in the District of Columbia (Baltimore, ?), p. 16 - 18
82.) Sun, July 28, 1863, page 1

Chapter 5
The Slave Jails

83.) Ibid, January 6, 1845, p. 4 and December 16, 1852, p. 4
84.) Ibid, January 1, 1850, p. 4
85.) Laws of Maryland, March 10, 1845, chp. 340
86.) Sun, August 24, 1849, p. 2
87.) Ibid, August 10, 1850, p. 1
88.) Ibid, September 30, 1850, p. 1

89.) Ibid, December 18, 1852, p. 1
90.) Ibid, January 1, 1856, p. 4
91.) Ibid, June 19, 1856, p. 1

Chapter 6
Fugitive Slaves - Modes of Escape

92.) The Emancipator, June 7, 1849
93.) Ibid
94.) Henry Box Brown to Gerrit Smith, September 13, 1850. The Abolitionist Society Papers, Enoch Pratt Free Library, Baltimore, Maryland.
95.) Ibid
96.) Sun, April 23, 1845, p. 2
97.) Ibid, May 2, 1845, p. 2
98.) Laws of Maryland, April 1839, chp. 375
99.) B+O Minute Books, November 4, 1840
100.) Ibid, August 4, 1841
101.) Sun, March 20, 1864, p. 1
102.) Ibid, January 1, 1856, p. 4
103.) Ibid, February 10, 1858, p. 1
104.) Ibid, April 15, 1858, p. 2
105.) Ibid, January 26, 1854, p. 1
106.) Ibid, March 4, 1856, p. 1
107.) Ibid, November 1, 1860, p. 1
108.) Ibid, June 27, 1859, p. 1

Chapter 7
Fugitive Slaves - Frequency

109.) Ibid, June 28, 1850, p. 2
110.) The Liberator, August 30, 1850, p. 3
111.) Ibid, October 5, 1855, p. 3
112.) Ibid, May 27, 1846, p. 3
113.) Sun, August 25, 1858, p. 3
114.) Ibid, July 28, 1848, p. 2
115.) Clayton, *Black Baltimore 1820 - 1870*, p. 17
116.) Sun, July 28, 1848, p. 2
117.) Ibid, June 9, 1849, p. 2
118.) Ibid, December 15, 1855, p. 1
119.) Ibid, July 1, 1856, p. 1

120.) Ibid, August 4, 1856, p. 1
121.) Ibid, December 30, 1856, p. 1
122.) Ibid, June, 1857
123.) Ibid, August 7, 1858, p. 1
124.) Ibid, December 29, 1848, p. 2
125.) Ibid, March 8, 1849, p. 2
126.) Ibid, January 1, 1857, p. 1
127.) Ibid, April 10, 1857, p. 1
128.) Ibid, June 4, 1857, p. 1
129.) Ibid, August 11, 1857, p. 1
130.) Ibid, September 7, 1857, p. 1
131.) Ibid, February 16, 1858, p. 1
132.) Ibid, August 18, 1860, p. 1
133.) Ibid, August 28, 1860, p. 1
134.) Ibid, December 29, 1860, p. 1
135.) Richard Wade, Slavery in the Cities, (NY, 1964) pp. 214 - 215

Chapter 8
The Kidnapping of Free Blacks

136.) U. S. Bureau of the Census, fourth through eighth census; 1820 - 1860, population.
137.) Leroy Graham, Baltimore - The Nineteenth Century Black Capital (Washington, 1982), pp. 48 - 60
138.) The Colored American, March 21, 1840, p. 1
139.) Ibid,
140.) The Liberator, February 9, 1949, p. 2
141.) Ibid
142.) Sun, August 25, 1857, p. 1
143.) Ibid
144.) Ibid, January 25, 1858, p. 1
145.) Ibid
146.) Ibid, August 17, 1860, p. 1
147.) Ibid, August 8, 1860, p. 3
148.) Ibid, August 30, 1860, p. 1
149.) Ibid, September 25, 1860, p. 1
150.) Ibid, December 16, 1850, p. 2
151.) Ibid, December 20, 1850, p. 1
152.) Ibid, May 6, 1852, p. 1
153.) Ibid
154.) Sun, March 8, 1859, p. 1
155.) Ibid, December 20, 1853, p. 1

Notes to Pages -

156.) Ibid, December 4, 1860, p. 1
157.) Ibid, November 18, 1852, p. 1; November 19, 1852, p. 1 June 2, 1860, p. 1; August 1, 1860, p. 1; August 3, 1860, p. 1; August 6, 1860, p. 1; September 24, 1860, p. 1

Chapter 9
The Sale of Free Blacks and Slaves For Crimes Committed

158.) Jeffrey Bracket, The Negro in Maryland, p. 126
159.) Ibid, p. 125
160.) Laws of Maryland, March 10, 1845, chp. 340
161.) Ibid
162.) Ibid
163.) Sun, May 3, 1850, p. 2
164.) Ibid, May 6, 1854, p. 3
165.) Ibid, January 29, 1853
166.) Ibid, December 29, 1855, p. 1
167.) Clayton, *Black Baltimore 1820 - 1870*, p. 8
168.) Ibid, p. 7
169.) Bracket, The Negro in Maryland, p. 126
170.) U. S Bureau of the Census, Seventh and Eighth census of the United States, 1850 1nd 1860, Population, Baltimore City, ward 8
171.) Laws of Maryland, March 11, 1858, chp. 324
172.) U. S. Bureau of the Census, Eighth Census of the United States, 1860, Population, Baltimore City, ward 8
173.) Sun, January 1, 1859, p. 1
174.) Ibid, April 4, 1860, p. 1

Bibliography

Books

Bancroft, Frederic. *Slave Trading in the Old South*. Baltimore, J. H. Furst and Co., 1931.

Brackett, Jeffrey. *The Negro in Maryland*. Baltimore, Johns Hopkins University Press, 1889.

Clayton, Ralph. *Black Baltimore 1820-1870*. Bowie, Maryland, Heritage Books Inc., 1987.

Graham, Leroy. *Baltimore - The Nineteenth Century Black Capital*. Washington D.C., University Press of America, 1982.

Ingle, Edward. *The Negro in the District of Columbia*. Washington, D.C., Books for Libraries Press, 1893.

Wade, Richard C. *Slavery in the Cities*. New York, Oxford University Press, 1964.

Wesley, Charles H. *Neqro Labor in the United States*. New York, Russell and Russell, 1967.

Woodson, Carter. *Free Negro Owners of Slaves in the United States - 1830*. Washington, Negro University Press, 1924.

Secondary Sources

Fowler, Fred. "Some Undistinguished Negroes." *Journal of Negro History* v.5 (Oct. 1920):477

Stockbridge, Henry Jr. "Baltimore in 1846." *Maryland Historical Magazine* v.6 (1911):126

Newspapers

The Port Tobacco Times 1856
The Baltimore Sun 1840-1864
The Baltimore Sun September 13, 1936
The Liberator 1850-1860
The Baltimore American 1860
The Emancipator 1849
The Colored American 1840

Bibliography

Documents and Primary Sources

Laws Of Maryland 1806-1888
U.S. Bureau of the Census, Fifth Census of the United States-1830
U.S. Bureau of the Census, Sixth Census of the United States-1840
U.S. Bureau of the Census, Seventh Census of the United States-1860
U.S. Bureau of the Census, Eighth Census of the United States-1860
Mortality Schedules, U.S. Bureau of the Census, Seventh Census of the United States-1850
Slave Schedules, U.S. Bureau of the Census. Seventh and Eighth Census of the United States-1850 and 1860
    Field Assesser Work Books. Baltimore City 1858
    General Property Tax Records. Baltimore City 1858
    Petitions (#129) Baltimore City Archives
    8+0 Minute 8ooks 1840, 1841
    Baltimore City Directories 1831-1860
    Ordinances, Baltimore City 1852
    Applications For Certificates of Freedom 1845-1864

Special Collections

Enoch Pratt Free Library (Baltimore, Maryland), The Abolitionist Society Papers.

Enoch Pratt Free Library (Baltimore. Maryland), Leeds Anti Slavery Series #9 (Schomburg Collection).

Enoch Pratt Free Library (Baltimore, Maryland), The Frederick Douglass Papers.

INDEX TO SLAVERY, SLAVEHOLDING, AND THE FREE BLACK POPULATION OF ANTEBELLUM BALTIMORE

ABSENTEE OWNERSHIP (of slaves): 13-15

AFRICAN AMERICANS *see also* FREE BLACKS: as slaveholders, 9-11

ALLEY LIVING: by slaves, 14; as contributing to the poor health of the Black community, 328

AUCTIONS: of free Blacks committing crimes, 56 57

AUCTIONEERS: as part of the slave trade hierarchy, 29

BILLS OF SALE: reflecting the sale of slaves, 59

BOXES: uses of, by escaping slaves, 37 38

CERTIFICATE OF FREEDOM *see also* FREEDOM PASS

CHOLERA: outbreak of, in Black community, 328

CITY DIRECTORIES: as a research tool for identifying the slaveholder, 63

CITY ORDINANCE: as regulating the monetary value of slaves, 75

COMMISSION MERCHANTS: part of the slave trade hierarchy, 29

CONSUMPTION: as the leading cause of death in the Black community, 328

FEDERAL CENSUS SCHEDULES: as a research tool for identifying the slaveholder, 59

FELLS' POINT: slave ships off of, 31

FIELD ASSESSOR TAX BOOKS: as a tool for identifying the slaveholder, 64; records of, for Baltimore's 11th ward in 1858, 76-80

FREE BLACKS *see also* AFRICAN AMERICANS: intermixing with slaves in Baltimore, 45; kidnapping of, 45-48; implicated in the fraudulent sale of themselves as slaves, 49 50; sold for committing crimes, 52 53; lack of public education of, before the Civil War, 58; shift of living quarters of, before the Civil War, 58

FREEDOM PASS: used by slaves escaping by railroad, 39; required by State Legislation, 147; applications for, as a

Index

research tool for studying slavery, 147; applications for, reflecting the free Black ownership of slaves, 147
FUGITIVE SLAVES: escapes of, in boxes, 37 38; financial loss in Maryland, incurred as a result of, 41; large escapes of, 41; turned in by free Blacks, 44
GENERAL AGENTS: as part of the slave trade hierarchy, 29
GENERAL PROPERTY TAX RECORDS: as a research tool for identifying slaveholders, 63
HIRING OUT: (of slaves) 1, 13; by slave traders, 19; examples of, in field assessor's work books, 19-20; examples of, in slave schedules, 20-23
IMMIGRATION: impact of, on male slave labor, 15; impact of, on the Black community, 57; census figures concerning, 57
INSURRECTION: impact of, on the free Black community, 57
KIDNAPPING: of free Blacks in Baltimore, 45-48
MARYLAND COLONIZATION SOCIETY: newspaper articles concerning, 169-176
MOUNT VERNON (Baltimore): slaveholding in, 63; real estate value in, 75
MORTALITY SCHEDULES: as a research tool for studying the Black community, 327; statistics of, in the Black community, 329
NEW ORLEANS: and the slave trade with Baltimore, 31; as the main port of destination for the slave trade from the upper South, 32
OMNIBUSES: used for the transportation of slaves, 31
PENITENTIARY: slaves incarcerated in, 51, 52; free Blacks incarcerated in, 52; population statistics of, 52; sentences served by whites and Blacks, 53; lists of Black prisoners in, in 1860, 53-56
PLANTATION ACCOUNT LEDGERS: as a research tool for the study of slaves, 59
POPULATION: statistics of, in Baltimore, 45
RAILROAD: used in the slave trade, 30 33; used as a means of escape by slaves, 38 39; legislation involving, 38 39
REAL ESTATE: value of, in Baltimore for 1863, 76; statistics of, owned by free Blacks in Baltimore, 261
RUNAWAYS see FUGITIVE SLAVES
SHIP'S MANIFEST: reflecting slave shipments, 32
SLAVE JAILS: description of, 31; functions of, 35; cost of housing slaves in, 35; slaves incarcerated in, as runaways, 35 36
SLAVE LISTS: as a research tool for the study of slaves, 59
SLAVE SCHEDULES: reflection of slave traders in, 34; as a research tool for the study of the slaveholder, 61, 75;
SLAVE TRADERS: profits of, 29; false advertisements by, 29; as part of the slave trade

Index

hierarchy, 29; association with the New Orleans Market, 30 31
SLAVE TRADING: as big business, 29; between Baltimore and the New Orleans market, 31
SLAVEHOLDERS: occupations of, 1-4; long term slaveholding by, 6-9; African Americans as, 9-11
SLAVEHOLDING: decline of, in Baltimore, 80
SLAVES: occupations of, 17 18; sales of, in hotels, 25 26; sales of, by administrators of estates, 27; value of, in adver-

SLAVES (continued)
tisements, 28; transportation of, by train, 30, by steamboat, 30, by omnibus, 31; sale of, for committing crimes, 51 52; monetary value of, in Baltimore, 76
STEAMBOATS: use of, in the slave trade, 30; use of, by escaping slaves, 40
TYPHOID: outbreak of, in the Black community, 328

www.ingramcontent.com/pod-product-compliance
Lightning Source LLC
Chambersburg PA
CBHW072132220426
43664CB00013B/2225